Renewals can be made
by internet   www.fifedirect.org.uk/libraries
in person   at any library in Fife
by phone   08451 55 00 66

Thank you for using your library

Assassinated!: Assassinations that Shook the World

Georgian House

George IV

Station to Station

Palladian Style

The Georgian House in Britian and America

Regency Style

Adam Style

THE LIFE OF THE AUTOMOBILE

A New History of the Motor Car

Steven Parissien

Atlantic Books

LONDON

This paperback edition first published in Great Britain in 2014 by Atlantic Books.

First published in hardback in Great Britain in 2013 by Atlantic Books,
an imprint of Atlantic Books Ltd.

10 9 8 7 6 5 4 3 2 1

A CIP catalogue record for this book is available from the British Library.

Hardback ISBN: 9781848877054
Ebook ISBN: 9781782390213
Paperback ISBN: 9781848877078

Printed and bound by CPI Group (UK) Ltd, Croydon, CRO 4YY.

Atlantic Books
An Imprint of Atlantic Books Ltd
Ormond House
26–27 Boswell Street
London
WCIN 3JZ
www.atlantic-books.co.uk

Contents

Illustrations

1

Pioneers

Henry Ford died, with exquisite irony, during a power failure on the dark and stormy night of 6–7 April 1947, whilst sleeping fitfully at his vast Dearborn, Michigan, estate. On the 9th, his body lay in state in his mansion's cavernous ballroom while almost one hundred thousand people filed by to pay their last respects. The next day, twenty thousand spectators gathered in silence, and in the pouring rain, outside St Paul's Episcopal Cathedral in Detroit's Woodward Avenue. Inside the cathedral were assembled not only every leading figure from the global automobile industry but also key members of Harry S. Truman's administration. It was as if a great international statesman had passed away. Outside, the whole of the city of Detroit came to a halt. Detroit City Hall hung a thirty-foot portrait of Ford outside its doors, and thousands of citizens lined the route of Ford's funeral cortège as it made its way to Dearborn's Ford Cemetery, stoically ignoring the rain. The only jarring note, aside from the disappointing weather, was the car chosen to act as the hearse: it was, for some inexplicable reason, not a Ford but a Packard. Someone had clearly blundered.

Sadly, few of the mourners who came to Ford Cemetery that day had much personal affection for the late magnate. His obituaries were generally polite and kind; only New York's *P.M.* dared to describe Ford's philosophy as 'a jungle of fear and ignorance and prejudice in social affairs'. In truth, even most of Henry's family were relieved that he had finally passed. Nevertheless, the motor mogul had become the most famous man in the world. In Russia, the word for 'Americanize' was, literally translated, 'Fordize', while in Hitler's Third Reich, so recently laid waste by the allied bombers that Ford's plants had helped manufacture, Henry Ford had been revered almost as a god.

Henry Ford left his vast automotive empire to be administered by the Ford Motor Company's board, then still dominated by the Ford family. Notoriously frugal and miserly, Henry also left his heirs a cash windfall of $26.5 million, which he had kept hidden for decades in a private bank account. Yet in his pockets on the day he died were found not the prized possessions of the world's most famous industrial magnate but, as historian Robert Lacey has observed, 'the paraphernalia of a little boy': a comb, a penknife and a simple Jew's harp.

Despite much subsequent American mythology, Ford did not actually invent the car; that honour properly goes to the German engineers Karl Benz and Gottlieb Daimler. Indeed, Ford did not even create the first American gasoline-powered vehicle. Three years before Ford's first car appeared, Charles and Frank Duryea were demonstrating their gasoline-powered 'motor wagon' around the streets of Springfield, Massachusetts, and it was not until 1896 that the young Henry Ford launched his revolutionary, if fragile, Quadricycle. But Henry Ford is rightly lauded as the man who created and developed the key to modern mass production, the assembly line. Ford's early years of struggle saw the transformation of the car's curious but prescient Victorian forebears into the most important mass-marketed phenomenon of the twentieth century. In many ways, the inherent contradictions of Ford's character mirror the history of the car itself: daringly innovative, yet at the same time intrinsically conservative; brashly aggressive, yet apprehensive and hesitant; socially progressive, yet politically reactionary.

. . .

The men who were responsible for the creation and development of the global car industry were, for the most part, enthusiastic experts or fast-talking salesmen – or, like Henry Ford, a bit of both. Many of the first auto pioneers were larger-than-life characters, perpetual chancers who drove their cars as fast as they could and took vast risks with other people's money. It was only in the 1930s, when the automotive industry reached its respectable maturity and the weaker firms had gone to the wall, that the salesmen were edged out (or went bankrupt) and the money men took over.

The father of the modern car was Karl Benz, an engineer from the province of Baden in south-western Germany. In 1885, at the back of a Mannheim bicycle shop, he created the first petrol-powered motor vehicle. Equipped with three bicycle-like wire wheels (not carriage-like wooden ones), a revolutionary four-stroke engine, an equally advanced electric coil ignition, and a transmission comprising two chains connecting the engine to the rear axle, Benz's invention was patented on 29 January 1886 and was known thereafter as the *Benz Patent Motorwagen*. Subsequent road tests proved very successful. Indeed, in 1888 his wife, Bertha, took their two sons (supposedly without Karl's knowledge) on the first long-distance car trip, a 65 mile journey from Mannheim to Pforzheim. Bertha Benz dealt adeptly with minor breakdowns on the way, bought more gasoline fuel at pharmacies she passed, and calmly telegraphed Karl to announce her arrival at Pforzheim in the evening.[1] Benz's Model 3 impressed visitors at the 1889 Paris Exposition Universelle – an event that also showcased the brand-new Eiffel Tower – and over twenty-five *Motorwagen*s were built between 1886 and 1893. In 1894 sales soared and Benz sold 136 Model 3s. The age of the car had arrived.

Benz was not the first man to invent a horseless carriage. All previous experiments had, however, been steam-powered and distinctly uncommercial. In 1704 the French physicist Denis Papin – a refugee from Louis

---

1 Today her epic journey is celebrated every two years in Germany in the Bertha Benz Memorial Route, a rally of vintage cars.

XIV's persecution of the Protestant Huguenots, who had moved to Kassel in Germany – invented a rudimentary steam piston engine which he used to power a small boat, thus creating the first mechanically powered vehicle. Sadly, Papin's achievement was never recognized and he died destitute in London in about 1712. Over fifty years later, his fellow Frenchman, army engineer Captain Nicolas Cugnot, used the motion of a steam piston engine to power a ratchet-operated driving mechanism which in turn drove a small but heavy three-wheeled car, which Cugnot called a *fardier à vapeur*. (A *fardier* was a sturdy, two-wheeled, horse-drawn cart for transporting bulky equipment; Cugnot's nomenclature thus became the first example of the automotive industry borrowing equine etymology.) Cugnot's two-ton vehicle of 1769, which was allegedly capable of just over 2 mph, was the first mechanically powered automobile. It may also have been responsible for the first mechanized road accident: in 1771, it was reported to have gone out of control and demolished a wall. This accident did not help convince the French army of its usefulness, and development of the *fardier* was discontinued. Cugnot survived on a royal pension, but this evaporated with the outbreak of the French Revolution in 1789. Cugnot would have emulated Papin's fate, dying penniless and forgotten, had he not been invited back to Paris by a sympathetic Napoleon, shortly before his death in 1804.

Cugnot's breakthrough encouraged Regency innovators to experiment with steam cars. The talented and underrated Scottish engineer William Murdoch built two 'road locomotives' in Redruth, Cornwall, in 1784 and 1786 – inventions that his friend Richard Trevithick exploited to create the world's first steam-powered railway locomotive in 1804. Trevithick's steam locomotive, alas, proved too heavy to use on roads. And frequent boiler explosions, together with conservative health and safety legislation, made steam power seem unviable. Britain's notorious Locomotive Acts of 1861 and 1865 stipulated that all steam cars should be occupied by at least three people, should be able to stop in an instant, and should be preceded by 'a person walking at least twenty yards ahead, who in case of need shall assist horses . . . and who will carry and display a red flag'. Steam cars were thus condemned to a speed slower than walking pace and were regarded as inherently dangerous modes of transport, liable to explode at any moment and kill or maim both driver and passers-by.

The quest for a safer, and faster, mechanically powered road vehicle gained enormous impetus after 1859 when the Belgian engineer Étienne Lenoir (surely one of the world's most famous Belgians) patented the first petrol-driven internal combustion engine. Over the next thirty years, French and German engineers perfected Lenoir's breakthrough. In 1880, Karl Benz himself patented a reliable, two-stroke, gasoline-powered engine, and five years later installed his petrol engine in the world's first true motor car. While the vehicle was only able to travel marginally faster than walking pace – Benz's 1885 machine would actually have gone quicker if it had been pulled by a pony rather than powered by its tiny engine – it was a landmark achievement.

Benz was not the only German to be working on petrol-powered vehicles in 1885. In the same year the engineer Gottlieb Daimler – who lived in Schorndorf, in Württemberg, only sixty miles away from Benz in Mannheim, although the two men never met – harnessed a four-stroke petrol engine designed by his partner Wilhelm Maybach to a bicycle, thus creating the world's first motorcycle.[1] Daimler's engine was far better than Benz's – as the journalist L. J. K. Setright has noted: '800 rpm was very fast by the standards of 1884'. Daimler, however, used an antiquated incandescent tube to start the ignition, whereas Benz's car had an electric ignition.

In 1886 Daimler and Maybach fitted an even larger engine to a stage-coach, thus inventing the world's first motor coach. Three years later, they exhibited their engines at the Paris Exposition. Then, in 1890, having obtained sufficient finance from a group of bankers and munitions makers, they formed a public company, Daimler-Motoren-Gesellschaft (DMG), to build and sell gasoline engines, with Maybach installed as its chief

---

1 Daimler's former boss, Dr Nikolaus Otto, had developed the first true four-stroke petrol engine in 1876, but forbade Daimler to use it, and the two had soon parted company.

designer. That same year, Daimler licensed the French firms of Panhard et Levassor and Peugeot to build DMG engines. The following year the company sold a similar licence to the US-German piano makers Steinway and Sons (who soon found that building cars was a little more difficult than building pianos), and in 1892 DMG sold its first four-wheeled car. In 1898 a Daimler car used the first-ever four-cylinder petrol engine, and two years later Maybach invented the first modern-style 'honeycomb' radiator, again for use in a Daimler car.

DMG was soon helping to create the British car industry, too. Britain was not in the forefront of car manufacture in the early years, relying solely on French and German imports. In 1889, the Englishman Frederick Simms, British-born but brought up in Hamburg, met Daimler and was sufficiently inspired to import one of Daimler's cars into England – probably the first car ever seen in Britain. Four years later Simms created a subsidiary of the Daimler firm in England, which sold German Daimlers and French Panhards. Simms then started producing the cars in Coventry, and successfully advertised them by running one from Land's End to John o'Groats in seventeen days, with no mishaps. While the first British-built car was also made in Coventry, it was not one of Simms's Daimlers or Panhards but a Bollée manufactured under licence by a subsidiary of the British Motor Syndicate, through which the crooked entrepreneur Harry Lawson hoped to control the embryonic British motor industry. Simms and his fellow automotive pioneers eventually managed to wriggle free of the strangling embrace of Lawson, who was trying to exercise legal ownership over all cars built in Britain. Lawson was eventually tried for fraud and served twelve months' hard labour.

Frederick Simms died in 1944, a successful and wealthy man. Daimler and Maybach, however, never enjoyed the riches their pioneer labours deserved. Maybach was forced out of DMG by the firm's powerful banking trustees, although Daimler continued to use him as a consultant for a while. Daimler himself suffered a heart attack in 1892 and the following year was bought out by his fellow directors. It was only thanks to pressure from Simms, whose association with DMG provided them with badly needed financial stability, that Daimler and Maybach were rein-stated to the board in 1895. Daimler, who never fully recovered from his heart problems, died prematurely in 1900, while Maybach left DMG after being demoted by the firm's ruthless and short-sighted directors (in what today would be a straightforward case of constructive dismissal) in 1907. Maybach was replaced on the DMG board by Paul Daimler, his former colleague's son, who proved far more amenable to the directors' whims than Maybach had been. (It was Paul Daimler who commissioned, and perhaps designed, the firm's three-pointed star logo in 1908.) Maybach, meanwhile, founded his own engineering company, which made engines for Zeppelin airships during the First World War and, after 1919, created large, luxury cars.

Wilhelm Maybach died in 1929, having never personally owned a car. After 1940, his eponymous firm made tank engines for the German army. Only just surviving the lean post-war years, the firm struggled on until 1960 when it was bought, predictably, by Daimler-Benz. In 2002, the successors of DMG finally, if belatedly, made amends for a shameful episode in their company's history by reviving the Maybach name as a brand for super-luxury limousines. Without Maybach, there may never have been a Mercedes.

Karl Benz suffered a similar fate to his rival, Daimler. Although he had improved his cars by inventing the radical horizontal 'boxer' engine in 1896, Benz was forced into retirement by his fellow directors in 1903, although he was allowed to remain notionally on the board until his death in 1929. Once again, the careful money men had triumphed over the visionary engineers.

Benz did at least live long enough to witness his company evolve into of one of the world's automotive giants, created by the 1926 merger of the Daimler and Benz operations. He also presided over the first Mercedes brand car. One of Benz's most important early customers was the Jewish entrepreneur Emil Jellinek, the Austro-Hungarian consul in Nice. Jellinek had been happy to help Benz market his cars in the 1890s, but found the Teutonic badge a handicap in a country still smarting from its comprehensive defeat by the Prussians twenty years earlier. Accordingly, he persuaded Benz to adopt a brand name for marketing purposes. Jellinek had recently met and married a vivacious new wife, the exotic Rachel Goggmann Cenrobert, in Morocco. Their daughter, born in 1889, was christened Adrienne but nicknamed 'Mercédès', a Spanish word meaning 'mercy' – the adoption of which, in hindsight, seems highly appropriate. By 1900, Jellinek was already using the name Mercedes for his private racing team, as well as for his yacht. He now persuaded Maybach to build him a new sports car using the same name. Rather presciently, Jellinek asserted that the Mercedes automobile should not be 'a car for today or tomorrow [but] the car of the day after tomorrow'.

The 35 hp Mercedes that Maybach built, which was first sold to the public in 1902, was revolutionary: it featured the first-ever gate gear-change, a honeycomb radiator, and a steel (not wooden) chassis. It was, as design historian Stephen Bayley has noted, the model in which 'the fundamental architecture of the car [was] established'. The prototype Mercedes dominated Nice Speed Week in March 1901 and was enthusias-tically backed by prominent patrons such as Baron Henri de Rothschild. The director of the French Automobile Club announced that: 'We have entered the Mercedes era.'

At the time of the Daimler-Benz merger in 1926, the Mercedes name was extended to the whole of the company's output, thus preventing any bitterness at the seeming triumph of either the Benz or the Daimler brand. Sadly, Mercédès herself died of cancer, aged only thirty-nine, in 1929, the same year that Benz died. She was thus spared witnessing the grotesque incongruity of cars named after a young Jewish girl being used to haul the anti-Semitic hierarchs of Nazi Germany around the Third Reich.

While the automobile was invented and perfected in Germany by Benz and Daimler, it was in France that it was developed into the vehicle we know today. One of the first French automotive pioneers was Armand Peugeot. Born into a family of Franche-Comté metalworkers, Armand was inspired by a visit to the factories of Leeds in 1881 and the following year not only set up a bicycle manufacturing business but also began experimenting with Benz-type gasoline engines. In 1889 he exhibited a steam-powered tricycle – in truth, more of a motorbike than a fully fledged car – at the Paris Exposition, and in 1896 he built a factory at Audincourt to make petrol-powered cars. By the time Armand retired in 1913, two years before his death, Peugeot was the largest car manufacturer in France, producing over ten thousand vehicles per year.

It was Peugeot's rival Émile Levassor, however, who did most to shape the design of this new mode of transport. In 1886, Levassor, newly licensed to build Gottlieb Daimler's Phoenix engine, had started building petrol engines in partnership with his friend, the engineer René Panhard, as Panhard et Levassor. By 1890 the pair, who had both graduated from the prestigious École Centrale des Arts et Manufactures, were building whole cars – again, under licence from Daimler. Indeed, Levassor, Peugeot and Daimler all met in 1888 at Peugeot's Valentigny factory to share their knowledge, a summit that led Levassor and Peugeot to cooperate in experimenting with Benz and Daimler engines. However, Levassor gave more thought to the design and operation of the new car than had Benz, Daimler or Peugeot, all of whom had been more concerned with introducing a successful engine into what was still basically a small carriage. With his Daimler-powered Panhard et Levassor of 1891, Levassor introduced a series of innovations that effectively created the modern car. He moved the engine from the rear to the front of the car, and cooled it via a front-mounted water radiator rather than relying, as had been customary, on natural aspiration, which was often insufficient. He also introduced a crankshaft to link the engine with the gearing, eschewing the bicycle-style belt drive of previous cars; and he installed a clutch pedal and a gear stick, situated between the seats, to operate the gearbox, thus creating the first modern transmission.

Levassor's brave challenge to the convention that cars should be disposed in the same basic format as their horse-drawn predecessors, by siting the engine not under the chassis but at the front of the vehicle, provided far more room for passengers, as well as easier access in and out of the automobile. The resultant configuration – which, unfortunately

for Levassor, was soon called the *système Panhard*, after the Panhard et
Levassor company rather than its actual progenitor – became the standard layout for all cars throughout the ensuing century.

Levassor was no studious engineer in the mode of Benz and Peugeot.
Bold and ambitious, he hugely enjoyed his new creations. It was largely
due to his efforts that his firm, in alliance with Peugeot, organized the
world's first car race, staged between Paris and Rouen in 1894. However,
Levassor's passion for racing was to lead to his untimely demise. Whilst
driving in the Paris–Marseilles rally of 1896, he swerved to avoid a dog
and crashed the car. He never recovered from his injuries, and died the
following year.

Soon after Levassor's death, his firm's early lead in the field of automobile production was overtaken by De Dion-Bouton. This pioneering
French auto manufacturer was founded in 1883 by an eccentric, aristocratic motor enthusiast, Jules Félix Philippe Albert, Marquis de Dion, a
playboy who was better known as a notorious duellist, and the engineer
Georges Bouton. By 1900 this unlikely combination had made their firm
into the world's biggest car maker. De Dion-Bouton's tiny Voiturette of
1899 was not a radical advance in the manner of Levassor's groundbreaking model of eight years before. However, it *was* the first 'people's car': a
cheap runabout aimed not at the idle rich, who had previously been the
only sort who could afford motor cars, but at the middle classes. By the
time of the outbreak of the First World War in 1914, De Dion-Bouton
was supplying engines to French rivals Peugeot and Renault, as well as
to foreign competitors such as Humber in Britain, Opel in Germany and
Packard in America. The Marquis de Dion, meanwhile, had fostered his
reputation as a right-wing maverick, assaulting the French president with
his cane at a Parisian racecourse (the anti-Semitic marquis was incensed
at President Loubet's moderate stance over the Dreyfus scandal, which
had split French society right down the middle), and bankrolling a variety
of ultra-conservative periodicals.[1]

---

1 De Dion's embryonic media empire included *Le Nain Jaune* ('The Yellow Gnome'),

In 1899 another new French car maker, Renault Frères, was founded in Paris. Little attention was paid at the time to the launch of yet another French manufacturer in what was then the global centre of car production. Yet, while Panhard et Levassor and De Dion-Bouton both prospered in the first decades of the twentieth century, only to stumble after 1918,[1] the Renault firm lasted the course to become, by 2000, one of the world's most successful car makers. Its founder, however, was no daredevil in the mould of Émile Levassor. A born engineer, Louis Renault was undersized, odd-looking and distinctly unsociable. But his Renault Voiturette had a revolutionary three-speed gearbox connected to a crankshaft, rather than to a bicycle-style chain drive, and was consequently smoother, faster and more reliable than its competitors. When Louis's dashing brother Marcel was killed in the Paris–Madrid motor race of 1903,[2] Louis took control of the company, remaining at the helm until 1942.

Few would have predicted in 1900 that, in less than two decades, America would have overtaken France as the world's leading producer of cars. This astonishing achievement – from a nation that, in contrast with France and Germany, came late to car manufacture – was largely due to the energy and vision of two very different men: Henry Ford and William Durant.

When Henry Ford was born in Dearborn, Michigan (then a small settlement outside the modestly sized town of Detroit), on 30 July 1863, America was still in the midst of the Civil War. Ford's was not an impoverished childhood, his father had become a prosperous farmer. But from his earliest years, Henry was a loner who did not get on well with the rest of his family and who seemed to follow his own star. His mother died in

---

which the unrepentant marquis admitted 'served no particular purpose'.

1 De Dion stopped making cars in 1932 and in 1955 what remained of the company was bought by a motorcycle manufacturer, while in 1965 the failing Panhard company was absorbed by Citroën.

2 The race was so disfigured by the deaths of drivers and spectators that it became the last such competition until 1927.

childbirth when he was only thirteen years old, and for ever afterwards Henry revered his late mother's memory – while marginalizing his father, whose mechanical aptitude he had clearly inherited – and always attributed the organization of his factories to her tidiness and cleanliness.

In 1878 the young Henry began work as an apprentice at Flower Brothers' machine shop, owned by friends of the Ford family. This was a lowly job, which Henry later exorcized from his résumé. He then moved to the Detroit Dry Dock engine works, which he left in 1882 to strike out on his own. In 1888 he married Clara Bryant, who was also from local farming stock, and three years later moved to Detroit itself. Here he began work at the Edison Illuminating Company, which also allowed him some space at the factory to continue his own mechanical experiments. By 1893 Henry was increasingly interested in the motor cars that German and French engineers were producing, and in 1896 he unveiled his own response, the Quadricycle. Ford's Quadricycle had no brakes and no reverse gear, and was steered by a tiller. But it did have four wheels – albeit bicycle wheels – and an engine, and an electric bell. And it had a top speed of 20 mph, which was very fast by the standards of the time.

By 1898, having won financial backing from a family friend, Detroit mayor William Maybury, Ford was producing a proper, German-style car, with high wheels, padded bench seats, brass lamps and running boards. And on the back of this breakthrough, he boldly founded the Detroit Automobile Company in August 1899. Yet only fourteen months later the company had ceased trading. Henry had simply never delivered to his new plant a finished car design; unable to adapt his obsessive working practices to industrial deadlines, he simply stopped coming into the factory. His employees saw less and less of him, and eventually found themselves out of work. It was not an auspicious start.

Ford was not one to give up easily. A new automotive manufacturer – the Henry Ford Company – was set up a year later, in November 1901. By that time, Ford had become an enthusiastic racer and thought only of building faster racing cars. Once again, the company seemed close to collapse after only a year. This time, however, Ford's fellow directors seized the initiative. They actually sacked Henry before he could walk away, and restructured the company around director Henry M. Leland, renaming it the Cadillac Automobile Company – a name borrowed from the legendary French adventurer Antoine Laumet de la Mothe, Sieur de Cadillac, who had founded the city of Détroit in 1701.

Having had two companies shot from underneath him, Ford tried yet again in 1903, with the Ford Automobile Company (later retitled the Ford Motor Company). This time he actually had a car design to put into production: the sturdy, practical Model A, built in two- or four-seat formats, though only available in red, and with a top speed of 28 mph. Even so, the firm was virtually bankrupt by the time the first Model As appeared. Although its assets amounted to just $223.65 in July 1903, the company survived – largely because the Model A proved an immediate success, which in turn encouraged banks to lend on the strength of its sales. Ford's automotive empire was finally launched.

Henry Ford was no inventor. Indeed, if he had died in 1907, he would have been dimly remembered as just one of the many pioneers of the early auto industry, one who had endured repeated financial failures only to strike lucky when all seemed lost. Ford's pivotal role in twentieth-century history derives instead from his development of the first mass-market car, which was soon being made by the world's first mass-production manufacturing system.

Ford's 'Tin Lizzie', the Model T, was first introduced in 1908. Its four cylinders were cast all in one block and not separately, as was then common. It had three speeds, like the Model A (though one of these was reverse). It was not the cheapest car available in 1908, but it was the only one to combine innovation with reliability and value. It was hardly festooned with gadgets, either: production models came without a speed-ometer, windscreen wipers or even doors. But the lack of refinements meant that owners were free to personalize their Model Ts. By 1922, as Robert Lacey has noted, the Sears, Roebuck and Co. catalogue, America's mail-order bible, contained 'no less than 5,000 different items that could be bolted, screwed or strapped to the vehicle'.

By September 1909 over ten thousand Model Ts had been sold, representing a 60 per cent increase in the company's sales. Ford even had to stop taking orders for nine weeks in order to catch up with demand. Farmers bought the Tin Lizzie as a cheap form of transport; its crude but effective suspension meant that Model Ts coped with ruts, potholes and off-road conditions far better than their rivals. The car could connect the farmer and his family easily with the nearby town – and the doctor, and the family church. The advertisements vowed that the Model T was 'designed for everyday wear and tear' by the average American farmer. 'Anybody can drive a Ford,' promised Henry, who also reassured his agricultural constituency that it was *never* a sporting car'. Indeed, the Model T could be used for just about anything. T. E. Lawrence ('Lawrence of Arabia') stated that the only cars that had been of any use to him in his desert campaigns were the Rolls-Royce Silver Ghost and Ford's Model T; while John Steinbeck, in his 1945 novel *Cannery Row*, recalled how 'most of America's children were conceived in Model T Fords and not a few of them were born in them'.

Spurred by his success, Ford decided to put all his eggs into one, crudely sprung, basket. He dropped all his other car models and concentrated just on the Model T. He also made the car more affordable, at a time when other car makers were struggling to keep pace with Ford's runaway success. Thus in 1912 the Model T's price, which had started out at $825, fell to just $575. For the first time, a car cost less than the average annual wage.

A vehicle that was now within reach of the purse of almost everyone, the Model T was effectively the first global car. And Ford prospered mightily; until the mid-1920s it appeared that Ford's low-price, single-model strategy would be the way ahead for the world's car makers. By 1918 Ford's American market share stood at an astonishing 49 per cent, while 40 per cent of cars on British roads were Model Ts. By 1921 the Model T commanded 60 per cent of the new car market around the world – a dominant position that no car maker, or car, has ever enjoyed since. By 1913 Ford's US dealer network covered virtually every town of reasonable size, and the company boasted more dealerships and agents than any other car maker in the world. Ford also dispatched Model T kits all over the world for local assembly. After the end of the First World War he extended his global supply empire by buying up rubber plants in Brazil, coal mines in Kentucky and West Virginia, a fleet of cargo ships, and glassworks in Pennsylvania and Minnesota. By the time production of the Model T was stopped in 1927, 15 million cars had been sold – a record that stood until Volkswagen's Beetle and Golf surpassed it decades later.

The Model T was the car of the century, transforming motoring for millions. Its cheapness and flexibility meant that the car became less a symbol of wealth and leisure than an affordable adjunct to the everyday life of even the humblest worker. And the key to its cheapness was its revolutionary production method.

Henry Ford's introduction of a moving assembly line at his recently built Highland Park factory in 1913–14 transformed the way cars were made and sold. Highland Park's pioneering system was based on a metal conveyor belt, operated by flywheels, which enabled workers to assemble magnetos, then transmissions, then whole engines. The initial drawback of this revolutionary approach to manufacturing was that the swifter production of these elements quickly swamped the final chassis assembly at the end of the factory. It was only when every process had been adapted to assembly-line working that massive savings in time and labour could be achieved. In 1913–14 production of Model Ts almost doubled – while the plant's workforce diminished by 10 per cent – as the assembly time was reduced from 12.5 hours per man to an amazing 1.5 hours. The pace was quickened even more when, in 1914, Ford famously prohibited his cars from being painted any colour except black. Meanwhile Ford's new, all-steel bodies meant that there were fewer parts to assemble; while the company's pioneering use of vanadium steel, which gave greater strength for less weight, also added to the cars' performance. Highland Park was, unsurprisingly, the envy of every industrialist in the world.

The home for this new assembly line, Albert Kahn's Highland Park factory, was as revolutionary as its product. Kahn was a rabbi's son who, aged eleven, had emigrated from the Rhineland to Detroit, where he set up his own architectural office at the tender age of twenty-six. He pioneered the use of reinforced concrete, a cheap, fireproof and immensely strong material which could be used to span vast areas. Beginning with his Packard factory of 1905–7, Kahn's concrete-vaulted buildings changed the face of Detroit forever. His new factory for Ford, built in 1909 in the inner-city suburb of Highland Park, comprised a vast open space spanned by a reinforced concrete roof and lit by fifty thousand feet of grid windows – a feature that led journalists to dub it 'Detroit's Crystal Palace' when it opened in December 1909. Eight years later, Kahn designed the even more capacious Rouge River plant for Ford at Dearborn, a few miles to the south-west of downtown Detroit, creating a factory complex a half-mile long. As a coda to his illustrious career in the city, in 1928 Kahn also gave Detroit's downtown its most outstanding structure, the art deco skyscraper of the Fisher Building. (Ironically, after 1930 Kahn's most lucrative client was to be the Soviet Union, which Henry Ford had come to loathe.[1] However, that did not prevent Ford from hiring Kahn back in 1942 to design what was to be his last building, the giant Willow Run plant at Ypsilanti.)

Mass production at the Highland Park factory spelled the end of the primacy of the skilled worker. European factories still retained a high proportion of skilled labourers during the 1920s, but by the mid-1930s the economics of manufacture, coupled with the crippling effects of the Great Depression, only allowed niche luxury and sports models to be made by skilled craftsmen. While in 1914 most European car makers were generally producing cars at a rate of one per man per year, Ford's factories were producing twelve cars per man-year – and this was before the moving assembly line had been fully perfected. As late as 1927, French car workers were taking on average three hundred man-days to make a car, whereas their American counterparts at Ford and GM needed only seventy.

---

1 Of Kahn's six hundred factories worldwide, 521 were built for Stalin.

The US, with its vast internal market, low raw material costs and no great tradition of skilled labour, was well suited to the techniques of mass production. The history of the car industry in Europe – and in particular in the cradle of the Industrial Revolution, Britain – can be directly linked to the painful erosion of the status and importance of skilled craftsmen. In America, however, that shop-floor war was never as charged or as significant. Yet the employment and wealth that Fordization brought came at a high price: the inevitable dehumanization of the workforce not only sounded the death knell for the skilled worker but also consigned thousands of car workers to a slave-like existence.

In his pursuit of mechanization, Ford enthusiastically adapted the fashionable new ideas of the time-and-motion pioneer Frederick Taylor, whose peculiar philosophy attempted to apply standardized scientific measurement to almost every aspect of life. But, at least at this stage, Ford was no Taylorist tyrant. He was also very keen to retain, and indeed to grow, his workforce, introducing a system of high wages and attractive benefits. In 1905 every Ford worker received a huge Christmas bonus of $1,000. In 1911 workers at Ford's new British factory at Trafford Park, Manchester, were paid £3 for a six-day week – twice the average industrial wage in the UK. In 1913 wages in US plants rose on average by 15 per cent. In January 1914 Ford unveiled his greatest industrial relations coup yet: he publicly guaranteed a minimum rate of $5 for a day's work, assuming the worker in question met his production targets. The $5 rate was significantly more than any other major employer was currently offering to semi-skilled industrial workers, and it won him worldwide publicity and applause. Yet Ford's new payroll strategy was not born of altruism. He reasoned that, with more money to spend, his workers would lavish a substantial proportion of it on Ford cars. And the inflation of the wartime years meant that by 1918 the much-lauded $5 per day was actually worth only $2.80 in 1914 terms. In addition, in order to qualify for their $5 day, Ford's workers had to knuckle down to the tough new regime being imposed at Highland Park. The camaraderie and cross-departmental relationships that had flourished in traditional engineering firms had gone, to be replaced by a system of snoopers, or 'spotters', who ensured that the new shop-floor regulations were rigorously observed. Workers were not allowed to sit, smoke or talk on the job. (Some learned to move their lips, in what became known as the 'Ford whisper', while keeping their faces immobile – the freezing of their features being nicknamed locally 'the Fordization of the face'.) Ford officials even visited workers' homes to check on their dietary and recreational habits, financial health and moral well-being. Any individuals who failed to conform to the Ford code, and were found guilty of 'malicious practice derogatory to good physical manhood or moral character', were sacked. In return for their new-found affluence, Ford's workers were, for the most part, treated as automata.

Seeing that the assembly-line experiment at Highland Park had been a success, in 1916 Henry Ford began building a vast new automated complex on the banks of the River Rouge in western Detroit. The Dodge brothers – major shareholders in the Ford Motor Company who also ran their own, modest, car manufacturing business – tried to halt the expansion, alleging that Ford's profits should be diverted as dividends to shareholders (such as themselves) rather than invested in a new plant. In 1917 Ford's lawyers shrugged off the challenge, although they were unable to avoid the subsequent judgement that Ford should pay an extra special dividend – an unhelpful ruling that convinced the enraged Henry Ford to rid himself of all his minority shareholders. The Dodge brothers were not a thorn in Ford's side for long, as they both died in 1920. By the time of their death Ford had successfully converted his growing car-making empire into a family-owned and family-managed business.

Ford did not have a good First World War. A right-wing populist pacifist by nature, he strongly opposed conscription and anything that smacked of benevolence towards the allied cause, at least until America's own entry into the war. His much-vaunted Peace Ship Expedition to Europe in 1915, designed to publicize American isolationism and, rather more naively, to promote 'universal peace' between the warring European powers, predictably proved a political and public relations disaster. President Wilson took an instant dislike to the brash, opinionated car maker and wisely refused to sanction the project, while the media had a field day with Ford's ill-conceived and incoherent press conferences. The *Springfield Republican* labelled him 'God's Fool', while the *New York Tribune* responded to his bizarre proposal to organize a Europe-wide general strike of armies and workers on Christmas Day 1915 with the sardonic headline 'GREAT WAR ENDS CHRISTMAS DAY: FORD TO STOP IT'. The 'Peace Ship', meanwhile, never sailed further than the neutral nations of Scandinavia, and none of Ford's absurd pacifist ambitions was ever realized.

When, after America entered the war in April 1917, Ford did grudgingly lend his factories to the war effort, it was too late. The sixty Packard-powered, Eagle-class patrol craft that the Rouge River plant produced, out of an original US Navy order for one hundred boats, arrived too late to see action. By 1 December only seven had been delivered to the navy, which never asked Ford to supply it again. And while Ford had publicly affirmed that he would provide all Ford-made boats and munitions 'without one cent of profit', decrying those who accepted such 'blood money', he was later accused of making outrageous profits from the Eagles that were never delivered. These charges became even more resonant when it was revealed that Henry Ford's only son, Edsel, had managed to avoid serving in the armed forces during the war. These draft-dodging accusations certainly helped Henry Ford lose the US senatorial election for Michigan in November 1918. Three years later allegations were made to the US Treasury that Ford had avoided paying any federal tax on his wartime profits – a tax bill that may have been as large as $29 million. The issue was still being hotly debated in the mid-1930s and remains unresolved to this day.

While Ford was creating the greatest industrial enterprise the world had ever seen, across the city of Detroit another automotive pioneer was binding a bizarre, ramshackle collection of struggling car makers into a cohesive conglomerate that would one day overtake Ford as the world's biggest vehicle manufacturer.

William Crapo Durant died in April 1947, just a month before Henry Ford. But Durant's was not a rags-to-riches story like Ford's; his grandfather had not only been a rich and successful lumber merchant, but had risen to become governor of Michigan. Nor was Durant obsessed by cars, as Ford was. He invented many other machines – some successful, such as the Frigidaire electric icebox; and some not, like the Samson tractor, which you had to walk patiently behind – but always remained an enthusiast rather than a zealot. Ford was a businessman who loved to run his manufacturing empire and was loath to let it go; Durant was a fast-talking salesman who tired of businesses once he had acquired and developed them. His business strategy was exactly the opposite of Ford's: he believed in consumer choice, rather than in selling the same single product at a rock-bottom price. And Durant was very different from the calculating, bullying tycoons who dominated the car industry after 1945. He was charming, handsome, creative – and easily distracted. Unlike contemporaries such as Ford, Chrysler or Chevrolet, he was also surprisingly modest and reticent. He has been called 'the Great Gatsby of car making'. He made and lost two fortunes, and on his death was worth a mere $250.

Durant grew up in the little town of Flint, Michigan, the subsequent growth of which into one of the principal motor centres of America was largely his doing. He graduated from making delivery carts, which he soon made into the town's biggest industry, to making cars, capitalizing the fledgling Buick company and making Flint one of the fastest-growing towns in America.

David Dunbar Buick was a Scottish plumber turned inventor who became a car maker at the relatively advanced aged of forty-five. Born in Arbroath, on Scotland's east coast, his parents emigrated to America when David was two years old. Aged fifteen, Buick began to work for a plumbing fixtures firm in his native Detroit, which in 1882 he was able to rescue after it folded. Selling the firm in 1899, he invested in engine manufacture with his partner, Walter Marr, and together they built the first Buick car in 1903. Buick himself was never a ruthless businessman in the mould of countless Scots-American emigrants. In 1900 he had actually sold Marr the rights to the Buick Automobile name, and in 1903 sold 99 per cent of the rights in the new Buick Motor Car Company to the Briscoe brothers, Frank and Benjamin. Yet he and Marr were nothing if not persistent, and in 1904 they came up with the first saleable Buick, the Model B. Attracted by the Model B, William Durant offered to help bankroll the struggling new car maker, and in 1906 he built a new factory in Flint which was then the largest and most modern in the world.

Durant's flair, energy and seemingly inexhaustible self-belief helped him to establish a small dealership network for Buick. However, he soon became convinced that only by the large-scale capitalization of an alliance of leading car makers could the fledgling US motor industry find the investment necessary to make a big success of the automobile. Accordingly, in the winter of 1907–8 Durant began negotiations with the fabulously wealthy and successful banking house of J. P. Morgan with a view to securing multi-million dollar backing for a group of manufacturers, which he called the United Motors Corporation. Durant later discovered that a United Motors Car Company already existed in New Jersey, and he and his partners thereupon agreed on the straightforward if insipid name of General Motor (GM).

J. Pierpont Morgan was the nation's premier banker. Born in 1837, the year Queen Victoria came to the throne, he had built up an enormous banking fortune over sixty years, and in 1895 his personal guarantees had saved President Cleveland's administration from bankruptcy. Morgan originally believed the automobile was a passing fad, and after his first meeting with the Tigger-ish Durant he dubbed the auto entrepreneur 'an unstable visionary'. Durant nevertheless eventually convinced him otherwise, and was able to proceed on his quest with qualified backing from Morgan. What followed was a period of astonishing growth, as the banks nervously financed Durant's rapid assembly of the world's first car combine. Oldsmobile's Fred Smith later declared that no one else but Durant, 'the master salesman of all time', possessed the vision to recognize that a 'strong combination' was exactly what the auto industry needed, and affirmed that Durant was the only man who could have created such an ambitious conglomerate: 'No man ever lived who could sell such a variety of commodities in so short a space of time, cigars, buggies, automobiles and himself, believing wholeheartedly in his wares and in the last item especially.'

On 16 September 1908, Durant incorporated GM in New Jersey and sold Buick to himself as GM's first car marque. He then swiftly bought the W. F. Stewart body plant in Flint, Albert Champion's Detroit spark plug factory, and the nearby Oldsmobile plant, and additionally made the first cross-marque transfer, giving Oldsmobile the best-selling Buick Model 10 to rework as a premium product. Within months he had also purchased the Oakland Company, a car maker sited in Pontiac, to the north of Detroit, and run by his friend Edward M. Murphy, a former buggy maker whom Durant had helped to convert to the idea of automobile manufacture in 1907. Murphy was actually less than enthusiastic with the buyout than his eager partners, but found he could not argue with the $201,000 offer that Durant's GM made for his tiny company, which in 1926 was formally renamed Pontiac. Within months, Durant had also added the budding auto manufacturer Cadillac to his growing portfolio of brands. In this instance, however, the indefatigable impresario found that he was facing a far tougher opponent than Murphy – one who, while seemingly at the end of his professional life, could still drive a hard bargain.

In 1893 the fifty-year-old precision toolmaker Henry M. Leland, who ran a company making bicycle gears and steam-tram power units, opened an automotive workshop on Detroit's Trombly Avenue. In 1899 he merged his firm with the newly bankrupt Detroit Automobile Company and named the resulting business the Cadillac Automobile Company. In 1903 Leland unveiled his first Cadillac car, with the Sieur de Cadillac's antique coat of arms fixed to the radiator cap. By 1908 Leland's premium-priced Cadillac 30 was selling exceptionally well, emboldening the car maker to devise what became the brand's enduring slogan: 'The Standard of the World'. Leland also attracted the attention of the irrepressible Durant, who in 1909 found he had to offer far more for Cadillac than the $201,000 with which he had snared Oakland. The final negotiated price for Cadillac was $4.5 million, which even the resourceful Durant needed ten days to find.

By the beginning of 1910 GM was selling fifty thousand cars annually. But this was still way short of the 170,000 Model Ts that Henry Ford was producing every year. Nevertheless, in a gesture of amazing effrontery, Durant attempted to raise $8 million to buy the Ford Motor Company from under Ford's nose. Ford's directors agreed, but Henry Ford himself held firm and successfully blocked the deal.

Seeking other outlets for his expansionism, Durant floated a million-dollar stock issue and made his first overseas purchase, Bedford Motors, in London, which formed the kernel of what by 1912 was known as Bedford Motors (Europe). Not all of Durant's purchases were as perceptive, though. He bought many companies for the engines or parts that they made, only to find that the businesses were on the brink of collapse and needed an injection of far more cash than they were worth.[1] At the same time, Durant eschewed cash reserves, relying on income from sales to pay his operating expenses and to seal new acquisitions.

By the summer of 1910 the General Motors empire comprised twenty-five companies. Predictably, Durant's seemingly endless spending spree and GM's lightning growth had unsettled the banks. Durant's creditors estimated Buick's debt alone to be worth in the region of $7 million dollars, and at the end of 1910 resolved on a stop to new acquisitions and 'a restriction of enthusiasm'. The Buick, Cadillac and Oldsmobile factories were temporarily closed. Durant went on the road and managed to borrow $8 million from an assortment of small country banks, dazzling their executives with his boundless enthusiasm and the paper value of GM's constituent elements. But the big banks refused to play ball. Summoned to meet key investment bankers at the Chase National Bank on 25 September 1910, Durant was repeatedly upbraided for his debts and was refused any further loans. GM was only saved from receivership

---

1 For example, Durant paid $7 million for the Heany Lamp Company in order to acquire a patent for an incandescent light which turned out to be fraudulent.

by an expertly professional presentation by Henry Leland, whose Cadillac division was at the time the most profitable part of the combine. The bankers decreed that GM be put into the hands of five trustees – bankers all, led by the deeply conservative 'Boston Brahmin' James Jackson Storrow – with Durant retained only as vice president.

Durant was predictably dismayed to lose control of his own creation. Thirty years later, in notes he wrote for an autobiography which, typically, he never finished, he remembered: 'I saw some of my cherished ideas laid aside, never to be revived. Opportunities that should have been taken care of with quickness and decision were not considered. The things that counted so much in the past, which gave General Motors its unique and powerful position, were subordinated to "liquidate and pay".'

GM had been saved – in a year in which eighteen car manufacturers collapsed. But its founder had been marginalized. One of the principal authors of Durant's downfall, GM's new president, James Storrow, later astutely (if condescendingly) recalled Durant as an irresponsible enthusiast: 'In many respects he is a child in emotions, in temperament and in mental balance, yet possessed of wonderful energy and ability . . . He is sensitive and proud, and successful leadership, I think, really counts with him more than financial success.' Storrow himself did not last long. Having established a GM listing on the New York Stock Exchange, after only two months at the helm he reluctantly ceded the GM presidency to Charles Nash, who was supported by a raft of Detroit businessmen who thought they knew more about car making than the Boston banker.

In the meantime, Durant had found himself a new playpen. He bought the old Flint factory where Buick had started, hired a former Buick manager, and launched the Mason Car Company in August 1911. In the same year he met Louis Chevrolet, a man whose press releases described him as 'one of the speed wonders of the day'. It was subsequently announced that the two would 'establish a factory in Detroit for the manufacture of a new high-priced car'.

Louis Chevrolet looked just like a caricature Frenchman. He was a huge, bear-like man, built like a rugby prop-forward, sporting a bristling moustache and seeming to have a cigarette permanently attached to his lower lip. Chevrolet was actually Swiss by birth, though the son of a watchmaker of French origin; his family had moved to the French town of Beaune, in the heart of the Burgundy wine country, when he was only eight years old. There the young Louis discovered his passion for engineering, assisting a blind wine merchant by building him a revolutionary new wine pump. Chevrolet never lost that childish glee at being able to dismantle and reassemble a machine. In 1900 he emigrated to Montreal to work as a mechanic and as a chauffeur, before moving again, this time to New York. Here the ever-restless Chevrolet began working in the Brooklyn workshop of the French manufacturer De Dion-Bouton, at that time the world's largest car maker.

Chevrolet, like Durant, could never keep still. In 1905 he was hired by Fiat as a racing driver, and a year later was approached by a wide range of car makers who were keen to prove their new products on the racetrack. Among them was Billy Durant, and Chevrolet was soon racing for Buick. At the same time, Chevrolet started designing his own engine. Highly impressed by his industry, Durant backed him to found the Chevrolet Motor Car Company in 1911, employing a stylized version of the Swiss cross as its corporate logo. The firm's big, luxurious Classic 6 was a great success, and even Louis Chevrolet himself was pressed into helping market the model, inviting journalists to place a pencil tip against the car's bonnet while he revved the engine – the stationary pencil demonstrating the smoothness of the new engine.

Chevrolet and Durant were completely dissimilar characters, both physically and temperamentally, and it was no surprise to most observers when they fell out. Durant used the runaway success of Chevrolet's cars to buy up GM stock and, ultimately, to buy his way back to overall control of General Motors in 1915 – buying out shareholders who were disgruntled with their stock's lacklustre performance in the hands of the conservative, steady-as-she-goes bankers who had run GM since 1910. But he did this without Louis Chevrolet. Chevrolet returned to France in the summer of

1913 and in his absence Durant moved the production of Chevrolet cars from Detroit to Flint. When Chevrolet returned he was furious. Relations deteriorated even further when Durant suggested that the chain-smoking Chevrolet replace his beloved Gauloises with cigars, the image of which was so much more stereotypically American. The two also quarrelled over the design and marketing of Chevrolet's automobiles: the self-educated, rough-hewn Chevrolet wanted his name to be used for a big, meaty car with a powerful engine, while the smooth, fast-talking Durant merely wanted to build cars cheaply and quickly. By the end of 1913 Chevrolet had resigned from the company that bore his name; and by 1915, the year in which Durant returned in triumph to the summit of the conglomerate, he had sold Durant all his shares in GM – stock that, had he held on to it, would have been worth many millions of dollars by the time of his death in 1941. In 1917 Durant quietly folded the business into General Motors, making Chevrolet the largest division of the corporation, producing the kind of affordable, everyday cars that Louis Chevrolet, ever the romantic racing driver, loathed.

Chevrolet himself, meanwhile, had reverted to his first automotive love and started building racing cars. In 1916 he and his younger brother, Gaston, started the Frontenac Motor Corporation, whose products frequently competed in the Indianapolis 500 race, with modest success. Sadly, though, success in business always eluded the impatient racer. Gaston died in a racetrack accident in 1921, and the brothers' company was declared bankrupt in 1924. After this failure, Louis ventured into boat and aircraft building, again with little success. By the early 1930s he was penniless and he and his wife were eking out a living in a small Florida apartment. Embarrassed by his plight – and aware of the public relations disaster that would ensue if the media were to rediscover the man who had lent his name to GM's most profitable division – General Motors agreed to provide Chevrolet with a small pension in 1934. Seven years later, he died after a botched leg operation. Louis Chevrolet was buried not in his native Switzerland, nor in France, nor even in Detroit, but in Indianapolis, where his happiest moments had been spent at the wheel of a racing car.

Ransom Eli Olds was yet another pioneer American car maker who, like Benz, Daimler and Chevrolet, found himself sidelined in the industry's rapid dash for growth. In 1892 Olds was selling gasoline engines to customers in America and Britain, and a year later tested a buggy powered by one of these engines on the streets of his native Lansing, Michigan. Olds so impressed local lumber and copper magnate Samuel L. Smith that the latter eagerly invested in his new Olds Motor Vehicle Company.[1] Initially, Olds met with little success, and all seemed lost when his Detroit factory burned to the ground in 1901. However, the single car that Olds had managed to save from the flames – a little 4 hp vehicle with a curved dashboard – was put into production in 1902 and proved an immediate hit. Orders topped one thousand when test-driver Roy Chapin drove the car across Canada to Detroit and then on to New York.[2] Olds, however, soon found himself almost as temperamentally unsuited for the world of big business as Louis Chevrolet. Disagreements with Smith and his son culminated in Olds's sacking in 1904. Ironically, the following year the company finally adopted the colloquial name for the Olds cars and began officially calling them Oldsmobiles – a brand that, with the help of Smiths' financial backing, became one of the constituents of Durant's General Motors in 1908. The Oldsmobile name survived for almost a century before being axed by its parent company in 2004.

Alone once more, Olds had founded his own automobile manufacturer, named REO after his own initials, in 1905. REO's stylish and innovative cars won many admirers, but Olds found himself elbowed

---

1 Legend has it that Olds intended to establish his new factory in Newark, New Jersey, but that he met a mining engineer on the platform of Detroit station who offered to bankroll his operation at a nearby location.
2 Chapin went on to found the Hudson Motor Car Company in 1908. In 1954 Hudson merged with Nash-Kelvinator to become the American Motor Corporation (AMC), a firm that Roy's son, Roy Chapin junior, later led. Chapin senior, however, was to earn notoriety as President Herbert Hoover's last Secretary of Commerce in 1932–3.

out yet again; removed as general manager in 1923, he remained only as nominal president of his eponymous firm. Unlike Chevrolet, Olds at least ensured that his enforced retirement was not a penurious one. He turned to architectural patronage, financing the Olds Tower in Lansing, the tallest building in Michigan's state capital;[1] and adding to his mansion on Lansing's South Washington Avenue, where one of his many domestic innovations was to design a garage turntable that allowed him to drive his car in at night and leave again the next morning without having to engage reverse gear. Four years after his death in 1950, the struggling REO company was declared bankrupt; and in 1972, with a flagrant disregard for America's architectural and industrial heritage that was so typical of the times, Olds's fine Lansing mansion was demolished to make way for Interstate 496 – a highway which, in a hideous irony, was named after Ransom Olds himself.

Durant, meanwhile, continued his roller-coaster ride. On 16 September 1915, having engineered Chevrolet's reverse takeover of the much larger GM, he returned to the top job at General Motors, jubilantly informing a shaken James Storrow: 'I'm in control of General Motors today.' Storrow and Nash were soon persuaded to resign. (Charles Nash went on to found the Nash Motor Company, which by the 1920s had become a successful niche car maker.[2]) Over the next few years Durant installed Ford-style assembly lines at GM's plants and saw the combine produce its millionth car (an Oldsmobile). Meanwhile he continued buying companies, among them Delco electronics; the Guardian Frigerator Company, whose electric icebox Durant memorably christened the Frigidaire; Fisher car bodies; and the ball-bearing manufacturer Hyatt, whose president, Alfred P. Sloan, now found himself on the GM board. In June 1919 work was begun on a new GM corporate headquarters in Detroit, designed by the car makers' Palladio, Albert Kahn. However, Durant was soon to be faced with an

---

1 It is currently known as the Boji Tower.
2 In 1954 Nash merged with Hudson to form AMC.

obstacle far more implacable than Storrow or Nash, and was about to get his final comeuppance.

Across the Atlantic, in Britain, the success of Ford and Durant in the years before the First World War encouraged other automotive enthusiasts to try their hand at car making. Not all of them, however, proved as success-ful as the lions of Detroit.

Of the early British auto pioneers, London-born Frederick Lanchester initially seemed to be the man most likely to succeed. The son of an architect, Lanchester began work as a humble draughtsman's assistant in Birmingham in 1887. Soon he had risen to become assistant manager of the local gas works. However, while on a visit to Paris in 1889 he caught the automotive bug. From 1895 he began experimenting with his own car designs, introducing pneumatic tyres, water-cooling, overhead valves and, in 1903, disc brakes.

Lanchester's cars were a cut above those of his competitors: they rode smoothly, were well built, and as a result were far more reliable than most vehicles currently on the roads. They were also unusually spacious; Lanchester (like Alec Issigonis forty years later) sought to concentrate the engine as far forward as possible in order to create as much internal space as he could for the car's occupants. But Lanchester, like Chevrolet, was no businessman. His first car company went bankrupt in 1905, just as he was introducing his superb 20 hp model. Lanchester, however, a good-humoured man with a fine singing voice and an excellent reputation as a public speaker, never seemed to let such setbacks affect him. He first became a consultant for Daimler and then restarted the Lanchester busi-ness. Sadly, in 1913 he was forced to resign – just as Benz, Daimler and Olds had been – by his impatient fellow directors. After 1913 he turned his attention to producing aircraft engines during the First World War and to developing radio, and he acted as a consultant to Coventry's car makers.

Where the impeccably middle-class Lanchester failed with his luxury models, farmer's son Herbert Austin succeeded with his everyday runabouts. Working as an engineer in Australia in his twenties, Austin met the Dublin emigrant turned sheep-shearer Frederick Wolseley, who had patented new sheep-shearing machinery in Victoria in 1876, and in 1889 had brought his Wolseley Sheep Shearing Machine Company (WSSMC) back to Birmingham. Wolseley invited Austin to manage the WSSMC works, which he did very successfully, centralizing production and replacing antiquated machines. Indeed, Austin so impressed the WSSMC directors that, after he had seen his first cars in Paris in 1893, they agreed to his proposal to invest in this new mode of transport. Two years later Austin's first car was born: a three-wheeled, 2 hp Wolseley model, which was one of the first British-designed automobiles to run on British roads. A year later WSSMC, in collaboration with the Daimler syndicate, invested in a new car plant; and in 1900 the third Wolseley car, the Voiturette, won the first public motor trial – a gruelling 100 mile ride along bumpy roads and tracks, organized by the Auto Club of Great Britain. Nevertheless, Wolseley's directors saw the car as merely a bit of fun and soon refused to invest any more of their money in Austin's 'hobby'. Austin, however, quickly found another, more visionary backer: the armaments tycoon Sir Hiram Maxim funded Austin's break from WSSMC and, in 1905 (together with the Midland Bank and, curiously, the German steel giant Krupp), financed an Austin factory seven miles south of Birmingham, on the site of a derelict print works at Longbridge.

Austin was criticized for his new factory's remote location, but he argued that at Longbridge there was lots of room for expansion, unlike at the cramped car shops of Birmingham and Coventry, and that the absence of urban air pollution would assist in the application of paint and varnish. The space Austin enjoyed at Longbridge also, crucially, enabled him to add an on-site body shop, whereas the majority of his rivals had their car bodies made elsewhere. And here Sir Herbert (he was knighted for his services to the war effort in 1917) was the absolute ruler, sincerely believing that his interests would always be the same as those of his workforce – who would, he assumed, value engineering more than equality.

While Austin was making a name for himself as the builder of small family cars in Birmingham, fifty miles away, on the other side of the Midlands, the unlikely partnership of Rolls and Royce was succeeding, where Frederick Lanchester had stumbled, in establishing a British luxury car business to rival those of Benz and Cadillac.

F. H. Royce was a miller's son from Cambridgeshire who had only had three years' schooling when, on the death of his father in a London poorhouse, he was forced to seek work – which he found first as a news-paper boy for W. H. Smith and then (aged only twelve) as a telegram delivery boy for the Post Office. A kindly aunt financed an apprenticeship at the Great Northern Railway (GNR) works at Peterborough, but Royce had to leave the GNR when his aunt's money ran out. Instead he joined a machine-tool firm in London and attended evening classes at Finsbury Polytechnic. Moving to Liverpool to work on theatrical lighting, his newly invented electric dynamo came to the attention of the automotive world, including a would-be aristocratic entrepreneur, the Hon. C. S. Rolls.

Charles Rolls's background was as far removed from Royce's as could be imagined. He was the third son of Lord Llangattock, a wealthy Welsh landowner whose family seat was near Monmouth, while his mother was the daughter of a rich Scottish baronet. Rolls was a tall, confident man – he stood at 6 foot 5 inches – who was always impeccably dressed and was a natural salesman.[1] From Eton – a school he detested, and where his developing interest in engineering earned him the nickname 'Dirty Rolls' – he scraped into Trinity College, Cambridge, via a crammer school. At Cambridge he was more interested in cars and bicycles than in his degree course in Mechanical and Applied Science, and won a half-blue in cycling. In 1896, at the age of eighteen, Rolls brought a Peugeot Phaeton back to Cambridge, the first car the ancient city had ever seen. He joined the Self-Propelled Traffic Association, became a founder member of the Automobile Club, and built an engineering workshop in his parents'

---

1 He was also, however, notoriously mean with money and never paid for anything he could get for free.

garden. On his graduation, Rolls shocked his family by getting a job at the London and North Western Railway workshops at Crewe, albeit in a rather more elevated position than Royce had been able to find with the GNR at Peterborough. In 1903, with the help of £6,600 provided by his father, he started one of Britain's first car dealerships, at Fulham, in west London, where he sold imported Peugeots from France and Minervas from Belgium.

Rolls and Royce's historic meeting, at the splendid Midland Hotel in Manchester on 4 May 1904, was facilitated by a mutual friend at the Automobile Club. Rolls could see the potential in Royce's new two-cylinder car and agreed to sell all the cars Royce could make. The two were like chalk and cheese: Rolls urbane, unruffled and sociable; Royce coarse, reticent and obsessed with engineering. (Royce would no doubt have been pleased that his statue in Derby is merely inscribed 'Henry Royce, mechanic'.) But the partnership worked.

The first Rolls-Royce car, the 10 hp, was unveiled in Paris in December 1904; and in 1906 Rolls and Royce formalized their partnership by creating Rolls-Royce Ltd, with Rolls providing the financial backing and salesmanship to complement Royce's engineering expertise. Their first cars were built on the principles of lightness, speed and quality. Royce, like Lanchester, was shocked by how poorly built most contemporary automobiles were, and was determined that his vehicles would be made to last. Rolls, meanwhile, put much effort into publicizing the quietness and smoothness of Royce's superb cars, and at the end of 1906 he travelled to the US to promote the new automobiles, unlocking a market that was to sustain the firm ever after. By 1907 the company was winning numerous awards for the quality and reliability of its cars, and in 1908 it was able to afford to begin production at its new factory in Derby, bought after Derby City Council, seeking to lure embryonic car makers away from Coventry, offered the partners all the cheap electricity they needed.

By 1909 Rolls's personal interest in the car business was waning, having been superseded by his fascination with the new fad of flying. On

2 June 1910 he became the first man to make a non-stop double crossing of the English Channel by air in his Wright flyer, for which achievement he was awarded the Gold Medal of the Royal Aero Club and memorialized with imposing statues in both Monmouth and Dover. But it was flying that was to cut Rolls's glittering career tragically short. On 12 July 1910, at the age of just thirty-two, he was killed in an air crash at Bournemouth when the tail of his Wright biplane broke off.

After Rolls's death, Royce, a workaholic who made himself ill with overwork, became increasingly unwell and was advised to spend most of his time at West Wittering in Sussex, on the warm south coast of England, or in southern France. As a result, Rolls-Royce was effectively run by its canny business director, Claude Johnson, a publicity-conscious enthusiast and former museum curator who, as secretary, essentially ran Britain's Automobile Club. By 1914 Johnson was nicknamed (behind his back) 'the hyphen in Rolls-Royce'.

After the Model T, perhaps the most famous car in the world in the years in the years before the First World War was the Rolls-Royce 40/50, first introduced in 1906 and later named the Silver Ghost. This legendary car, as motor historian Jonathan Wood has noted, 'more than justified the firm's claim that it was "the Best Six Cylinder Car in the World"'. The Silver Ghost was emphatically Claude Johnson's creation. Royce tended to lose interest once he had created a car design and always wanted to move on to the next challenge. It was Johnson who produced and marketed the Silver Ghost; in Johnson's hands it was – in sharp contrast to Ford's products – promoted as an unambiguously premium product, retailing at prices up to £2,500 at a time when Ford's new Model N was available for £125. Reassuringly, customers considered the high price quite justified, and the success of the Silver Ghost help to make Rolls-Royce a byword for build, resilience and longevity.

Rolls-Royce's reputation for fine luxury cars was cemented by the First World War. As early as 20 August 1914, only sixteen days after Britain had declared war on Germany and Austria, Claude Johnson arranged for twenty-five Silver Ghost owners to cross by ferry with their

cars to Le Havre and drive to Picardy, where they were soon chauffeur-
ing the generals of Sir John French's British Expeditionary Force. Silver
Ghosts were also provided with basic armour plating to protect key air-
fields for the Royal Naval Air Service. As a result, when the first Royal
Naval Armoured Car Division was formed in September 1914, it used
adapted Silver Ghosts fitted with armour and a turret, the car's resilient
chassis happily taking the extra weight. Quiet, reliable and well built, and
capable of up to 63 mph, the Silver Ghost served as the ultimate British
staff car and was selected to carry King's Messengers around the Western
Front. Most famously, T. E. Lawrence immortalized the Silver Ghost during his 'Revolt in the Desert' of 1917–8. Writing about the campaign after
the event in his classic account *The Seven Pillars of Wisdom*, Lawrence
of Arabia's tales of driving militarily adapted Silver Ghosts through the
desert at over 60 mph did wonders for Rolls-Royce's international image.
The cars were 'more valuable than rubies', Lawrence enthused; 'we knew
it was nearly impossible to break a Rolls-Royce'. When, after the publication of the *Seven Pillars*, Lawrence was asked by a journalist what in life
he most valued, he replied: 'I should like my own Rolls-Royce car with
enough tyres and petrol to last me all my life.' You couldn't buy that sort
of publicity. And Lawrence's encomiums helped to ensure that the Silver
Ghost survived the vicissitudes of the post-war years as one of the world's
most prestigious cars. The last Silver Ghost rolled out of the Derby works
in 1925, two years before Henry Ford ceased production of the Model T.
Together these two, vastly different, vehicles helped ensure that the motor
car was definitely no passing fad.

By the time Lawrence was haring across the desert in his Silver
Ghost, Rolls-Royce had already adopted its famous radiator mascot, the
Spirit of Ecstasy, designed in 1911 by Charles Robinson Sykes. The Spirit's
lithe, sinuous figure was allegedly based on Eleanor Thornton, the secretary and mistress of John, 2nd Lord Montagu of Beaulieu, a pioneer
of the automobile movement and editor of *The Car* from 1902. Eleanor,
who had a child by Montagu, died in 1915 when the passenger ship on
which she was travelling, the SS *Persia*, was torpedoed by a German

U-boat. Interestingly, Royce himself hated the mascot, asserting that it impaired the driver's view, and he refused to carry it on his own cars. Nevertheless, Sykes was subsequently brought back to Rolls-Royce to create a lower, more aerodynamic version of the mascot for the firm's new sports saloons. (The resulting 'kneeling lady' mascot was first used on the Phantom III of 1936–9.) Today's Spirit of Ecstasy – also known as the Silver Lady, although the figures were never made wholly of silver, and in the US as the Flying Lady – is mounted on a spring-loaded mechanism, designed to retract instantly into the radiator shell if struck from any direction.

It was not only the Spirit of Ecstasy that made the Silver Ghost into one of the most instantly recognizable models on the road. The car's prominent architectural radiator also helped create the luxury marque's iconic status. Shaped in the form of a classical pedimented portico, Rolls-Royce's radiator used the same principle of entasis – the vertical members tapering imperceptibly inwards in order to counteract the apparent distortion of the grille's straight lines – that the ancient Greeks had used for their stone temple columns. Both the mascot and the radiator soon became distinctive and invaluable brand properties – assets that were, as we will see, to take central stage during the undignified auction of Rolls-Royce Motors at the end of the twentieth century.

In hindsight, we can see how the Ford Model T and the Rolls-Royce Silver Ghost pointed the way forward for the development of, respectively, the family and the luxury car. However, in the years before the First World War the future was not so transparent. The motoring enthusiast of 1914 would have been surprised to learn that, a century later, the names of great contemporary automotive pioneers such as Durant and Lanchester would be almost wholly forgotten, along with such household brands such as De Dion-Bouton and Panhard. He or she may also have been surprised at the global prevalence of the petrol-driven internal combustion engine. For as late as 1900 it appeared that steam-powered vehicles, rather than those run on oil-based fuels, would provide the transport of the future.

The years of optimism for steam power were brief, however. In 1903 the Connecticut-based Locomobile Company of America, which had been making steam cars since 1899, switched to gasoline engines; seven years later the White Motor Company of Cleveland, Ohio, followed suit. The principal reasons for the flight from steam were safety and the constant need for a nearby fuel supply (the same problem that plagues plug-in electric cars today). A few high-profile explosions of steam boilers did nothing to help. In 1906 the public endorsement of the gasoline engine by the city officials of San Francisco proved the final nail in the coffin for the steam car; in that year two hundred private cars, fuelled by fifteen thousand gallons of petrol donated by Standard Oil, were pressed into service to rescue people trapped or hurt in the San Francisco earthquake. The city's fire chief declared to the media afterwards that he had been sceptical about the value of the car before the disaster, 'but now give it my hearty endorsement'. The internal combustion engine had proved its worth, and the steam car was left wallowing in its wake.

Electric vehicles took longer to be vanquished by the petrol motor. Even while steam cars were beginning to be viewed as a liability, electric autos were becoming increasingly popular with pioneer drivers. The Electric Cab and Carriage Service was launched in New York in 1897 by two Philadelphia engineers, Henry Morris and Pedro Salom, and backed by the Electric Storage Battery Company; in 1899, against a background of encouraging sales, it renamed itself the Electric Vehicle Company (EVC). Yet the lead-acid batteries that the EVC vehicles carried were disproportionately heavy, weighing around 1,600 pounds each, and the cars' tiny engines could barely cope with the added weight. Moreover, the batteries tended to leak corrosive fluid, while charging facilities were few, at least outside Manhattan. In 1907, predictably, EVC folded. Electric cabs continued running in New York City until 1912, but by 1914 few manufacturers or operators were continuing with electric cars. By 1919 just 1 per cent of all US commercial vehicles, and virtually no private cars, were electrically powered. The search was on to find a lightweight alternative to the heavy lead-acid battery, but it was a quest that would take almost seventy years to reach its goal.

2

Snakes and Ladders: Europe between the Wars

In the turbulent years after the First World War, some famous European car-making names from before 1914 disappeared entirely, while newer manufacturers built worldwide reputations. It was a time of boom and bust; some manufacturers died impoverished and disappointed, while others became immensely rich. And those firms that had survived the tough years immediately following the war often prospered in the later 1920s, only to fall victim to the catastrophic depression that gripped the globe in the years following the Wall Street Crash of October 1929. Most of those that did survive tended to follow the example of Ford and Rolls-Royce, building a reputation for reliability and longevity, and aiming their products squarely at either the popular or the luxury end of the market.

One of the principal British casualties of the Great Depression was Frederick Lanchester. In 1931 what was left of his firm was merged into Coventry's Daimler. Three years later, and almost sightless, Lanchester was diagnosed with Parkinson's disease. He was only able to continue living in his Birmingham home through charitable donations, which helped him to pay his mortgage. In 1946 he died, blind, impoverished, and largely ignored by the motor industry.

Some car makers actually managed to profit from the rising tide of company failures. Surveying the collapse of so many famous pre-war concerns, from the mid-1920s the Rootes brothers sought to build an automotive empire by buying up failing companies at rock-bottom prices. Billy and Reggie Rootes were not engineers but car dealers. Billy, the natural salesman of the family, started his working life as a fifteen-year-old apprentice at Singer's Coventry factory. At the end of the First World War he persuaded his bookish brother Reginald to leave his post at the Admiralty and help expand the family's Maidstone-based dealership network into car manufacture. In later years Billy often joked that 'I am the engine and Reginald is the steering and brakes of the business' ... 'I think up the ideas, and then Reggie tells me whether they will work.' It was a combination that initially seemed to work well. In 1926 the brothers put a marker down on their ambitions by establishing an impressive new central London showroom on the site of the old Devonshire House, opposite the Ritz Hotel on Piccadilly. The two then proceeded to use this prestigious headquarters as a base for an ambitious campaign of acquisition, which was funded not from their own limited resources but by the mighty purse of Prudential Assurance, which the rapacious Rootes brothers had persuaded to back them. In 1928–9 Rootes bought Hillman, Humber and Commer, renowned brands which were struggling in the tough post-war trading environment. Not everything went to plan, however. In 1931, at the height of the Great Depression, Billy Rootes unveiled the new Hillman Wizard at a grandiose launch for a thousand people, held in the cavernous Royal Albert Hall. The guests consumed 278 bottles of champagne and 199 bottles of hock, and a message of congratulation from the Prince of Wales was read out. The upwardly mobile Billy Rootes had already insinuated himself into Edward, Prince of Wales's notoriously raffish set; he often shot with the prince and was a frequent companion of his former mistress, Freda Dudley Ward, after the prince dropped her for the American heiress Wallis Simpson. The ever-persistent Billy had ensured that the prince had bought a series of Rootes cars. However, no amount of royal patronage or premium champagne could disguise the fact that the Wizard was the wrong car at the wrong time. Billy, though, was always quick learn from his mistakes: the Hillman Minx small family car of 1932 was cheaper and more conventional than the doomed Wizard, and proved an enduring success.

As the Depression eased in the mid-1930s, the Rootes brothers recommenced their spending spree. They harvested the venerable coach-builder Thrupp and Maberly, a firm that could trace its lineage back to 1790: Karrier commercial vehicles, British Light Steel Pressings of Acton, Talbot, and the prestigious Sunbeam company, then best known for its racing cars. Unfortunately, once the Rootes brothers had acquired new car makers, they did not really know how to market them. They contented themselves with badge-engineering, creating a range of similar-looking, down-market marques based on Rootes' run-of-the-mill Hillman plat-forms. The brothers were, it seemed, keener on new markets than on revolutionizing the car industry.[1]

Wolverhampton-based Sunbeam was a good example. Sunbeam had, in 1920, absorbed the famous French firms of Darracq and Talbot to form STD Motors (one historic marque that seems unlikely to be revived). During the 1920s, Sunbeam cars won numerous Grands Prix and established four land speed records. STD's luxury products, however, did not fare well during the Great Depression of the early 1930s and the firm was bought cheaply by Rootes after going into receivership in 1935. Thereafter, Rootes initially used the name only for mediocre cars based on Hillman chassis. Even the flowing, streamlined 1948 Sunbeam-Talbot 90 was little more than a Hillman under its stylish skin.

One British car maker that seemed ripe for takeover after the war but which by the late 1920s had completely turned its performance around – thus evading the tentacles of the Rootes octopus – was Austin. Sir Herbert Austin was as different from Reggie Rootes as could be imagined: an austere, conservative, puritanical man, who disliked outward show or display and who, crucially, never wanted to think too far ahead. While he was happy to open showrooms across England, Austin, in dramatic

---

1 In 1939 Billy Rootes even chatted enthusiastically to Hitler, Göring and Goebbels at the Berlin Motor Show about bringing his cars to Germany, seemingly oblivious to the fact that war was imminent in Europe.

contrast to the Rootes brothers, shunned advertising and publicity and refused to exhibit his cars at any of the new motor shows which were beginning to proliferate across Europe. Thus, though Austin did well out of the First World War, making shells, guns, aircraft and armoured cars for the Ministry of Munitions, his lack of forward planning meant that, when peace came in November 1918, Longbridge had all the wrong machine tools to restart car production. As a result, Austin was unable to compete with the deluge of American-made imports (mostly Model T Fords) which flooded into the country after 1919, and had to rely on his high-priced, medium-sized Austin Twenty for sales growth. At the end of 1921 the Longbridge factory was mortgaged and the Austin Motor Company went into receivership.

Thankfully, one of Herbert Austin's talents was his uncanny ability to attract funding. Having impressed the banks with his no-nonsense approach to business, Austin ensured that Longbridge was reborn. Sir Herbert himself appeared belatedly to have learned the lessons of the Model T, and now sought make a low-price utility car along the lines of Ford's Model T rather than relying on inappropriate mid-size models like the Austin Twenty. The result was the tiny Austin Seven of 1922, Britain's first 'baby car' and one of the twentieth century's most important automotive breakthroughs.

There had been smaller British autos before the Austin Seven, but they had not really been true motor cars. The Rover Eight of 1919, for example, was really a hybrid cycle-car. Neither was the Austin Seven Europe's first utilitarian small auto; that accolade properly goes to the Peugeot Quadrillette of 1921. What Austin did, however, was to create a vehicle that was bigger and thus more adaptable than a Quadrillette, but smaller and thus more economical than a Model T.

It was a good time to introduce a small car into Britain. Foreign imports were still handicapped by the swingeing McKenna duties of 1915, which added up to a third of their value in tax;[1] and Austin was additionally

---

1 In September 1915 the Liberal Chancellor of the Exchequer, Reginald McKenna,

aided by the 1921 road fund licence, a horsepower tax which meant that high-powered US imports such as the Model T were effectively penalized in favour of low-powered British rivals.

Launched as 'the Motor for the Million' – 'so cheap to run it makes walking foolish' – the Austin Seven was initially aimed at the motorbike and sidecar market. Austin declared that the car could be bought by 'the man who, at present, can only afford a motorcycle and sidecar, and yet has the ambition to become a motorist', and it initially cost only £25 more than a top of the range BSA motorcycle and sidecar. Firmly wedded to principles of utilitarian design and sound engineering – the motor industry was not, Austin reminded his dealers in 1922, 'a fancy trade' – the simple Austin Seven was Sir Herbert's ideal car. But the runaway success of the £165 'Baby Austin' encouraged even the cautious car maker to be more ambitious in his marketing strategy. The Seven soon proved to be a classless and gender-free automobile (just like the Mini, forty years later) which was bought by both aristocrats and shop workers. Working families bought it as essential transport; wealthy households that already owned a large car bought it as a fashionable runabout.[1] It also appealed to women. By 1930 the Austin Motor Company was advertising the Seven as 'the first small car to give the woman driver everything she wants', and was producing a well-upholstered saloon version, the Ruby, specifically for a female market. Herbert Austin even forgot his prejudice against racing and agreed to enter the car in a variety of motor races and hill climbs. Nevertheless, he was still wary of advertising and failed to exploit the car's triumphs in a manner that fellow car makers such as Morris, Chrysler and Citroën would have found puzzling. What advertisements Austin did

---

introduced a 33¾ per cent duty on imported cars at the urging of the nation's hard-pressed motor manufacturers, who felt they were being swamped by wartime imports from France and, increasingly, from neutral America. The McKenna duties remained in force long after the end of the war and were only finally removed in 1956.

1 Austin himself believed that the breakthrough in the upscale market came when Cambridge University's vice chancellor bought an Austin Seven as his second car, thus giving the model a prestigious social cachet overnight.

agree to release stressed the Austin Seven's dependability, rather than its versatility or fun.

As he had already proved, Austin was no natural businessman. Reluctant to tamper with an apparently winning formula, he strenuously maintained that the path to success lay in small profit margins on a high volume of sales. (This voodoo economics was to have serious repercussions for the Austin Seven's equivalent, the evergreen Mini, in the 1960s, and indirectly led to the bankruptcy of British Leyland.) The result was that Austin's cars effectively stayed the same for years and, as Ford had found with his Model T, ultimately became obsolescent. By 1939 even Lord Austin – Sir Herbert was ennobled as Baron Austin of Longbridge in 1936 – had come to realize that his firm was dangerously over-reliant on the success of the Seven.

By 1932, the year in which Austin-led exports had secured the UK a 28 per cent share of the world car market, the Austin Seven had become the Model T of Europe. Even Adolf Hitler had bought one. The car was licensed for production around the globe. In Germany it was made by Dixi (which was bought by BMW in 1928), and in France by Rosengart. In America it was made by an Austin subsidiary, and in Japan a locally built Austin Seven became, in 1925, the country's first export car (six years later Austin's Japanese licensee, Jidosha Seizo of Yokohama, became Nissan). In production until 1939, the jaunty, economical Austin Seven was Britain's best-selling car of the inter-war years, and, after the Model T, the most successful automobile of its day. Admiring the Seven's achievements, the mighty General Motors even made an offer for Austin Motors – a flattering proposal which Austin's senior managers curtly refused.

Longbridge's founder, sadly, never really seemed to enjoy his success. A dour and colourless man, Sir Herbert never recovered his spirits after the death of his only son on the Western Front in 1915. Austin was the typical British car pioneer, fascinated by engineering perfection and dismissive of business expertise. Humourless and gruff, remote and brusque, he made few friends. (William Lyons of Jaguar, which made bodies for Austin in the late 1920s, later declared that the car maker 'was not a noted respecter of persons'.) Austin had no leisure pursuits apart from listening to music, and never seemed to be off-duty; an inveterate workaholic, he was often to be found prowling around the factory floor on a Sunday in his shabby suit, his trademark trilby hat pushed firmly to the back of his head. Austin did become Tory MP for King's Norton but, typically, never spoke in the House of Commons. His devotion to his company initially earned him the respect of his workforce, but his resolute anti-union stance and campaigns in favour of longer working hours and against the forty-hour week had served to make Longbridge a centre of industrial discontent by 1939. In that year Austin withdrew from day-to-day involvement with the firm and passed over the reins to his nominated successor, the ruthless Leonard Lord, who cleared out what he called the 'Longbridge gerontocracy' of Austin's senior management. 'You'll need a couple of coaches to take them away before I'm finished,' Lord defiantly declared.[1]

Notwithstanding Austin's signal success with the Seven, in inter-war Europe the car magnate par excellence was his Oxford-based rival, William Morris. Born in Worcester in 1877, six years before Daimler perfected the first successful petrol engine and eight years before Benz made the first car, Morris was the son of a shop manager from Witney, Oxfordshire, and was brought up in a humble brick-built terraced house in Oxford. In later years Morris tended to reinvent his past; a central element was his tendency to exaggerate his father's achievements and qualities while omitting any mention of his mother. In 1937 he described his father (whose school William had already converted into a primitive car factory) as 'a great accountant [and] a financial brain', who had sought his fortune in Canada, where he had lived for a time with a native tribe. In truth, Frederick Morris was a mercurial lost soul who moved rapidly from job to job and migrated around the south Midlands. After a mysterious accident

1 Lord Austin himself died of a heart attack in May 1941.

on the London Underground in 1880, which was never fully explained, his health was permanently impaired, and a simple job was found for him as bailiff for his father-in-law at Wood Farm in east Oxford. Yet the truth about his father appears to have been expunged from his son's memory. William also later maintained that he was 'always known as William or Will' and that he had always had a particular dislike of being called Bill. However, a number of childhood acquaintances distinctly remembered him as Bill or Billy. William Morris's curious insistence on reimagining his background was, as his biographer Martin Adeney has subsequently suggested, part of an attempt to 'cut deliberately away from his origins'.

Morris was the archetypal self-made man. By the age of sixteen he was repairing bicycles for a living and attempting to use his income to support his family, his father having had to retire from his bailiff's job owing to severe asthma. However, in 1904 Morris's Oxford Automobile and Cycle Agency collapsed, a disaster that was to colour his whole attitude to life and business. Nevertheless, the determined, wiry Morris set out to re-establish himself as quickly as possible. He started a new cycle business at his workshop in Oxford's Holywell Street and developed a new motorcycle, and in 1908 he sold the company and used the resulting profits to build a handsome new workshop-cum-showroom just around the corner in Longwall Street, which he christened The Morris Garage.[1] Unusually for the time, he displayed the motor cars he built here in a nearby showroom window, sited in the shopping area of Queen Street.

Morris's approach to car manufacture differed considerably from that of Ford or Austin. He did not seek to build cars from scratch, but aimed to become an assembler of other companies' products, relying on his own mechanical skill to source and combine the best components currently on the market. Oxford was not far from established West Midlands car makers such as Humber, Singer and Standard, and Morris soon compiled an impressive list of suppliers all over the country. Crucially, his car-making philosophy minimized the amount of investment Morris, always mindful

---

1 The *Oxford Mail* called it 'The Oxford Motor Palace'.

of his 1904 bankruptcy, needed to stake. As he often told his acolytes, this strategy helped him to survive the post-war depression of 1920–2, a time when many other automobile firms went to the wall. In truth, though, Morris Motors only survived due to a generous injection of cash by a prominent local landowner, the Earl of Macclesfield. Lord Macclesfield had originally contacted Morris in order to threaten legal proceedings after his car had been in an accident with one of Morris's hire cars. As Martin Adeney has described it, the car maker gleefully pointed out 'that the hire car had three chief constables as its passengers and any claim was unlikely to succeed'. Despite this bumptious reply, Macclesfield took to the energetic young man and in 1912 supported his reformed car business with £4,000 of investment. Seven years later, Macclesfield pumped over £32,000 into the business, allowing Morris to expand his factory and his model line just at the time when other car makers were contracting or folding.

While Morris's policy of assembling other people's parts served him very well up until the Second World War, the absence of any real vertical integration within his company, in the manner of General Motors, meant that after 1945 Morris's car operation looked dangerously vulnerable and antiquated. By 1939 Morris had in fact bought up many of his former suppliers. But, always fearful of over-commitment, he was a cautious investor even when he was doing well. The result was that in 1952 the forward-looking Austin operation took over the stagnating Morris Motors – a result that would have surprised anyone looking at Morris's mighty automotive empire in the 1930s.

While he remained reluctant to change his business model, Morris was no technical conservative. He eschewed luxury models and, following Henry Ford's Model T philosophy,[1] stuck to cheap, reliable products like the famous Bullnose Morris Oxford (which owed its name to its pleasingly rounded radiator). Morris, like Ford, wanted his cars to be cheap

---

1 The Model T was first imported into Britain in 1909, and was assembled from imported parts at Trafford Park in Manchester from 1911.

and reliable – and he succeeded. In 1913 *Autocar* lauded the Bullnose Morris as, 'a miniature motor car, possessing all the attributes of a full-size car but . . . made with all the care that is bestowed upon the highest priced cars'.

William Morris continued to dog Henry Ford's footsteps. Shortly after the First World War, Morris introduced Ford's mass-production methods to Europe at his Cowley factory in east Oxford. To compete with Ford's bargain-basement Model T, Morris planned a second model, the Morris Cowley, which was designed to a lower specification than the existing 8 hp Morris Oxford. Moreover, Morris wanted this Ford-beater to be made, as the Model T was, on an automated assembly line. His plan was to have this up and running by 1915, but the war intervened. In the event, the Cowley still became Europe's first mass-produced family car, albeit after 1918. Moreover, the British government's horsepower tax of 1920, combined with the McKenna duties on imported cars, helpfully gave the Cowley a distinct advantage over its imported rivals.

After the First World War, Morris began to experiment with sportier autos. His racier version of the Morris Cowley, a 1923 model that boasted an open, two-seater body made by Carbodies of Coventry, was not a great success – partly, perhaps, because of its name, the Morris Chummy. But the following year Morris adapted the Chummy into a closed-body car which was re-badged as an MG, which stood for Morris Garages. This 'vee-front' saloon was adorned with an octagonal MG badge, a logo that the firm's accountant, Edmund Lee, had designed in a spare moment from his ledgers. By 1928 the MG brand had grown sufficiently to merit its own factory at Abingdon in Berkshire, only six miles from Morris's main Cowley plant. MG, though, was still owned personally by Morris, who regarded it as his private hobby. It was only when funds ran short in 1935 that he sold MG to the main Morris Motors operation.

In 1926 Morris joined forces with a Philadelphia steel body manufacturer to create the Anglo-American Pressed Steel Company. Car bodies no longer had to be made by coachbuilders but could be mass-produced as a single unit. Pressed Steel's British factory was predictably located next to the Morris factory at Cowley, but did not make bodies solely for Morris; car makers across the Midlands sought Pressed Steel bodies. When Morris realized that his personal stake was holding back the firm's growth – many would-be clients came to see the Pressed Steel plant as merely another tentacle of the Morris octopus – he altruistically withdrew his investment. As a result, the firm remained proudly independent – while still being very handily placed to meet Morris's needs – until it was caught up in the merger mania of the 1960s.

Morris always retained his eye for a good deal, even if he never really escaped his bicycle-maker roots. Sensing the mood of the Great Depression, in 1931 he was the first manufacturer to offer a model with a rock-bottom price tag, of £100. He also bought up bankrupt car makers: famous names such as Wolseley (acquired in 1927) and Riley (bought in 1938), whose marques he used to bolster the premium end of what had until then been a very limited and low-cost Morris model range. He also thoroughly understood the importance of marketing. Morris was the first car manufacturer to publish a magazine for existing customers: *Morris Owner*, launched in 1924. To run it, Morris hired Miles Thomas, a journalist from *Motor Trader* magazine, who soon displayed a flair for public relations (and who soon married Morris's secretary). In the early 1930s, as the world sought to extricate itself from the Great Depression, Thomas, with Morris's enthusiastic backing, launched what Morris himself boasted was 'the largest concentrated advertising campaign ever issued in this country'.

By 1936 Morris was operating the biggest car plant outside of America, at the heart of what was then the largest auto-producing country outside the US.[1] Morris's giant Cowley complex was a plant where, in emulation of the great Detroit factories, discipline was rigid, the needs of the assembly line were paramount, and independent thought was discouraged. University graduates, if they were discovered, were instantly

---

1 Largely thanks to Morris and his principal British rival, Austin, Britain had in 1932 overtaken France as the largest car manufacturing nation outside the USA, an accolade it held on to until 1955.

sacked by the vehemently anti-intellectual Morris – the man who, ironi-cally, went on to found an Oxford college.

However, Morris also made mistakes. In 1924 he bought the Le Mans-based French car maker Léon Bollée. It was thought at the time that Morris was responding to Citroën's rumoured arrival in Britain;[1] but a Morris executive later admitted that the boss had not done his homework and that 'we built the wrong car at the wrong price'. By 1928 even Morris was admitting that he might have made a mistake, and the Bollée fac-tory was closed in 1931. The Empire Morris 16/40 of 1926, intended for the imperial market, also flopped disastrously, proving far too fragile and feebly powered for the tough conditions of the Australian outback and the Canadian Rockies. By 1928 hundreds of Empires were being returned from Australia unsold (Morris blamed the colonial roads) and the Morris Motor Company lost over £100,000. The original tiny Morris Minor of 1928 was another disaster which signally failed to dent the market of its main rival, the all-conquering Austin Seven. Bizarrely, twenty years later Morris insisted that the tarnished Minor brand should be reused for Alec Issigonis's highly successful Mosquito project.

Notwithstanding these setbacks, the humbly born mechanic was doggedly ascending the social ladder. In 1929 Morris was made a baronet by King George V; four years later he created a suitably appropriate home for himself and his wife in the village of Nuffield in south Oxfordshire.[2] In 1934 Morris was made Baron Nuffield (he chose the title Nuffield because both Morris and Cowley were already in use), and was promoted yet fur-ther, becoming Viscount Nuffield, by Neville Chamberlain's Conservative government in 1938.

Morris always believed he knew best and, like so many other auto-mobile magnates of the time, brooked no dissent. One misty November morning in 1913, for example, he unilaterally introduced motor buses to the ancient streets of Oxford, with no council sanction whatsoever, and

---

1 In fact, it was not until 1926 that Citroën began to assemble cars in Slough.
2 In 2011 his relatively modest home of Nuffield Place passed into the hands of the National Trust.

then simply ignored the flood of complaints and the ineffectual protests of Oxford City Council. Morris was also ruthless in his personal relationships, suddenly dropping supposed friends and allies for the most trivial of reasons – figures such as Frank Grey, who had supported his Oxford bus network and even canvassed for Morris in the 1919 general election; Reginald Hanks, Morris's vice chairman during the 1950s; and even Lord Macclesfield, whose financial investment had been invaluable to Morris's success. In 1922 Macclesfield suddenly found himself *persona non grata* at Morris Motors because Morris believed he was interfering too much in the business. Morris bought Macclesfield's shareholding and brusquely severed his link with the company the blameless earl had done so much to rescue.

While he became immensely rich, and was subsequently a generous philanthropist, Morris frequently denounced what he saw as 'extravagance' in others. His publicity chief, Miles Thomas, later recounted how his boss had reacted to finding a piece of soap left in a full basin in a plant washroom (without asking what Morris was doing checking the factory toilets in the first place): 'That bright-eyed little man fumed and swore and became tremendously hot under the collar.' Morris recorded all his personal expenditure down to the last penny right up until his death, while his eating and drinking habits were notoriously abstemious (as, indeed, were those of his wife, who allegedly gathered scraps from the Cowley canteen for her chickens at Nuffield Place and then sold their eggs to the Morris workforce at the plant gates). Morris's only extracurricular activity was golf – together with the mysterious, unidentified, Australian mistress he seems to have visited every winter.

Morris was also socially clumsy and a poor communicator. Thomas later noted that: 'Bill Morris was at his unhappy worst at a meeting . . . He lost his temper easily, wriggled in his chair and on numerous occasions simply had to leave the boardroom. Of these shortcomings he was acutely aware and avoided both calling and attending round-table discussions.' A shy workaholic – 'a self-centred withdrawn introvert', in Miles Thomas's words – who was always moving and full of nervous energy,

Morris's attitude to his workers was benevolently paternalistic. He paid above the statutory wage rate – attracting agricultural labourers from all over Oxfordshire to his Cowley factory with his munificent salaries – and before 1939 he prided himself on knowing most of his workforce by name. But he always had to have his own way, and towards the end of his life he became increasingly unsociable. Designer Alec Issigonis recalled that he only met his boss twice, 'and the second time was eleven years later when we'd made a million Morris Minors'. Even in his declining years, having made a vast amount of money from his car business, Morris remained a cold and ruthlessly competitive man. At the same time, however, he was an extremely generous benefactor to hospitals and health charities. His Nuffield Foundation gave generously to the local Oxford hospitals; and, as an inveterate smoker, Morris provided a fund in October 1939 to buy cigarettes for troops based overseas. By the time of his death Morris had given much of his fortune – over £25 million, a vast sum in those days – to charitable causes, particularly those that sought to alleviate the conditions of the 'deserving poor'.

Always eager to point out that he had had no formal schooling past the age of fifteen, Morris affected to despise 'intellectuals' – particularly those with a university background. 'I've lived long enough to know that it is not always the men who have an expensive education who do things,' he was fond of declaring. He was never seen to read a book, and he only skimmed the front page of his newspapers. More seriously for the Morris Motor Company, the boss's anti-intellectual bias led him to spend almost nothing on market or product research. Only in 1949, at the very end of his reign, did Morris reluctantly appoint an 'experimental engineer'.

It was somewhat surprising, then, when William Morris founded a new college at Oxford University. In 1926 he had funded university chairs in anaesthetics and Spanish, but for very specific reasons: the former because he had suffered from poorly anaesthetised operations early in his life; the latter because he sought to win over the motoring enthusiast King Alfonso XIII of Spain, whom he had recently met, and after whom the chair was named. (King Alfonso, Morris thought, would provide a useful conduit to the Iberian and Latin American markets for Morris cars; Alfonso was deposed five years later, however, and Morris's plans evaporated.) Then in 1937 Morris proposed creating a new institution devoted to engineering, which would be built on an empty site he had just bought to the north of Oxford Castle. In the event, the University's shrewd vice chancellor, the philosopher A. D. Lindsay, adeptly managed to steer his benefaction away from engineering and towards the social sciences. Morris later claimed that Lindsay had cheated him out of his expressed wish for an engineering college; but in the late 1930s he seemed happy to go along with Lindsay's proposals. Morris did, though, object strongly not only to the college's proposed design but also to its first head, the socialist philosopher G. H. D. Cole, and, after 1943, to the absence of any engineering courses from its curriculum. In his last years he rarely visited Nuffield College. The first Nuffield dons appear to have got their own back on their problematic patron by choosing as their college motto a punning reference to one of the Morris's major European competitors: *Fiat Lux.*

One of Morris's greatest achievements, for good or ill, was permanently to change the face of the ancient university city. By 1936 Oxford was no longer merely one of the world's most esteemed centres of higher education. It was also home to one of the biggest car factories in the world, a plant that employed almost thirty thousand workers – far more than worked for Oxford University. As John Betjeman observed of Morris in his 1938 book *An Oxford University Chest*: 'It has always occurred to me that the great black wall of the University has shadowed his life. He has stormed it and won. Oxford is no longer primarily a university town but primarily an industrial town. The shade of the wall may now seem grateful to Lord Nuffield. He is able to bolster its crumbling bastions, to mortice it with gold.'

Having cowed the city and bought the grudging approval of the university, Morris decided to involve himself in politics on a national scale. However, his political interventions were, like those of Henry Ford, clumsy, ill-informed and inappropriately right-wing. As a result he was, like Ford, rarely taken seriously, even by conservative politicians. In 1930–1 Morris bankrolled the New Party then being set up by former Labour minister Sir Oswald Mosley, who later described the tycoon as 'our chief backer'. After the New Party had metamorphosed into the British Union of Fascists in 1932, and Mosley had adopted Mussolini as his model, Morris ostensibly ended his financial support for his activities, and he later strenuously denied any involvement in the fascist movement. However, Martin Adeney has uncovered evidence suggesting that Morris surreptitiously channelled money to Mosley's fascists throughout the 1930s. Given Morris's adamantly right-wing views and his staunch belief that he was always right, this should perhaps not come as a surprise.

William Morris's Italian equivalent, Giovanni Agnelli, was cut from very different cloth. While as politically conservative as Morris, and similarly keen to exploit the burgeoning inter-war market for small, economical family cars, Agnelli's social and political acumen, and in particular his uncanny ability to rub along with the government of the day, ensured that while Morris Motors is long gone, the firm that he founded is as prominent as ever, happily taking its place among the world's top-ten car makers.

The Agnellis were Piedmontese gentry who, by 1899, were living in a sumptuous Turin villa. In that year 33-year-old Giovanni Agnelli, an intense former cavalry officer with a pronounced weakness for women, joined the new car-making partnership soon to be known as *Fabbrica Italiana di Automobili Torino*, or FIAT, as its managing director. By 1906 Agnelli had persuaded most of Fiat's original partners, laid-back Torinese aristocrats, to sell him their shares. Three years later he found himself on trial for fraud, accused of falsifying the company's accounts and misrepresenting its share price. But, exhibiting the good luck with which he was always associated (and that seems to have been crucial for any budding car maker at that time), he was mysteriously acquitted and swiftly returned to his role at Fiat.

Agnelli soon showed that he was not just a talented auto executive but also a consummate politician. He established close ties with the Italian Liberal premier Giovanni Giolitti, and in return received lucrative government contracts for military vehicles and aircraft engines during the First World War, with the title of *Cavaliere al Merito del Lavoro* thrown in for good measure. The canny car maker then ensured that he covered all his political bases by simultaneously allying both with Giolitti's left-of-centre Liberals and with the up and coming firebrand Benito Mussolini, then a radical socialist. By 1917 Agnelli was one of Mussolini's biggest benefactors.

Like Morris Motors, Fiat – and Agnelli – did very well out of the First World War. By 1918 Fiat was the third biggest company in Italy, its profits not only helping swell the massive salaries of Agnelli and his fellow directors but also enabling the company to build a new car factory at Lingotto, outside Turin. When Giacomo Mattè-Trucco's revolutionary Lingotto plant was finally opened in 1923 it was not just the largest car factory in the world, but also the first true example of purpose-built automobile architecture. Made, like Kahn's Ford factories, primarily of reinforced concrete, and looking like a huge ocean liner, it was planned vertically: raw materials entered at ground level, cars were assembled on the building's five floors, and the finished vehicles emerged on the rooftop, where they could be put through their paces on a test track. The modernist architectural guru Le Corbusier called Lingotto 'one of the most impressive sights in industry' and 'a guideline for town planning'.[1]

Revolutionary unrest after the First World War prompted Agnelli to choose between his increasingly disparate political allies. When in 1920 his friend Giolitti declined his request to use troops to quell a communist-led sit-down strike in the Fiat factories, Agnelli turned to Mussolini for help. By the time of Mussolini's stage-managed March on Rome and his

---

1 Sadly, Fiat's failure to update the plant meant that after 1945 it fell behind its competitors, and it was demolished in 1982.

subsequent seizure of power in October 1922, the two men were closely linked. (Agnelli's daughter later unconvincingly argued that her father had never been serious about supporting Mussolini's fascism: 'Putting on those black Fascist uniforms was a great joke to him,' she maintained, asserting that Giovanni's fashion sense prevented him from embracing Mussolini's dictatorship, 'just think of the bad taste of those people who designed the Fascist uniforms.') Mussolini helpfully disbanded the commission investigating Fiat's 'excess' wartime profits, Fiat continued to win significant government contracts, and in 1923 Agnelli himself was made a government senator. Where William Morris chose to criticize government from outside, Agnelli preferred the cosier environment inside the regime.

Secure in his political backing, Giovanni Agnelli's Fiat created a series of outstandingly novel and influential cars in the mid-1930s. The revolutionary 1500 of 1936 was swiftly followed by the endearing 500, dubbed the Topolino after Disney's Mickey Mouse, and the larger 1100, the Millecento. These three models were, along with Volkswagen's contemporary Beetle, the direct antecedents of the modern small car. Dante Giacosa, a Piedmontese engineer who had joined Fiat in 1928 and had become engineering manager by 1937, gave the 500 hydraulic brakes and independent front suspension, while Rudolfo Schaffer styled the car in a manner that suggested a far larger vehicle. The resulting Topolino was far better built, and performed far more impressively, than cheap and cheerful predecessors such as the Model T and the Austin Seven. Giacosa's Millecento of 1937, which slotted in between the 1500 and the tiny 500, was not only simple, frugal and strong but enjoyed better roadholding and performance than most contemporary sports cars.

Austin, Morris and Fiat were not the only European success stories to make millions out of the mass manufacture of small, popular cars in the inter-war era. Renault and Citroën of France had, by 1939, become major players in the same market, as we shall see. But not every successful

European car manufacturer was based in the West. Indeed, one Eastern European firm had become a household name across the continent by 1939.

The founder of the Škoda firm, Emil Škoda, had himself never made cars. By the time of his death in 1900 he had made the Škoda works at Pilsen (Plzeň), near Prague, one of the largest arms manufacturers in Europe. Only in 1919 did the Škoda plant turn to cars, producing Hispano-Suizas under licence, using their own Czech-built engines. It was the engineers Václav Laurin (1865–1930) and Václav Klement (1868–1938) who turned the successful arms producer into a leading car maker. Laurin was retiring, modest and hard-working; Klement was ebullient and ambitious – and together they made an ideal partnership. Their first car, the Type A Voiturette, appeared in 1905 and sold respectably; Laurin and Klement also did very well out of the First World War, making military vehicles and ambulances for the Austro-Hungarian Empire. In 1926 they had made enough money to be able to absorb Škoda – sensibly retaining the well-known Škoda brand rather than substituting their own – and proceeded to carve out a niche market in small, handsome family cars. The Škoda 633 of 1931 and the 420 Tudor of 1933 were particularly successful, being just what Central Europe needed at a time of economic uncertainty.[1]

By 1938 Škoda was making cabriolets, coupés and a streamlined two-door saloon, the Rapid, that looked a lot like Porsche's new *KdF-Wagen*. (Skoda's aerodynamic, rear-engined 935 also owed a lot to Porsche and Ledwinka's designs.) And early in 1939 Škoda unveiled its best and biggest car yet: the impressive four-door Superb saloon. Sadly, the Superb was to be the last great car Škoda was to make for almost sixty years. In 1939 the invading German army occupied the Škoda works; in fact, the acquisition of Škoda had been one of the principal reasons why Hitler was so keen to overturn the Munich agreement of 1938 and absorb all of Czechoslovakia.

---

1 The origin of the eccentric Tudor name is mysterious; one suggestion is that it derived from the English term 'two-door', but Škoda was soon applying it to four-door cars, too.

Over the next six years, the Škoda plant became notorious not as the producer of cheerful, sturdy family cars but as one of the Nazi regime's most efficient producers of military vehicles and equipment.

Škoda's equivalents in France were the Paris-based companies of Renault and Citroën. However, while both car makers focused on the popular end of the market, there the similarity ended. The nature of both concerns derived from the personalities of their founders, bitter rivals whose temperaments were at opposite ends of the spectrum.

Whatever his achievements, Louis Renault could never be said to have been an endearing character. Indeed, Renault was as far removed from his cinematic namesake – the ineffably charming, incorrigibly roguish chief of police in Michael Curtiz's legendary 1943 film *Casablanca* – as could possibly be imagined. One colleague described him as 'always in bad humour, irritable, tense and . . . aggressive because of his natural shyness'. Outside the cockpit of his beloved racing cars, Renault felt vulnerable and awkward, and he did not relish working with others or delegating, even to senior managers. Like William Morris and Henry Ford, he was impatient and fidgety, and rarely kept still. But he was also tough, wiry and able to do anything his workforce did – which he often proved on the shop floor. He was a mechanic who had made good, and he always behaved as if he still *was* that mechanic. Like Morris, he was highly suspicious of finance and rarely borrowed from banks unless it was absolutely necessary. When in 1931, at the height of the Great Depression, Renault ran out of spare cash, it took a government act (popularly known as *la loi Renault*) to force him to accept state aid.

Renault's home life, like Morris's, was remarkably austere. Highly reclusive by nature, he and his young family (he married his wife Christiane when he was forty and she was twenty-one) bought a remote country estate and chateau at Herqueville in Normandy – but not before he had paid to have the local inhabitants removed and their homes demolished, and had down driven the price of the property by claiming that the government intended to make a compulsory purchase of the land. He even took advantage of his brother Fernand's failing health to buy him out of the family firm at an extraordinarily low price, leaving his widow and three children almost destitute when Fernand finally died in 1908.

Yet Louis Renault – again, like Herbert Morris – was undoubtedly a gifted engineer. Renault's early cars had live axles, rather than being chain-driven, as most of the early autos (taking their cue from the bicycle) had been. His transmission system soon became the industry standard, at least until Cadillac introduced synchromesh in 1928. At the same time, he was fully aware of the importance of marketing. By 1909 he was selling cars not just across Europe but also in America, Japan and Russia. In Britain, King Edward VII, the architect of the historic 1904 Anglo-French rapprochement popularly known as the *Entente Cordiale*, swiftly cemented the new alliance by buying a Renault.

But, talented mechanic though he was, Renault's business methods always left something to be desired. In order to obtain room to expand his factory at Billancourt, for example, he offered the neighbours derisory prices for their land and homes. If they refused, he would noisily test his cars outside their doors until they capitulated. In this way he was able to extend his works across the River Seine, ultimately colonizing the whole of the mid-river Île Seguin.

Renault prospered from the First World War. Along with Panhard, he championed the use of the car for military purposes, a passionate advocacy that appeared to be vindicated when Renault taxis played a central, and highly publicized, role in the Miracle of the Marne, when the Anglo-French armies halted the seemingly irresistible advance of the German army in September 1914. Paris's military chief, General Gallieni, requisitioned all the taxis in Paris (having promised their drivers the meter fare plus 27 per cent) – amounting to some six hundred-odd Renaults. Louis Renault found himself an accidental hero and capitalized on his new-found celebrity. Soon his firm was making aircraft engines and shells, and by 1918 the Billancourt factory was churning out large numbers of the successful FT-17 light tank, which he himself had helped design.

Renault's uncompromisingly conservative views made him a leading standard-bearer for the right in the 1930s. The traditionalist magnate was particularly vocal in his denunciations of Léon Blum's left-wing Popular Front coalition of 1936; he sacked 2,500 workers on the suspicion that they were Popular Front communists and, during the short lifetime of the Popular Front, Renault's resolutely anti-union stance led to numerous strikes and stoppages at Billancourt.

Yet not all of the motor moguls of the 1920s and 30s were anti-social dictators or autistic engineers. Louis Renault's great rival, André Citroën, was an ebullient *bon vivant* who actually did not like driving – a sharp contrast to those automotive rivals who had graduated from racing cars to running boardrooms. And he was good company. An inveterate gambler – the London *Daily Sketch* reported on 24 September 1924 that Citroën had won £162,000 (around £3 million in today's money) in a few hours at a Deauville casino – who also liked being seen with beautiful women, Citroën's numerous friendships extended to many of the leading celebrities of the day, such as Charlie Chaplin and Josephine Baker. Citroën's senior staff at the company's Quai de Javel plant displayed great loyalty and affection for their colourful chief, creating an *esprit de corps* very different from the sombre mood at Renault's Billancourt complex. Citroën often visited the shop floor to talk to his staff and, unlike Renault, was happy to delegate major decisions to his senior managers.

Citroën and the austere, cold Renault were never close. Renault was callous, calculating, lugubrious and autocratic; Citroën was warm, generous, humane, and always visibly enthusiastic about his cars and his workforce. Citroën was also Jewish, and after 1933 was increasingly worried by the growth of anti-Semitism not just in Germany but in France, too. (During the Second World War, over one hundred members of the Citroën family were to perish in Hitler's gas chambers, the majority of them deported from France by the Vichy authorities.) As we have seen, Louis Renault never shrank from expressing anti-Semitic opinions. Although he did, in February 1932, deign to invite Citroën to his new, vastly expanded works at Billancourt, it was largely to gloat over Citroën's discomfort at Renault's massive new trans-Seine complex; typically, the two auto barons lunched frugally in Renault's office rather than at one of the flagship Parisian restaurants that were André Citroën's habitual haunts.

The Citroën family had originated in Holland. André's grandfather had sold lemons, and had used his trade as the basis for his somewhat curious change of name (*citroen* means 'lemon' in Dutch.[1]) André's father committed suicide when his son was only six years old, yet André still managed to enrol at the prestigious École Polytechnique in Paris in 1898. From then on, his fortune seemed assured. After operating a successful munitions business during the First World War, in 1919 he founded a new auto company which immediately acquired a reputation for brave, if not eccentric, innovation. He built Europe's first car assembly line in 1919, on which he built Europe's earliest mass-produced car, the Type A Tourer, the first low-priced car in the world to incorporate an electric starter and electric lighting. Citroën's simple, utilitarian 5CV of 1922, nicknamed 'Le Petit Citron' after the yellow paintwork often used for its bodywork, became the French farmer's car of choice – and the first French car to be widely bought by women. (Citroën's wife, a close friend of Coco Chanel, was a pioneer of women's driving and a founder of the Automobile Club Féminin de Paris.) A francophone rival to the Model T and Austin Seven, the highly successful 5CV was the ancestor of the legendary post-war 2CV.

The restless Citroën was always looking for new challenges and, in particular, for ways to adapt the accepted form of the automobile. In 1920, working with the engineer Adolphe Kégresse and advised by British tank pioneer General Sir Ernest Swinton, he developed the world's first half-track car, popularly known as the Citroën-Kégresse caterpillar.[2] These rugged vehicles conquered both the Alps and the desert, crossing three

---

1 The addition of the diaeresis, changing 'Citroen' to 'Citroën', came after the family moved from Amsterdam to Paris in 1873.
2 Swinton himself was made a director of Citroën in 1926, the year in which the firm built its British factory in Slough.

thousand miles of the Sahara in just one week. (In 1923 Citroën even persuaded England's Queen Mary to ride in one during the British army's manoeuvres in Aldershot.) Meanwhile, Citroën's B2 taxi had become a common sight on the streets of French cities, undermining Renault's earlier domination of this lucrative market. By the late 1920s Citroën's factory was producing a car every ten minutes, a rate unheard of outside of Detroit.

Perhaps Citroën's greatest achievement, however, was his astonishing Traction Avant of 1934. This car was undoubtedly the most innovative product Citroën had yet developed. Designed by Flaminio Bertoni and André Lefèbvre, the dashing former racing car driver, who had joined Citroën from Renault in 1933,[1] it brought luxury car engineering to a mass-produced family runabout. The world's first front-wheel-drive, steel monocoque production car, it was constructed using a unitary, or 'monocoque', body rather than, as had long been the custom, a coach-built body lowered on to a chassis, making the car enviably light, fast and low. The Traction Avant's graceful lines made it an instant design classic, and the star of countless French films of the 1930s and 40s. And its distinctive, double-chevron logo, which now spanned the radiator grille, ensured that no one was in any doubt that this was a Citroën car (not that the Traction Avant looked like anything else on the road, anyway). Its intrinsic lightness also made it frugal with petrol, while the low-slung arrangement of the car eliminated the need for running boards to step into or out of the vehicle. These features made the Traction Avant ideal for use as a limousine or taxicab, and it was enormously popular with drivers and passengers alike.

The interior of the car was equally innovatory. The gear change was set in the dashboard, with the gear lever protruding through a vertical, H-shaped gate alongside pendant pedals, an umbrella-type handbrake control, and front bench seats. This all made for a very spacious interior

---

1 Lefèbvre had not enjoyed working for the autocratic Louis Renault, and on arriving at Citroën gleefully remarked that he had evidently moved from an empire to a republic.

with a flat and unobstructed floor of the type more usually associated with modern-day MPVs.

Rivals cast doubts on the resilience of the new car's monocoque construction; Citroën accordingly staged a public relations event in which a Traction Avant was driven off a cliff and (unlike Chrysler's Airflows) was found to be still intact, if a little bruised and bent, at the bottom. Citroën was a master of PR, initiating direct-mail marketing straight to potential customers and making extensive use of poster and print advertising. In his advertising, Citroën was once again way ahead of his time, preferring to communicate the qualities of the Citroën brand rather than those of a single product. He had his cars photographed in genuine outdoor venues, which no one had ever done before. Imitating Morris, he also launched a company magazine, the *Bulletin Citroën*, with illustrations featuring some of the best French graphic artists of the day. At the launch of the Paris Motor Show of 1922 he even had an aircraft emblazon his name in the sky above the Eiffel Tower, the first example of skywriting ever seen in Europe. And between 1925 and 1934 his name was flashed in 100-foot letters created by a quarter of a million electric light bulbs wired to the Eiffel Tower, a brazen advertisement which could be seen from sixty miles away. He also paid for Paris's Arc de Triomphe and Place de la Concorde to be permanently illuminated.

Citroën's public relations coups were not just limited to his native France. At the Berlin Motor Show of 1933 – the first since Hitler's seizure of power – the Club Citroën hospitality centre dominated the event. (Hitler ordered that such a national embarrassment, particularly one perpetrated by a foreign Jew, was never to happen again in Germany.) And when King George VI visited Paris in 1938, Citroën presented his two daughters – one of whom was the future Queen Elizabeth II – with working miniature right-hand-drive Traction Avants, made in England at Slough. After 1945 the firm went out of its way to stress that its right-hand-drive Citroëns were 'made in England', staging publicity shoots for Slough-built Traction Avants – badged throughout the British Empire as Citroën Twelves and Citroën Fifteens (or 'Big Sixes') – at quintessentially English venues such as the idyllic Cotswold town of Chipping Campden.

Production of the Traction Avant continued until 1957 and thus overlapped with Citroën's other legendary large car, the DS. When production of Slough-built, right-hand-drive versions of the Traction Avant restarted in 1946, *Motor* magazine commented that it 'was the car we could not overturn' and hymned its 'extraordinary stability and exceptional roadholding and riding comfort'. *Autocar* was similarly ecstatic, noting that 'the car can be driven at amazing speeds over a pot-holed surface that you would not take at more than a cautious 20 mph in the average car'.

The importance of the Traction Avant, and the sheer genius of André Citroën, cannot be underestimated. All other car manufacturers of the period stood by the principle of rear-wheel drive. The Austrian engineer Ferdinand Porsche went even further, insisting that for optimum traction both engine and gearbox should be located right at the back, behind the rear axle, a solution found in Porsche designs from the legendary VW Beetle to the Porsche 911. Only Citroën dared to challenge the accepted wisdom, insisting that front-wheel drive gave better tyre adhesion, improved directional stability and easier steering control. In short, front-wheel-drive cars were, Citroën insisted, safer. But it was not until the 1950s that his rivals warily began to forsake rear-wheel for front-wheel drive.

Tragically, the high development costs of the revolutionary Traction Avant ruined a company already weakened by the aftershock of the worldwide depression (which devastated the market for Citroën's larger models), a crippling factory strike of March–May 1933, and over-optimistic sales forecasts. The end came when Citroën's supplier of Bakelite steering wheels submitted a winding-up petition to the French courts in November 1934. Citroën's bankruptcy was announced on 21 December, and a creditors' committee was appointed only nine months after Citroën had unveiled his first Traction Avant. Thankfully, Citroën's largest creditor, the tyre manufacturer Michelin, stepped in at the last minute to purchase the company, reassuringly promising to maintain the firm's reputation for innovative excellence.

Michelin had been Citroën's sole supplier of wheels and tyres since 1919, and the surviving Michelin founder, Édouard (his brother and business partner André had died in 1931), understood and admired Citroën's vision and methods. The resulting purchase was negotiated with tact and decorum by Édouard's son, Pierre, on condition that Citroën himself did not leave the company to start another manufacturing operation. (It was widely rumoured that the automotive genius was planning to team up with Ettore Bugatti.) Thereafter, Michelin took care to keep the tyre and car concerns wholly separate. More worryingly, Michelin also swiftly terminated most of Citroën's flamboyant marketing campaigns – a strange decision from the company that as early as 1898 had popularized the Monsieur Bibendum trademark – and established a secretive management method completely at odds with Citroën's jovial transparency. Austere and devout Catholics, the Michelin family ensured that no outsider was admitted into the inner sanctum of higher management. Certainly no Michelin was ever seen at a racecourse, casino or nightclub.

Crushed by the ignominy of his bankruptcy, André Citroën died of cancer only seven months after his company's sale, on 3 July 1935. Two years later, Citroën's friend and the saviour of his firm, Pierre Michelin, was killed in a car accident while at the wheel of his Traction Avant. This double tragedy meant that neither man lived to enjoy the huge success of Citroën in the years after the Second World War, a time that saw the firm not only produce one of the most popular automotive workhorses the world has ever seen but also, exactly twenty years after André's death, launch a vehicle that is still hailed as the most beautiful and advanced automotive design of all time.

While most of the successful European car makers of the 1930s were those who concentrated on the middle-class market for small family cars, a few firms did manage to prosper at the other end of the scale – at least until full effects of the Depression were felt in the early 1930s. By 1939, though, the continent boasted very few luxury car makers. Of those, even fewer survived the vicissitudes of the coming war.

Rolls-Royce was one glowing exception to the string of inter-war failures and motored serenely on. Following Claude Johnson's untimely death from pneumonia (contracted at the funeral of a friend) in 1928, he was succeeded by the able Arthur Sidgreaves, who had made his name developing aircraft engines. Royce, meanwhile, visited Britain less and less often, preferring to work with Sidgreaves on the firm's new aviation projects. Royce quietly expired in 1933, two years before Rolls-Royce's legendary Merlin aero engine was finally perfected. In that year, too, the 'RR' emblem atop all the firm's car radiators was permanently changed from red to mourning black – but not, as is often thought, in memory of Royce; rather, the red colour was thought to clash with the tones of many of the new car bodies and the decision to change the colour had actually been taken before Royce's death.

The strength of the Rolls-Royce brand enabled it to outlast the Great Depression. At the 1931 London Motor Show, the Rolls-Royce Phantom II was, astonishingly, the only British-built premium car to be exhibited. The company's famous sporting counterpart, Bentley, had already succumbed to the recession; indeed, it had now become part and parcel of Rolls-Royce.

Like Royce and Rolls, Walter Owen Bentley began his working life in a railway workshop – in his case, in the GNR's vast Doncaster complex. As a wealthy former public schoolboy, however, he could choose his desired path, as C. S. Rolls had done, rather than having to fight for a job, as working-class boys such as Henry Royce had to do. In 1912 he and his brother Henry set up an agency to sell and repair French cars – still then regarded as the gold standard of the automobile world – and during the First World War they successfully converted their workshop to the manufacture of aircraft engines. Then, in 1919, the restless Bentley founded his own car works.

Bentley's personal life was a bit of a mess. His first wife, Leonie, died of influenza in 1919. His second wife, Audrey, was a fun-loving society girl who hated factories. Bentley, though, was a homely, modest worka-holic who was prone to depression and loved to spend his weekends in the plant. Predictably, the marriage was a disaster. Walter only found last-ing happiness with his third wife, Margaret.

His professional life was rarely smooth, either. An engineer dedi-cated to motoring perfection, who preferred testing and racing cars to checking budgets, he was never a real businessman and always hovered on the brink of bankruptcy. Bentley's target was the performance end of the specialist market. As Martin Adeney put it, his products 'were racing cars adapted for the road'. His classic 3 litre of 1921 was made famous by a group of rich playboy motorists, known popularly as 'the Bentley Boys', led by the diamond and gold tycoon Woolf Barnato, whose outrageous exploits entranced the media. Barnato was so impressed with the 3 litre that in 1925 he bought a majority shareholding in Bentley and became its chairman.

Woolf Barnato was one of the great characters of the age and his dar-ing exploits epitomized the post-war passions of the Roaring Twenties. He inherited a multi-million pound fortune at the age of just two, on the mysterious suicide of his father, Barney Barnato, the music hall enter-tainer turned South African mining king. Woolf was an early convert to the charms of the motor car and raced Bentleys to great acclaim. He was also an excellent cricketer; between 1928 and 1930, while he was Bentley's chairman, he also kept wicket for Surrey County Cricket Club. Even away from the stumps, Barnato's adventures rarely failed to hit the headlines. His most famous feat came in 1930 when he raced the *Train Bleu* and *Flêche d'Or* express trains from Cannes to London in his Bentley 6½ litre Speed Six – and won, beating the train by forty-five minutes.

From 1925, thanks to Barnato's vast injections of cash, Bentley's cars got bigger and bigger – and their bonnets longer and longer, as they were redesigned to accommodate ever-larger engines. Bentley models pro-gressed from the excellent 4½ litre of 1926 to the massive 8 litre of 1930. Bentleys also became hugely successful on the racetrack. From 1927 until 1930 Bentley cars won the Le Mans 24-hour endurance race – part driven, from 1928, by the fearless Barnato himself. Nothing seemed to stand in the way of Bentley and Barnato, either on the track or on the road.

However, while Bentley's cars were more than able to cope with the racetrack challenges of Bugatti, Alfa Romeo and Mercedes, they were unable to survive the Great Depression of the early 1930s. The 8 litre was launched in 1930 as the most luxurious Bentley ever, capable of 100 mph. It was the largest production car ever made in Britain, and was designed to eclipse its contemporary rival, the massive Bugatti Royale (which boasted a vast, 15 litre engine and an endless bonnet), and to elevate Bentley to the position of the world's supreme manufacturer of luxury cars. However, the Depression made it almost impossible to sell luxury behemoths such as the 8 litre and the Royale. Bentley only managed to sell sixty-three models before production was stopped. (Bentley had done relatively well: only three Bugatti Royales were sold. Even then, Ettore Bugatti famously refused to sell a Royale to the notorious King Zog of Albania, claiming that 'the man's table manners are beyond belief'.) Barnato himself lost a fortune; Bentley's orders dried up and Bentley himself was promptly sacked by Barnato. In 1931 Bentley Motors was declared insolvent and was snapped up in secret by Rolls-Royce.[1] Walter Bentley, humiliated by the company that bore his name – he was even asked to return his personal Bentley 8 litre – recovered from depression sufficiently to join Lagonda after they emerged from receivership in 1935. And unlike Rolls and Royce, Bentley lived until a ripe old age. He died in 1971, aged eighty-three. Today, the rights to make Bentley cars are owned by the German giant Volkswagen.

Bentley and Bugatti were not the only luxurious marques to find illusory prosperity in the inter-war years. In 1898 a Spanish artillery captain, Emilio de la Cuadra, began making electric cars in Barcelona. Four years later Swiss engineer Marc Birkigt joined him to form Fábrica Hispano-Suiza. By 1911 a second factory had been set up in France, and during the

---

1 Rolls's agents had posed as the British Equitable Central Trust so as not to inflate the firm's price or to alert rival bidders Napier.

First World War both the French and Spanish sides of the firm gained an international reputation for building excellent aircraft engines. Birkigt, later hailed as the Henry Royce of Spain, cleverly capitalized on this military fame, introducing a stork mascot on to the front of the bonnet of each Hispano-Suiza car, in imitation of Rolls-Royce's Spirit of Ecstasy and derived from the Alsatian stork emblem adopted by French fighter ace Georges Guynemer, who himself was an enthusiastic Hispano-Suiza customer.

In the immediate post-war years, Birkigt swiftly stole a march on his arch-rivals at Rolls-Royce. Where Rolls-Royces were boxy and staid, Hispano-Suizas were long and slender, and far more powerful. Birkigt's H6 of 1919, with a six-cylinder engine based on his successful wartime V-8, eclipsed the Crewe car maker's already legendary but now somewhat elderly Silver Ghost, and prompted Rolls to adopt, under licence, a number of Hispano-Suiza's patented features, such as power brakes.

By 1930 the name of Hispano-Suiza was, like Rolls-Royce and Bentley, synonymous with quality and power. King Alfonso XIII of Spain was a regular customer until his deposition in 1931. The J12 of 1933 possessed a massive 9.4 litre V-12 engine under its endless bonnet and was a favourite with heads of state around the world, while the Type 68 of 1933 weighed a massive two tons. Moreover, unlike Bentley, Hispano-Suiza managed to survive the Depression years of the early 1930s. However, the outbreak of the Spanish Civil War in 1936 saw the firm abandon car manufacture to return to aircraft engines. Birkigt himself fled to France, but refused to collaborate with the Nazis after 1940 and returned to Spain. There he worked on Hispano-Suiza aircraft engines with the disgraced French car maker Émile Dewoitine (who faced imprisonment for collaboration if he returned to France), until his death in 1953. Hispano-Suiza's French arm continued to produce engines for German aircraft during the Second World War, with the result that the name was considered too tarnished to resurrect after 1945. Nor did its Spanish parent ever recommence car production; instead, its factory was used as a base for General Franco's new state-owned auto conglomerate, the ancestor of Seat.

By the time Birkigt escaped from Franco's Nationalist Spain to seek refuge in France, many of his fellow automotive pioneers were dead or forgotten. However, the cars they had created had, in the space of just forty years, completely transformed the developed world. From Benz to Birkigt, the inspired engineers and businessmen who had developed the automobile into the principal mode of human transport during the first decades of the twentieth century had succeeded in altering the global land-scape beyond all recognition. It was a world the young Gottlieb Daimler or Billy Durant could only dream of in 1900. And it was an environment that, thanks to the car, was still changing with frightening speed.

3

The Big Three

However successful and important were the European motor magnates of the inter-war decades, by 1939 even William Morris and Louis Renault would have admitted that they stood in the shadow of the Big Three of Detroit. The Americans who had forged the industrial giants of Ford, General Motors and Chrysler had not only come to dominate motor manufacture in the US, but had irrevocably changed the face of the whole world.

At General Motors, the seat-of-the-pants salesmanship of Billy Durant was inexorably giving way to a cooler, more professional approach to company management. Legendary GM boss Alfred Sloan's subsequent assessment of Durant was that, while he recognized that Durant 'had created and inspired the dynamic growth of General Motors', he judged that Durant 'was too casual in his ways for an administrator, and he overloaded himself. Important decisions had to wait until he was free, and were often made impulsively.' Undoubtedly, by 1920 Durant's reliance on intuition rather than consultation maddened senior GM board members – most notably Pierre Samuel DuPont.

DuPont was a shy, retiring man who preferred balance sheets to people. A scion of the Wilmington-based industrial giant, E. I. du Pont de Nemours and Company – founded as long ago as 1802, and which now embraced chemicals, armaments and steel – Pierre graduated from MIT with a major in chemistry and duly worked his way up the corporate ladder, becoming president of the family firm in 1915. He had already been invited on to the General Motors board by the bankers' trust and had brought along with him his financial wizard, John J. Raskob, who subsequently became vice president for finance of both GM and DuPont.

A DuPont efficiency expert judged in 1920 that Durant 'has complete charge of all the planning and dictates largely the policies', and that 'in a great many cases there seems to be no one else in the organization that is the final arbitrator for the various plans for new developments'. His conclusion was: 'There is no system similar to our work order system for making suggestions, or no central engineering organization. There is, I think, also a certain lack of cooperative spirit between the different plants, [which] are practically independent as regards their purchasing, accounting and other organization, [with] no central organization directing them, except in the most general way.'

Durant's impulsiveness had led to his summary firing of Cadillac's Henry Leland early in 1917, ostensibly over the issue of the war. The pro-British Leland had wanted to make aircraft engines for the RAF, while Durant viewed the war simply as a distraction from car making in the US. Now in his mid-seventies, Leland financed a wholly new auto factory and began to produce luxury cars on the Cadillac model, which he named after 'the greatest American', Abraham Lincoln. In 1922 Leland finally retired and sold the Lincoln marque to Ford.

Meanwhile, DuPont continued put more money into GM,[1] while becoming increasingly worried about the company's increasing debt and mounting stocks of unsold cars. During the post-war slump of 1919–20, as GM's share price plummeted, Durant resorted to his accustomed panacea of personally buying up company stock, using borrowed money.

---

1 Only in 1958 was DuPont forced to sell its sizeable stake in the company, under pressure from Eisenhower's administration.

But Durant was rapidly approaching personal bankruptcy. In November 1920, after he had admitted launching a wholly unredeemable $34 million stock issue using promissory notes, DuPont promised a further cash injection for GM only if Durant resigned as president. DuPont, Raskob and the bankers from J. P. Morgan raised the $27 million necessary to shore up GM in the short-term; DuPont loaned Durant $1.7 million to pay off his pressing personal debts, and also offered him a share in GM's new holding company (over which he would have no control). Morgan's bankers made no secret of their belief that Durant was unfit to run an automobile company and that GM's founder had no option but to walk the plank. On 1 December 1920, Durant resigned from General Motors.

This time there was to be no Hollywood-style comeback. In April 1921 Durant launched yet another new car maker, Durant Motors, which he financed with $5 million of GM stock. But, after initial successes, the company foundered in 1931. (GM eventually bought its deserted factory in Lansing.) Durant himself went into semi-retirement, supported only by his GM pension after he lost most of his money in the Wall Street Crash of 1929. He put much of his declining energy into building a mock-castle residence in northern Michigan, which mysteriously burnt down just before he and his wife were due to move in. (Rumours of arson have subsequently pointed the finger at a number of candidates, from the United Auto Workers' union to GM itself.) Felled by a stroke in 1942, Durant managed a bowling alley in Flint until his death in 1947.

Over in Dearborn, it soon seemed as if Henry Ford might follow Durant's example and be ousted (once again) by his own board. Ford liked to think of himself as a lonely genius, who needed no one's advice. However, in the 1920s he was to be proved spectacularly wrong in two key areas: the company's model range (or lack of it), and its expansion into Europe.

By 1923 it was obvious to most automotive experts that Ford's obsessive concentration on just one model was beginning to turn sour. Sales of the Model T were flagging and the car, even with a variety of bodywork changes, was beginning to look old and antiquated in the face of new competition from GM's multi-marque line-up. In 1924 the Model T was finally made available in colours other than black: Empire Grey, Orriford Lake or Cobalt Blue. But underneath the bonnet the Model T was intrinsically the same car that Ford had launched in 1908. Chevrolet's new closed-body K sedan of 1925, available in a rainbow of DuPont's new Duco lacquer colours, made the Model T seem dull and obsolete. And while Ford spent almost nothing publicizing the Model T, GM was spending an average of $10 per car advertising the Chevrolet K. Meanwhile, Highland Park and 'the Rouge' (as the Rouge River colossus was popularly known) were losing workers to GM and other Detroit-based rivals, as Ford's wages slipped significantly below the US industrial average.

In 1927 the decision was finally made to end production of the Model T and to switch to a more modern product, the Model A. However, with just one car being produced by Ford's titanic factories, this necessitated a complete shutdown of all Ford plants while $45 million worth of Model T machine tools were junked and replaced with a similar value of new tools – including remarkably advanced electric welding machines, the ancestors of the assembly-line robots of the 1980s – for the new Model A. Ford's plants were shut for six months, during which sixty thousand people were thrown out of work. Meanwhile, Ford's hard-pressed dealers had to eke out the supplies of outmoded Model Ts they already had on their forecourts. Ford took years to recover from this setback, and seven decades to regain the ground it lost to its principal competitor, General Motors.

Ford also shot himself in the foot in Europe. Ford Motor Company's senior British representative, Percival Lea Dewhurst Perry, had come from humble English working-class stock. In 1896 he had left the Birmingham lawyer's office where he worked as a clerk to seek his fortune in London. There he became attracted to the glamorous if precarious world of the automobile makers, and by 1906 had become managing director of Ford's British agency, the Central Motor Company. When in 1911 Henry Ford sought to establish a car factory in Britain, at Trafford Park in

Manchester, the amenable, dependable Perry was the obvious choice to head the operation. While Ford pursued his doomed pacifist agenda, Perry astutely volunteered his British factory for the production of munitions and military cars, and was made deputy controller of mechanical warfare at the Ministry of Munitions in 1917, for which work he received a knighthood. However, his adept handling of Ford's notoriously militant pacifism, together with his insistence that the Model T needed to be adapted for the European market, merely enraged his boss. In 1919 Ford summarily sacked him.

Ford's loss was Slough's gain. From 1920 Perry began to build up what became the largest trading estate in Europe at Slough in Buckinghamshire,[1] and in 1923 he persuaded André Citroën to build cars there, thus helping the French firm to evade the draconian McKenna duties on vehicles imported into Britain. Meanwhile, bereft of Perry's sure hand, Ford's British operation went rapidly downhill. Against cheaper and more technically advanced small cars such as the Austin Seven and the Bullnose Morris, Ford had no answer. Ford's British market share plummeted and it looked as if the firm would be permanently eclipsed by its home-grown rivals.

In an unparalleled admission that he may have been wrong, Henry Ford finally swallowed his pride and made two spectacular policy U-turns. In 1927, as we have seen, he finally admitted that the Model T was no longer viable. And in 1928 he crossed the Atlantic to ask Percival Perry back to run Ford of Britain.[2] It was Perry who decided that Ford needed a brand-new plant nearer to the capital and close to Europe's principal shipping lanes, and in 1929 not only bought a large tract of Thames-side marshland for that purpose but also persuaded the London County Council to build rented housing for twenty-five thousand families nearby. Henry Ford's son, Edsel, was present alongside Perry at the ground-breaking

---

1 In 1974 Slough passed into Berkshire as part of the Heath government's county boundary changes.

2 A trip that, it must be admitted, also took in tea with King George V.

ceremony for the new Dagenham works in 1932, but only as a substitute for Perry's new friend, the Prince of Wales, later King Edward VIII.

In 1938 Percival Perry was made Baron Perry of Stock Harvard, named after the charming Essex village where he now lived. And in the immediate post-war years the impressive capacity of the Dagenham factory – now under the control of Perry's successor, the rumbustious Irishman Sir Patrick Hennessey – proved its worth, as Ford's sales in Britain surged. The Dagenham-made Ford Eight of 1932 and Ford Popular of 1935 set the European standard for basic, no-nonsense family cars, a tradition Ford continued in the post-war years with Dagenham's Anglia, Cortina, Escort and Fiesta.

There was also a dark side to Henry Ford's character, one that became more pronounced as he grew older and richer. Ford mass-produced not just Model Ts but also venomous anti-Semitic propaganda, which he channelled initially through a newspaper he had acquired in 1918 to further his gubernatorial campaign, the *Dearborn Independent*. Ford's notorious article of 22 May 1920, 'The International Jew', cheerfully repeated the calumnies of *The Protocols of the Elders of Zion*, a tsarist tract of 1903 alleging a worldwide Jewish conspiracy, which had already been revealed as a forgery by the London *Times* in 1921. This malicious piece presaged weekly diatribes in the *Dearborn Independent* detailing the corrupting effect of Jews on American life, tirades that denounced jazz, short skirts and inflation as the inevitable results of the international Jewish conspiracy. Ford seemed to have forgotten that the architect of his world-famous automobile plants, Albert Kahn, was a Jew – as, indeed, were a large proportion of his own workforce.

Ford's anti-Semitic rants of the 1920s proved a significant inspiration to a little-known right-wing activist on the other side of the Atlantic. Adolf Hitler frequently cited Ford as an early inspiration; indeed, several passages from his incoherent apologia, *Mein Kampf*, appear to have been adapted from Ford's writings. Henry Ford was certainly the only American to be cited in the pages of that lengthy harangue. (Hitler wrote how 'only a single great man, Henry Ford' had resisted the Jews' attempts to make themselves 'the controlling masters' of America.) In 1922 Hitler installed a life-size portrait of Ford behind his desk in his office at the Munich Nazi party headquarters, while his waiting room carried multiple copies of Ford's series of pamphlets, *The International Jew*, translated into German. He even offered to lend Ford some of his storm troopers to support his presidential ambitions. In return, Hitler hoped for funding from the wealthy car magnate for his fledgling Nazi movement. It is uncertain whether this was forthcoming, although we do know that in 1939 Ford sent Hitler a cheque for $50,000 on his birthday. However, on laying the foundation stone for Ford's new Köln factory in 1929, Henry Ford happily declared: 'What Europe needs is leaders' – a statement that most listeners took to mean dictators in the mould of Italian strongman Benito Mussolini and, in hindsight, totalitarians such as Adolf Hitler. Significantly, after 1933 the leader of the pro-Nazi German-American Bund, a deeply unpleasant proto-fascist named Fritz Kuhn, was maintained on the payroll at Dearborn, although there is scant evidence to show that he ever did any work there.

By the mid-1930s Henry Ford was finding it politic to deny in public that he was anti-Semitic. He had shut down the *Dearborn Independent* as early as 1927, and ordered all unsold copies of *The International Jew* to be destroyed, not because he regretted its message but because he realized that its notoriety had ruined his bids for senatorial and presidential office. Yet on his seventy-fifth birthday, on 30 July 1938, months after Hitler's Nazi government had ordered 3,150 V-8 trucks to be built by Ford's plant at Köln, Henry Ford proudly received the Grand Service Cross of the Supreme Order of the German Eagle from the German consul in Detroit, for 'making autos available to the masses'. This award had been personally created by Hitler as 'the highest honour given by Germany to distinguished foreigners'. Its first recipient had been Mussolini; Ford was only the fourth. Two years later, in an unguarded moment, Ford told an American reporter that 'international Jewish bankers' had caused the outbreak of war in Europe – rather than his friend and ally, Adolf Hitler.

By the end of the 1930s, as Henry Ford's grip on reality was slipping, he still refused to give way to a younger generation. From the time of his sixtieth birthday, in 1923, Ford kept hinting that he would soon retire from the company, but it soon became clear that he was not serious. His only child – the easy-going, patient, diligent Edsel, who collected luxury cars and worked hard to try and infuse Ford's models with a little more class and style – remained obediently in the wings, bullied and marginalized by his tyrannical father. Henry's programme of 'toughening up' his son involved undermining all of Edsel's key decisions and achievements behind his back, a cruel policy which merely added to his son's levels of stress. Robert Lacey tells how a new series of coke ovens that Edsel had commissioned for the Rouge River plant were torn down on Henry's orders 'within days of their completion', just so Edsel would be reminded who was boss.

In contrast to his philistine father, Edsel Ford was very conscious of the importance of aesthetics in selling cars. From 1922 he attempted to introduce elegance and panache into a Ford auto range that had previously been known just for its everyday functionalism. It was Edsel who commissioned Mexican artist Diego Rivera to paint 'Detroit's own Sistine Chapel', the unmistakably socialist 'Detroit Industry' frescoes that Rivera painted on to the walls of the Ford-funded Detroit Institute of Art.[1] And it was Edsel who was instrumental in developing the Lincoln brand into a sophisticated rival to Chrysler and Cadillac. Edsel's liberated regime at Lincoln – an island of common sense and creativity in the increasingly oppressive Ford empire – authorized the creation of the twelve-cylinder Lincoln Zephyr of 1936, an aerodynamic gem designed by Dutch immigrant John Tjaarda and gifted ex-GM designer Eugene 'Bob' Gregorie, who built a close relationship with Edsel Ford at Lincoln in the pre-war years but left the company after Edsel's premature death in 1943.[2]

---

1 The city was outraged by the frescoes' overtly political content, but Edsel resolutely stood by Rivera.
2 Briefly enticed back to the firm by Henry Ford II, Gregorie recognized that the Ford he had known from Edsel's Lincoln division no longer existed. In 1946 he left Ford for

Instead of gradually handing over the succession to Edsel, Ford came to rely on Harry Bennett, a thuggish former sailor and ex-boxer who knew nothing about cars or the car industry. Bennett preferred to spend his office hours shooting at targets with his air pistol, and liked to bring pet lions and tigers to work to reinforce his tough-guy image. Henry Ford let Bennett do what he liked, and soon the latter's growing band of goons, euphemistically named the Service Department, were enforcing a brutal discipline across all of Ford's plants through a network of shop-floor spies and gangsterish heavies. Bennett's 'empire of darkness' soon enveloped the whole of the Ford company. Even Edsel was genuinely frightened of him and dared not step out of line. Until 1933 Service Department appa-ratchiks ruthlessly enforced Prohibition legislation, which the company's pro-temperance chairman enthusiastically supported – Henry Ford once threatened to close his factories if Prohibition was ever repealed – while simultaneously making themselves fortunes as underground bootleg-gers. Soon Bennett and his henchmen became inextricably embroiled in the criminal underworld, from which source Bennett often hired his new recruits.

By the mid-1930s Ford's plants were run on fear and had the worst reputation of any of Detroit's car makers – none of which were exemplary employers at the best of times. In 1932 Bennett personally led his thugs out to combat the Ford Hunger Marchers and, in the subsequent stand-off, a nineteen-year-old Young Communist League activist, Joseph York, was shot by Service Department goons as he tussled with Bennett, and another three demonstrators were later gunned down.[1] Five years later, on 26 May 1937, Bennett's henchmen confronted senior union negotiators, including the respected labour leader Walter Reuther, as they crossed the Miller Road overpass to the Rouge plant, and beat them to a pulp in broad daylight.[2] Fortunately for the union team, no one was killed,

---

good, aged only thirty-eight, and never designed another car.

1 Fifteen thousand people subsequently turned out to mourn the four 'Ford martyrs'.

2 Reuther recovered to become president of the UAW in 1946. By the 1960s he had become a prominent civil rights activist and supporter of Martin Luther King.

although one man's back was broken. Equally fortunately, press photographers were on hand to record the incident, though many of those, too, were beaten up by Bennett's hoodlums and their cameras confiscated. The 'Battle of the Overpass' represents the low point of Ford's history and remains a lasting stain on American industrial relations. Edsel Ford was horrified by the event and pleaded with his father to recognize the unions and to fire Bennett. But his pleas were ineffectual; Bennett, secure in the unquestioning protection of Henry Ford, remained the power behind the throne. Historians have estimated that Bennett and his men removed over $1 million of Ford property from company premises during their reign of terror. Yet, basking in the president's favour, Bennett seemed untouchable. He later wrote, with intentionally cruel candour: 'I became [Ford's] most intimate companion, closer to him than his only son'.

Ford and Bennett proved themselves to be the most ruthless union-busters of an age not noted for its professional ethics or comradely ethos. While Henry Ford blithely turned a blind eye to Bennett's semi-criminal activities, the latter did not shrink from using violence to end strikes and dilute opposition. Even after the appalling publicity garnered by the Battle of the Overpass, Bennett's goons routinely beat up union officials and cowed the activists of the United Automobile Workers Union (UAW), which was still unrecognized at Ford, even though both GM and Chrysler had formally acknowledged it in 1937. Even Bennett's thugs, however, could not prevent the massive strikes that erupted at the Rouge in April 1941. The ageing Ford, now with his back against the wall (and winning little sympathy from Roosevelt's federal government), was finally persuaded by Edsel – who, for once, was standing up to his father – that the company must grant Ford workers a ballot on union recognition. Henry grudgingly agreed, his autocratic paternalism leading him to assume that his loyal workforce would reject all union blandishments and agree to keep Ford a non-union shop. Bennett, meanwhile, hoped to use his Service Department to intimidate workers into voting no. In the event, only 2.7 per cent of Ford workers voted against union membership, a result that flabbergasted Henry and seemed to drive him even more into the land of the bewildered. (Ford executive Charles Sorenson later wrote that the vote was 'perhaps the greatest disappointment [Ford] ever had in all his business experience', and observed that 'he was never the same after that'.)

Bennett tried to alter the (remarkably generous) terms of the subsequent contract with the UAW; but Henry's robust wife, Clara, appalled by the psychological damage the dispute was having on both her husband and her beloved son, threatened Henry that she would leave him if he did not accede to all the UAW's demands. A shattered Henry Ford duly caved in and signed the agreement. Edsel, however, was now seriously affected by stomach cancer – an illness exacerbated, if not caused, by the stress of being constantly bullied by both his father and Bennett. When Edsel died in May 1943, his father successfully resisted pressure from Washington to relinquish the reins at Dearborn and took back the day-to-day running of the Ford Motor Company at the age of eighty.

Thankfully, not all car tycoons were aggressive bullies in the mould of Henry Ford. The career of Ford's contemporary, Walter Chrysler, proved that you did not have to be a tyrant to succeed in the automotive industry. Chrysler's astonishing achievements proved, reassuringly, that nice guys did not always finish last.

Walter P. Chrysler was born twelve years after Ford, in 1875. He started his working life as a locomotive engineer in Kansas, from which humble beginnings he rose to manage the American Locomotive Works in Pittsburgh. However, on a visit to the 1908 Chicago Automobile Show he caught the automotive bug. When General Motors' James Storrow asked him to come to Flint to run Buick, on half of his Pittsburgh salary, he eagerly accepted. Chrysler remained in office, with substantially increased remuneration, after Durant's corporate coup of 1915, on condition that he answer only to Durant. However, Durant's tendency to make snap decisions on his own infuriated Chrysler, who believed himself seriously undermined. In March 1920 he resigned from GM, taking with him $1.5 million in stock options.

Chrysler initially made a name for himself as an industry troubleshooter. In 1920 he was enlisted to save the struggling firm of Willys-Overland and proceeded to shut down uneconomic plants, slash management and other white-collar staff, and move production from Ohio to the suburbs of Detroit, where labour was cheaper. But when, in November 1921, Willys went into receivership (actually a desperate ploy by John Willys to regain control of his company from his banker creditors), the firm decided it could no longer afford Chrysler's substantial salary.

Finding himself jobless once more, Chrysler decided to launch his own marque. For this he adapted the Detroit factory of the bankrupt Maxwell Motor Company, in which Chrysler had taken a controlling interest in 1921. His first breakthrough vehicle was the Chrysler Six of 1924; adapted from a design Chrysler had begun for Willys in 1920, it was smooth and reliable, a fusion of European quality with American ruggedness. The model's success enabled Chrysler to convert Maxwell Motors into the Chrysler Corporation in 1925; three years later he bought up the bankrupt Dodge Brothers Company, which he intended to use as the basis for an ambitious challenge to the mighty General Motors brands.

John and Horace Dodge started in the automotive business by making transmissions for Olds and Ford. But by 1913 John Dodge was claiming that he was 'tired of being carried around in Henry Ford's vest pocket', and in 1914 they began production of their own car: a tougher, larger version of the Model T, the Model 30. This car acquitted itself well in the Mexican War of 1914, and earned celebrity status in a well-publicized raid at Sonora, in which a Lieutenant George S. Patton led ten soldiers and two civilian guides into battle in three Model 30s – and returned with three dead Mexicans (including revolutionary leader Pancho Villa's key adviser) tied to the bonnets of each Dodge. In 1920, however, both Dodge brothers died, John from pneumonia, Horace from cirrhosis. Without their guidance, by 1928 their eponymous company was on its last legs and was duly bought up by the ambitious Chrysler. Existing Dodge models were retained, although in 1930 Dodge cars lost their 'Brothers' suffix. Inventing two new marques – the low-priced Plymouth and a more upmarket brand, De Soto – Chrysler expanded his firm's operation to become a mirror of GM's, with each Chrysler brand – Plymouth, Dodge, De Soto and Chrysler – directly competing with a rival GM division.[1]

Not every Chrysler product was a success. The streamlined Airflow of 1934 was not only daunting-looking but was equipped with an unreliable engine, and proved a disaster in the marketplace. It was not designed by stylists but was the work solely of Chrysler's engineers, and it showed. Looking heavy and bloated, with tall doors and small windows, the Airflow hardly suggested power or speed. Public relations stunts involving Airflows being thrown off cliffs probably did little to help sales; GM's exultant publicity department merely bought space to denounce 'ill-timed' or 'dubious' experiments. But Chrysler was now buoyant enough to shrug off such failures. In 1936 the company overtook Ford as America's second largest car maker – ironically, just as Ford launched their own streamlined car, the Lincoln Zephyr.[2] The Airflow saga did at least convince Chrysler that he needed to pay more attention to styling, as GM was doing.

By 1939 Chrysler had captured 20 per cent of the US automobile market and was regarded as one of the American automotive industry's Big Three, alongside GM and Ford. Only in the nadir of the Great Depression, in 1932, did the energetic new combine fail to make a profit. The low-priced Plymouth marque helped the firm through the Depression years (by 1933 Chrysler's Plymouth division accounted for half of the company's sales), as, too, did Walter Chrysler's own irrepressible optimism. The lofty mast of William Van Alen's astonishing Art Deco masterpiece, the Chrysler Building in New York – built in 1928–31 and paid for out of Chrysler's own pocket – publicly testified to Walter Chrysler's hubris and success.

------

1 In 1955 the number of Chrysler brands was increased to five, as the top of the range Chrysler Imperial metamorphosed into the Imperial marque, designed to challenge Cadillac and Lincoln head-on.

2 The Zephyr did surprisingly well and helped to revive the dormant Lincoln brand.

Chrysler's boss was no monomaniac in the mould of Ford or Morris. He was popular on the shop floor, and never attempted to micromanage or undermine his senior managers, as was common at Dearborn and Cowley. As early as 1926 Chrysler began grooming K. T. Keller, a workaholic engineer who had begun his working life at Westinghouse in Pittsburgh in 1906 and whom Chrysler had lured from GM to become his general manager, to succeed him when he retired. And as he grew older, Chrysler increasingly spent much of his time in the opulent home he had built for himself – a house that was not located close to Detroit, where most his fellow car makers tended to congregate, but in far-off Cambridge, Maryland. There Chrysler hunted and sailed, played the piano or the cornet (he was a natural musician), drank (he was instrumental in the successful campaign to repeal Prohibition, to which he lent both his voice and his money), and womanized. Showgirls were a particular passion for Chrysler: in the late 1920s he fell madly in love with the notorious actress and gold-digger Peggy Hopkins Joyce, while she was married to the first of her six husbands. When Chrysler did emerge from his Maryland home, it was more often than not to inspect the rising storeys of his Chrysler Building in New York rather than to inspect any of his automotive plants.

In 1935, as he always had said he would do (and as Henry Ford had repeatedly refused to do), Chrysler retired, passing the presidency of the firm to his protégé, Keller. When Chrysler died of a stroke, on 18 August 1940, there were no crocodile tears at his funeral, as there were to be for Henry Ford seven years later. Both his employees and the general public seemed genuinely distressed at the passing of this generous, irrepressible and multi-talented American.

Looking at the soaring spire of the Chrysler Building today, or indeed at Ford's massive global headquarters at Dearborn, it is difficult to imagine that there was anyone in the global car industry who had achieved more. Nevertheless, it is clear in retrospect, even if it was not wholly evident at the time, that the considerable accomplishments of Walter Chrysler and even of Henry Ford were eclipsed by the outstanding successes of the quietly spoken man across town who sat impassively at the helm of General Motors. Perhaps the most influential and successful of all the twentieth century's automotive tycoons, Alfred P. Sloan was the man who, even more than Henry Ford, can be said to have created the modern auto business. He ruled General Motors with a rod of iron for over thirty years, and under his direction GM became the largest, most successful and profitable, industrial enterprise the world had ever known. Yet, in contrast to Ford and Chrysler, today he is a largely forgotten figure, even within the car industry.

Alfred P. Sloan was no greasemonkey or groundbreaking engineer in the vein of Henry Ford. The first of the motor industry's all-powerful 'grey men', Sloan was born only a month after Chrysler; but he came from a very different background, one dripping in money and privilege. Having joined the Hyatt Roller Bearing Company of Harrison, New Jersey, after graduating from MIT, he found himself its president when his father rescued Hyatt from bankruptcy. Sloan was careful not to present the image either of an irresponsible enthusiast, like Durant, nor of a despotic bully, like Ford. Readers were quick to identify the car maker hero of Sinclair Lewis's 1929 novel *Dodsworth* with Sloan, but in truth Lewis had made Alex Kynance in the image of the schoolboyish Billy Durant.

After Pierre DuPont had ousted Durant from the presidency of GM in 1920, it was DuPont who drew the ire of GM dealers and Durant sympathizers across America. But it was Sloan who was effectively running the company, and Sloan to whom, in 1923, DuPont formally handed control of the growing combine. Sloan then proceeded to dominate the car giant until his retirement as chairman in 1956 – a reign of thirty-three years.

After 1923 Sloan, safe in the backing of the company's principal shareholders (still led by DuPont), proceeded to remodel GM's structure in accordance with sound business principles. One of his first acts was to hire Ford's cast-off number two, William Knudsen, to run Chevrolet,

GM's premier brand. Knudsen was a shrewd acquisition; his people skills had something of Durant about them, and he forged valuable relationships with dealers and plant workers – the sort of relationships that were beyond the retiring, academic DuPont or the cold, calculating Sloan.

Alfred Sloan's General Motors was far more businesslike than Durant's restless, cobbled-together creation. It was Sloan who introduced the policy of refreshing its models every year, in stark contrast to Henry Ford's stubborn reliance on the Model T. In 1925 Henry Ford, having blamed his dealers for the pronounced loss of market share to GM's Chevrolet division (they were, he raged, all 'fat and lazy'), denounced Chevrolet for bringing out new cars every year: 'We want the man who buys one of our products never to have to buy another. We never make an improvement that renders any previous model obsolete.' Under Sloan's direction, GM's multiple brands were matched with every definable market category, in contrast to Ford's outdated credo of doing just one thing well. Every year GM models were rejuvenated and relaunched, having been equipped with whatever new technology was affordable. In 1912 Cadillac introduced the electric starter; and by 1920 all GM cars had acquired hydraulic brakes for all four wheels, along with enclosed bodies and quick-drying pyroxylin varnishes, which enabled them to be offered in a wide variety of colours, not just Henry Ford's ubiquitous black. In 1928 a Cadillac car introduced synchromesh, while in 1934 all of the GM range, from Cadillac down to Chevrolet, offered independent front suspension.

In marked contrast to Henry Ford, Alfred Sloan was keen to promote technological advance as well as aesthetic development in his cars. In 1919 he hired the gifted engineer Charles Kettering, who had invented the electric starter motor, to run GM's industrial research laboratory, a facility that by 1939 was enjoying a vast annual budget of $2 million. In 1927 he engaged Harley Earl as the first chief of a new 'Art and Color Section', effectively GM's design studio. Earl's designs not only transformed the look of GM's cars, but changed the way cars were regarded by both manufacturers and customers. No longer were autos to be mere utilitarian objects, as the plain old Model T had been; now they were objects of beauty, envy and power.

The annual model update that Sloan promoted was not cheap. Sloan himself estimated that it cost GM $35 million to remodel its cars every year, in an effort to instil the principle of 'planned obsolescence' into its customers. (In 1955 Harley Earl declared: 'Our big job is to hasten obsolescence. In 1934 the average car ownership was five years; now it is two years. When it is one year, we will have the perfect score.') But Sloan believed it was worth it – provided, of course, that existing GM customers upgraded to GM cars. The high cost of the annual process also dissuaded smaller car makers from imitating GM; most of them, if they tried, went bankrupt. And Sloan's dictum that every model needed a complete redesign every three years also made engineering and economic sense, since many of the car's original machine tools would have worn out by then and needed replacing anyway.

Sloan's greatest achievement, alongside the introduction of the annual upgrade, was to seek to cater for almost all customers within one company – a strategy predicated, once again, on the assumption that car buyers, once hooked, would not buy outside the GM family. Sloan's hierarchy of GM divisions made sense of Durant's jumble of competing companies. None of GM's marques was to duplicate another; the customer would gradually ascend the five steps of GM's brand ladder, trading up each time. The first-time buyer would, ideally, buy a downmarket Chevrolet, and then graduate via a more superior Oldsmobile, to a Pontiac, a Buick and, it was hoped, eventually to that ultimate American status symbol, a Cadillac. Yet every rung on the ladder was to be clearly differentiated. As Sloan himself later wrote: 'Each line of General Motors cars produced should preserve a distinction of appearance so that one knows on sight a Chevrolet, a Pontiac, an Oldsmobile, a Buick or a Cadillac.' All of the five divisions overlapped a little, since Sloan wanted to promote a degree of internal competition, but he ensured that the heads of the 'GM Five' met frequently with him and his key managers to iron out any potential confusions. He also ensured that each division had a Fisher body plant

Karl Benz driving his 1885 Motorwagen.

Gottlieb Daimler riding in the world's first four-wheeled automobile, 1886. His son Wilhelm is driving.

(*Top left*) A 1910 poster by Henri Thiriet for one of the most successful of the early auto makers: De Dion-Bouton. The car is the Model K; the figure of the (somewhat unamused) black chauffeur was modelled on the Marquis de Dion's Abyssinian man-servant. (*Top right*) Henry and Clara Ford in 1946, riding in Henry's 1896 Quadricycle.

René Panhard (in the back, with Mme Levassor) and Emile Levassor (with his hand on the tiller) in their licensed Daimler, 1886.

The tiny Austin Seven of 1922.

Woolf Barnato and his Speed-Six Bentley at Brooklands in 1930.

One of the first cars to be produced by Rolls-Royce: their 20 hp model of 1905. The Hon. C. S. Rolls himself is seated at the back, to our left.

GM's President, Alfred P. Sloan, peers uncertainly into the engine of a 1911 Cadillac Model 30 in 1936, flanked by GM's Head of Research, Charles F. Kettering, and Nicholas Dreystadt, then boss of GM's Cadillac division. They are posed to commemorate Kettering's invention of the self-starter twenty-five years earlier.

(a company that GM eventually bought outright) sited conveniently next door.

Even Ford knew Sloan was right. In 1939 Edsel Ford finally persuaded his father to mimic Sloan's brand ladder by introducing a new mid-priced marque called Mercury. Customers were not fooled, however. Ford was too mean to launch a wholly new brand, and early Mercurys looked little different from the bargain-basement Fords to which they were supposed to be significantly superior. Ford never grasped Sloan's basic business philosophy: do it properly, or not at all.

Alfred Sloan, while far from being a natural salesman in the Durant mould, also recognized the importance of advertising and marketing. He was the first car maker to encourage his dealers to offer trade-ins and payment credit (soon known as 'hire purchase'). He invested heavily in advertisements and public relations – again, unlike Henry Ford. Yet he was no believer in the inherent wisdom of the market. For example, he subtly exploited GM's industrial might to cross-subsidize his upmarket Cadillac and Buick divisions during the Depression, with the result that Cadillac was one of the very few upmarket brands to survive.

Countless luxury and sports car makers perished during the 1930s, no matter how impressive or revolutionary their products. Gordon Buehrig's impressively aerodynamic Cord 810 was the fastest American car on the road, set a land speed record of 107 mph, and was promoted by film star Sonja Henie. But the impressive qualities of the 810 did not prevent Cord from going bankrupt in 1937 – joining Stutz, Duesenberg and other famous American luxury marques on the scrapheap. Sloan was determined that his premium Cadillac brand should not go the same way. While American luxury auto sales plummeted from 150,000 per year in 1929 to barely 10,000 in 1937, Sloan kept Cadillac afloat (much as Arthur Sidgreaves was doing across the Atlantic with Rolls-Royce). Sloan lowered the prices of all GM's cars – something that small producers like Cord could not afford to do – and thus kept sales and market share, if not income, relatively buoyant. Sloan did not suddenly have to switch to making cheaper, smaller cars, as Packard was now attempting to do;

GM's Chevrolet division already made inexpensive cars that had a large and loyal following. What Sloan was prepared to do was to use the same basic body for his Cadillacs *and* for the bigger Buicks, thus saving tooling and production costs. As a result, GM's luxury marque was one of the few exclusive American automobile names to be still in business at the end of 1930s.

Sloan additionally acknowledged the importance of export markets. As he was to note in his (ghosted) autobiography, always the question was not whether he should or should not export, but 'whether to build up our own companies or to buy and develop existing ones'. Sloan invariably plumped for the latter. In 1919 he targeted the new Citroën concern in France, but withdrew on judging that the ambitious new car maker's management was 'weak' (an epithet Sloan employed for most auto makers' managements other than his own and Ford's). Five years later he almost bought Austin of Britain. Then, to everyone's surprise, GM bought the modest British firm of Vauxhall of Luton, a luxury car maker that up until 1925 had – strange as it may seem now, in the days of the Vauxhall Astra – sought to compete with Rolls, Bentley and Bugatti. Vauxhall had been limping along in the slow lane under the benign but hopelessly amateur leadership of Old Etonian Leslie Walton. Overnight, GM changed Vauxhall's corporate strategy completely, remodelling the firm to concentrate not on the sort of luxury cars that Walton had liked to own but on profitable smaller cars and light trucks. With GM's technical know-how behind the company, Vauxhall introduced the first synchromesh gearbox to Britain, in 1931. Two years later, Vauxhall launched its first successful small car, the Light Six, and began to make money for GM.

Three years after buying Vauxhall, Sloan added the far larger German firm of Adam Opel to GM's portfolio, making GM overnight the largest car maker in Germany. In 1937 Opel launched its first mass-produced small car, the Kadett (the equivalent of Vauxhall's Light Six). From then on, both Vauxhall and Opel anchored their product lines on cheap and simple models; any thought of competing with the likes of Rolls-Royce and Mercedes had long since faded from memory.

In his personal life, Sloan was not unlike Morris, Austin and Renault: a cold, reserved and isolated figure. He admitted to few friends, and even referred to himself as a 'narrow man'. (In later years, though, he was curiously close to two larger-than-life figures whose extrovert personalities could not have been further removed from his own: rival car tycoon Walter Chrysler and design guru Harley Earl.) He did not associate with movie stars (nor starlets), did not own a yacht, and was not interested in motor racing. He was prudish and censorious; senior GM executive John J. Raskob, for example, was asked to leave the company after Sloan heard that he had been seen in Atlantic City in the company of a woman who was not his wife. He was remote: he never once appeared on a factory floor, and was simply not interested in the concerns or lives of most of his workers. And he could be surprisingly mean-spirited at times. Thus, while he was happy to be seen publicly with Durant when GM's twenty-five millionth car was rolled out in 1940 – Sloan publicly took the aged Durant by the hand, declaring that 'we often fail to recognize the creative spirit' – he could not be bothered to attend Durant's funeral seven years later, an absence that was widely noted both inside and outside the industry. The calculating magnate clearly did not want to be seen to be associated with failure.

Nor was Sloan a misguided paternalist in the mould of Henry Ford or William Morris. He left the amenable William Knudsen – who, in 1937, became the company's president – to sort out GM's labour relations and strikes.[1] Predictably, Sloan's political leanings were definitely towards the right. A friend of the last Republican president of the inter-war years, Herbert Hoover, Sloan loathed his successor, Franklin D. Roosevelt, and (like Henry Ford) despised all that he stood for. Alongside Ford, he campaigned bitterly against the New Deal, and tried to prevent

---

1 In 1940 President Franklin D. Roosevelt lured Knudsen away from GM to head up America's war production effort. Knudsen was later made a lieutenant general in the US Army for his wartime services – the only civilian to join at such a high rank. Sloan, who had persistently resisted government interference in GM's wartime operations, received nothing.

Roosevelt's presidential nomination in 1936 via a hateful campaign run by the far-right American Liberty League. Even after the League issued a pamphlet carrying supposedly damning photographs – showing Eleanor Roosevelt in the company of African-Americans, shots that the League gleefully described as 'nigger pictures' – Sloan continued to bankroll its disgraceful activities. Sloan also supported an even more shadowy right-wing group, the Sentinels of the Republic, whose members' anti-New Deal campaigns carried over into overt anti-Semitism (one Sentinel labelled the New Deal 'Jewish communism') and public demands for an 'American Hitler'.

Like Ford, Sloan, too, was at best agnostic about Adolf Hitler and the brutal Nazi regime. Hitler's minister of production, Albert Speer, later said that the German army could not have invaded Poland in 1939 without GM's technical help. As a result, Sloan has been branded by some historians as 'Hitler's car maker'. While this soubriquet may be a little unfair, he was certainly happy to appease the Nazis after 1933, acquiescing to the Nazification of Opel's plants and management, with the anodyne comment that 'politics should not be considered the business of the management of GM'. Sloan said nothing as the Nazis purged all the Jewish employees from his German factories and dealerships, and did not interfere as Opel's new Brandenburg plant was forcibly converted to make military trucks. When the European war broke out in 1939, he famously declared that 'we are too big to be inconvenienced by these pitiful international squabbles'. The following March, GM president William Knudsen admitted: 'I have to report with some regret that Mr Hitler is the boss of our German factory.'

By 1939 Alfred Sloan presided over the world's largest corporation. GM not only sold more cars than any other company, it also built the majority of America's buses and railway engines. It even controlled a major aircraft manufacturer, North American Aviation. For all its worldwide expertise and apparent knowledge of the German market, however, GM overlooked one of the most important cars of the century. The launch in 1939 of Ferdinand Porsche's 'Strength through Joy' car caused barely a ripple of interest in Detroit. Six years later Sloan's henchmen passed up the opportunity to acquire both the car and its factory. It was a mistake that GM would come profoundly to regret.

4

The Age of Gasoline

In 1916, while Europe was convulsed by the carnage of the First World War, Henri Deterding, the boss of oil giant Royal Dutch Shell, prophetically announced: 'This is a century of travel, and the restlessness which has been created by the war will make the desire for travel still greater.' At the time, Deterding's prediction may have seemed unduly optimistic. For until the 1920s – the era of the Model T and the Austin Seven – most people simply did not drive. It was just the pampered few who did, a wealthy minority who were hugely resented by everyone else. However, by 1930 Deterding had been proved right: the car was now within reach of the many, rather than just the few. The automobile had truly arrived.

The cars produced by the pioneer auto makers before 1914 were, for all their promise and potential, initially just seen as rich men's toys. In Britain, King Edward VII rode in Daimlers from Coventry; in Spain, motoring enthusiast King Alfonso XIII delighted in driving his own De Dion-Bouton. By the late 1920s Duesenbergs and Cadillacs in America and Rolls-Royces, Hispano-Suizas and Bugattis in Europe were *de rigueur* accessories for any pretentious plutocrat and bywords for excess, sophistication and opulence. In India the profligate and sadistic Maharaja of Alwah, Sir Jai Singh, commissioned a Lanchester Forty – a car that cost more than a Rolls-Royce Silver Ghost – converted into a replica of the British royal coach, complete with postilion seats for two footmen and gold-leaf crowns on the doors.[1]

Motorists' societies, such as America's Automobile Association of 1902 and the Automobile Club of Great Britain of 1897, were emphatically elite organizations. The latter earned a royal prefix from Edward VII in 1907, and used this as an excuse to build a pompous new headquarters on London's fashionable Pall Mall.[2] Even the more ostensibly egalitarian Automobile Association (AA) of 1905 was initially concerned with protecting its wealthy members from the pitfalls of legislation; the first AA men would cycle down the road looking for police speed traps and would then warn oncoming drivers where they were located. (Both RAC and AA representatives were also required to acknowledge passing members. As Eric Newby observed: 'If they failed to salute, members were advised to stop them and ask the reason why.') And in America, Britain and France, well-heeled motorists were provided with a luxury, 24-hour service of hire car facilities and chauffeurs, together with, on occasion, well-appointed bedrooms for the weary driver.

As a symbol of wealth and sophistication, in its earliest years the car was seen by many less privileged citizens as a particularly pernicious weapon in the class war. Rural communities often threw glass or tacks over country roads to stop passing traffic, and in some instances even barbed wire was strung from tree to tree. Any driver hitting an animal, let alone a small child, was liable to be set upon by a howling mob of locals. Compensation litigation, dealing with cars that had frightened horses and caused accidents and injuries, was soon common across Europe and North America. The first motorist to drive up New York's Broadway, Philip Hagel, had to pay $48,000 in damages to the owners of horses terrified by the sight of his stately De Dion-Bouton.

As cars got faster and faster, public opinion became increasingly concerned about road safety – more worried, it has to be said, about the

---

1 Singh was deposed by the British for his extravagance and corruption in 1933 and died in exile in Paris four years later.
2 Designed by classical architects Mewès and Davis and completed in 1911.

danger to pedestrians than any risk to the car's invariably affluent occupants. In 1896 the national speed limit in Britain was raised from 4 to 14 mph, and thirty-three drivers celebrated with an 'emancipation day' drive on 14 November from London to Brighton. The same year, however, also saw the first British motor accident, when a woman pedestrian was run down and killed while walking in the grounds of the Crystal Palace in south London. Three years later came the first American road death, as H. H. Bliss was struck by an automobile after alighting from a New York City trolley car. By 1902, the year in which the Society for the Protection of Pedestrians (SPP) was founded in Britain, the reputation of the car had been firmly established on both sides of the Atlantic as a rich man's plaything which posed a serious hazard to working families. The death in 1905 of a small boy in Markyate, Hertfordshire, run over by a chauffeured car which simply sped off, turned into a national crusade, and the influential *Daily Mail* offered a £100 reward for catching the 'motor criminals' responsible. (With delicious irony, the perpetrator of the accident turned out to be a vehicle owned by Hildebrand Harmsworth, the brother of the *Mail*'s proprietor.) The following year, as the Royal Commission on the Motor Car confirmed the suspicion that many local communities were sabotaging roads against the speeding rich, the case of the Duchess of Connaught (born Princess Louise Margaret of Prussia), whose chauffeured car had hit and killed a small boy who had run heedlessly across the road, received considerable publicity. Neither the duchess nor her driver was ever prosecuted – the former was, of course, a member of the British royal family – but the incident did nothing to cool passions. Shortly after this tragedy the novelist Kenneth Grahame made his famous *The Wind in the Willows* character Mr Toad into a faddish, prosperous, yet terminally irresponsible motorist, a 'Terror of the Highway' who was, unlike the Duchess of Connaught's chauffeur, both arrested and imprisoned.

Early apologists for the automobile were quick to advertise the health benefits of the car over the horse. Cars, they pointed out, did not spread the diseases or foul smells that emanated from horse dung, stables or the dead horses that frequently littered the roads. And runaway horses, it was alleged, actually caused more accidents than did the first cars. (One British writer has estimated that the number of people seriously injured in road accidents in London was the same in 1872 as it was in 1972.) In the event, it was the motoring lobby that triumphed. In Britain, despite protests from organizations such as the SPP, the Motor Car Act of 1903 raised the national speed limit to 20 mph – a threshold that, surprisingly, remained in force until 1930.[1]

The wealthy motorists of the Edwardian era were often attracted to the bewildering array of city-to-city contests that proliferated in Europe after the groundbreaking Paris–Bordeaux race of 1895. (Most of the grand international races of this period either started or ended in Paris, a tacit acknowledgement of France's status as the world's leading car maker.[2]) Yet many of these less-than-idle rich suffered injury or even death as a result of their participation. The 1903 Paris–Madrid race claimed not just the life of Louis Renault's brother, Marcel; altogether the race claimed eight dead (three drivers and five spectators), with many more spectators injured – a casualty rate that prompted the French government to shut down the race when it reached Bordeaux. Yet the carnage of 1903 failed to prevent more rich young men risking their lives at the wheel.

The most ambitious, daring and expensive competition of all was the Peking–Paris race in 1907. Organized by the French daily newspaper *Le Matin*, it was won by that paradigm of the aristocratic motorist, Prince Luigi Marcantonio Francesco Rodolfo Scipione Borghese. The prince drove a Turin-made Italia, which was powered by a huge 7.4 litre engine. With his erect bearing, calm demeanour, aloof manner and pith helmet, he looked every inch the epitome of Edwardian sangfroid and

---

1 The same piece of legislation also introduced registration plates, the driving licence and a minimum driving age of seventeen.
2 By 1913 there were 175,300 cars on British roads, almost double those in France (88,300) and Germany (about 70,000). But the French still boasted Europe's largest car industry, making around 45,000 cars in that year, compared with Britain's 26,238 and Germany's 17,162.

the patrician auto pioneer – even though his chauffeur, Ettore Guizardi, actually did most of the driving, while a gang of Chinese coolies was hired to carry the car across rivers and up and down mountains. Prince Borghese was also unusual in that he survived his many races; having published a book on his Peking–Paris triumph, he joined Italy's Radical Party as an MP and, after 1915, added a distinguished war record to his already impressive career.

While aristocrats like Prince Borghese were content to drive faster and faster, the spread of car ownership across all classes of society gradually made road safety more of a civic priority. A manually oper-ated, gas-powered traffic signal, using red and green lanterns, had been sited outside London's Palace of Westminster since 1868 – although in 1869 the gaslight assembly blew up, injuring the duty constable. The earliest electric two-colour (red and green) traffic lights were erected at the corner of East 105th Street and Euclid Avenue in Cleveland, Ohio, in the fateful month of August 1914.[1] Three-colour lights were intro-duced, appropriately enough, in the Motor City itself, Detroit, in 1920. Two years later the first automated, interconnected traffic light system appeared, in Houston, Texas. Yet the first European traffic lights – sup-plemented by a gong that was operated by a traffic gendarme to alert dozy motorists – did not appear until 1923, when they were installed in Paris. By that time, traffic light systems were common across the USA, one of the most successful patents being that taken out by the remark-able African-American inventor and entrepreneur Garrett Morgan, who in 1923 installed three-colour sets, arranged on T-shaped poles, in downtown Detroit.

Where America pioneered traffic lights, Britain led the way with foot junctions. The 'zebra' pedestrian crossing – originally comprising blue and yellow stripes; the famous black and white pattern came later – first appeared in the early 1920s and was mentioned in the National 'Safety First' Association's *Safety Hints for all Motorists* (the ancestor of today's

---

1 The basic concept had actually been patented by a Utah policeman two years earlier.

Highway Code) in 1924. This crossing type was formalized in 1935, when the Ministry of Transport added amber beacons at each end of the crossing (at the same time introducing a formal driving test).[1] These globes, first installed at Wigan in Lancashire, were soon dubbed Belisha beacons, after the current transport minister, Leslie Hore-Belisha.[2] It was not until 1951, however, that zebra crossings with lit Belisha beacons were given the force of law.

By the time Hore-Belisha's beacons appeared, the role and status of the motor car had changed enormously since the pioneer days of motoring before the First World War. By the mid-1920s the car had become the transport of the middle-class family and the working man, not just the preserve of the idle rich. As the Lexington Motor Company claimed in 1920: 'The Motor Car is the Magic Carpet of Modern Times.' In 1900 there were eight thousand car owners in America; this had grown to 912,000 by 1912, 3.4 million by 1916, 23.1 million by 1930, and 32 million by 1940. In 1929 the US made 5.3 million cars, ten times the output of the rest of the world put together. Cars were also being driven ever further; a yearly average mileage per car of 4,500 miles in 1919 had grown to 7,500 by 1929. Anyone, it seemed, could afford a motor car. America's Hire Purchase Act, designed to protect consumers from unscrupulous salesman who hid their vast profits behind complicated hire purchase deals, specifically exempted the automobile from its controls.

In 1929 Frederick Lewis Allen wrote that 'the age of steam was yielding to the age of gasoline':

Villages that had once prospered because they were 'on the railroad' languished with economic anemia; villages on Route 61 blossomed with garages, filling stations, hot-dog stands, chicken-dinner restaurants, tearooms, tourists' rests,

---

1 The flashing lights were a later addition.
2 Subsequently a reforming, though controversial, minister of war; in 1940 he was sacked from his post, largely as a result of widespread anti-Semitic feeling in both the army and the government. Six years earlier, it was Hore-Belisha who had been responsible for raising the speed limit to 30 mph.

camping sites and affluence. The interurban trolley perished . . . By the end of the decade . . . red and green lights, blinkers, one-way streets . . . parking ordinances, and still a shining flow of traffic that backed up for blocks along Main Street every Saturday and Sunday afternoon.

Doctors particularly prized their cars, which speeded up their home visits no end. Libraries found they could now take their books out to communities. Mail services improved immeasurably, and mail-order businesses boomed. Smaller schools closed as parents found they could bus or drive their children to alternative sites. Agricultural workers, particularly during the Depression of the early 1930s, deserted the countryside for the growing cities, whole families moving in cars or small trucks. And the hire car business had taken off: Hertz was founded in Chicago in 1923 (when it absorbed a car hire business of 1918), while Godfrey Davis was founded in Britain in 1925.

By the mid-1920s, cheap cars like the Model T, the Austin Seven and the Peugeot Quadrillette had made motoring available to all. The age of the aristocratic 'touring' car, with its open body, was over; now customers expected closed-body saloons, or sedans, designed for everyday wear and tear, whatever the weather. Pre-1914 automobiles often could not bear the weight that closed bodies imposed, as their engines were simply too weak to drive the resultant burden. But more efficient post-war engines made the closed body possible, while improved steel-casting methods, which enabled larger pieces of steel to be supplied to the world's car makers, allowed saloons' glasshouses (the car's window area) to get bigger and bigger. The car of the twenties had come a long way from its carriage-based ancestors.

The car was now more than a luxury; it was an essential form of transport and an incarnation of freedom, equality and escape. It also offered individual independence; after the carnage of the First World War advertisers promoted the 'joy of the open road' and, as *Motor* headlined in July 1919, 'Freedom Regained'. Two weeks after the Armistice of 11 November 1918, both themes were combined in *Light Car and Cyclecar* magazine,[1] which pictured a woman driving a car 'Out of the Fog of War into the Light of Peace'.

The car additionally revolutionized holidays – indeed, it almost created them. Vermont was a quiet, remote backwater until the car and its highway came along. In 1911 the Vermont Bureau of Publicity began marketing the state to motorists not just for 'leaf-peeping' in the fall but also for the newly popular sport of skiing. Ski resorts and summer camps opened near to the new highways, and 1928 saw the opening of the 262 mile Green Mountain hiking trail, a long walkers' path whose devotees invariably came by car. In the early 1920s roadside cabins and camps of the sort immortalized in Frank Capra's 1934 hit film *It Happened One Night* began to appear all over America, soon to be followed by more sophisticated accommodation. The motel first appeared in California and France in the mid-1920s; the first 'mo-tel' surfacing in San Luis Obispo, California, in 1926, while the Halte-Relais Hôtel was unveiled at the 1925 Paris Exposition. Cars also fuelled the inter-war craze for 'auto-camping', camping by tent or (preferably) wheeled caravan in once remote sites which were suddenly accessible by car. Henry Ford himself was an enthusiastic auto-camper, as was President Warren Harding. Harding's FBI chief, J. Edgar Hoover, though, condemned the new cabin camps as 'camouflaged brothels'. By 1929, despite Hoover's reservations, 45 million Americans were driving to their holiday destinations each year.

By the early 1930s the car had irrevocably changed the way we live. The first drive-in restaurant, Royce Hailey's Pig Stand, opened in Dallas, Texas, in 1921. The first drive-in movie theatre followed in 1933, at Camden, New Jersey; the site could fit four hundred cars in seven inclined rows, to watch a screen measuring 40 × 50 feet. In 1922 the world's first car-dependent shopping mall was built outside Kansas City, Missouri – optimistically called the Country Club Plaza. And the first modern-style, self-contained suburban mall appeared in 1931 in Highland Park, Dallas.

---

1 A publication that traced its origins back to 1912 but did not survive the 1930s.

At home, garages began to be incorporated into the architectural shell. Le Corbusier's famous modernist villas of the 1920s, such as his Villa Stein of 1927, gave lots of space and much visual prominence to garages which were now sited at the front, rather than the side or rear, of the home.[1] By 1935 progressive architects were designing homes with integrated garages in the modernist idiom, with Le Corbusier-style pilotis screening the ground-floor parking area. But these car-oriented homes did not have to be modernist in conception. C. W. Stephenson's neo-Georgian 'motorcentric' house, built in Hartford, Connecticut, in 1935 by architects Adams and Prentice, gave over the whole, five-bay ground floor to garages; visitors had to ascend a staircase to reach the main rooms. For those who could not afford a garage integrated into the fabric of their house, in 1925 the auto manufacturer William Morris offered two versions of a prefabricated asbestos garage, while in 1928 the US manual *Home Builders* illustrated sixty different types of free-standing garage.

While individuals began to contemplate adding a garage to their home, cities began to invest in concrete multi-storey car parks, bulldozing whole blocks to accommodate these vast and ungainly edifices. London's first multi-storey car park arrived in 1906, in Soho's Wardour Street, and rose to five floors; it was subsequently advertised at the fifth international motor exhibition as 'The Largest Garage in yhe World'. Hotels, too, began to erect garages at the side or rear, often on the footprint of the stable area. Underground car parks followed in the 1930s; Britain's first was not in London, but in seaside Hastings, in 1931.

Hydrocarbon man also changed the landscape of whole continents. The creation of suburbs accelerated in the 1920s as the vast increase in car use made downtown living seem irrelevant, cramped and dirty. By 1940 there were 13 million Americans living in car-dependent suburban communities with no form of public transport. Ribbon development linked communities, filling stations and motels along newly widened highways.

---

1 Le Corbusier's 1922 plan for La Ville Contemporaine envisaged a wholly car-dependent metropolis, comprised only of tall tower blocks.

And suburbs grew exponentially, especially in America. During the 1920s the upmarket Beverly Hills suburb of Los Angeles grew by a phenomenal 2,480 per cent, while its equivalents in Detroit, Grosse Point Park and Ferndale, grew by 725 and 690 per cent, respectively.

Filling stations were a particularly intrusive feature in the cityscape or countryside. Before the First World War, most motorists had carried spare supplies of petrol with them in large cans. By 1910, however, the first kerbside petrol pumps had appeared in the US. In Britain, the first kerbside pumps were installed in Shrewsbury in 1915 by the American pump manufacturers S. F. Bowser & Co., and the first filling station was built at Aldermaston in Berkshire in 1919. Post-war, the Automobile Association opened ten filling stations across the country, each with a Bowser pump and a 500 gallon underground tank. Other entrepreneurs followed with filling stations in urban locations, often with multiple pumps, and in 1921 the oil giant Shell started erecting its own pumps. And in 1924 came the first combined garage-cum-showrooms. (The first built in Britain, the Blue Bird Motor Co. Filling Station of 1926, on London's King's Road, still survives, albeit converted into a restaurant and shop.) By 1929 there were over fifty-five thousand filling stations in Britain, with local authorities now empowered to prohibit them in sensitive areas.

These early installations were invariably phrased in comforting architectural idioms to reassure the motorist. Early urban examples were often designed in a stripped classical style, while British rural stations of the 1920s and 30s were sometimes thatched, despite the obvious risk of fire. In 1928 the British government passed the Petroleum (Consolidation) Act, which attempted to regulate the design and signage of filling stations in locations of historic importance, but no other nations followed suit. But in 1931 the Royal Institute of British Architects was still warning of the need to 'keep hold on future developments', citing the 'many awful examples already existing' of petrol stations and parking garages. In 1933 Bowser offered a service to design and equip oil companies with a 'typical filling station', which was invariably phrased in a vaguely modernist-cum-Art

Deco ('Moderne') style. By 1939 filling stations were being incorporated into new residential blocks in urban areas.

America's landscape, too, was by 1930 littered with filling stations (or 'service stations', as they were called west of the Rockies). The first multi-pump 'super station' opened in Fort Worth, Texas, in 1921, by which year the US boasted about twelve thousand gas stations. During the 1920s, first Shell and then the other major oil companies standardized their filling stations, plastering them with existing or newly contrived brand logos, from Shell's eponymous and ubiquitous crustacean (invented in 1930) to Sinclair Oil's improbable brontosaurus. Service stations now offered free oil and water checks – although employees were forbidden to comment on other aspects of the car's mechanics, for fear of litigation.

Oil companies began to promote motor tourism as a way of increasing their sales. In Britain, Shell was especially active, launching its 'See Britain First – On Shell' pamphlet and poster campaign from 1925. The company followed this with 'Everywhere You Go' and 'Visit Britain's Landmarks' in the 1930s, and commissioned poster designs from the leading artists of the day, from Edward McKnight Kauffer and Rex Whistler to Paul Nash and Graham Sutherland. In 1934 the firm launched the first of its Shell Guides to the cultural highlights of Britain's counties: John Betjeman's *Cornwall*. Not everyone was happy with the proliferation of the automobile, however; many agreed with the premise of C. E. M. Joad's *The Horrors of the Countryside* of 1931, in which he described in passionate detail how motorists, 'in no frame of mind for aesthetic enjoyment', were ruining the English landscape.

Automobile production also created the world's first 'motor cities': Detroit and Coventry. Detroit had been founded by the French at the dawn of the eighteenth century, as Fort Pontchartrain du Détroit. Appropriated by the British in 1760, during the Seven Years War of 1756–63, its name was shortened to Detroit. Its fertile soil made it an agricultural centre, the Great Lakes had an abundance of fish, and its position on the Great Lakes made it a strategic strongpoint. As a result, when the USA won its independence in 1783 the British clung on to Detroit, which was only occupied by American troops in 1796 (and then briefly recaptured by the British in 1812). In the nineteenth century Detroit developed as a centre for mechanical trades, fed by the newly built Erie Canal which linked the Great Lakes to New York. From 1847 until the 1880s the Detroit area led the world in copper production, boasted the largest seed company in the world (D. M. Ferry), and was a major exporter of lead and salt. In 1896 the first refrigerated railcar was made in Detroit, enabling meat and other perishables to be transported across the continent. By 1890 it had become the tenth largest city in the US, and by 1920 the third largest. By 1900 it had also become notorious for the unscrupulous activities of the Employers' Association of Detroit, whose strike-breaking and union infiltration activities had encouraged a number of companies suffering from labour trouble to relocate to the city; one of these was the Packard Motor Company, which left Warren, Ohio, for Detroit in 1903. Already playing host to a large number of diverse small-scale industrial enterprises, the city was well equipped to offer the embryonic auto industry the cheap, skilled labour and machine shops it needed. It also offered good water transport for the import of coal and iron ore. There was, however, an element of coincidence in Detroit's establishment as America's – and the world's – Motor City: it just happened that most of the early pioneers of the US motor industry, men like Ford, Durant and Leland, either came from or moved to the city. During the 1920s and 30s black workers migrated to Detroit from the impoverished South, attracted by the high wages and steady jobs being offered by Ford and his competitors. By 1922, the year Berry Gordy's parents made the journey, 3,500 per month were making the trek to Michigan.[1]

. . .

---

1 Black workers were still denied jobs at some Detroit plants. When three African-Americans were hired for skilled posts at Packard in 1943, all of their white colleagues downed tools.

The role of advertising in selling cars became something that few car makers could afford to ignore by the mid-1920s. Posters and print advertisements were soon supplemented by newer forms of marketing, such as in-house magazines and billboards. And in America, Edward ('Ned') Jordan broke the advertising mould when in June 1923 he produced his *Saturday Evening Post* ad for his (rather unfortunately named) Playboy car:

SOMEWHERE west of Laramie there's a bronco-busting, steer-roping girl who knows what I'm talking about. She can tell what a sassy pony, that's a cross between greased lighting and the place where it hits, can do with eleven hundred pounds of steel and action when he's going high, wide and handsome. The truth is – the Playboy was built for her. Built for the lass whose face is brown with the sun when the day is done of revel and romp and race. She loves the cross of the wild and the tame. There's a savor of links about that car – of laughter and lilt and light – a hint of old loves – and saddle and quirt. It's a brawny thing – yet a graceful thing for the sweep o' the Avenue. Step into the Playboy when the hour grows dull with things gone dead and stale. Then start for the land of real living with the spirit of the lass who rides, lean and rangy, into the red horizon of a Wyoming twilight.

Sadly for Jordan, few customers wanted to join the lean and rangy lass in the Wyoming twilight. In this case advertising definitely did not work: sales actually fell after this press promotion appeared. Jordan's company managed to survive through the 1920s, but failed to survive the Depression and collapsed in 1931. Jordan himself descended into alcoholism and was abandoned by his wife. After a stint as an advertising executive on New York's Madison Avenue, he sought redemption in the rum-fuelled bars of the West Indies. But his revolutionary new approach to promotional copy changed automobile advertising for ever.

In 1922 William Durant astutely predicted that 'most of us will live to see this whole country covered with a network of motor highways'. Yet twenty years earlier that prophecy would have seemed like the words of a madman. In most places around the globe the car was unable to go fast, owing to the appalling state of the roads, which had been designed for slow horse and carriage traffic. France was the only country in the world with a network of properly metalled roads; everywhere else, the first automobiles had to battle with mud, rocks and tree stumps. In 1903 less than 10 per cent of roads in the US were paved.

America, at least, was quick to recognize the deficiencies of its primitive road network. In 1913 work was begun on the Californian end of the first modern American road, the National Old Trails Highway, later to metamorphose into the National Trails Highway and, more famously, US Route 66 – the legendary east–west route which was brutally removed from the map by the automata at the American Association of State Highway and Transportation Officials in 1985. The same year also saw the launch of the Lincoln Highway, an ambitious scheme to create the nation's first 'high-speed' road, connecting New York and San Francisco via fourteen states, 128 counties and over seven hundred communities. The man behind the Lincoln Highway was automotive pioneer Carl Fisher, manufacturer of the Prest-O-Lite carbide-gas headlights used on most early cars, who also opened what was possibly the first car dealership in America (in Indianapolis) and was one of the principal investors in the Indianapolis motor racing track. Fisher's high-profile backers included his friend the legendary inventor Thomas Edison, former US president Theodore Roosevelt, and the current president, Woodrow Wilson, who was the first occupant of the Oval Office to make frequent personal use of the car.[1] With their ostentatious public support, money flowed in and work progressed swiftly. The first section, from Newark, New Jersey, to Jersey City, was opened in December 1913, and by 1924 the highway was largely complete. Fisher had maintained that the Lincoln Highway would 'stimulate as nothing else could the building of enduring highways everywhere that will not only be a credit to the American people but that will

---

1 The highway itself was, of course, named after the most celebrated of American presidents.

also mean much to American agriculture and American commerce'. In this he was largely proved right; by the mid-1930s (by which time it had been segmented into a confusing numerical array of new federal route designations), the road was popularly known as 'America's Highway'. Fisher himself had lost most of his fortune in the Wall Street Crash of 1929 and ended his days as an odd-job man in Miami Beach and, ultimately, as a nightclub owner in Key Largo.

Motoring enthusiast President Wilson supported the first tranche of federal funding for America's highways, declaring: 'The happiness, comfort and prosperity of rural life, and the development of the city, are alike conserved by the construction of public highways.' The Federal Road Aid Act of 1916 offered match-funding to states to build car-friendly roads as part of a $75 million highways package; the states raised their half of the funds through gasoline taxes, which most motorists shrugged off (the majority of car owners were still, at this time, comfortably off).

Highway construction gathered pace after the First World War. In New York the Bronx River Parkway, completed in 1925, was the first highway in the world to offer only limited access, with overpasses eliminating potentially dangerous intersections, and the first, too, to separate the two directions of traffic by a central reservation. Three years later Woodbridge, New Jersey, became the site of the first-ever 'cloverleaf' junction. And in 1932 Alfred Sloan of General Motors organized the first National Highway Users Conference, which successfully lobbied Herbert Hoover's outgoing administration to provide 100 per cent federal funding for new national highways. Hoover did not need much persuading; already, like President Wilson, a big fan of the car, he appointed the president of the Hudson Motor Car Company, Roy D. Chapin, as his last Secretary of Commerce.

America's highways never stopped growing. Roosevelt's 1938 Federal Aid Highway Act authorized a feasibility study for a national network of multi-lane, limited access superhighways on the model of the Bronx River Parkway. Before these deliberations had been completed, though, the 160 mile Pennsylvania Turnpike opened, on 1 October 1940, as the world's first long-distance superhighway. (At the grand opening, two black cats were sent across the drying tarmac as a superstitious precaution before cars were allowed to rush down it.) There were tolls on the Pennsylvania Turnpike, but no speed limits; as in Germany and Italy, you could go as fast as your car could manage. *Time* magazine described the new road with gushing enthusiasm: 'A 10-foot centre strip, soon to be hedged with small fire trees, divides the four lanes into two. No signboards mar the way or confuse the eye – its only borders are the misty, pine-edged hillsides of the Alleghenies. Ten smart Esso stations, finished Pennsylvania-Dutch fashion in native wood and stone, specialize in restroom toilet seats sterilized by ultraviolet ray after every use.' In 1944 the federal government followed Pennsylvania's example and passed a Highway Act to promote a federally funded network of superhighways, which would henceforward be free, although each state could still build its own toll roads.

America was not the only country contemplating superhighways. Most of the other Western democracies, however, were a good deal slower in implementing them. As early as 1902, British civil engineer B. H. Thwaite had argued for a four-lane toll road for cars and motorbikes 'from London, through the centre of England' to Scotland. His proposal was supported by the aristocratic motoring enthusiast John, 2nd Baron Montagu of Beaulieu, who promoted it in the pages of his glossy magazine *The Car*. In 1905 Lord Montagu's new periodical, *The Motor Car Magazine*, proposed a 'great system of motor roads . . . linking all the principal centres of the United Kingdom', which would begin with 'a London to Brighton Motorway'. And in 1906 came the first proposal for a multi-lane superhighway with 'cloverleaf' intersections at grade, formulated by the French engineer Eugène Hénard. However, all these early schemes failed to find sufficient financial backing. In 1923 Montagu tried again, this time promoting the idea of a privately run London to Birmingham motorway,[1] a scheme backed by Eagle Star Insurance, Shell Oil and, oddly enough, Coventry-based aircraft manufacturers Armstrong Whitworth. Yet even this powerful syndicate failed to lobby sufficient parliamentary support,

---

1 This road was, eventually, to be extended northwards to Salford and Liverpool.

and the scheme was deemed dead in the water even before the incoming Labour administration of 1924 dealt it its death blow. That year the well-known writer Hilaire Belloc called for the creation of 'a very few arterial roads joining up the main centres of population', 100 feet wide and with intersections at grade – effectively, a modern motorway. However, the first superhighways in France and Britain were not completed until 1946 and 1956, respectively.

Early cars, as manifestations of speed, style and wealth, invariably became symbols not just of status but also of implied sexual magnetism. The styling of cars from the late 1920s onwards exaggerated their carnal characteristics: the bonnets of luxury sports cars – Bentleys, Cords and Bugattis – became impossibly long; while the pointed nose – by 1937 almost all American cars had V-shaped front ends – and expanded front grille became aggressive tropes of macho aggression.

Unsurprisingly, given this sexual context, the automobile was gendered from its first years. While 'car' was a masculine noun in France, in Britain and the US autos were emphatically feminine. As *Autocar*'s reviewer rhapsodized in March 1899, the 'extreme tractability, the ready and pleasant response to my guiding hand, varied by occasional fits of moodiness, not to say stubbornness, disappearing as rapidly as they appeared, make the appellation of the gentle sex particularly suitable to the motor car'. While reinforcing sexual stereotypes, however, cars also served to liberate women from their Victorian roles and restraints. Sometimes they merely seemed to facilitate a journey from the frying pan into the fire: the *Harmsworth Monthly Pictorial Magazine* of July 1898 illustrated the story of the 'Motor-Car Elopement' of 'heiress Kitty and fearless Jack'. More helpfully, *Car Illustrated* of August 1904 pointed out that the car enabled women to travel independently; women drivers 'could shop 20 miles away, lunch 40 miles away and still have time to return home for dinner'. The introduction of the electronic starter, which became common after 1918, also made the process of driving much easier for women, who now did not have to grapple with stiff, heavy hand-cranks in order to start the engine.

Women drove cars from the earliest years of the automobile age. (Interestingly, though, historian Sean O'Connell points out that only 13 per cent of British women possessed a driving licence as late as 1965.) Dorothy Levitt, the first woman racing driver, was competing in British road races as early as 1903. Levitt confounded the current stereotype of sportswomen: short, slight and shy, she proved that you did not have to be a loud-mouthed, virile male to drive a car well. Yet while the new Automobile Association happily admitted female members after 1905, the more aristocratic Royal Automobile Club refused, forcing the establishment of a ladies' equivalent.

By the 1930s not only were many cars specifically aimed at the female market – not just the perennial Austin Seven, but also newer models like the Hillman Minx of 1935 – but women were racing cars and driving them on endurance expeditions. In 1931 Barbara Cartland organized a race for MG Midgets at the famous Brooklands racing track in Surrey to prove that women could drive, and race, as well as men. And as early as 1935 the *Daily Express* was noting that women drivers were seen as better insurance risks than men.

The car also had its own complex etymology by 1930. The very word 'car', adapted from the railways and the carriage trade, had been in use since the 1880s. 'Automobile', 'autocar' and 'motor car', particularly common terms in America and France, had also survived from the carriage age; whereas 'locomobile', a term coined for the car in the 1890s, had not (the word survived into the twentieth century in Britain and France only as a designation for steam automobiles; confusingly, there was also an American car manufacturer called Locomobile, which survived until 1929.) Despite much subsequent mythologizing, the phrase 'horseless carriage' was never officially adopted on either side of the Atlantic. Indeed, in October 1895 the London *Daily Chronicle* was bemoaning the fact that 'a name has not yet been found for the horseless carriage'. That same year, an enterprising Chicago newspaper held a competition for the best name for the car, offering a $500 prize to the winner. Among those submitted were 'self-motor', 'petrocar', 'autobat', 'autogo', 'autowain' (shades of John Constable), 'diamote' and 'pneumobile', which would have been interesting challenge for English speakers. The winner was – 'motocycle'.

Neither 'motocycle' nor 'locomobile' stuck. The first popular word for the car on both sides of the Atlantic was 'automobile', a word first recorded in France in 1876, nine years *before* the appearance of the first true car. In 1899 the *New York Times* raged against this pernicious French appellation: 'The French, who are usually orthodox in their etymology if nothing else, have evolved "automobile", which being half Greek and half Latin is so near indecent that we print it with hesitation.' At first, the word was anglicized in a manner of which the *New York Times* would have approved, neatly separating its Greek and Latin roots, as 'auto-mobile'. But by 1895 the London *Daily News* was referring to the arrival of a new 'automobile carriage' from Milan.

Soon 'automobile' and 'car' were being employed interchangeably. The English word 'car' had long been used to denote a wagon, chariot, carriage or railway carriage. By 1896 the term 'auto-car' was being used by both the British and the French to denote a petrol-powered vehicle; and by 1900 the British had simply shortened this term back to 'car'. In America, however, 'car' remained in use solely for railway carriages. Confusingly, by the late 1890s both Americans and British were using the term 'motor car' (sometimes hyphenated as 'motor-car') to describe both a powered railway vehicle and a highway automobile. By the 1920s, 'motor car' had become standard in the UK, if not in the US. 'Automobile' was shortened to 'auto' in Germany and Italy, and stuck – although the forward-looking Italians came to prefer *macchina* ('machine'), while the more traditional Germans also used the old word for carriage, *Wagen*.

Many early types of car borrowed their nomenclature from the carriage forms of the nineteenth century. Car makers used familiar carriage terms in order to lend the product status and lineage, or simply because many automobile coachbuilders used the old carriage terms with which they were familiar. A 'landau' – from the Rhenish town of that name – had been a light, four-wheeled, convertible carriage, first made in the mid-eighteenth century and highly fashionable across Europe by 1840. The landau carriage featured facing seats either side of a dropped footwell, all of which could be covered with a soft folding top, divided into two sections, and its low-slung nature made it a popular choice for ceremonial occasions. By 1900 the term 'landau' was also being employed by the first car makers to indicate a convertible car. But generally the landau configuration, with the hood in two sections, was not a style that transferred well to the automobile. The expression was disinterred by American manufacturers in the 1920s to denote a fixed-roof sedan in which the rear quarter of the glasshouse was covered with fabric in an attempt to make it look like a real convertible. By the 1950s the word had become completely meaningless and was used indiscriminately by GM and Chrysler merely to give their models some vaguely European chic.

As landaus grew rarer, their half-landau cousins, 'landaulets', enjoyed a brief vogue. A landaulet's body had a convertible top over the back seat – the rear half of the landau's two-part folding top – while the front seat was either roofed or left open. Since a landaulet was always intended to be a chauffeured car, the style was never popular in the mass market, and after 1918 was reserved for celebrity or official transport. Since the 1960s Mercedes have made special landaulets for the popes John XXIII, Paul VI and the German pontiff, Benedict XVI. As recently as 2007 their Maybach division displayed a 'landaulet concept car' at the Middle East International Auto Show, which found itself added to the production roster in 2009.

A 'brougham' was a light, four-wheeled, horse-drawn carriage of the nineteenth century. Originally designed in 1830 for Britain's Lord Chancellor, Lord Brougham and Vaux, it was smaller and nimbler than the usual heavy coach, with an enclosed, two-door body which usually sat only two people (though it sometimes carried an extra pair of foldaway seats in the front corners), a glazed front window allowing its occupants to see forwards, and a box seat for the driver and companion in front. The 'brougham' car of the Edwardian era was basically the same, with an outside seat in front for the chauffeur and an enclosed, hard-top cabin behind for the passengers. Cadillac first used the name in 1916 and kept reusing the term throughout the century. By the 1930s, though, a 'brougham' simply meant – for Cadillac as well as its American imitators – a well-appointed, two-door sedan. Cadillac's GM stablemate Oldsmobile sold a Regency Brougham until the demise of the marque in 2004, and even Ford used the term during the 1970s.

Other motor-related words soon entered the everyday vocabulary. The American word 'limousine' – meaning, literally, from the Limousin region of France – indicated, by 1902, a car with a closed passenger cab but an open driver's seat, later covered by an extension of the roof.[1] By 1930 the word was being applied more generally to larger automobiles, and after the Second World War to large or long cars with a chauffeur, whose seat could be portioned off from the rest of the interior. Limousines were soon being connected with service to and from US airports.

By the end of the 1930s, that peculiarly Anglo-Saxon invention the 'station wagon' (a phrase first used in the US in 1929), 'estate wagon' (used in both the US and the UK) or 'estate car' (UK only) indicated a car that was large enough to accommodate both people and goods. The 'station wagon' took its title from the horse-drawn buggies or carts that used to greet passengers from railway stations. The British 'estate car' was later called the Traveller or Countryman by Morris and Austin. A 'shooting brake' was a peculiar, British term for a two-door estate car, used up until the 1930s. The single word 'brake' had been used for large country wagons in the late nineteenth century, and was used by francophone countries to denote their (fairly rare) versions of 'estate cars' (*un break*) until the 1960s. In 2012, Jaguar issued a 'Sportbrake' estate version of its XF luxury saloon.

Some of the new words and phrase stuck. The name popularly used in America to describe a fixed-top car with two rows of four or more seats,

---

1 The tortuous etymology of the term suggests it originated from the Limousin-style cloak worn by the car's exposed chauffeur.

'sedan', comes from the covered, transportable chairs of the seventeenth and eighteenth centuries – and not, it seems, from the French city of the same name. The US periodical *Motor World* was using the word 'sedan' in 1912, and it soon became common in America. The equivalent British term, 'saloon', derived from the Georgian name (itself derived from the French 'salon') for the most elegant public room of the house. This rather overused word was by 1840 also being employed for a large, well-appointed room on a ship or train and, by 1908, for an expensive car. The French persisted with a term derived from the age of the carriage, 'berline', from the fast Berlin carriages invented in the late seventeenth century. The Germans, confusingly, stuck with *die Limousine*. The window area of a saloon or sedan was by the 1930s termed a 'turret top' or a 'glass-house' – an industry term that caught on mainly in America. The supports for the roof were called pillars and were lettered from front to back; thus the framing supports for the windscreen were the A-pillars, those behind the front door the B-pillars, and those framing the rear window the C-pillars.

As the automobile industry grew more diverse and complicated, so did its terminology. By 1930 a sedan or a saloon car had ample room for passengers, and accordingly featured a trunk (US) or a boot (UK), or a *coffre* (France) or *Kofferaum* (Germany). The impact bar at the front of the car was either a 'bumper' in Britain (a usage derived from wooden logs used to protect ships' hulls from damage) or, in America, a 'fender' (which originated as another nautical term, describing pieces of cork designed to protect the hull).[1] The American slang term 'fender-bender' was already in use by 1884, to denote a carriage accident, while the house magazine *Morris Owner* was in February 1926 describing 'the front face of the bumper bar'. Above the bumper or fender lay the bonnet and windscreen (UK), hood and windshield (US), *capote* and *pare-brise* (France), or *Motorhaube* and the onomatopoeic *Windshutzscheibe* (Germany). Below

---

1 In French the word for 'bumper' or 'fender' is plural, *les pare-chocs* (although the English 'bumper car' translates as *une tamponneuse*); in German the term is *Stoßstanger*.

was the gearbox (UK) or transmission (US and France). The engine was powered by petrol (UK) or gasoline (US).[1] Emissions came from the tailpipe in the US, the exhaust pipe in the UK, the *pot d'échappement* in France and, delightfully, the *Auspuffrohr* in Germany.[2] But a cabriolet was a convertible coupé in Britain, France *and* America – although 'coupé' lost its acute accent when it travelled across the Atlantic.

Many other motor terms happily crossed national linguistic boundaries. A 'Spider' or 'Spyder' was an Italian term which originally meant a two-seat sports car with a folding hood – a vehicle that could also be called by most of the world's nations a 'roadster', though this usually signified a convertible with four proper seats and (sometimes) four doors. Convertibles with hard tops were called, unsurprisingly, 'hard-tops'.[3] The French word 'tonneau' was, and is, employed across the world for the soft or hard covers used to protect the empty seats of convertibles, roadsters or Spyders. And the English term 'sports car' means the same in any language.

Looking back at the automotive vocabulary of the pioneer years, some terms have, inevitably, disappeared; while the fact that some others were ever considered at all now seems incredible. There are no more 'berlines' or 'landaulets', and the 'locomobile' and the 'petrocar' have been consigned to history. Some expressions, though, have managed to survive: American luxury marques still occasionally use the term 'brougham', and even the 'shooting brake' has made an unlikely comeback. Meanwhile, we have a new set of terms to absorb, from crossovers and mini-MPVs to hybrids and e-cars. And while the English term 'sports car' is still in widespread use, today most sports cars are actually made not in Britain or even America but in Japan, a statistic that would have been unthinkable

---

1 *L'essence* or *pétrole* in French; *das Benzin* across the Rhine. The Italians followed the Germans, with *benzina*, while the Spanish followed American practice, adopting *gasolina*.

2 *Auspuff* means 'emissions'.

3 By 1960 ostensibly fixed hard-top roofs could often be electrically retracted; today the practice is common and threatens to smother the demand for soft-top convertibles.

in 1939. When the Second World War broke out that year, the world was to change forever – and it was a change that would be largely shaped by the car.

5

The People's War

Adolf Hitler adored cars – though he never learned to drive. In 1936 the *New York Times* reported that the German dictator was believed to 'reel off a higher annual motor mileage than any other ruler or head of state'. On becoming chancellor in 1933, Hitler made three symbolic gestures to raise the status of the automobile in Nazi Germany: he personally opened the annual Berlin Motor Show (a task he cheerfully repeated every year until 1939); he declared that his government would begin a state-sponsored programme to create a 'people's car'; and he announced that his Nazi administration would help Germany's luxury car makers to dominate world motor racing. Three years later Hitler used the platform of the Berlin Motor Show to announce (somewhat prematurely, as it turned out) that Germany had 'effectively solved the problem of producing synthetic gasoline' and never need be dependent on foreign oil imports. Hitler's minister of propaganda, Josef Goebbels, then echoed his master by declaring that 'politics shows the direction applied science is to take' and that 'the twentieth century is the era of the motor car'.

During the 1920s and 30s, Britain and France dithered over the provision of improved multi-lane highways for the new, democratic phenomenon of the car (from 1918 until 1927 Britain built only 127 miles of new road), whereas the new totalitarian states of Germany and Italy enthusiastically embraced the potential of the automobile. In 1926 Mussolini's Italian government hosted the fifth International Road

Congress, and prominent civil servants and journalists from Britain, France and America were very impressed by fascist Italy's new *autostrade*. Mussolini touted these impressive multi-lane superhighways as a fitting symbol of the technological advance and energy of fascist Italy (while ignoring the fact that the *autostrade* system had been begun in 1921, a year before came to power). And after having seized power in 1933, Hitler was quick to follow Mussolini's lead. The new German Führer authorized the construction of 4,300 miles of *Autobahnen* along with three thousand new bridges, an Italian-style network that served several purposes at once. Not only did the project closely associate the Nazi regime with the speed and strength of the automobile, delivering valuable symbols of technological progress to promote Germany's image abroad (in 1938 Nazi labour chief Dr Fritz Todt asserted that 'the great importance of the Reich motor roads has long since been recognized in foreign countries'), but construction of the *Autobahnen* also created thousands of new jobs. The rapid motorization of Germany under the Nazis was, automotive historians such as R. J. Overy and James J. Flink have suggested, just as important as military rearmament in stimulating Germany's economic recovery after 1933. Most crucially, the road network provided Hitler's armed forces with broad new routes for fast and easy deployment.

Hitler's ministers made much of their new *Autobahnen*. In 1934 Nazi Germany hosted the seventh International Road Congress, and in 1936 the second International Congress for Bridges and Overground Structures. A government propaganda magazine extolling the virtues of the Nazis' highways, *Die Straße* ('The Road'), was launched. And in April 1936 Reichsminister Göring opened the new *Autobahn* out of Berlin by racing down it at high speed in his massive duck-egg blue Mercedes 540K Special Roadster – on the wrong side of the highway. (A misty-eyed Hitler later reminisced that Göring always 'made a point of always driving on the left-hand side of the road. In moments of danger, he used to blow his horn. His confidence was unfailing . . .')

The following year the German government persuaded a large delegation of experts from Britain's Automobile Association, Royal

Automobile Club, British Road Federation and, crucially, the parliamentary road group to come and admire Germany's motorways, a trip that climaxed with a brief meeting with both Hitler and Mussolini. The starry-eyed British delegation's report of January 1938, which relied heavily on skewed statistics provided by Todt's *Deutsche Arbeitsfront*, naively lauded German achievements and declared its 'firm opinion that a national scheme should be framed without delay for a series of motorways' along German lines. But some observers were not deceived by the Nazis' utopian rhetoric. While post-war historians have tended to downplay the military role of Germany's *Autobahnen*, some Western commentators of the late 1930s believed that Hitler's motorways were primarily designed to carry military traffic. As early as 1938, the editor of Britain's *Geographical Magazine* noted that: 'Dictatorship expresses itself naturally in grandiose public works, of which the German *Autobahnen* afford a striking example. Democratic governments, subject to critical opposition and accountable for every item of expenditure, cannot afford to burden the exchequer from motives of self-advertisement, still less for the sake of unavowed aims.'

Hitler was eager to build automobiles that would match the technology of his impressive new *Autobahnen* and the social aspirations of his classless National Socialist state. From 1914 until 1938 Germany had made few viable everyday cars; German automobiles were built largely for the luxury and performance car markets, and the country relied on foreign manufacturers such as Austin (whose Seven was, as we have seen, built under licence in Germany) to provide more modest personal transport. Hitler aimed to change all that. One strand of his government's motor manufacturing policy was to subsidize a new big car programme, using the factories and expertise of Mercedes and Auto Union to create impressively grand cars for the *hohe Tiere* (the 'big cheeses') of the Nazi regime, as well as sportier derivatives to dominate the international Grand Prix circuit. The other strand was to make a car for all classes, a Model T for Germany. A 'people's car' would, Hitler insisted, prove 'the instrument for uniting the different classes, just as it has done in America, thanks to

Mr Ford's genius'. The Führer saw such a car as the embodiment of the egalitarian Nazi ideal, an automobile that would sweep away old social and political divisions and help create a harmonized, obedient National Socialist Germany. It would be built 'for the broad masses'; its purpose would be 'to answer their transport needs and it is intended to give them joy'.

The first of Hitler's automotive ambitions was swiftly realized. By 1935 Germany's 'silver arrow' cars, as they were known,[1] were dominating the Grand Prix and European championship circuits, beating Bugattis, Bentleys and Alfas almost every time, as vehicles such as Mercedes' superlative W125 of 1937 carried all before them. On the roads, too, voluptuously finished products of the Daimler-Benz and Auto Union factories, such as the giant Grösser Mercedes series, were utilized as symbols of power and virility by Hitler and his henchmen. Hitler's own armour-plated Mercedes 770K W50 II of 1939 weighed more than five tons and, with its supercharged eight-cylinder engine, could reach 112 mph. Daimler-Benz did not even attempt to sell their automobiles to the Nazi leaders, but loaned the party all the Mercedes cars it needed. Bolstered by the Nazi hierarchs' ostentatious support, these luxurious and bullet-proof behemoths were also sold to dictators and monarchs across the globe, from King Zog of Albania to General Franco of Spain and Emperor Hirohito of Japan, who ordered seven of the vast Grösser Mercedes models.

Fast, virile German sports cars were soon also being made in Bavaria. Founded in 1916 to make aircraft engines, after the First World War the Bayerische Motoren Werke had originally concentrated on making motorcycles. Until 1932 those saloon cars that BMW did manufacture were generally made under licence from Austin. After Hitler's seizure of power in 1933, however, BMW began to make home-grown models and by the late 1930s had become renowned for its streamlined coupés. The BMW 328 of 1937 was particularly admired, and was copied by British sports car manufacturers such as Frazer-Nash and Bristol. Yet as Hitler

---

1 After 1934 German racing cars, formerly in white, were left unpainted.

expanded Germany's war machine, the production of aero engines once again took precedence, and BMW built a series of fine aircraft engines for the Luftwaffe along with a heavy, 2-litre, jeep-type military transport, the BMW 325, for the Wehrmacht.

Hitler's second goal was more complex. The Nazi government initially sought to pursue their objective of creating a 'people's car' by gaining control of Germany's existing volume car manufacturer, GM-owned Adam Opel. After Hitler gained power in 1933, his new administration substantially cut the profits GM was able to take out of the firm, gained control of the factory council at Opel's main plant, in Rüsselsheim, and launched their own National Socialist in-house magazine, *Der Opel Geist* ('The Opel Spirit', later renamed *Der Opel-Kamerad*, 'The Opel Comrade'). Wilhelm von Opel, the son and heir of the firm's founder, saw which way the wind was blowing and joined the Nazi party. All Jewish Opel dealers and employees were purged by 1938, and a brutal SS officer was appointed to head the firm's internal security service. Yet Opel's willing subservience to the Nazi regime failed to earn the company the commission to build the new 'people's car'. Ferdinand Porsche was far closer to Hitler than Wilhem von Opel and effortlessly secured the contract. And Opel's candidate for the classless auto, their conventional P4, looked positively antiquated when compared with Porsche's revolutionary new design. However, GM's Opel subsidiary continued to operate at the Nazis' whim. The closeness of this relationship was amply demonstrated in October 1940 when Göring attempted to use GM officials, led by the automotive giant's astonishingly naive head of overseas operations, James D. Mooney, as intermediaries in a peace bid to Britain. The overture was swiftly rejected, and Mooney hurriedly disowned by his Detroit masters.

Thanks to Hitler's promotion of the automobile, car ownership doubled in Germany between 1934 and 1938. In 1936 Daimler-Benz produced the world's first civilian car to use diesel fuel, the 260D. (Citroën had produced their Rosalie diesel car three years earlier, but had been forbidden from manufacturing it because of the French government's fears about the volatility of the fuel.[1]) But the first 'people's car' did not go on sale until shortly before the German invasion of Poland in 1939 triggered the outbreak of the Second World War.

In May 1934, Austrian engineer Ferdinand Porsche met Hitler to discuss his plans for the classless auto.[2] The two got on famously; Hitler enjoyed talking about cars with his fellow Austrian and they chatted for hours over sausages and beer. It was eventually agreed that the new 'people's car' would be capable of 60 mph and 40 mpg, have four seats and be air-cooled. Most important of all, despite this racy specification it would only cost a modest 1,000 Reichsmarks – then the equivalent of about £50.

Ferdinand Porsche had been born in 1875 in a German-speaking enclave of Bohemia, in what was then the Austro-Hungarian Empire (now the Czech Republic). He joined the imperial coach-makers Jakob Lohner & Co. in Vienna in 1898, and helped to create Lohner's first car – rather optimistically named the Toujours-Contente – in the same year. Drafted into the Austrian army in 1902, he served for a time as chauffeur to the emperor of Austria's heir, Archduke Franz Ferdinand, but returned to civilian life two years later, and thus was not at the wheel of the 1911 Gräf & Stift Double Phaeton in which the archduke and his wife were assassinated on 28 June 1914.

In 1906 Porsche was recruited by Daimler subsidiary Austro-Daimler as their chief designer. By 1916 he was managing director, and the following year was awarded an honorary doctorate by the Technical University of Vienna. After the war he designed a successful series of racing cars for Austro-Daimler before leaving the company in 1923 to join the main Daimler company in Stuttgart. Impatient as ever, he left for the Austrian car maker Steyr in 1929. However, like most of Germany's car makers, Steyr was soon laid low by the Great Depression (in 1934 it was finally

---

1 Britain's first diesel-powered car did not arrive until 1954's Standard Vanguard.
2 Not, strictly speaking, 'Dr Porsche', as he is often described. Porsche's doctorate was merely an honorary one, bestowed for his wartime work for Austro-Daimler in 1916, and thus should not be used as a formal title.

absorbed into the empire of Porsche's old employers, Daimler-Benz), and in April 1931 Porsche founded his own firm back in Stuttgart. The new Porsche company not only made its own small racing cars but also acted as consultant for larger firms. In this capacity, Porsche became Hitler's favourite automotive designer, working not just on the prototype 'people's car' but, from 1937, on Germany's new monster tank designs.

In June 1934 Porsche received a contract from Hitler to build three prototypes of the 'people's car' from designs he had already been working on, such as his Type 12 car of 1931. In October 1936 three prototypes of the *KdF-Wagen* ('strength through joy car') were revealed to Nazi bosses and their media acolytes. However, the design Porsche unveiled – which had actually been worked up from his master's concept by Franz Reimspiess, one of the few employees who was prepared to stand up to the autocratic Porsche – appeared to owe a lot to the ideas of Porsche's fellow Austrian, Hans Ledwinka, who worked for the Czech car maker Tatra. Ledwinka's Tatra T97, which had been introduced earlier that same year, was also cheap, simple, streamlined and provided with a rear-mounted engine. Indeed, from the front it looked strikingly similar to Porsche's *KdF-Wagen*. Hitler is known to have admired the Tatra – 'it's the kind of car I want for my highways,' he had announced – and it has been alleged that the Führer personally provided Porsche with a detailed drawing of the T97 with which Ledwinka had presented him. Inevitably, Ledwinka and Tatra were furious at the obvious plagiarism and attempted to sue Porsche for damages. Hitler said he would settle the matter – which he did somewhat dramatically, in March 1939, when units of the German army (which had already occupied the German-speaking Sudetenland in October 1938, following the conclusion of the Munich agreement) rolled their tanks over the undefended Czech border, annexed the rump of Czechoslovakia and closed the Tatra factory.

After 1945 the Tatra plant, now controlled by the Russians, restarted production of the T97 and disinterred Ledwinka's 1937 lawsuit. Porsche himself sheepishly admitted to having 'looked over Ledwinka's shoulders' while designing the 'people's car', and in 1961 Volkswagen finally paid

3 million Deutschmarks in settlement to Tatra's successor. However, although Porsche spent twenty months in a French jail at the end of the war, on his release, with his reputation restored, he returned to car manufacture. Ledwinka, in contrast, was jailed for five years by the Czech authorities for collaboration with the Germans (he had made powerful staff cars and munitions for them after 1939) and, after his release in 1951, refused to work for any car maker at all up until his death, an embittered and angry man, in 1967. Ledwinka was only posthumously rehabilitated by the Czech government in 1992, after the fall of the Iron Curtain. Ledwinka was not the only car designer whose work influenced Hitler and Porsche. The low-cost Standard Superior, which Hitler admired at the 1933 Berlin Motor Show, and which was designed by German-Hungarian engineer Josef Ganz, not only looked suspiciously like Porsche's later design for the *KdF-Wagen* (particularly in its more curvaceous, production form), but Standard Fahrzeugfabrik of Berlin subsequently promoted it as the 'Deutsche Volkswagen', the 'people's car'. As a Jew, however, Ganz was easily sidelined; he was arrested in 1933 and fled to Switzerland the following year.[1]

Having appropriated Ledwinka's and Ganz's ideas, the wily Austrian engineer was lauded with Nazi honours. Herr Porsche was, indeed, the ideal National Socialist. Abstemious and obedient, he swiftly complied with the Nazi interdiction on church attendance, though he had formerly been a devout Catholic. Strict and austere, he rarely bestowed praise on his employees and he ran his plants with a rod of iron, brooking no criticism or contradiction. Already designated *Reichsautokonstruktor* (state car designer) by Hitler, in 1938 he was awarded the Nazi equivalent of the Nobel Prize, alongside aircraft manufacturers Heinkel and Messerschmitt and labour chief Fritz Todt. At the awards ceremony Porsche smiled beatifically while Goebbels conjured a motorized future and Hitler delivered one of his customary anti-Semitic rants.

---

1 Ganz's subsequent career in Switzerland was mired in lawsuits and disappointments. He died in Australia in 1967.

In 1938, too, Hitler finally unveiled the first production 'people's car', the *Volkswagen*, at the Berlin Motor Show. A new city, the unimaginatively named Stadt des KdF-Wagens, had been built to produce the new car at Fallersleben, near Brunswick in Lower Saxony. The car plant was financed by confiscated union funds and run by a company created by the German Labour Front. Initially, its workforce comprised Italian 'guest workers', although after 1941 this was to change. Hitler himself laid the foundation stone for the factory, which was consciously modelled on Ford's giant Rouge River plant which Porsche had visited the previous year. Porsche not only built the car; his firm was even given the contract to plan the new city, although he quickly contracted out this task. After the war, the city was hastily renamed Wolfsburg, and still serves as the world headquarters of Volkswagen.

Even before the first Volkswagen appeared, the Reich's citizens had been encouraged to make down payments towards a new VW. By 1939 a staggering 336,668 had done so – although very few of those had actually received their completed cars. Instead, the KdF factory produced war materiel using slave labour – mainly, after 1941, captured Russian soldiers. Most of the credulous investors never saw their money again. In 1945, 280 million marks belonging to VW depositors were discovered in the Bank of German Labour in Berlin, and were promptly seized by the occupying Russians. And in 1954 the compliant West German authorities absolved Volkswagen from any responsibility for the pre-war *KdF-Wagen* contracts. However, the public outrage of the gulled *KdF-Wagen* investors forced the West German government to back-pedal, and in 1961 they offered investors either 600 Deutschmarks towards a new VW or 100 Deutschmarks in cash.

Hitler's Volkswagen was destined to transport millions of Ayran *Volk* across their expanded homeland. Yet large-scale production of the *KdF-Wagen* had not even begun when Germany invaded Poland in September 1939. A few civilian examples were made in 1940, but they were mostly given to senior Nazi officials. The flexible Porsche, meanwhile, adapted the *KdF-Wagen* for military use as a staff car, the Kübelwagen, and, more ambitiously, as the Type 166 *Schwimmwagen*, an amphibian four-seater.[1] The former was a great success and performed with distinction on all fronts. Rommel used one as his staff car in North Africa and in 1942 personally thanked Porsche for saving his life: 'Your VW *Kübelwagen* which I use in Africa crossed a minefield without setting anything off.'[2] In 1944 the American army even issued a manual, *The German Jeep*, describing how to use a *Kübelwagen* if it was captured. (It is worth noting, though, that whereas America produced 660,000 Jeeps during 1941–5, the *KdF-Wagen* plant only managed to make just over fifty thousand *Kübelwagens*.) Some historians even suggest that the creation of the military *Kübelwagen* was the original purpose of the *KdF-Wagen* project, with the civilian Volkswagen as merely a useful peacetime front – and the duped civilian investors a useful source of cash.

During the war Porsche was made chairman of the Panzer Commission under the new minister of labour, Albert Speer, and helped to design some of Germany's heavy battle-tanks, including the Tiger I of 1942, the Tiger II (which the allies called the 'King Tiger') of 1944, and the Type 205 Panzer VIII. The last-named, at 200 tons, remains the heaviest tank ever built. As big as a house, it was given the ironic nickname *Die Maus*, the mouse. It carried a monumental 128 mm gun and 18 inches of armour. Too heavy to cross bridges, it was expected to swim or snorkel across rivers. Only two prototypes had been completed by the time the Russians overran the factory. Porsche himself was arrested a few weeks later, on 30 May 1945. Twenty years on, however, his 'people's car' had managed to shed its Nazi associations to become the Beetle (*Der Käfer*), a counterculture icon and lovable star of the 1969 Disney movie *The Love Bug* – which, dispiritingly, was the world's highest-grossing film that year.

With the advent of war, Hitler's championing of the automobile was revealed as only so much window-dressing. The Daimler-Benz

---

1 The *Schwimmwagen*, unfortunately, was not such a triumph as its land-based cousin, since its thin skin could easily be penetrated by a rifle bullet.

2 Unlike Rommel's accompanying Horch armoured cars, which mostly blew up.

and Auto Union factories were closed, and existing Mercedes and Auto Unions adapted to serve as staff cars for high-ranking army and SS officers. The *KdF-Wagen* factory turned to making not just *Kübelwagens* and *Schwimmwagens* but also tanks and, from 1944, parts for the Fieseler Fi 103, better known as the first of Hitler's 'vengeance weapons' and the world's first self-powered missile, the V-1 flying bomb. By this time, however, Germany's critical lack of fuel (the Reich's synthetic fuel production had never reached significant levels) meant that those civilian models that still survived were unable to take to the road. By 1945 the Nazis' grandiose ambitions for the automobile were a faint folk memory.

The Second World War did, however, provide a stage for the graduation of the car from utilitarian runabout and luxury racer to essential transport and symbol of rank. Daimler-Benz was not the only manufacturer to convert its models into military staff vehicles. General Montgomery famously used a Humber as his staff car in North Africa and Italy. (The car can still be seen today in Coventry's excellent Transport Museum.) General Eisenhower, the allied supreme commander in Europe, and General MacArthur, army commander in the Pacific, both rode in a specially adapted Packard Clipper. The ambitious, extrovert General Patton inevitably had to go one better than his boss, Eisenhower, and appropriated a grand Cadillac. (It was while riding in his well-appointed Cadillac 75 in December 1945 that Patton was mortally injured when the car was hit by a 2½ ton truck.) By 1942, Detroit's Big Three were competing to make staff cars for the American top brass; GM's contender was the Buick Century Series 60, to which Ford replied with the C11 Fordor and Chrysler with the Chrysler Royal. Chrysler also made a smaller rival, aimed at the larger market of mid-rank officers: the highly successful and, by 1944, ubiquitous Plymouth P11.

Aside from adapting models for staff use, however, car makers in combatant countries were forced to abandon civilian auto production and switch entirely to the manufacture of war materiel. Car use dwindled as petrol rationing and the blackout encouraged many private motorists to keep their cars at home. In Britain, pedestrian deaths, caused largely by the blackout, soared from the peacetime annual figure of 3,800 to 4,800 in 1941, a disturbing trend which was only reversed when petrol rationing was introduced in July 1942.

In occupied Europe, auto manufacturers were made to serve the military needs of their German conquerors. For some motor bosses this was not too much of an imposition, provided they and their firms still made a reasonable profit. Given, for example, that the majority of the French car makers of the pre-war era were of a distinctly right-wing political persuasion, it is not surprising that many of them greeted Marshal Pétain's collaborationist Vichy government with enthusiasm and their new German masters with equanimity. Thus Peugeot's Sochaux plant continued in operation after 1940, making parts for Porsche's military vehicles, tanks and V-1s. The company's president, Jean-Pierre Peugeot, had always got on well with Ferdinand Porsche, and this relationship now began to pay handsome political and financial dividends. Even Ford's French plant at Poissy, under its malleable boss, Maurice Dollfus, proved extremely helpful to the Vichy regime and its German masters. Unsurprisingly, Dollfus's overt collaboration also won Henry Ford's wholehearted approval.

By the time the war broke out in 1939, Louis Renault in particular was deeply mired in anti-Semitic and pro-German politics. In 1938 he had met Hitler at the Berlin Motor Show and had declared that he hoped there would be no further wars between their two countries. Renault also referred to his great rival André Citroën in unrelentingly anti-Semitic terms, and delighted in identifying him as *le petit Juif* ('the little Jew').[1] By then, Mme Renault had become a close friend of the right-wing writer Pierre Drieu la Rochelle, who since 1936 had been the chief ideologue for Jacques Doriot's fascist and unapologetically anti-Semitic Parti Populaire Français (PPF), and who after 1940 was one of France's most strident and enthusiastic collaborationists.

---

1 Renault bought land opposite Citroën's Javry factory on which he erected huge billboards bearing the name 'RENAULT'.

Renault spent the early months of the war complaining about the mobilization of some of his workers, yet seemed unperturbed by the drastic fall in production of Renault tanks and aircraft engines. He even cheerfully diverted some of the resources earmarked for war production to the development of a small family car. Visitors to Renault's Billancourt factory commented on a depressing lack of urgency; but when the government complained about his firm's lackadaisical war effort, Renault alleged that it was trying to nationalize his company.

Following the fall of France in 1940, Renault's choices were stark. He could cooperate with the Germans, preventing them from taking over his company; already, in June 1940, he had been forced to accept senior executives from Daimler-Benz at Billancourt. Or he could resist the Germans, a path that would inevitably lead to the Nazis' seizure of his automotive empire, the removal of his factories' equipment to Germany, and his possible arrest. Renault chose the path of collaboration, finding many political soulmates in Marshal Pétain's supine Vichy government. Having impressed Pétain himself in an interview with the aged *Maréchal* in 1942, he was left in charge of his factories, despite widespread calls from younger critics for his retirement.

In 1945 Renault maintained that he was never responsible for 'external' relations with Vichy's German masters. Nevertheless, between the collapse of France in June 1940 and the allied liberation of August 1944, Renault's plants manufactured 34,232 vehicles for the Germans. His argument at the time was that 'by staying in operation he had saved thousands of workers from being transported to Germany'. To his colleagues, he insisted: 'It is better to give them the butter, or they'll take the cows.' To many, though, Renault incarnated Vichy's craven policy of collaboration. In 1943 he confirmed that impression when he refused to provide any financial aid for the rapidly growing French Resistance. Few noted that he simultaneously denounced the lawless activities of Doriot and Drieu la Rochelle's increasingly despised far-right PPF.

Following the allied liberation of France, Renault realized that his world had changed forever. His antisocial personality rebounded on him as a series of fellow industrialists (who had, like Renault, previously supported the Vichy regime, but now hastily attempted to wrap themselves in the Free French flag) suddenly remembered that they had never liked Renault and, seeking a scapegoat, eagerly denounced his willing subservience to the Germans. On 21 August 1944, as allied tanks stood at the gates of Paris, Renault visited the Billancourt factory to be insulted and spat at on the shop floor. The next day he took shelter in a friend's house, finding his home had become a target for Resistance reprisals. Three weeks later, following a vicious campaign against him in the newly liberated press ('He made six billions in his transactions with the Boche', screamed *l'Humanité*; 'The unanimous opinion of the Resistance is that Louis Renault must pay for the deaths of our allied soldiers'), Renault surrendered to de Gaulle's de facto government 'on condition that he would not be jailed until indicted'. On 22 September he was finally arrested for 'trafficking with the enemy'.

Renault denied that his firm had received millions of marks from the Germans, and asserted that he had kept his plants going at the request of the more moderate members of the Vichy government in order to keep its materials and equipment out of Nazi hands, and, more importantly, to save his workers from deportation. However, while being kept in the notorious prison at Fresnes – previously a Gestapo jail, where members of the Resistance and the British SOE had been tortured and murdered – his health collapsed. Renault had already suffered a mental and physical collapse in 1942; now his interrogators used his physical and mental deterioration to prise a confession from him. On 5 October he was moved to a psychiatric hospital at Ville-Evrard, and then to a nearby private nursing home. There he lapsed into a coma, and died on 24 October 1944, four weeks after his incarceration and still awaiting trial.

General de Gaulle's new provisional government immediately nationalized his company (Renault's wife and his son, Jean-Louis, who together owned 95 per cent of the company stock, received nothing in compensation), and Louis Renault was charged posthumously with 'guilty enrichment obtained by those who worked for the enemy'. Some years later Christiane Renault, who always maintained that her husband had been murdered, had his body exhumed for a proper autopsy, which had not been conducted in 1944. Doctors found that the 67-year-old Renault had in fact had been severely tortured and beaten while in prison. A nun who had been working at Fresnes prison in 1944 came forward to testify that she had seen Renault collapse after being hit over the head by a jailer 'wielding a helmet', an allegation corroborated by a subsequent X-ray which showed that the vertebrae of Renault's neck had been broken. In 1967 Jean-Louis Renault received minor compensation for his personal losses. Yet during the celebrations in 1999 for the centenary of the original Renault Frères company, the executives of Régie Renault pointedly ignored the grandchildren of their founder. Today both the car maker and the French government continue to fight the family's demands for financial compensation for Renault's untimely death.

Not all French motor manufacturers were like Peugeot and Renault. Marcel Michelin, the second son of the founder of the great tyre-making firm, André Michelin, and a pillar of the new Michelin-Citroën combine, was arrested by the Germans in 1943 for organizing a Resistance cell in Puy-de-Dôme. He died in Ohrdruf concentration camp in January 1945, only two months before the camp was liberated by the Americans. Two of Marcel's sons escaped to England and flew with the RAF; the other two were killed working for the French Resistance. André's son, Bernard, having been dismissed from the Vichy air force in February 1941 for being Jewish, walked across the Pyrenees to Barcelona. Twenty weeks later, and still on foot, he reached Lisbon; from there he travelled to England, where he subsequently flew Douglas Bostons with 324 Squadron. The late André Citroën's nephew, Louis-Hugues, became a Resistance leader in Marseilles, but was captured at Nîmes in November 1943 and executed at Auschwitz. Many more from the Citroën family perished at Auschwitz, including two of André Citroën's nieces. With hideous irony, the Gestapo chose to cruise round occupied France in black Citroën Traction Avants they had requisitioned from local citizens.

At the Citroën plants, company boss Pierre-Jules Boulanger took his cue from the Michelin and Citroën families and took care to distance himself as much as possible from France's German occupiers. He refused to meet Nazi motor supremo Ferdinand Porsche and insisted on dealing with the Germans, who had requisitioned his factories in order to build lorries for the Wehrmacht, only through intermediaries. As the war went on, Boulanger slowed production as far as he dared, and sabotaged an attempt in 1944 to transplant Citroën's machine tools to Germany. He was also an early supporter of de Gaulle – in marked contrast to most of his fellow car makers, most of whom were eager Vichyites. Unsurprisingly, Boulanger appeared on the Nazi blacklist of sixty-seven prominent Frenchmen who would be immediately executed in the event of an Allied invasion or a French rising.

Across occupied Europe, car plants were put to more sinister use by the Germans. Hitler had been delighted to acquire the famous Škoda works outside Prague without a fight in the spring of 1939, and the plant was soon producing light tanks for the Wehrmacht (the Panzer 35 and 38), along with countless guns and shells. While civilian auto production was now subjugated to military needs, Škoda was also commissioned to produce the Type 903 command car, the ubiquitous transport of Nazi generals, and a would-be rival to the American Jeep, the Type 923. However, during the furious fight for Prague between the Germans and the advancing Russians of 6–11 May 1945, much of the Škoda plant was destroyed.

The motor manufacturers of Hitler's Axis partners also played their part. In Italy, Giovanni Agnelli's pampered grandson (also called Giovanni, but popularly known as 'Gianni') actually fought for Mussolini's army on the Russian front. When Italy surrendered to the allies in 1943, Gianni, like many of Italy's combatants, swiftly changed sides and enthusiastically welcomed his country's British and American 'liberators'. His grandfather, however, was too deeply mired in fascist politics to execute such a neat about-turn. Somewhat fortunately for Fiat's post-war reputation, the 79-year-old Giovanni died in December 1945, just as the allies were beginning to examine Fiat's suspiciously intimate ties with Mussolini's deposed fascist regime.

In Germany, Ford's subsidiary was doing Hitler's bidding as early as July 1939, two months before the invasion of Poland precipitated the conflict and over two years before Hitler's declaration of war on America, on 11 December 1941. As German armies advanced across Europe, Ford's other European outposts were added to this ersatz Ford empire.

Meanwhile, GM's Opel subsidiary made the three-ton Blitz truck for the Wehrmacht and also helped to make parts for the Junkers Ju-88 fast fighter-bomber. Despite the company's key role in providing vital equipment for the Wehrmacht and the Luftwaffe – the Blitz truck was the mainstay of the German army's mechanized transport – Alfred Sloan remained on the Opel board during the entire duration of the war. After 1945 he even had the gall to demand compensation from the US government for allied damage to Opel's plants. Insisting that all US personnel had resigned from Opel 'as early as October 1939', and that the American parent had ceased to have any connection with its German affiliate after September 1941, while conveniently ignoring the fact that the legal connection between Detroit and Rüsselsheim was never severed, in 1967 GM successfully extracted $33 million from the US government in reparations for 'troubles and destruction' to their German factories during the war.

Allied car factories also became essential weapons in the fight for survival. In Britain, new 'shadow factories' were built in the Midlands and the north of England, sited near to existing car plants but generally outside urban centres so as not to attract the attention of enemy bombers. Run by established car makers, they were to build tanks, aircraft and munitions. As early as 1936, William Morris had agreed to operate the vast new Castle Bromwich shadow factory, built adjacent to an existing airfield to the east of Birmingham. Castle Bromwich became the most successful of the shadow factories and the aircraft it produced played a

major part in sustaining Britain's war effort. The plant made the superlative Supermarine Spitfire (over twenty thousand of which were made
there, making Castle Bromwich the largest producer of Spitfires in the
country) and later added an assembly line for the equally successful Avro
Lancaster heavy bomber. However, by the time the tools for the Lancaster
had begun to appear in the factory, Morris's involvement in the site had
been terminated, his limitations as an industrial dynamo having been
swiftly revealed. Having been made director general of maintenance of
the RAF at the beginning of the war, Morris childishly refused to come to
London and instead stayed in his Morris offices at the Cowley works in
Oxford. By the time the Germans invaded Holland, Belgium and France
in May 1940, it was clear that Morris's assembly-line mentality was unable
to encompass factors such as the constant alterations that had to be made
to machine tools for complex aircraft like the Spitfire and Lancaster, of
which many disparate marks were made. The autocratic Morris had met
his match in the minister of aircraft production, Lord Beaverbrook, who
could be just as ruthless and demanding as the automobile tycoon. When
Morris rang Beaverbrook to complain about the RAF's constant requests
for modifications, the car maker finally erupted with the threat: 'Maybe
you would like me to give up control of the Spitfire factory?' Beaverbrook
instantly seized his chance, replying: 'Nuffield, that's very generous of
you. I accept.' He slammed the phone down. Morris, seething, stormed
up to London and confronted Prime Minister, Winston Churchill, over
the issue, tactlessly reminding the premier how much money Morris had
in the past donated to Churchill's Conservative Party. But Churchill stood
by his pugnacious minister and Morris had to retreat to Oxford with his
tail between his legs. (Miles Thomas later commented that thereafter
Morris 'seemed to lose the vital force that drove him inexorably to greater
and greater things'.) The running of Castle Bromwich was handed by
Beaverbrook to Vickers, since 1936 the owners of Supermarine. Vickers
ironed out the production difficulties and produced twenty-two different types of Spitfire during the war years. Meanwhile, Morris himself
displayed little interest in the sterling work his Cowley works played in

making Tiger Moth trainers and repairing and refitting damaged aircraft, a vital task so memorably captured by artist Paul Nash in his evocative wartime paintings.

Morris Motors also failed to distinguish themselves at their other shadow factory. On the Birmingham site of the former Wolseley plant, the Nuffield Organization's military arm, Nuffield Mechanization and Aero, designed and built the uninspiring Covenanter tank of 1939. On the outbreak of war, Morris adapted this into a model which was little better, the Crusader VI tank of 1940. Fast, but lamentably under-gunned and notoriously prone to breakdowns, the Crusader's shortcomings were cruelly exposed in North Africa in 1941. Its thin armour made it easy prey for the Rommel's Panzers, and its appalling unreliability – an ominous trait that was to plague Morris's civilian products after the war – led to its withdrawal from front-line service during 1942. The Crusaders were replaced by American Grants, Lees and Shermans, and, less successfully, by British Cromwell tanks (designed by Leyland Motors and made at the Rover Car Company) and Churchill tanks (made by Morris's GM-owned rival, Vauxhall Motors). Morris Motors' subsequent 'improvement' of the Crusader format, in the shape of the Cavalier, proved even more inadequate. It is strange that a nation that produced so many outstanding aircraft during the Second World War could never design and build a good wartime tank.[1]

Morris's rivals proved far better at managing their shadow factories than the ageing viscount. Daimler of Coventry initially missed the point of the shadow factory scheme by building one directly behind their existing works at Radford, but then erected a second plant to the west of Coventry at Brown's Lane in Allesley. Rootes and Standard also built shadow plants on the fringes of Coventry, at Stoke and Ryton (Rootes) and Canley and Banner Lane (Standard). Churchill was so impressed with Billy Rootes's energy that he made the car maker head of Coventry's reconstruction

---

1 The excellent Centurion tank, powered by an engine designed by Rolls-Royce and built by Rover, only reached the allied front line in May 1945, just as the war was ending.

committee following the destruction of much of the city in the Blitz of 1940–1, chairman of the National Supply Council and a knight of the realm. (Sir William Rootes, as he now was, repaid Churchill's faith by leading a successful fund-raising campaign for a new RAF squadron, later numbered 154, entirely financed by the motor industry.) Rover built shadow plants at Acocks Green in Birmingham and in Solihull, and was also asked to manage a new plant at Speke in Liverpool, designed to manufacture Blenheim light bombers.[1] Ford used the site of its old plant at Trafford Park in Manchester to make Rolls-Royce Merlin engines and the Avro Lancaster bomber, while its principal plant at Dagenham made trucks, vans and tractors for the rear and Bren-gun carriers for the front, and its V-8 engines were used in almost everything from landing craft to barrage-balloon winches.

The wisdom of building shadow factories was soon evident. Traditional production centres such as Coventry and Birmingham were heavily bombed, but the outlying plants emerged largely unscathed and were able to continue manufacturing. In 1940–1 the centre of Coventry was subject to forty air raids; the most serious of these, on the night of 14–15 November 1940, killed 554 people and wrecked the medieval city centre, including the magnificent church of St Michael, since 1918 designated a cathedral. The Alvis car plant was completely destroyed (its wartime production was, as a result, dispersed all over England, from Hinckley in Leicestershire to Ealing in west London), while Daimler's Radford factory also suffered very badly. But while the city lay devastated, the shadow factory sites offered the prospect of a miraculous, phoenix-like industrial rebirth.

Even as Coventry was being blitzed, many months before its formal entry into the war, in December 1941, America was being hailed by the allies as the Arsenal of Democracy. Early in 1942 President Roosevelt formally banned the manufacture of civilian cars; from then on, America's

---

1 When Speke was opened in 1937 the Bristol Blenheim was the fastest light bomber in the world, but by 1939 it was sadly obsolescent.

mighty car makers were directed to concentrate solely on fulfilling military requirements. GM began making munitions in 1941 and by 1942 had switched all of its numerous plants over to war production. Chrysler plants made the Martin B-26 Marauder, Swedish-designed Bofors guns, Wright Cyclone engines, parts for B-17 and B-29 bombers, Helldivers and Corsairs, and their own Dodge trucks. From June 1942, Chrysler also manufactured America's principal tank, the M4 Sherman, which was powered by a Chrysler engine; and by 1945 the company had added an assembly line for the new, heavy M26 Pershing tank. As we have seen, Ford built and ran the vast Willow Run plant,[1] where B-24 Liberators were made, while the Rouge, Highland Park and other Ford plants churned out aircraft, tanks and shells. When the Japanese bombed Pearl Harbor on 7 December 1941, Winston Churchill privately recognized that no other country or alliance in the world would be able to compete with or resist America's vast military-industrial complex, a manufacturing base that relied heavily on the nation's vast automotive industry.[2] America's car makers helped to make the allied victory certain.

Ford's wartime record as a munitions supplier was initially disappointing. Critics were quick to point out that the *Ford-Werke* in Germany appeared happily to be supplying the enemy with hundreds of trucks (indeed, Ford and GM-built trucks and half-tracks made up 70 per cent of the Wehrmacht's motorized transport during the Second World War), while back in the US the conversion of Ford plants to wartime production moved agonizingly slowly. Although Ford agreed to make Pratt and Whitney aircraft engines under licence as early as November 1940, the incorrigible isolationist dragged his heels as much as he could, even after the Japanese attack on Pearl Harbor, on 7 December 1941, and Hitler's senseless declaration of war on the US four days later. Henry Ford blocked the proposed manufacture of the peerless Rolls-Royce Merlin engine,

---

1 The Detroit Industrial Expressway, completed in 1942, was built to carry twenty thousand workers per day from metropolitan Detroit to Willow Run.

2 'So we had won after all!' was Churchill's comment in his diary at the time, later immortalized in his memoirs.

the power plant of the Supermarine Spitfire fighter and Avro Lancaster bomber,[1] on the grounds that the company should not be making engines for the British – despite Edsel Ford's own enthusiastic backing for the project and the glaring fact that Ford's German subsidiary was churning out large quantities of munitions for the Nazi war machine. Albert Kahn's massive Ford-run bomber plant at Willow Run, Michigan, took far longer than planned to finish – the architect himself died before it was completed – and the first Consolidated B-24 Liberator bomber only emerged from the new factory in September 1942.[2]

Even after 1942, as historian James J. Flink has noted, the increasingly paranoid Ford 'feared that the military personnel at Willow Run were spies sent by Roosevelt to assassinate him and [he] took to carrying an automatic pistol under the cowl of his car'. When Roosevelt came to open Willow Run in 1942, Ford tried to hide from the president and was only introduced into the welcoming line-up under protest. Unsurprisingly, the US Army Air Force, exasperated by Henry Ford's constant interference in bomber production, was soon urging the federal government to take control of the firm. The final straw came when the ageing autocrat let it be known that he intended to make the universally loathed Harry Bennett his sole successor. It was only the threat of Edsel's widow, Eleanor, together with his own wife, the indefatigable Clara Ford, that they would sell all their company shares if Henry did not step down, thereby ending decades of family control, that induced the old tyrant finally to retire. He reluctantly accepted that Edsel's son, the 26-year-old Henry Ford II, should be plucked from his naval training and given an immediate role in senior management with a view to his succeeding to the company presidency in 1945. Henry II was not happy with the idea, hoping to be posted to the Pacific, but was persuaded to go along with it for the time being.

Predictably, the company's founder was determined not to go quietly. Between 1943 and 1945, as the federal government contemplated

---

1 And, later, of the superlative American-built P-51 Mustang.
2 The Liberator's stirring name, originally applied by the RAF, was subsequently taken up by the USAAF.

taking over the poorly managed Willow Run plant, Henry began to exhibit an irrational distrust of his grandson, and simultaneously allowed Harry Bennett to tighten his grip on the corporation's throat. Bennett was even permitted to oust Ford's long-serving production chief, Charles Sorenson (aided in this instance by Clara Ford, who feared Sorenson was trying to usurp her grandson). Henry also attempted to create a board of trustees, which would have been dominated by Bennett as board secretary, to control the company after his death, 'until Henry II and the other grandchildren were old enough to manage the company themselves'. Fortunately, Henry II discovered the plot and forced Bennett to withdraw the plan. (Bennett later admitted to Ford's chief lawyer that the document creating the board was no longer a legal entity, as 'Mr Ford had carried the instrument around in his pocket for a long time and had made a lot of scribblings on it, including verses from the Bible'.)

As Henry II attempted to wrest control of the firm from Bennett, the Service Department chief found he could count on the founder's support less and less, as Henry Ford spent most of his days in impenetrable reveries. When in a lucid moment, on 20 September 1945, he formally told his grandson that he could take over as president of the Ford Motor Company, Henry II only agreed, he later recalled, 'if I had a completely free hand to make any changes I wanted to make'. Young Henry's first executive act was, unsurprisingly, to fire Harry Bennett. Henry Ford's reaction to this news was to exclaim: 'Well now, Harry is back where he started from.'

As Henry Ford's mind was failing, so was his body. From 1938 he suffered a series of strokes and spent increasing amounts of time withdrawn and silent. Even when he was more alert, he expressed a growing enthusiasm for reincarnation and began to announce that his son Edsel was not really dead. On the rare occasions when he was conducted around the Ford factories, Henry did not seem to have any idea what was happening there. ('What are all those people doing?' he once asked in the middle of the Rouge's engineering department.) On the evening of 6 April 1947, the 83-year-old Henry Ford spoke his last recognizable words, to a maid at his Fair Lane mansion: 'I'll sleep well tonight. We're going early to bed.' Hours later it was evident that he was actually sleeping very badly, and Clara Ford summoned the doctor. By the time medical help arrived, Henry was dead.

By the summer of 1944, as the allied armies were advancing across France, the Russians were beating down German resistance in the east, and Admiral Nimitz and General MacArthur were island-hopping their way towards Japan, most American auto companies were beginning to think of dusting down their 1941 ranges in order to have something to offer their customers when the war ended. Only one military vehicle, however, managed to make the transition from wartime to peacetime – the Jeep. In the ensuing years this basic form of transport established a reputation that became as classless and durable as Porsche's 'people's car', and outlived its creators to become a valuable brand in its own right. This rugged, four-wheel-drive equivalent of the Volkswagen became the people's off-roader, the ancestor of all of today's sports utility vehicles (SUVs), and a household name.

The modest auto manufacturer Willys-Overland had been founded in Toledo, Ohio, in 1902, but had already gone bankrupt twice (in 1920 and again in 1933) by the time the Japanese attacked Pearl Harbor. Today, Willys is only remembered because, to its great good fortune, it was the only firm that tendered for the US War Department's little-noticed contract to manufacture a small military truck from a prototype recently designed by the American Bantam company of Butler, Pennsylvania.

Bantam was even less well known than Willys. The company had started life in 1929 as American Austin, the US subsidy of Britain's Austin Motors, which concentrated on making American versions of the best-selling Austin Seven. Following its bankruptcy in 1935, the company was split from its British parent and renamed American Bantam, after the name of their Baby Austin derivative (which the firm still retained a licence to make). The car maker's only claim to fame in these pre-war years came when a young animator named Walt Disney adapted a 1938

Bantam as the basis for a car for his new cartoon character Donald Duck. Even when, in 1940, Bantam seemed to strike gold by securing the War Department's tender for a quarter-ton, four-wheel-drive, small truck for 'command reconnaissance duties', the firm proved too small and under-resourced to reap the benefits of its success. Bantam had originally developed the contract-winning vehicle with the help of freelance engineer Karl Probst (who always resisted post-war claims that he was the 'Father of the Jeep', insisting that the design was a Bantam team effort). But Bantam had only made 2,675 of the miniature trucks before the federal government decided that the operation was far too small to produce the vehicle in the numbers they needed. (Bantam had already had to stop production of all of its civilian cars to work on the new army contract.) Willys was instead awarded the commission to adapt the Bantam vehicle and produce it on a far larger scale. In the event, the runaway success of the car meant that even Willys was not big enough to fulfil the US Army's orders, and Ford was appointed as a back-up manufacturer.

Originally designated a General Purpose Vehicle (GP for short), it soon became known by the affectionate name of Jeep, a designation Willys formally trademarked in 1943. This marvellously simple and rugged four-wheel-drive runabout carried privates and presidents, and could go just about anywhere. Six hundred and sixty thousand were made during the war. In 1945 Willys bravely began making a civilian version, the CJ (Civilian Jeep), which was subsequently manufactured under licence by Hotchkiss in France and even by Mitsubishi and Toyota in Japan. Few in 1945, though, would have predicted that it would be the wartime Jeep brand that, sixty years later, would keep one of America's legendary automotive giants afloat.[1] As we will see, by 2000 it had proved almost as powerful and iconic a brand as the immortal Volkswagen.

---

1 The Jeep brand survived not only the purchase of Willys by Kaiser in 1953 (the company actually renamed itself Kaiser-Jeep in 1963) but also its transfer to American Motors in 1970 and Chrysler in 1987.

6

Austerity Britain

The car industries of Western Europe emerged in a shaky condition from the debilitating trials of the Second World War. Most models that they offered in the immediate post-war years came from pre-war antecedents. In those European countries that still possessed car factories that had managed to survive years of bombing, there were generally too many small plants making too many models, and too many cars that were grossly underpowered, built according to the conditions and expectations of 1935 rather than of 1945. On top of all that, petrol rationing continued throughout much of Europe for many years, while petrol taxes were increased, ensuring that car ownership remained a luxury rather than a necessity. As if this were not enough, aside from the wrecked Axis powers of Germany and Italy, Europe was severely handicapped by its elderly road system which included no motorways and few dual carriageways.

In Brave New Britain, car manufacture fell well below housing and health on the long list of national priorities. Most cars were diverted by the government for export, in order to earn hard cash, although many British models failed to cope with testing foreign roads. Those models that did well abroad were rarely seen in Britain; few of the racy, boat-tailed Jaguar XK120s, which took America by storm after 1948, for example, were ever spotted on British roads; while all of the first forty-seven thousand Austin A40s produced at Longbridge were sold overseas. MG's TC Midget of 1946 was not as fast as it looked, but it still held the road better than its

American rivals and proved a vital earner of US dollars for cash-strapped Britain. Its successor, the uprated MGA of 1955, did even better. As late as 1952 Jaguar was exporting 96 per cent of its annual output, mostly to the US.

While the British government (effectively broke by 1947) still desperately needed foreign currency, it was also aware of the pressing need to improve Britain's antiquated highway infrastructure. In 1946 Labour's minister of transport, Alfred Barnes, announced a ten-year plan for the reconstruction of Britain's road network, including the provision of several new multi-lane motorways. The key role motorized transport had played in winning the war, and the evident success of the American parkways, had softened the image of superhighways, which before 1939 had been inevitably associated with the totalitarian regimes of Mussolini's Italy and Hitler's Germany. However, bankrupt Britain was in no state to build hundreds of miles of new highways. The route of the country's first motorway, the London–Yorkshire M1, was not published until 1955, and work did not start on the road until 1959.

Attlee's post-war government did manage to abolish the notorious horsepower tax, in 1946. But it retained the swingeing purchase tax of up to one third of a car's value (two thirds after 1947), and petrol remained rationed until 1950. Added to this, the need to fulfil export quotas meant that many prospective car owners had to wait over five years for their vehicles. (Motor historian Michael Sedgwick remembered that 'My family ordered a Morris Oxford in November 1948; it was not ready until 1954, by which time we could no longer afford it.') Successive post-war governments tacitly kept to a low-growth, low-investment strategy for Britain's largest manufacturing industry. The result was that by the early 1970s, when the oil crisis changed the motoring world forever, British car makers were crippled by appalling under-investment in plants, models and ideas. By 1974 annual investment in British Leyland was two thirds that of state-owned Renault and under half that of Volkswagen.

The hand-crafted tradition of the pre-war British motor industry was just too expensive to maintain for all but the super-premium car makers.

One pre-war Cowley worker recalled that it took him seven hours just to make one seat for a Vanden Plas. Now, in austerity Britain, mechanization and rationalization were the order of the day. Morris merged its mid-size Morris and Wolseley ranges; and in 1952 Morris itself was absorbed by Austin into a conglomerate known as the British Motor Corporation (BMC). While Ford of Britain had one principal factory in 1952, BMC had fourteen.

Many British car makers took advantage of the shadow factories that the government had built near their old plants during wartime by buying them after the war. Some, such as Standard-Triumph, abandoned their old, bomb-damaged factories in city centres altogether and moved whole-sale into the shadow plants, which were usually on the peripheries of urban areas. However, post-war governments of all political hues would only allow new car plants to be built in areas of high unemployment, and would withhold the necessary Industrial Development Certificate if this criterion were not met. As a result, many car factories were built where there was no tradition of skilled labour of the sort needed to manufacture such a complex animal as a car.

While many motor manufacturers eagerly moved into new factories, industrial relations in Britain remained in the stone age. French and German car makers now involved their workers, to varying degrees, in the process of decision-making; but the autocrats of Britain's motor industry disdained any such newfangled notions. As the chairman of Austin, Leonard Lord, revealingly declared in 1947: 'With whom are we going to cooperate – the shop stewards? The shop stewards are communists.' The result was shop-floor strife and a ten-fold increase in days lost to strikes between 1948 and 1973.

Nevertheless, for a time Britain became, almost by default, the world's leading car exporter, as its former European rivals sought to rebuild their shattered factories and American car makers concentrated on the home market. Ominously, when British car production was overtaken by a European nation, in 1956, it was the Germans who took the number one slot.

In Coventry, Britain's motor city, Standard's chairman, Sir John Black, sought to learn from the example of Germany's Volkswagen (a car he had originally dismissed) by decreeing that his firm would thereafter concentrate on just one model. Accordingly, the Standard Vanguard – ominously named after Britain's last battleship,[1] launched two years earlier – was unveiled in 1948 as the company's hope for the future. The Vanguard was surprisingly advanced, with a three-speed synchromesh gearbox, hydraulic brakes, coil-spring front suspension and a new 2 litre engine. But it looked like an American car that had been involved in a rear-end collision. Walter Belgrove's deliberately Atlanticist design made it resemble a contemporary Plymouth, with no trunk. Few bought the Vanguard at home, while the crucial export sales were non-existent. Black, and Standard, had put all their eggs in the wrong basket.

Sir John Black was one of the car industry's most eccentric characters. A clerk's son, he had joined Hillman in 1919, married one of the Hillman heiresses (William Hillman had six daughters, each of whom inherited a share in the business), and rose from being just one of the sales managers to the lofty heights of managing director. When Rootes absorbed Hillman in 1929, he left the firm and joined Standard Motors as its managing director. His wartime role as chairman of the Aero Engine Committee won him a knighthood, and in 1944 he engineered Standard's takeover of the bankrupt Triumph operation. But Black was also a dictatorial autocrat who, like Ford and Morris, brooked no criticism. He was tall, extrovert, immensely vain, bullying and worryingly unpredictable. Most of his managers were terrified of him. He was always accompanied by his butler – a similarly statuesque man – and was prone to sudden whims. On returning from a business trip or holiday, he would often announce that there were too many staff and promptly sack some of them. And every year, when the first snow fell, he insisted on being dragged round the Standard factory behind a car on a pair of skis.

---

1 HMS *Vanguard* was also the best of a long line of twentieth-century Dreadnought battleships. Sadly, she was prematurely scrapped in 1960.

Unconventional and overbearing as Black was, many of his decisions – such as proceeding with the Standard Vanguard and the Triumph Mayflower, a bulky, poorly made car that was supposed to take America by storm – were simply wrong. In 1953 Black was seriously injured at the wheel of a prototype Triumph sports car which crashed, and after the accident his behaviour became even more outrageous. At the works Christmas party a few weeks after the mishap, whilst very drunk (and possibly still feeling the after-effects of his collision), he declared that there were just too many managers at Standard-Triumph and began naming those who should go – including his second in command, Ted Grinham. For the firm's senior officers, this was the final straw. On New Year's Day 1954 the company's board finally summoned up the courage to travel en masse to Sir John's palatial home at Bubbenhall, outside Coventry. There they politely asked Black to sign his own resignation letter, which used his recent accident as a convenient excuse for his departure. Black was to leave the firm immediately, and to be paid off with £30,000, his company Bentley, access to the company bungalow in Wales, and (in a somewhat double-edged gesture) an unsold Mayflower.

With Black out of the picture, Standard-Triumph was able to abandon its disastrous one-model policy. But by then the Standard brand was irretrievably associated with unreliability and poor performance. In 1959 Standard put its own name quietly to sleep and announced that all future models – beginning with the perky, boxy Herald – would carry the Triumph marque. Black's promotion of the Standard Vanguard was not wholly without merit, however. Its engine was reused in Triumph's first successful sports car, the fast TR2 of 1953, which won the RAC Rally and proved a smash hit in America – something that, sadly, could never be said of the Vanguard itself.

Standard-Triumph's great Coventry rival was Rootes, whose post-war model range began to look suspiciously like that of the American manufacturer Studebaker. This was not terribly surprising, as Studebaker's Raymond Loewy was by then advising the Warwickshire combine and helped design both the Hillman Minx Magnificent of 1948 and Rootes'

Audax range of 1955. Yet in 1954, just when the market for premium cars was picking up, Rootes pulled out of the luxury car business altogether, ending production of the Humber Pullman and Imperial at Ryton.[1] The Rootes brothers' lack of foresight merely encouraged government departments and other corporate limousine buyers to go to other firms. Rootes' assault on America in the shape of 1953's Hillman Californian, a two-door coupé version of the Minx, was equally disastrous. And when Rootes made yet another purchase in 1955, of Singer, the latter's outdated models, and its cramped Birmingham factory,[2] were of little help to the ramshackle group.

In 1953, however, Rootes got it right, unveiling a variant of the Sunbeam 90 in the shape of a two-seat roadster powered by a gutsy 2267cc Rootes saloon car engine. Rootes called this the Sunbeam Alpine, a model that they aimed primarily at the American market. The rakish Alpine was designed by Kenneth Howes, who had originally trained as an apprentice at the Great Western Railway works at Swindon and had subsequently worked for Studebaker and Ford in the US. The result was an instant classic that became a Hollywood favourite. Grace Kelly drove Cary Grant up the winding Riviera roads in an Alpine mark I in her last film, Hitchcock's *To Catch a Thief* of 1955; Elizabeth Taylor drove a similar car in *Butterfield 8* in 1960; and later marks of Alpine were used by Sean Connery in the first Bond film, *Dr No* of 1962. Michael Caine drove a Sunbeam Alpine both in the engaging Hollywood comedy-thriller *Gambit* of 1966 and in the gritty British gangster classic *Get Carter* of 1971, during which a 1968 Alpine disappeared into the murky waters of a Tyneside dock with the car's owner, Glenda (played by Geraldine Moffat), unconscious in the boot.

In typical British fashion, though, Rootes' managers were caught completely unawares by the Alpine's success. In three years Rootes

---

1 The celebrated, handsome Humber Super Snipe series was not introduced until 1958 – and prematurely axed by Chrysler in 1967.

2 Singer had persisted with the Fiat model of 1923, producing its cars vertically: parts were fed into the bottom of the factory and the finished cars were rolled out at the top.

made just 1,582 Alpine Mark I–IIIs, with the result that demand far out-
stripped supply. And while a highly successful redesign by Howes and
Jeff Crompton in 1956 (following which the Alpine looked uncannily
like 1955's Ford Thunderbird) made the Alpine even more popular, the
revamped car was based on the mediocre platform of the Hillman Husky
and the running gear of the portly Sunbeam Rapier – which was itself,
despite its much-vaunted 'Studebaker' curves, little more than a glamorous Hillman Minx.

Not every British auto maker was prepared to take the financial risks
that Billy Rootes did. Vauxhall and Opel, under a tight rein from their
GM parent, produced no distinguished models at all during the post-war
years. Their cars remained in thrall to American styling concepts, resulting in a design idiom that often seemed sadly out of place in the austere
world of rationing and the Marshall Plan. Historian Anthony Pritchard
has called Vauxhall's American-styled Victor of 1957 (which soon became
notorious for corrosion problems) 'the warthog of the motoring world . . .
all lumps and bumps'.

Even Ford of Britain initially offered little new to its post-war customers. Its models were much the same as in 1939, blandly styled and
mechanically conservative. The 1950 Consul was hailed as a stylish
new development but was in reality merely a conduit for watered-down
and scaled-down American styling.[1] All that could be said of the 1953
Ford Popular was that it was, in the venerable tradition of the Model
T, very cheap, undercutting all its rivals. Savings had been achieved on
the Popular by using Henry Ford's famous principle of 'thrifting'; thus
the car had only a few instruments, tiny headlamps, one windscreen
wiper, heavy fuel consumption and a derisory top speed of 50 mph. But
between 1953 and 1959 Ford sold more examples of the Popular – and
its marginally more sophisticated stablemates, the Anglia, Prefect, Escort
and Squire – than BMC sold small Austin or Morris cars. Britain thus

---

1 The Mark II Consul range of 1956 was a substantial improvement in visual terms but
still looked too American to prove a runaway success.

became the only market worldwide in which Ford cars outsold those of GM.

Worryingly, Ford of Britain's exemplary pre-war record in industrial relations (which had been a sharp contrast to those at its Detroit parent) was soon badly tarnished following the acquisition of the problematic supplier Briggs Motor Bodies in 1953. The notorious 'bell-ringer dispute' of 1957, when production at Dagenham was stopped because a shop steward had been disciplined for attending a union meeting (which he eventually convened in his lunch hour), signalled the start of a period of growing conflict. This was only halted when Ford sacked seventeen activists in 1962 and simultaneously began to improve pay and conditions, particularly for skilled workers.

Austin's post-war offerings from its Longbridge works, the 8HP and 10HP, were similarly conservative and underpowered models, whose ancestry could be traced well back into the 1930s. Indeed, Austin's new chairman, the irascible Leonard Lord, cared more about getting one over on his rival and former employer, Lord Nuffield, rather than about producing competitive and modern cars.

Lord was a notoriously difficult man with a pronounced inferiority complex, who suffered few other people, let alone fools, gladly. A Coventry-born engineer who was, in the best British automotive tradition, brusquely dismissive of financial controls and marketing campaigns, he rose through the ranks at Daimler, Hotchkiss and Morris. Like his talented if eccentric protégé, the engineer-designer Alec Issigonis, Lord was deeply, indeed obsessively, devoted to his mother.[1] He was rude, abrupt and unpleasant, and rarely bothered to remove his ubiquitous lit cigarette from his lower lip. Morris's suave and cultivated publicity chief, Miles Thomas, later asserted of Lord that 'everyone admired his methods if not his manners'. However, from other contemporary accounts it seems that Thomas may have been too kind. Certainly, some of the blame for the collapse of the British motor industry can be laid directly at Lord's

---

1 Unlike Issigonis, Lord did marry, and had three daughters.

feet, since it was he who presided over the stagnation of BMC and was responsible for the firm's criminal failure properly to exploit successes such as the Mini and the Minor.

Lord's big break came in 1929 when Morris promoted the opinionated and abrasive manager to reorganize Wolseley Motors, which Morris had recently bought following Wolseley's bankruptcy. Lord's success, and his seeming indifference to the unfavourable impression he made upon people, quickly recommended him to the antisocial Morris. He modernized the Cowley factory, launched the small and tidy Morris Eight, which quickly became the best-selling small car in Britain, and mapped out a new model range. Yet Morris's failure to retire, as he had promised, and his mean-minded rejection of Lord's justifiable demand for a greater share of the firm's profits (after all, Morris Motors' fortunes had been transformed by the success of Lord's Morris Eight), led to Lord's ill-tempered resignation in 1936. Then he enraged Morris still further when he joined Morris Motors' bitter rival, Austin, as general manager in 1938.

Lord's perception that Nuffield had treated him very shabbily in 1936 left such a bad taste in his mouth that he vowed to 'take Cowley apart brick by brick'. And after 1952 he effectively did just that. On Herbert Austin's death in 1941, Lord had assumed complete control as chairman at Austin. And when, eleven years later, the Conservative government persuaded Austin and Morris, Britain's two leading car makers, to join together as BMC, Lord ensured that what was ostensibly a 'merger' was in fact an Austin takeover of the Nuffield Organization. He placed Austin executives in charge of every major division of BMC and went out of his way to demean even those Morris directors who had supported the merger. As motor historian Gillian Bardsley wrote, Lord 'made the most of every opportunity to belittle the former directors of Morris Motors and ensure that Austin was the senior partner in every way'. This unpleasant atmosphere was too much for the talented Alec Issigonis, who left even before the creation of BMC could be publicly announced and joined the small Coventry car maker Alvis. William Morris himself was encouraged to retire after a brief stint as non-executive chairman, while Morris

Motors' entire engine programme was scrapped. Cowley was very much the junior partner in the supposed coalition. Yet Lord also negligently allowed Austin and Morris cars to continue to compete for both home and export sales, and Longbridge and Cowley each retained its own set of dealers. Thus, when Issigonis's Mini was launched in 1959, virtually identical Austin and Morris versions of the car were made, marketed and sold by the two separate companies – an extremely wasteful use of BMC's resources which did nothing to help the car's profitability. This was a crucial mistake that GM would never have made.

Despite his notorious irascibility and his hijacking of BMC, by the time of his retirement in 1961 Lord had, somewhat puzzlingly, come to dominate the British motor industry. He had been knighted for his services to the industry in 1954 and was raised to the peerage as Baron Lambury (rather than Lord Lord) in 1962. His rise and dominance over the automotive trade is perhaps a testimony to the poor standard of British car executives at the time. While American, French and German rivals encouraged leading graduates to enter the industry, in Britain the engineer still held sway and graduates specializing in areas such as financial control, marketing and public relations were largely ignored.

In the years immediately after the Second World War, Austin's network of worldwide franchises meant that, however uninspiring the car, Austin products would continue to sell well. A venture into the American market, the Austin A90 Atlantic of 1951, flopped badly – a fiasco that merely encouraged Lord not to listen to the innovators. The performance of the tiny Austin A30 was abysmal when it was fully laden with four people, but the model continued to be exported well in to the 1960s. In a similar vein, a vehicle based on the Morris Oxford of 1954 – which historian Anthony Pritchard has labelled 'a car of unsurpassed ugliness' – is still produced under licence in India to this day.

Morris himself was unable to acclimatize to the post-war world and became an increasingly isolated figure. Inevitably, he regarded the Labour Party's landslide election victory of 1945 as a national disaster, and continually demanded the reduction of state powers and the reversal

The epitome of elegance: a Bugatti Type 41 Royale, pictured in 1930.

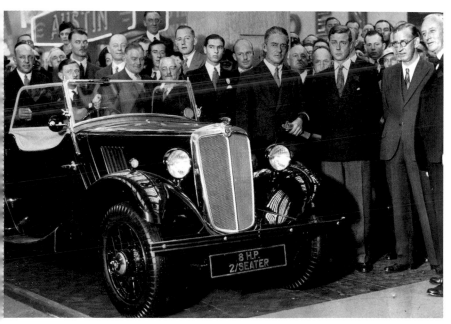

Lord Nuffield and Leonard Lord flank a distracted Prince of Wales (evidently unimpressed with the new Morris Eight) at the Olympia Motor Show of 1935.

Springtime for Hitler, 1938: Ferdinand Porsche (*left*) shows a delighted Führer where to find the engine in his new *Kraft durch Freude* people's car.

Wolfsburg's busy *Volkswagenwerk* in May 1949.

Production of André Citroën's groundbreaking and ground-hugging Traction Avant of 1934 continued until 1957. Three years later this oft-filmed model was showcased in the successful BBC TV series adapted from Georges Simenon's *Maigret* novels – this particular car being subsequently bought by the series' star, Rupert Davies.

Could this have been Britain's Volkswagen? Morris Motors attempts to sell the Minor to the world in 1949.

Harley Earl and a scale model of his stunning Buick Le Sabre concept car of 1950.

The sporty Ford Thunderbird of 1955, cheerfully endorsed by Frank Sinatra – who also lent his name and his voice to promote the disastrous Edsel two years later.

of the Attlee government's nationalization policy. 'All manufacturers,' he declared, should 'be given the opportunity to work out their own commercial salvation in their own way, unfettered and unhampered by red tape, restrictions and regulations.' Morris's laissez-faire economics and Victorian social attitudes failed to adapt to the challenges of nationalization and the welfare state, and his dissatisfaction seemed to grow with every month of Attlee's Labour administration. Miles Thomas later wrote:

Gradually we began to realize that in his increasing disenchantment and dislike of the immediate post-war frustrations of shortages of steel, continuing government controls, and all the trammels and trappings that chafe a man who has sat ... on the throne of a dictator, he was an unhappy man. He whose implicit wish became translated into a command to the executives of one of the most successful and fast growing businesses in the country, now had to bow to bureaucratic influence in business.

Like Ford, Morris also constantly reneged on his promises to leave the company to a younger generation. As early as 1932 Morris, then fifty-five years old, declared that he would be shortly stepping back from day-to-day supervision of the Morris Motor Company (which was formally retitled the Nuffield Organization in 1940); but, like Henry Ford, William Morris found he could not let go. As Miles Thomas wrote of the immediate postwar period: 'Although [Morris] had said long before that he was going to leave the running of the business to the board, he still persisted in exercising what was inappropriately, if undeniably, his right of destructive criticism.' The result was that talented senior managers such as Leonard Lord and Miles Thomas abruptly left the Nuffield Organization in fractious circumstances. Thomas had proposed rationalizing the firm's tangled web of factories and suppliers in 1945, but Morris, having returned from his annual holiday to Australia, senselessly axed the plan. Even the suave and mild-mannered Thomas decided that he could stand Morris's myopic tyranny no longer and resigned in November 1946. Leonard Lord had fallen out with Morris in 1938 and had promptly joined the 'enemy'; they never spoke again. Lord had finally had his revenge when Morris was unceremoniously kicked upstairs, first to the post of non-executive chairman of BMC and then, in 1954, that of honorary 'president'. For the last nine years of his life Morris had no involvement with BMC whatsoever, other than being summoned for the occasional publicity photo – for which he famously hated posing. By the time of his death in 1963, Morris, despite his fortune, appeared to be an unhappy man. He was particularly saddened by his failure to have children, writing: 'I have more money than any man can possibly want, and for what it is worth I have a title, but all that I have been dies when I die.' As indeed it did: the title of Viscount Nuffield was extinguished on his death. Today, few Britons born after 1975 remember Morris cars. The stone obelisk of the 'Nuffield Needle' in Cowley is all that remains of the old Morris works in Oxford, which once employed thousands of workers but was demolished in 1993.

Before its disappearance into the maw of BMC, however, Morris's declining empire was able to produce one excellent sports model, the MGA, which swiftly became the most popular sports car in the world and captured a large chunk of the American market, and one final outstanding small car, the Morris Minor. The latter's success, though, was achieved in spite of, rather with the aid of, the Nuffield Organization's eponymous founder.

Despite the Ministry of Transport's wartime ban on the production of cars for civilian use, in 1941 Miles Thomas, now managing director of Morris Motors, persuaded the government to allow work on a new small Morris car for peacetime, provided that this did not distract the plant's work on tanks, armoured cars and armaments. Given the wartime context, it is unsurprising that the project was code-named Mosquito, after the twin-engined, wooden-bodied de Havilland fighter-bomber, which became one of the outstanding aircraft of the war. The Mosquito car was not only to have a revolutionary pressed-steel body; it was also to be equipped with a new four-cylinder engine – soon labelled the 'flat-four' – which maximized output while minimizing (taxed) horsepower.[1]

---

1 Given the delays that Morris imposed upon the project, by the time the Minor was

When the war ended in 1945, Morris Motors was one of the very few car makers in Western Europe that was ready with a brand-new model. Miles Thomas gave the first Mosquito a spin and judged it 'by far the best prototype car I have ever been associated with'. But Thomas and the car's designer, Alec Issigonis, had reckoned without the interference of the increasingly reactionary Morris. The ageing, cantankerous viscount hated the car on sight and denounced its revolutionary, American-influenced body. 'It looks like a poached egg,' he barked; 'we can't make that.' The conservative tycoon preferred to extend the lifespan of the tried and trusted pre-war Morris Eight and did not want to introduce any new models. As the ever-diplomatic Thomas later wrote: 'Lord Nuffield was in no mood for changes. His argument was that we had more orders for the Morris Eight than we could cope with . . . I pleaded that the Morris Eight was rapidly becoming out of date, [and] the Morris Minor would give us a commanding lead. He was adamant. The frustration left a sour taste in my mouth.'

Morris also tried to delay the project by insisting on comprehensive restyling and demanding that the project name of Mosquito be dropped in favour of a name from Morris's pre-war past: the Minor. The mild-mannered but far-sighted Thomas could take no more, and resigned – a grave blow to the Nuffield Organization, which led directly to its 'merger' with Austin four years later. On 11 November 1948, Thomas was per-functorily thanked by the Nuffield board, given a cheque for £10,000, and shown the door. Two years later he joined the fast-growing British Overseas Airways Corporation (BOAC) as its chairman.

Thomas's abrupt departure finally stung Morris into reluctantly sanctioning the revised Minor. But he did insist that the radical separate rear suspension be dropped, on grounds of cost, and that the powerful 'flat-four' engine that had been designed for the car was replaced by a gutless pre-war engine from the Morris Eight.[1] The underpowered nature

---

launched Attlee's government had replaced the horsepower duty with a flat-rate car tax.
1 In 1956 a gutsier engine was finally installed, and the split windscreen with its primi-tive wipers was abandoned.

of the resulting model meant that it could not compete in the US, leaving the field clear for the reborn Volkswagen. At least Morris agreed to retain the Minor's revolutionary rack-and-pinion steering, while Issigonis's last-minute design intervention, splitting the prototype in half and adding an extra four inches in length, did succeed in making the car look less egg-like.

The Minor's rounded curves and flush bodywork were clearly influenced by the latest American models, by the Volkswagen Beetle (though no one at Morris would have admitted this), and by the Renault 750 (whose suspicious resemblance to the Beetle was not accidental: Ferdinand Porsche had been forced to work on the prototype while interned in France in 1945). Issigonis's design was even linked to Christian Dior's curvaceous New Look fashions of 1947. In short, even watered down from its original concept, the Morris Minor was still a winner. As Issigonis wrote in 1948 (with characteristic immodesty), this was a car that 'fits the economic conditions of this rather lean post-war era to perfection'. *Motor* magazine found it to be 'a very good 8 hp car indeed'.

Customers agreed and the Minor was an immediate sales success. Two new assembly lines had to be added at Cowley in 1949 to meet domestic demand, and in 1952 a wood-panelled estate version, the Morris Traveller (later immortalized as Dame Edna Everage's 'half-timbered car'), was introduced. Altogether 1.6 million Minors were made between 1948 and October 1970. The millionth Minor was rolled out in 1960, prompting BMC's public relations department to announce that a line of all the Minors made to date would stretch from Oxfordshire to the moon, and to make a series of films showing the Minor travelling thousands of miles through Canada and Germany.[1] There was a nod to Oxford's academic tradition, too: the millionth car's number plate was 1MHU, *mhu* being the ancient Greek abbreviation for a million.[2]

---

1 These films had a somewhat less than subliminal message: Minors were filmed continually overtaking VW Beetles.

2 The occasion was also marked by the production of a small batch of Morris Millions, identical to their parent Minors except for the name, which read Minor 1000000, and

Typically, though, first Morris and later BMC never properly exploited the car's potential. As motor historian Jonathan Wood has observed: 'Morris Motors unquestionably had the finest small car in the world with the Minor . . . Yet there is little evidence to suggest that the Nuffield Organization appreciated the quality of their talented designer's work, and although the car proved popular on the home market, the export one was never fully exploited.' Had Morris and Lord possessed the necessary vision, the Minor could have conquered the US marketplace before imports of the Volkswagen got going, and Issigonis's 'poached egg' could have achieved the worldwide iconic status of its rear-engined German rival.

Like the Minor, most British family models of the early 1950s were underpowered and poorly equipped. British motor manufacturers, like their continental equivalents, eschewed the automatic gearboxes that were taking the US by storm; nevertheless, the manual transmissions in British small cars were notoriously awful. Nor was the British car industry terribly bothered about their products' failings. As historian Martin Wainwright has observed: 'The prevailing attitude was epitomized at Wolseley, a Morris subsidiary, which received complaints about a model whose gear stick regularly snapped at the base. Complainants were sent letters effectively advising them to learn how to change gear more carefully'.[1]

At the end of the decade, BMC's management attempted to shake off some of their Little-Englander complacency and employed the Italian design house of Pininfarina to sex up some of their staid models. A few of the early results, like the Austin A40 of 1958, were undoubted successes. Pininfarina's clean, purposeful straight lines contrasted sharply with the curved, waddling forms of many of the less distinguished, American-inspired British vehicles. But not even Italian styling could disguise a dud car. The Morris Oxford V and Austin A60 Cambridge of 1959, for

---

their inexplicable lilac paintwork.

1 Even the Minor itself was knowingly supplied with a bonnet that did not lock properly, causing it to fly up on occasion when the car was in motion.

example, had sharp, clean lines from Pininfarina but offered appalling performance and abysmal roadholding. Such inherent defects encouraged even British buyers to look elsewhere, and helped ensure that in 1960 BMC lost its position as Britain's premier car manufacturer to Ford. Neither BMC nor its successors were ever to occupy the top slot again.

There were some bright spots in British motor manufacturing after the Second World War. The sleek, low Jaguar XK120 continued to wow American audiences, as did MG's compact sports models. Rolls-Royce consolidated their reputation as the world's premier luxury car maker. (Many of Rolls's rivals had perished before or during the war, while Mercedes' bomb-damaged German factories were in no position to offer any immediate challenge.) In 1949 Rover launched their new P4 (marketed as the Rover 60, 75 or 90, according to engine size), which over the years generated huge affection across Britain and its Empire on account of its portly but handsome lines, well-appointed interior and dogged reliability. There was the Morris Minor. And there was one outstanding British success, unveiled in the same year as the Minor: a Spartan utility vehicle based loosely on the Willys Jeep.

That quintessentially British classic, the Land Rover, was conceived by Rover's chairman, Maurice Wilks, who wanted a rugged, Jeep-type, off-road vehicle which could perform equally well on metalled roads and farm tracks. Wilks gave the brief to Rover's 32-year-old design chief, Gordon Bashford, who in a mere six months came up with one of the century's most successful and enduring vehicles. Bashford's Land-Rover (the title was initially hyphenated) used a Jeep chassis and the engine from the short-lived, old-fashioned Rover P3 of 1948–9. Launched at the Amsterdam Motor Show of 1948, the Land Rover was undeniably austere: not just seat cushions but even doors were considered luxurious extras. But it was simple, reliable – and successful. By 1955 the Land Rover was outselling Rover's conventional cars. The British army snapped it up, followed by armed forces across the world. Even the Queen bought one; from November 1953 Land Rovers were being used for royal tours in Commonwealth countries.

In 1958 Rover brought out a less austere variant, the Series II, which had actually received the attentions of a stylist, Rover's David Bache. The more comfortable Series II was more appropriate for the 'never had it so good' years of Harold Macmillan's post-austerity administration than its ascetic predecessor, and – along with its progeny, the IIA, IIB and Series III, all of which differed relatively little from the 1958 original – continued in production well into the 1980s.

By 1970 Land Rovers were a reassuringly common sight on the world's roads and trails. In that year Rover produced an upmarket companion to the Land Rover, which proved a huge and lasting success. That Rover and its new owners failed to capitalize on these impressive breakthroughs to dominate the vast off-road market by the end of the twentieth century remains, as we shall see, one of the great lost opportunities of automotive history.

7

Flight of the Phoenix

Along with most auto plants in continental Europe, France's car factories were in a sorry state in 1945. Peugeot's Sochaux factory had been wrecked when the Americans and Germans used it as a battleground in 1944. Panhard's Ivry works had been used as a bomb dump by the Germans. Bugatti's factory at Molsheim in Alsace, which had been requisitioned by the Germans in 1940, had also been deliberately razed when the Nazis retreated. It took years for the firm to re-establish its legal right to the site, and by the time it did, Ettore Bugatti, the man whose products had dominated motor racing in the 1920s and 30s, was gone; he had died, exhausted and dispirited, in 1947.[1] Indeed, the immediate post-war years proved the graveyard not just of Bugatti but of many other celebrated French marques. Firms that had relied on expensive luxury models and sleek, high-powered racing cars to sell their wares found that the shattered, straitened Fourth Republic was in no condition to support either market. The Paris-based luxury car maker Voisin did not survive the war at all, while the Hotchkiss management was accused of collaboration in 1944 and the firm never shook off the stigma; by 1953 it was producing a miserly 230 cars per year and was soon concentrating only on manufacturing Willys Jeeps under licence.[2] Delahaye, whose racing cars had

---

1 The Bugatti firm attempted to make a comeback in 1955, but their Type 251 Grand Prix car proved a grave disappointment and the company reverted to making aircraft engines.
2 In 1966 Hotchkiss was bought by armaments manufacturer Brandt. Hotchkiss's last

challenged the racetrack hegemony of the powerful Mercedes and Auto Unions before 1939, also struggled to find its feet, and in 1953 made precisely three cars before being taken over by Hotchkiss. The same year saw the demise of the famous luxury and sports car manufacturer Delage. Meanwhile, the French arm of the pre-war Anglo-French Talbot company (whose British arm had been absorbed by the Rootes Group in 1935) limped on until 1958, when it was taken over by the expanding, Fiat-backed Simca.

Some car makers simply gave up. Berliet, based outside Lyons, never made another car. In 1944 the firm, which had enthusiastically cooperated with the Germans, was summarily taken over by a self-appointed board of Resistance workers, who decided to stick to trucks. Berliet was finally taken over by Citroën in 1967.

Citroën itself, however, was one of the great success stories of the Fourth Republic. In 1948 the company unveiled the 2CV, the era's ultimate expression of stylish utilitarianism and a worthy successor to Ford's Model T and the Austin Seven. Much like the Model T forty years before, the 2CV was specifically aimed at rural customers who could not previously afford a car. Accordingly, its specification decreed that the car needed to be a low-priced, rugged, 'umbrella on four wheels', in which two peasants could drive 100 kg (220 lb) of farm produce to market at 60 kph (37 mph) – wearing clogs. It had to be able to negotiate across muddy, unpaved roads and, most famously, should be able to cross a ploughed field without breaking the eggs it was carrying. And it should average 3 litres of petrol to every 100 kilometres.[1]

When France was invaded by German troops in 1940, Citroën had two hundred and fifty prototypes of the 2CV chugging around roads all over the country. Citroën and its Michelin managers were well aware of the car's value either as a military transport or as a civilian equivalent to Nazi Germany's *KdF-Wagen*. Many of the prototypes were therefore

---

military vehicle rolled out in 1971.
1 The equivalent of 78 mpg.

hidden in secret locations all over France, some so secret that they had been wholly forgotten by 1945. (One prototype was successfully disguised as a light truck at the Michelin factory at Clermont-Ferrand.) Those that survived the war were ordered to be destroyed in 1948 by the austere, *Gitanes*-smoking Michelin supremo, Pierre-Jules Boulanger, who wanted to start from the drawing board and was embarrassed by these old, crude prototypes. Thankfully for posterity, Boulanger failed to find them all; three pre-war 2CVs were discovered in a barn near Citroën's test track at La Ferté-Vidame, to the west of Paris, as recently as 1994.

After the liberation, at a time when many French auto manufacturers were under investigation for collaboration, Boulanger, with his impeccable Resistance credentials, was able swiftly and painlessly to retake control of Citroën. Two prototype 2CVs were rescued, and Boulanger hired the designer Flaminio Bertoni to reconfigure the bodywork. Boulanger himself was never able to enjoy the fruits of his labour; he was killed in a car crash in 1950 (while driving, with cruel irony, a Citroën Traction Avant). Bertoni, however, went on to complete the 2CV and, subsequently, to design Citroën's legendary DS.

Bertoni had been a sculptor before the war, and the 2CV's sinuous, almost erotic, lines betrayed his sculptural insight. The 2CV was crude, it was agonizingly slow (the original, 9 bhp engine provided 35 mph on the flat, if you were lucky), and its suspension was laughably soft: the car tilted alarmingly round sharp corners and could be rocked from side to side by a small child. But, as Michael Sedgwick observed, 'it was properly made and enjoyed the backing of nationwide service'. And as the car's English biographer, John Reynolds, has noted: 'Conceived as a utilitarian vehicle, it was engineered to the highest technical standards. Seemingly crude and basic, with the frailest of bodywork, it was one of the most ingenious and sophisticated designs ever offered to the motoring public.' The 2CV's detachable seating enabled it to carry loads that seemed impossible. Its hydraulic brakes were a considerable improvement on the VW Beetle's primitive braking system, and it was also longer than its principal rivals, the Morris Minor and the fractionally more upmarket Renault 4CV. In its early years, the 2CV was also half the price of a Beetle. Moreover, the 2CV's relative lack of moving parts – a key element of the original design brief – made it very reliable and remarkably cheap to repair on the few occasions when it did fail.

In contrast to the engine-led attitudes of the great American and German car makers of the 1930s, who sought to maximize brake horse-power at the expense of everything else, Citroën was primarily concerned with safety and comfort. The 2CV was thus founded on the fundamental principle of guaranteeing excellent stability, even when the car was driven badly by an inexperienced driver. To achieve this, wheels were positioned at all four corners, and the engine and gearbox placed ahead of the front axle. The car was given the latest rack-and-pinion steering, which required only 2.3 turns from lock to lock. And since the body waas largely made of bolt-on aluminium panels, which had no load-bearing role at all, the 2CV was surprisingly light, assisting both handling and fuel economy.

Almost 8.5 million *Deux chevaux* (including derivatives such as the Dyane and Ami) were made in France before production was halted in 1988.[1] But the 2CV was not an instant hit. The car was at first heavily criticized – in print by the European motoring press, as well as on the stage by French comedy stars. In Britain, *Autocar* sniffed that the 2CV was 'the work of a designer who has kissed the lash of austerity with almost masochistic fervour', while Morris Motors insisted that their new Minor of 1948 was Europe's most economical *real* car, implying that the 2CV barely qualified as such. Yet Citroën was flooded with orders and there was soon a three-year waiting list. Sales peaked in 1974 when the old campaigner was given a new lease of life by customers panicked by the oil crisis; as late as 1979 a new, thrifty version was introduced with a fuel-efficient 602 cc engine (providing a mere 29 bhp). Right-hand-drive 2CVs were produced under licence in England from 1953 to 1964. In 1960 Citroën even produced an 'anglicized' version, called the Bijou, which must rank as one of the ugliest cars ever sold. Britons, though,

---

1 2CV manufacture continued for a further two years in Portugal.

never rallied either to the Bijou or its 2CV cousin. In 1966 Citroën shut its Slough factory, which was subsequently bought by the American confectionery giant Mars who converted the plant to make Milky Ways and Twixes.

The 2CV owed its timeless design to André Citroën's gifted protégé, André Lefèbvre. Born in 1894 and trained as an aircraft designer, Lefèbvre joined the idiosyncratic pioneer car maker and aircraft manufacturer Gabriel Voisin after the First World War. During the Great Depression the market for Voisin's hand-made luxury cars imploded, and Voisin generously offered his key designers, led by Lefèbvre, to Citroën. Here Lefèbvre established a reputation for innovation and eccentricity. Tall and debonair, he was rarely seen without his trademark glass of champagne, and usually dressed in a flying jacket and white silk scarf as if he were about to pilot one of Voisin's planes into the skies. Yet Lefèbvre was no engineer, dismissing car engines as *tournebroches* ('spits'), which merely served to dirty his sophisticated apparel. It was Boulanger who introduced the mechanical innovations to the 2CV, and who ensured that the car was frugal with fuel; Lefèbvre was there to lend it style and class.

In 1955, Lefèbvre and Bertoni helped Citroën create one of the most innovative, daring and stylish cars of the twentieth century, the DS19. The 'Goddess' – *déesse* ('DS') is the French word for a female deity – instantly became one of the outstanding cars of all time. Its wraparound windscreen, sloping nose and wheel at each corner made it look like nothing else. The 'thinking-man's car', and very much an engineer's vehicle, it boasted a detachable glass-fibre roof; a large glasshouse, making the car seem light and airy; a single-spoke steering wheel; new radial-ply tyres from Michelin; high-pressure hydraulics; nitrogen springing; disc brakes at the front; revolutionary, quick-release wheels; and radial tyres, which offered far better performance and a far longer lifespan than their competitors.

Most drivers, though, focused on the DS's new pneumatic suspension – the stuff of dreams. It made the car wonderfully comfortable; the

DS rose into the air when started, and sank gracefully on to its stream-lined haunches when at rest. And it automatically adjusted the car to the road conditions, from the bumpiest country track to the smooth new *autoroutes*. It could keep the car running even if it was operating on only three of the wheels.

Understandably, and in sharp contrast to the undemanding 2CV, the DS was a highly complex animal. Some French dealers actually terminated their relationship with Citroën after 1955, saying that the DS was too difficult to repair.[1] But it was always worth trying. As the magazine *Motor* commented, the DS may have been 'the most complicated car made anywhere in Europe', but it was also 'the most comfortable car made anywhere in the world'. As the champagne-coloured DS was revealed on the Citroën stand at 1955's Paris Motor Show, scenes of near-hysteria broke out as everyone sought a closer look. Lefèbvre and Bertoni's sinuous, aerodynamic lines gave the DS a timeless grace, light years removed from the chunky silhouettes of most contemporary European offerings. (The equally new Peugeot 403 on the adjacent stand – a boxy, Pininfarina-designed saloon – was completely upstaged by the DS, which made the Peugeot look hopelessly outdated.) By the end of the day Citroën had taken twelve thousand orders for this most exquisite of all motor cars. Two years later the vehicle was even entered as an exhibit at the International Exposition of Decorative Art in Milan, where it was shown suspended in the air with no wheels, like a spaceship.

After 1958 the DS became the epitome of the assertive, francophone individualism of de Gaulle's new Fifth Republic, helping to banish embarrassing memories of imperial decline and military retreat from the collective French memory. It became the default official car for President de Gaulle and his ministers (and star of the film of Frederick Forsyth's tale of the plot to assassinate de Gaulle, *The Day of the Jackal*, in 1973). In

---

1 In some ways those dealers were right. Not all early DSs worked as well as they looked: the hydraulic suspension system was notoriously prone to failure, as the hydraulic fluid overheated, while accessing the rear wheels and the hydraulic suspension behind the rear skirt was fraught with difficulty.

1958 independent coachbuilder Henri Chapron built a cabriolet version, and between 1962 and 1968 Bertoni updated the design, introducing quadrupled headlights behind glass covers. Citroën even introduced a luxury version, the DS21, and an estate variant, the Safari.

While it had no answer to the DS, Renault's recovery was almost as impressive as Citroën's. Following Louis Renault's death and the nationalization of the firm, Renault settled down to re-equipping its factories for civilian operation. Now that generous overtime payments were guaranteed by the government, the crippling strikes that had so plagued the company in the 1930s were a thing of the past and production soared. Equally significantly, the numerous administrations of the Fourth Republic ensured that the native car industry – or at least what remained of it by 1955 – was well protected by trade barriers. These were not raised until 1960; even then, the only model initially allowed into the country was the tiny Isetta bubble car, which had no equivalent in France.

The Renault 4CV was the firm's first post-war product. Unveiled in 1947, it had been quietly developed during the war; in 1946, as we have seen, the notorious Ferdinand Porsche was appropriated to work on its design. Clearly influenced by Porsche's *KdF-Wagen* – the 4CV was rear-engined, like the VW, while its tail looked identical to that of the Beetle – the 4CV's German ancestry was accidentally underlined when the first production models were painted in surplus sand-coloured paint which had originally been ordered for the vehicles of Rommel's wartime Afrika Korps. Early 4CVs were accordingly nicknamed *La Motte de Beurre*, the 'Lump of Butter'.

The sturdy, cheap 4CV soon became France's most popular car. It remained in production until 1961, although in 1956 it was officially replaced with the Dauphine. This racy, three-box design (front and rear ends were bolted on to a welded centre section) looked like a sports car but was actually a modest little family saloon which handled frighteningly badly at the high speeds its jet-age shape encouraged. Neither the Dauphine nor the 4CV ever challenged the export success of the Volkswagen.

Citroën and Renault were not the only French car makers to prosper in the post-war years. Simca (an acronym which stood for the Société Industrielle de Mécanique et de Carrosserie Automobile) had been founded in Nanterre, to the west of Paris, by the Franco-Italian entrepreneur Henri Pigozzi in 1935 as a French arm of Fiat. In 1951 it launched the first model not based on a Fiat design, the Aronde, and three years later felt strong enough to absorb Ford's nearby Poissy factory, which Dearborn was no longer interested in. As Ford retreated from France, however, Chrysler advanced. In 1958 Chrysler bought a 15 per cent stake in Simca, and five years later bought the controlling interest in the firm from Fiat. Chrysler's purchase of the British Rootes Group the following year (which, incidentally, reunited the two halves of the venerable Talbot marque) laid the foundations for the ill-fated conglomerate that became known as Chrysler Europe. By 1981 the ailing combine had, ironically, axed the Simca name in favour of the rejuvenated Talbot brand.

Post-war Italy was not the ideal market for the ambitious car maker. The Italian car industry had been ruined by retreating Germans and advancing allies alike. And Italy was still a poor nation; in 1950 only one in every eighty-two Italians actually owned a car. Nevertheless, the Italian love of motor racing soon reasserted itself. This, combined with the Italians' flair for design, and their inimitable gift for devising cheap, small cars, helped the major Italian auto makers to an enviably healthy position by 1955.

The flagship manufacturer of Italian sports cars in the fifties was, as before 1940, Ferrari. Helped by its successes on the racetrack – Ferraris won the majority of Grand Prix and major rallies after 1950 – the firm carved out a unique niche in the global auto industry. The company's founder, Enzo Ferrari, came from a humble background in Modena in northern Italy. Having fought in the First World War, and seen most of his family wiped out by the terrible influenza pandemic of 1918–19, he began work as a mechanic, joining Alfa Romeo in 1920. In 1923 Ferrari started racing Alfas, using (after 1932) the prancing horse symbol to adorn his cars.¹ In 1933 Depression-hit Alfa withdrew their financial support for Ferrari's team, but the indefatigable entrepreneur simply found an alternative patron in Pirelli, and continued to drive his 'race-red' cars (red was the official Italian racing colour in the inter-war years) for Alfa. When Italy entered the Second World War in 1940, Alfa found its plant confiscated by the government, but Ferrari's factory was too small to be considered for government requisition. Nevertheless, as an enthusiastic fascist, Enzo Ferrari, forced to move his factory from Modena to the small town of Maranello in order to avoid allied bombing, willingly made machine tools and aircraft parts for Mussolini's government, until Mussolini's fall in 1943. Ferrari then miraculously shed his fascist past when the allies arrived – a situation at which both the allied military government and the US Army, fearing communist insurgency, were happy to connive. Ferrari was thus allowed to reform his company and to begin racing again in 1948. When the Formula 1 championship was introduced in 1950, Ferrari cars, driven by legendary figures such as Juan Fangio and John Surtees, proceeded to dominate the races of the ensuing decade, while also performing spectacularly well in endurance races such as the Mille Miglia and the Le Mans 24-hour contest.

Enzo Ferrari only began to sell production road cars in order to fund his racing habit. The first Ferrari sports car, the 125S, was produced at Maranello in 1947. More influential, though, was the splendidly curvaceous and remarkably advanced 166 Inter of 1949, the company's first successful assault on the Grand Touring market, a sector with which Ferrari has been closely associated ever since. In 1962 Ferrari followed the 166 with the company's first supercar, and possibly the greatest Ferrari road car of all time, the 250 GTO. Today the GTO's successors serve as the enduring global benchmark for high-performance sports cars.

----

1 The *cavallino rampante* logo has a complex history, deriving from the insignia of the cavalry unit of the First World War's leading Italian aircraft ace, Count Francesco Baracca, which the count later emblazoned on his plane's fuselage. Its yellow background derives from the coat of arms of Enzo Ferrari's home city, Modena.

The cost of racing, however, finally proved too much for Enzo's pockets – as well as those of his main backer, Italian tyre giant Pirelli. By the mid-1960s Ferrari was on the verge of bankruptcy, and in 1963 Ferrari and Pirelli offered Ford a stake in the company. Ford's autocratic chairman, Henry Ford II, was delighted; but delight turned to fury when Enzo Ferrari, guessing that his independence would be seriously compromised once subsumed within the mighty Ford organization, had second thoughts and abruptly broke off negotiations. Henry Ford II retaliated to this public humiliation by launching a racing car division to challenge Ferrari.[1] By 1965, now fighting off a series of hostile takeover bids by angry Ford managers, Ferrari turned to Fiat. It was Fiat that provided the essential financial security to enable Ferrari to resist Ford, and in 1969 the Torinese giant increased its stake in the company to 50 per cent.[2] Thereafter, Ferrari prospered under the shelter of Fiat's umbrella; indeed, it was soon joined there by other famous, sporty Italian marques such as Lancia, Maserati and Alfa Romeo itself. Today, Ferrari is effectively the racing arm of the Agnellis' formidable empire.

In 1946 control of Fiat passed, with the allies' blessing, to the steely academic Dr Vittorio Valletta, who had been Agnelli's CEO since 1939. This transition was achieved despite the fact that the communist-dominated Turin unions had demanded Valletta's resignation on account of his complicity with Mussolini's administration. Valletta's avowed aim was to 'regain our former ascendancy, to re-establish the prestige of Italian technology and to safeguard our jobs'. And this he duly did: between 1947 and 1956 production at Fiat rose tenfold and the car maker was restored to financial health.

Not all of Fiat's new models were successes. The Fiat 1400 of 1950 was too much of a compromise; its bulbous styling seemed to owe more to America than to Italy, and although its revolutionary unitary construction

---

1 This Dearborn did very successfully in the late 1960s, when Ford's massive V-8 powered GT40s beat Ferraris in most of the major endurance races.
2 In 2006 Fiat cemented its relationship with Ferrari by buying a further 29 per cent of the legendary car maker's stock.

set the pattern for future Fiats, the conservative Fiat board would not allow the company's experienced designer, Dante Giacosa, to install the engine he wanted, decreeing that a big power plant would make the car too potent and too expensive to run. The 1.4 litre engine they chose instead was far too feeble to make the overall package attractive, and the car was a flop.

The Fiat 600, however, was an unqualified triumph. Giacosa introduced a new layout for the car, with the engine at the rear, as well as using the 1400's pioneering unitary construction. Significantly, the Italian government seized on the 600's launch in 1955 as a cause for national celebration, to mark ten years of reconstruction and redevelopment following the devastation and ignominy of 1945. The following year Giacosa adapted the 600 into yet another innovative new product, the Fiat Multipla. A six-seater miniature minibus which could carry a whole family, it was, in 1980s' parlance, the first multi-purpose vehicle (MPV), or people carrier. The engine was packed as far forward as it would go (an idea borrowed by the Mini three years later) and the front luggage compartment removed in order to accommodate three rows of paired seats. At the 1960 Rome Olympics, Multiplas, with their Tardis-like internal capacities, provided memorable transport for all of the event's officials and athletes.

In 1957 Giacosa produced his masterpiece. Reminding the motoring world of his classic Fiat 500 of 1936, he launched his brilliant, characterful Nuova 500, or *Cinquecento*. Over 3.6 million of these tiny, beautifully styled cars were built before production ended in 1975. Only 3 metres long and weighing less than 500 kg, the *Cinquecento* was originally powered by a diminutive 497cc engine, sited under the floor at the rear. But it proved practical, economical, and immensely popular. Many still survive today – although, as with all post-war Fiats, body rust soon grew to be a notorious problem. Fiat even made an estate version, surely one of the smallest station wagons ever to be mass-produced.

Like Ferrari, Alfa Romeo also rebuilt its reputation after 1945 through success on the racetrack. In 1950 1.5 litre Alfa Alfettas (in truth a pre-war design that had been updated and supercharged) came first, second and third in the world motor racing championship. Their second-placed driver was Juan Manuel Fangio, generally agreed to be the finest racing driver of all time.

Alfa had been founded in Milan in 1910, but had gone bankrupt in 1928. It was rescued by Mussolini's government, for which it made aircraft engines during the war, and only fully returned to civilian car production in 1954 when it launched the stylish, Loewy-influenced Giulietta two-door coupé. Concentrating on sports and performance car production in the 1960s, Alfa was, like Ferrari, always precariously balanced on the brink of bankruptcy and in 1986 finally fell into the ever-welcoming arms of Fiat.

Fiat was not the only great Italian success of the post-war era. Italy's independent car designers were by 1950 in great demand by the auto manufacturers of Western Europe, and even by America's Big Three. Mario Boano of Ghia in Turin worked not only for Alfa, Lancia, Ferrari and Turin's own Fiat in the 1950s, but also for Chrysler and Renault, for whom he created the Dauphine. As we have seen, Battista Farina's design consultancy Pininfarina, based just outside Turin at Cambiano, acted as design consultant for many British, French and American firms, and by the end of the 1950s had built a successful relationship with BMC. Perhaps the greatest stylist of them all, Giovanni Michelotti, worked with Standard-Triumph after 1958 and designed some of the classic cars of the fifties and sixties, including Triumph's Herald, Spitfire, TR4 and the marvellous Triumph 2000.

In the immediate post-war period, the German car industry was in a sorry state. Most of the now-divided nation's car plants, which since 1939 had largely been making tanks, guns, armoured cars or engines for Hitler's war machine, were ruined. Machinery that was still intact in the east was often carted away by the Russians as war reparations. Few Germans were even allowed to drive; in 1946 only those whose jobs made driving essential were allowed by the military governments to use their cars.

Nor, thanks to allied bombing and the devastation of the allies' invasion, were there many cars actually available to native Germans. As historian Michael Sedgwick has noted: 'Of the 40,897 private cars registered in Hamburg in 1938, only 7,147 had survived.'

Many of the famous German plants of the 1930s were handed over to the Soviets in 1945. The most prestigious was BMW's Saxon base at Eisenach in Thuringia, which continued to produce pre-war BMWs in small numbers until 1952, when the works was transferred to the new East German government and renamed EMW, or Eisenacher Motorenwerk. Four years later, the factory produced its first model under the new marque of Wartburg, a pioneer car maker of 1898–1904 and a brand that BMW had briefly resurrected in the 1930s. Eisenach's Wartburg became one of the two staple cars of Soviet-controlled East Germany, alongside Zwickau's Trabant. It continued to be powered by feeble two-stroke engines (fuelled by a mixture of petrol and oil) until shortly before the fall of the Iron Curtain in 1989, when Volkswagen assisted Wartburg in making its first four-stroke power plant. German reunification the following year spelled the end of the Wartburg car, which was not only hideously underpowered and dangerously polluting but also, thanks to its ancient production line, cost far more to make than equivalent Western models. The Wartburg factory was closed in 1991 and much of its workforce joined the new Opel factory that opened nearby the following year.

BMW's pre-war base at Milbertshofen in Munich was virtually destroyed in the war. But its second-string works, at Allach, was only lightly damaged. Since both sites were in the American sector after 1945, neither was immediately dismantled or appropriated. However, Allach had been run during the war by slave labour, much of which had been plucked from the nearby concentration camp at Dachau. As late as 25 April 1945, the SS listed 9,997 inmates of Dachau allocated to BMW at Allach. BMW, which had also been a key supplier of aircraft engines during the war and had latterly helped to make the lethal V-2 rocket, was accordingly high on the allies' blacklist in 1945. As the company's historian, Horst Mönnich, has noted: 'BMW was second after the I. G. Farben Dye Trust amongst those industrial companies charged with having been most responsible for the disaster that befell Europe and the world.' Yet on 3 August 1945 the American military government decreed that Milbertshofen, at least, was to be reconstructed. America had no wish to see Germany remain on its knees, especially when a new threat was emerging to the east. At the same time, the Americans rebuffed Daimler-Benz's cynically opportunistic proposal to take over the Allach plant.

While BMW was permitted to reconstruct its Munich factory, it was not until 1951 that the company was able to unveil its first post-war model: the big, burly 501, affectionately nicknamed 'the Baroque Angel'. Hardly the car for the shallow pockets of war-wracked Europe, it was no surprise when the 501 sold poorly. During the 1950s, indeed, BMW only survived through export sales of a vehicle that was as far removed from its pre-war sports cars as could be imagined.

BMW, Heinkel and Messerschmitt had spent the war years churning out powerful fighters, bombers and tanks for the Nazis. Now, desperate for any kind of sales success, they resorted to mass-producing the most unlikely vehicle ever to grace Europe's roads: the bubble car.

Messerschmitt, manufacturer of the superlative Me-109 fighter, was first off the chocks. But its three-wheeled Kabinenroller of 1953 was not a huge success, derived as it was from Fritz Fend's miniscule and fragile 38cc invalid carriage for disabled ex-servicemen. With its joystick steering and canopy adapted from the firm's two-engined wartime *Zerstörer* ('destroyer'), the Me-110, the diminutive Messerschmitt conveyed too many memories of the Luftwaffe to prove a success in the rest of Europe. What was more, its cockpit was incredibly cramped (just like that of the Me-110); the single passenger sat right behind the driver, legs straddling the front seat. To engage reverse, you had to stop the engine and start it again. Many export models simply had no reverse gear at all.

BMW produced the first bubble car that actually took off. Its iconic, diminutive *rollendes Ei* ('rolling egg') of 1955 had originally been made by the Italian motorbike and refrigerator manufacturer Isa, which BMW now approached with a generous licensing agreement. Recognizing a good deal when they saw it, the Italians were soon shipping all the model's tooling to Germany, in a grim parody of the enforced industrial relocations of the recent war. BMW, better known at the time for their motorcycles, then adapted the miniscule model into their own Isetta. The close-set rear wheels of the Isetta made many mistake it for a three-wheeler (one did indeed follow later). But in cash-strapped Europe, it was an instant hit. By 1957 the car was, in an ironic twist of fate, being assembled in Britain at the former works of the London, Brighton and South Coast Railway, which had suffered so grievously at the hands of BMW-engined German bombers after 1940.

BMW's unexpected success with the Isetta prompted Heinkel to follow with a similar model in 1956. It looked like a toad, but continued in production until 1964.[1] Fortunately, the appearance of BMC's Mini in 1959 soon consigned all of these hilarious, but inherently dangerous, bubble cars to the rubbish heap.

While BMW managed to keep afloat during the fifties on bubble car and motorbike sales, those German car makers owned by wealthy American combines were able to recover quickly and comprehensively. Despite the wholesale obliteration of much of the city of Köln, Ford was producing their pre-war Taunus there as early as 1948, the year Henry Ford II visited Germany (and failed to buy Volkswagen). Oddly enough, the Köln plant had escaped serious damage from USAAF bombers during the war. Indeed, locals had often taken refuge at the Ford works during bombing raids, as they knew it to be one of the safest spots in the city. (By 1945, German historian Winfried Wolf has recorded, the Ford works was popularly known as 'the bunker'.) Nineteen years later the Ford Motor Company, thanks to years of extensive lobbying, received $1 million in tax exemptions from the US government as compensation for the damage allied bombers had done to the Köln works – an astonishing victory given

---

1 It was also made under licence in England by eccentric small-car experts Trojan, part of bus and truck makers Leyland Motors.

the notoriously pro-Nazi leanings of Henry Ford and the importance of the plant's trucks to the German war effort.

Opel, backed by the resources of the mighty GM empire, also recuperated rapidly. In 1945 the company's principal plant at Rüsselsheim lay wrecked, and much of its tooling – including the whole production line for the successful pre-war Kadett – was taken to Russia as reparations. (The Kadett magically reappeared in post-war Russia as the Moskvitch 400.) All of the machinery from Opel's Brandenburg plant, formerly the home of the Blitz truck, was also swiftly removed to Soviet territory. But Opel's workforce helped clear Rüsselsheim by the end of 1945, and in 1946 production of the legendary Blitz restarted. In 1948 GM resumed full control of Opel (with no Germans on the senior management team), largely thanks to GM management's success in cultivating the military governor of Germany's US zone, General Lucius Clay. The same year, Opel produced its first post-war car, a reissue of the austere pre-war Olympia. Alfred Sloan was reluctant, however, to invest much new capital in Opel; accordingly, the new, 'Western' Kadett did not appear until 1962.

Opel's recovery was helped by a calm, collegiate attitude on the shop floor at Rüsselsheim. In the years after 1945 strikes were almost unknown in German car plants. Heinz Nordhoff of Volkswagen spoke for Germany's car industry, and indeed the whole German nation, when he warned that 'our grandchildren will curse us because we did not think of them but only of the present'. Nordhoff and his fellow auto makers thought nothing of introducing workers' representatives on to their company boards – in marked contrast to the antiquated attitudes to labour still held by their American and British rivals. What mattered were not differentials, conditions or perquisites, but getting the company, and West Germany, back on its feet.

Things were not quite so simple for those German car makers that were unable to benefit from American guarantees and investment. Auto Union had been formed in 1932 from four firms: Horch, created by former Benz employee Karl Horch in 1901; Audi, founded by Horch in Zwickau, in Saxony, in 1910, after he had left his original firm and a court had ruled he had no claim on the eponymous brand; DKW (Dampf-Kraft-Wagen – literally, 'steam-powered car'), founded in 1916, which by 1939 had not only become the world's largest motorcycle manufacturer but was also making cars at Audi's Zwickau factory; and Wanderer, founded in 1911 in the Saxon town of Siegmar (today a district of Chemnitz). The four companies were all struggling in the midst of Germany's appalling depression of the early 1930s and had huddled together for safety. (The new conglomerate adopted as its logo the symbol of four rings, for its component companies, which its successor, Audi, still uses today.) And the ploy worked: by 1936 Siegmar-based Auto Union was firmly in the black and its cars were challenging Mercedes for pre-eminence in international Grand Prix.

In 1933 Auto Union's aristocratic chairman, Baron Klaus-Detlof von Oertzen, sought to ingratiate himself with Germany's new chancellor, Adolf Hitler, by suggesting two state-funded projects – both of which Hitler eagerly embraced. The first, as we have seen, was the creation of a Nazi 'people's car' which, under the direction of Ferdinand Porsche (and not of Auto Union, as Oertzen had hoped), ultimately became the VW Beetle. The second was the launch of a state-sponsored motor-racing programme, at which Auto Union cars excelled.

Immense wartime damage, and the fact that most of Auto Union's plants lay inside the Russian zone of occupation, meant that in 1945 little survived of Auto Union's proud pre-war legacy. All of the firm's East German assets were appropriated without compensation. Wanderer's (and Auto Union's) former home town of Siegmar was renamed Karl-Marx-Stadt, and the wrecked plant there was never revived. The wretched remains of the Horch and Audi factories in Zwickau were allocated to the VEB (Volkseigener Betrieb, or 'People-Owned Enterprise'), which began to make poor-quality copies of old DKW models until halted by a West German lawsuit. In 1957 VEB began production of the Trabant, whose smoky, two-stroke, 594cc engine produced ten times the hydrocarbon emissions of comparable cars; and the manufacture of whose Duroplast body, made from an amalgam of recycled plastic, brown paper and shredded cotton waste, released toxic fumes which killed a number of factory workers and made many more seriously ill. Nevertheless, wealthier citizens of East Germany who wanted to buy a car had a choice of the Trabant or the equally appalling Wartburg. Trabants survived largely unchanged until 1989, when, following the collapse of the Berlin Wall, VEB belatedly installed the reliable 1.1 litre engine from the Volkswagen Polo under the bonnet. But the fall of the whole Eastern Bloc that year spelled the end for the Trabant. As restrictions on international trade and personal movement evaporated, East Germans opted for second-hand Western cars rather than the ghastly Trabants and Wartburgs. The Trabant factory closed in 1991, after which Trabant cars could be had for just a few marks. (A proposal to restart manufacture in Uzbekistan resulted in the production of just one car.) But such are the vagaries of fashion that ten years later Trabants had become collectors' items, with green-painted examples especially, if somewhat inexplicably, prized by nostalgic Germans as 'lucky' cars.

In West Germany, a new Auto Union slowly emerged out of the ashes of war. In 1949 a new factory was built in Ingolstadt in Bavaria, partly financed by American aid from the generous and far-sighted Marshall Plan. The new plant, partly staffed by workers who had migrated from old Auto Union plants in the east, began to make small, two-stroke cars, vans and motorbikes under the DKW label. However, the firm's products failed to make much of an impact, and in 1958–9 the struggling company was bought by Daimler-Benz. Despite building a brand-new factory at Ingolstadt, Daimler-Benz preferred to concentrate on building its prestige Mercedes brands and seemed strangely uninterested in Auto Union's far more humble products. In 1964 Daimler-Benz readily sold the company to Volkswagen, which dumped the DKW name, tainted as it was by association with low-powered, two-stroke models. Five years later VW merged Auto Union with niche German car maker NSU and badged all the resultant division's products as Audis. The first new Audi had already appeared the previous year: the strikingly impressive, fast and handsome Audi 100, which set an admirably high benchmark for the company's future output.

Auto Union was by no means the only producer to try and rebuild plants that had been devastated during the Second World War. By 1945 Daimler-Benz's vast works at Stuttgart was wholly ruined, and it was not fully functional again until 1947. Even then, the factory could produce only one Mercedes car: the pre-war, mid-size 170 saloon. It was not that the 170 was particularly special; it was just that the machine tools for this particular model were the only ones that had survived the allied bombing. However, by 1951 (the year in which German car production reached the pre-war levels of 1938), Mercedes had assembled a roster of innovative and reliable models, headed by the new 300 range. The 300 saloons, the ancestor of today's S-Class, were fast and sleek. Two-door cabriolet and coupé versions followed, the coupé developing into the gull-winged, high-performance 300SL coupé of 1954, allegedly the fastest production car of its day. 'SL' stood for *Sports Leicht* ('Sports Light'), and the 300SL's 3 litre engine and racy looks, developed from a non-production racing car of 1952, made it formidably powerful. The 300SL was also the first mass-produced car to use the fuel-injection system, a feature that enormously improved the engine's performance.[1] Mercedes was fortunate in that it had no home-grown rival in the family and sports car markets until 1954, when BMW finally resumed production at its Munich works. That same year, the far-sighted Mercedes management followed Alfa's example and returned to Grand Prix racing in order to provide a marketing platform for their sportier products. It was not until the 1960s, however, that Mercedes' recovery began in earnest, as their executive saloons – the 190s, the 220s (ancestors of the C-Class) and the 300s – began to conquer the world.

Mercedes was not the first German marque to make a decisive impact on the post-war global car market. Indeed, Stuttgart's success

---

1 Daimler-Benz had already pioneered this system in the wartime DB601 aircraft engine which had powered Messerschmitt's 109 and 110 fighters.

paled into insignificance compared with the astounding reincarnation of what became one of the most celebrated cars of the twentieth century.

In 1945 Volkswagen's enormous Stadt des KdF-Wagens, like most German auto works, lay shattered by Allied bombing. On the evening of 10 April 1945 the plant's SS guards fled into the night and the site's slave-labour workforce – Polish, French, Belgian, Dutch and, of course, Russian – proceeded to destroy what the Lancasters had left. As *Time* magazine, reported, when American troops arrived they found that 'every telephone had been torn from the walls, every typewriter had been sledge-hammered to junk, every file and record had been scattered and burned'. The workers then got uproariously drunk on appropriated schnapps and were only prevented from burning down the whole of the Stadt des KdF-Wagens by the intervention the next day of American tanks, summoned by the plant's chief engineer. The *New York Times* crowed that the US Army had captured 'the German Willow Run'.

By the summer of 1945 the American soldiers had been replaced by a British unit from the Royal Electrical and Mechanical Engineers (REME), as the Stadt des KdF-Wagens – now hastily rechristened Wolfsburg, after the adjacent historic settlement – was allotted to the British zone of occupation. REME found that what machinery had survived the allied bombing and the workers' destruction was due to be transferred to the Soviets as war reparations. Both the Americans – who, in the Morgenthau Plan of 1944,[1] had envisaged the complete eradication of all of Germany's heavy industry and the country's return to a predominantly agrarian, pre-industrial economy – and the Russians, keen to avenge their twenty million wartime deaths, sought to obliterate or repatriate the site. However, the 'people's car' itself was saved by the unlikely intervention of a young REME officer.

Ivan Hirst was a Yorkshire grammar-school boy, who had joined the army in the 1930s after the failure of his optical instruments business during the Depression, and had by 1945 risen to become a REME

---

1 Named after its author, US Treasury Secretary Henry Morgenthau.

major at the age of twenty-nine. It was Hirst who, when the Americans left, was made immediately responsible for the Volkswagen plant. He was well aware that the Americans and Russians had demanded the sale or destruction of the site. Even the Australians had tried to ship what remained of the plant home, while the aged Henry Ford had also waded into the debate, declaring that the factory lay too near to the communist peril to be viable as a future production centre. But having explored the ruined factory, Hirst found a pre-war prototype Volkswagen in a remote workshop and immediately saw its potential. Along with his commanding officer, Colonel Charles Radclyffe, he began to make plans for using the VW as an all-purpose transport for the British army. Some of the plant's machinery had survived the bombing, having been stored in various out-buildings, and some *Kübelwagens* (the military version of the VW) had survived. Cars began to be assembled from half-built *Kübelwagen* chassis and whatever other parts were to hand. The workforce was increased from 250 in April to over six thousand by the end of 1945, and almost eight thousand by August 1946, and by the end of the year the factory was producing about a thousand cars per month. Radclyffe asked engineer Rudolf Ringel to make him a two-seat roadster from old *Kübelwagens* and other spare bits and pieces, while Hirst had Ringel construct a four-door convertible version as his personal staff car.

To Hirst and Radclyffe, the promise of the Volkswagen was enormous. Together they persuaded the British military government to order twenty thousand Volkswagens over three years, and successfully cranked production up to over ten thousand cars by the end of 1946. By the end of 1945 the plant had produced 1,785 cars for the British army and the German post office. Hirst also resisted pressure to change the VW badge, and indeed its name, both of which were still associated in the allies' minds with the Nazi regime. And when a curious delegation from Renault visited the plant, Hirst deliberately showed their delegation the most damaged parts of the site in order to forestall a French takeover.

Predictably, the British car barons did not share Hirst's enthusiasm.

Wolfsburg was offered to Ford of Britain for free, but its chief, Sir Patrick Hennessey, told Henry Ford II in Köln: 'Mr Ford, I don't think what we are being offered here is worth a damn.' Hennessey's rival, Lord Rootes, told Hirst: 'If you think you're going to build cars in this place, young man, you're a bloody fool'. More damningly, Rootes actually judged the car technically deficient: 'The vehicle does not meet the fundamental technical requirements of a motor car. As regards performance and design it is quite unattractive to the average motor car buyer. It is too ugly and too noisy [and] to build the car commercially would be completely uneconomic nonsense. We do not consider that the design represents any special brilliance . . . and it is suggested that it is not to be regarded as an example of first-class modern design to be copied by the British industry.' Star-struck by the curvaceous, high-powered models then appearing in America, Rootes and his fellow car makers could not anticipate that a plain, functional, rear-engined vehicle would work.

Hirst, though, was not deterred, and painstakingly brought the factory back to life, scavenging parts and machinery from nearby industrial plants. He brought in new automotive experts: first, an RAF officer, Richard Berryman, who had worked for GM, and then, in 1947, a native-born German, who provided him with the managerial experience the plant so badly needed.

Heinz Heinrich Nordhoff had been technical director for Opel before the war. He had been partly responsible for the introduction in 1936 of their successful small car, the Kadett, and by 1942 had been made head of the Opel truck factory at Brandenburg. In 1945, however, he was tagged as a Nazi by the Americans to whom he surrendered. (Just before the war's end, Nordhoff had prudently fled westwards and attached himself to Opel's Rüsselsheim factory, in the American zone, rather than remain in Russian-held Brandenburg.) As a result, he found himself reduced to managing a local garage.

Despite Nordhoff's initial scorn for the VW – 'It had more faults than a dog had fleas,' he famously claimed – and his brittle personality, Hirst recognized that the former Opel executive was the man for the job, and appointed him VW's managing director. Soon Nordhoff, too, recognized what Hirst had seen in the car's potential. ('Once the fleas were gone,' he later declared, 'we found we had a pedigree dog.') Under Nordhoff's guidance, production of VWs topped twenty thousand in 1949, the year in which the British military government handed the plant back to the new West German authorities. He also resisted takeover attempts from his former employers at Opel.

Over the next two decades, Nordhoff ensured that the VW workforce shared in the model's success, keeping their wages high, involving them in senior management, and providing them with numerous benefits. The former Volkswagen sceptic became its biggest fan and built assembly plants across the world, from Brazil to the Philippines to New Zealand. By the 1960s, indeed, Nordhoff was widely criticized for being overly obsessed with just this one model. It is surely significant that VW's breakthrough replacement, the Golf, was introduced only after Nordhoff's death.

Nordhoff made the VW into a worldwide phenomenon, and one of the most influential cars of the century. It's nickname, 'the Beetle', was soon being used semi-officially, although it was also known in Germany by a variety of designations according to engine size (1100, 1200, 1500 and so on) and simply as the Type 1 in the rest of the world. In 1967 the American arm of VW bowed to the inevitable and began referring to it merely as the Beetle. And when Porsche's design concept was reworked on a Golf platform in 1998, the result was called the New Beetle.

The first post-war VWs betrayed their military origin. Their high clearance, for example, had been devised for use on the Russian front. But by 1946 they sat lower, and soon were provided with hydraulic brakes (1950), a 'sunroof' (actually a folding canvas strip), synchromesh and quarter-lights (1952), one-piece, oval rear windows (1953), and twin exhausts (1955). A coupé version was introduced in 1955, made by Osnabrück-based car maker Wilhelm Karmann (who had already made a cabriolet version for VW in 1949), with a body designed by Ghia of Turin. A microbus version of the Beetle, the legendary, cavernous Transporter – a van-cum-bus, forever associated with the hippies of the 1960s – appeared as early as 1950, having been adapted from the standard, rear-engined Beetle saloon by VW's Dutch importer Ben Pon.

As its price decreased, so the Beetle's success spread. In 1947 the first export Volkswagen was sent to Holland, and by 1952 41.4 per cent of all Beetles were being exported. By the mid-1950s the Beetle was America's favourite imported car, and in 1954 Volkswagen became, for a time, the fourth-largest car manufacturer in the world, after America's Big Three.

Wolfsburg's astonishing success soon attracted the attention of the Russians. The Soviet zone border was only a few miles to the east of the city and as relations deteriorated between the Soviets and their former wartime allies, Stalin's government began to cast covetous eyes on the phoenix-like plant. In 1948 the Russians even proposed that the border between the Russian and British zones be moved five miles to the west so that Wolfsburg would come under their control. Unsurprisingly, the British military government strenuously objected. The plan was shelved; instead, a year later the Soviets attempted to isolate allied-occupied Berlin from the West.

As the Beetle's fame spread, so the model's phenomenal sales encouraged the ever-cautious Nordhoff to stick to his policy of producing just this one model. In 1954 he declared that, while 'unfounded rumours arise of a new Volkswagen, the blessing lies not in bolder and more magnificent new designs, but in the consistent and tireless redevelopment of every tiny detail until perfection is achieved, which is the mark of a truly outstanding car'. In 1957 he was even more candid, comparing the whimsical design excesses of the American giants with the evergreen, homespun virtues of the plain VW: 'I am far more attached to the idea of offering people something of genuine value, a high-quality product with a low purchase price and an incomparable resale value, than to be continually pestered by a mob of hysterical stylists who try to sell people something which they don't really want.'

By 1960 VW production accounted for 42 per cent of all cars made in West Germany, and VW became a public company. The firm had already been building homes in Wolfsburg for its plant's workforce since 1953, and in 1961 the Volkswagen Foundation was launched to conduct technological research. The same year, sales of the VW reached the five million mark, and a new, upgraded, 1500 variant was launched. Three years later, VW felt confident enough to mount a successful bid for Auto Union, and afterwards converted the latter's Ingolstadt factory to VW production.

Noisier than its British and French competitors on account of its air-cooled engine (which did dispense with the laborious practice of topping up the radiator), the Volkswagen saloon outperformed fifties rivals like the Morris Minor and Renault Dauphine in almost every area. While British and French customers were understandably reluctant to buy this German machine in large numbers, Americans had no such compunction. Nordhoff prioritized exports to the US, and persuaded Chrysler to sell VWs from their showroom network. He also argued, somewhat convincingly, that the success of the cheap but reliable VW was a demonstration to America of West Germany's economic recovery, which would encourage further American investment in the young nation. In 1955, the year in which the millionth VW rolled off the Wolfsburg assembly line, thirty-five thousand Volkswagens were sold to America, making the US Wolfsburg's most important foreign market.

The decision by Carl Hahn, VW's inspirational American chief after 1959, to hire advertising agency Doyle Dane Bernbach (DDB) to produce campaigns of refreshing honesty and humour, helped to establish the Beetle as one of America's favourite cars during the sixties.[1] Shrewdly, DDB's campaign never mentioned Germany, and obviously avoided all references to the car's Nazi origins; instead, it emphasized the car's frugality, fun and lack of pretence. As a result, the Volkswagen became the first American 'people's car' since Ford's Model T. As early as 1960,

---

1 It also helped to cement Hahn's own reputation; in 1982 he became chairman of the entire VW combine.

Americans had bought their half-millionth Beetle, and by 1971 annual sales in the US were topping 1.3 million. In 1972 the Volkswagen overtook the Model T to become the world's best-selling car of all time. Beetle production lasted until 2003, giving the model a staggering sixty-five-year lifespan.[1]

Hirst, meanwhile, had left Wolfsburg for the Allied Military Security Board in Germany, where he became a regional industry director. (Radclyffe handed VW back to West Germany's federal government in September 1949, shortly after Hirst had departed.) He later joined the German section of the Foreign Office in London, where he stayed until 1955 before joining the international secretariat of the Organization for Economic Cooperation and Development (OECD) in Paris. On his retirement in 1975, Hirst returned to England and settled in Marsden, in Lancashire. Modest and reticent, he continued to play down his crucial role in the birth of the Volkswagen and preferred to emphasize instead the importance of Anglo-German collaboration at a time when the German car maker was running rings round its lacklustre British rivals. To his surprise, Hirst became something of a celebrity in his retirement and was increasingly asked to drive new VW models and speak to motor historians. Before his death in 2000, VW management and the people of Wolfsburg often invited him over to guest at major civic and company events. It was at one of these that Hirst was told that the eighteen-inch scale model of a Beetle with which he had been presented when he left Wolfsburg in August 1949 (he had modestly refused a full-sized version) had probably cost more than the real thing.

The Beetle's original designer had, like the car itself, also managed to extricate himself from any association with Hitler's regime. In December 1945 Ferdinand Porsche, having recently been released from an allied prison, was 'requested' to lend his expertise to France, the government of which had initially demanded that the VW plant be bodily moved to

---

1 Although in 1978, by which time the ageing model was faring poorly against newer European and Japanese competitors, production was transferred from Germany to Brazil and Mexico.

France as war reparations. Objections from French car makers put a swift end to this plan, but on 15 December 1945 the French authorities arrested Porsche as a war criminal and held him in prison for twenty months without trial – initially in a former Gestapo gaol in Baden-Baden and subsequently in Dijon. While in prison, as we have seen, he was persuaded to 'advise' the newly nationalized Renault combine on the design of the Renault 4CV.

Porsche was lucky that he did not suffer the same grim fate as Louis Renault. Tried by the French authorities in 1947 (the highly sensitive documents regarding which have, interestingly, been sealed for 100 years), charges against him were suddenly dismissed in August of that year and he was swiftly released. Possibly Porsche had simply revealed too much about French car makers' complicity with their German masters during the war.

Allowed to return to Germany, Porsche's consultancy work for the resurrected Volkswagen operation enabled him to recapitalize his own business. VW's generous offer to sell Porsche's own cars through its dealerships enabled him to sell small numbers of the petite Porsche 356, which his tiny workforce was painstakingly assembling by hand in an old sawmill in Gmünd, in Austria. By 1950 orders were beginning to multiply – 410 Porsche 356s had been made by the end of that year – and the firm's future seemed rosy. Yet Herr Porsche never witnessed his company's subsequent success. Having been presented with a black 356 on his seventy-fifth birthday on 3 September 1950, three months later he suffered a severe stroke. He died on 30 January 1951.

Porsche's 356 is perhaps best known today as the precursor of the legendary 911. While only a modest success in the early fifties, from 1955 the car's sales benefited from a well-publicized tragedy: the death of iconic film star James Dean at the wheel of a Porsche 550 Spyder, a racing model derived from the 356. The fact that Dean was not at fault and was not driving fast – a pickup truck, driven by one Donald Turnipseed, drove head-on into his vehicle – was ignored by the world's media. What caught the public's imagination was the thrill and glamour of the incident.

The wreck of Dean's 550 was even stolen from the train that was carrying it back east.

In 1963 Porsche's 356 was revised and repackaged by the firm's chief designer, Karl Rabe, as the 911,[1] a car that has proved a remarkably enduring success over fifty years. Rabe and his heirs ensured that their cars retained a family resemblance to the 356 of 1948, a policy that encouraged brand recognition and customer loyalty while also helpfully distancing the company from its competitors. As a result, the much sought-after Porsche sports cars of the twenty-first century are still recognizably the descendants of Ferdinand Porsche's post-war phoenix.

Porsche would surely have been delighted that not only does the 911 and its progeny set the gold standard for the modern sports car, but that his humble Volkswagen brand has merged with his eponymous car maker to form one of the world's strongest and most resilient auto combines. His life and legacy remain one of the industry's most remarkable legends.

---

1 The same year, surely coincidentally, 911 began be used as America's SOS telephone number.

8

The Golden Age

The Golden Age of the Car, effectively the mid- to late 1950s, was a fleetingly brief period of optimism, assurance and faith in the future. It was a time when the car came of age; when the automobile appeared to realize its potential and became a defining element of the modern world. More cars than ever were appearing on the world's roads. American car manufacture soared after 1945, and the world looked to the US auto industry to set the standard for design, innovation, comfort – and fuel consumption. New car types were introduced and new market sectors invented. Car ownership in the US alone rose from 45 million in 1949 to 119 million in 1972. Everyone wanted a car, and motoring seemed to offer limitless possibilities – and few drawbacks. No one in the fifties worried about emissions, about carbon footprints, or (except in the months after the Suez crisis in 1956) about the ready supply of cheap oil. Sports cars became popular once more, but were not now merely the preserve of the super-rich. In 1957 the French philosopher Roland Barthes hymned cars 'as the exact equivalent of the great Gothic cathedrals', a claim that fifty years before had been made for the world's great railway termini. Nothing, it seemed, could obstruct the onward march of the motor car.

It was in America that the Golden Age expressed itself most sumptuously and iconically. The American car industry was in far better shape than that of Europe to react to the post-war market. American car plants had never been bombed or shelled, and had been producing civilian automobiles as recently as 1942, whereas European manufacturers had to look back to their 1939 inventories for inspiration. Crucially, too, the big US car makers – even Ford – tried to ensure that their workforces remained solidly behind them, readily agreeing with the UAW's demands for a forty-hour week,[1] and offering pay rises geared to the cost of living. Some European car makers, notably in Britain and France, were still arguing over these principles twenty years later.

American auto producers enjoyed what the rest of the world's car industry greatly envied: a ready-made and burgeoning home market. This gave American manufacturers vast economies of scale. In 1950 the US made 75 per cent of the world's cars, and most of those vehicles stayed at home. By 1955 American cars still represented 67 per cent of the global market, with America's notoriously aggressive car dealers selling an astonishing seven million vehicles per year. Demand in the US was so high, and consumers' enthusiasm so buoyant, that salesmen were able to charge as much as they felt the customer could afford. (This increasingly disreputable practice was ended in 1958 with the Automotive Information Disclosure Act, as a result of which a list price became mandatory.)

Safety was still sidelined, because manufacturers were nervous of implying that their products were dangerous or prone to crash. Seat belts did become more common after 1953, while the spread of one-piece, wraparound windscreens and rear windows increased visibility substantially and reduced accidents. Similarly, the proliferation of fixed roofs – the 'hard-top' was now the rule rather than, as before the war, the exception – made fatal accidents less likely. Yet fashionable overhangs at front and rear made cars more difficult to steer, park and turn, while the fragile roofs of the newly fashionable 'hard-top convertibles' afforded little protection to the occupants in the event of a rollover.

Cars were increasingly seen as objects of beauty, with engineering – and performance – invariably subjugated to style. They could now be

---

1 Admittedly, this was only after crippling strikes in the winter of 1945–6 had brought production at GM, Packard, Chrysler and Nash to a halt.

delivered in a rainbow of colours; and from 1949 (when Buick began to paint its hard-top roofs a different hue from the bodies), two or even three colours could be employed on the same car.[1] American cars, and their European imitators, grew fins and headlamps, and sprouted chrome and wraparound bumpers. They were works of art; in 1951 the historian Arthur Drexler curated an exhibition entitled 'Eight Automobiles' at the prestigious Museum of Modern Art (MoMA) in New York, canonizing the car as a valid art form. Drexler's 'rolling sculptures' included a 1930 Mercedes, a 1939 Bentley, a 1941 Lincoln Continental, a 1948 MG TC, a 1951 Jeep and a 1949 Cisitalia.[2] And after the show was over, MoMA continued to acquire a collection of cars that they deemed instant classics, vehicles as varied as the Jaguar E-Type, John Barnard's 1990 F1 Ferrari, and the tiny Smart Car.

Cars were also now increasingly easy to drive and did not need to be handled by a strongman to get the best out of them. In the US, automatic transmission became widespread after the launch of Chevrolet's two-speed Powerglide system in 1950, while power steering, introduced into top of the range Chryslers and Cadillacs in 1951, had become common for more expensive models by 1955. American family car engines topped 5 litres; although the ability to brake quickly, which became increasingly problematic as wheels got bigger and bigger, got correspondingly worse. Tubeless tyres first appeared in 1948 and were customary by 1956. The use of an ignition key to start the engine electronically – far easier and safer than hand-cranking or the old 'pedomatic' system (manufacturers could never agree on which pedal to use) – was first applied on the Chryslers of 1949 and was widespread by the mid-fifties. Foot-operated parking brakes had reached GM's Buicks and Oldsmobiles by 1953. Powered hoods on convertibles were introduced back in 1942. Lincolns and Cadillacs had power windows by 1946; while GM's top of the range

---

1 From 1954 all of the Big Three began to use two-tone colour schemes for their whole range of models.

2 Drexler hymned 'that quality of animation which makes the Cisitalia seem larger than it is'. But only 170 examples were ever built.

Cadillacs received power seats in 1950, screen washers in 1953 and a power-operated boot lid in 1955. Car radios were less of a novelty by 1955, while some American luxury cars even added record players (not intended to be driver-operated while the car was in motion) to their list of optional extras.

Marques and models became worldwide brands in the manner of Coca-Cola and Heinz. As historian Michael Sedgwick has written, this was 'the age of the stylist, of the "intelligent buyer", and of global thinking'. Cars also began to be associated with national characteristics. American autos were seen as brash, large and loud; Italian as racy and flashy; British as well built and sedate. Never before had car manufacturers become so readily associated with the nation's economic health and technological aspirations. GM's Charles Wilson famously told the Senate armed forces committee: 'What is good for the country is good for General Motors, and what's good for General Motors is good for the country.' Twenty years later, in a more cynical and pragmatic age, few would take such pious corporate sentiments seriously.

By the 1950s it was clear that motoring had effected significant cultural and social change, and had forever altered conventions of travel and leisure. Between 1945 and 1954, nine million Americans moved to the suburbs, and by 1976 more Americans lived in suburbs than in down-town or rural areas, seeking the space, safety, autonomy, greenery and cleanliness that suburban life promised. The first planned out-of-town shopping centre opened in Raleigh, North Carolina, in 1949; the first enclosed, climate-controlled shopping mall appeared in Minneapolis in 1956; and by 1980 there were over twenty thousand major suburban shopping centres across the US.

Post-war, as the car plants got bigger, they moved to green-field sites at the edges of the expanding cities. In Detroit, the opening in 1956 of Eero Saarinen's soaring new GM Technical Centre in the suburb of Warren (which soon became the fastest-growing city in the state of Michigan) merely accelerated the 'white flight' of the inner-city population to the more spacious suburbs. Between 1955 and 1960 the city of Detroit lost as much as 25 per cent of its population to the outlying conurbations. The old city was left with a problem that just grew worse: a poor, predominantly black, residual population, with insufficient tax dollars to afford basic civic amenities. By 2010 what remained of the old city was 81.6 per cent African-American.

As the car liberated vast new travel and leisure opportunities, there was a corresponding growth in franchised motel chains. By 1960 Travelodge alone had 110 branches and the business had doubled in value during the past decade. In 1956 Memphis, Tennessee, witnessed the opening of the first Holiday Inn, a family-friendly, upmarket motel-cum-hotel which offered every facility for tired drivers and crotchety kids. Already, there were 160 Holiday Inns across America in 1960.

The car also engendered a revolution in eating, and is primarily responsible for ushering in the era of fast food. In 1948 the McDonald brothers introduced a drive-in retail method (the 'Speedee Service System'), based on the car assembly line, and a severely reduced menu at their restaurant in San Bernardino, California. But it was not until 1954 that, in association with milkshake-machine salesman Ray Kroc, they opened the first drive-in McDonald's outlet, in a Chicago suburb. Kroc forced the McDonald brothers out of the business, listed the company on the stock exchange, and made a fortune. Eating out was never to be the same again.

In America, by 1960 you could see a movie, buy your lunch and even attend church services in your car. Cars did not weaken church-going habits, as many clerics had feared; they actually strengthened them, as families found they could go to the church of their choice by car. Also by 1960, 90 per cent of American families took their holidays by car; and 95 per cent of visitors to America's national parks came by car.[1]

The vast increase in car use in the US also prompted a massive expansion in the road network. The building of the Los Angeles freeway system started in earnest in 1947 – the oil, car and tyre manufacturers

---

1 By 1970 this amounted to two million visitors per year.

having previously bought up and wound down the city's excellent suburban transit network. In 1949 work began on the New Jersey Turnpike, 'tomorrow's highway built today', the construction of which across miles of precious countryside would save motorists a grand one hour and ten minutes on their cross-state journeys. In the event, the superhighway's existence merely encouraged more driving: once opened, the Turnpike quickly became the busiest toll road in the world. And it hardly bore out state governor Alfred E. Driscoll's claim that it would 'permit New Jersey to emerge from behind the billboards, the hot-dog stands and the junkyards'. As one critic wrote at the time: 'It's difficult to obscure the major features of the landscape altogether, but the Turnpike manages it.'

In 1956 America began to build its interstate highways, funded from taxes on gasoline.[1] President Eisenhower told the American people that there was no choice but to embark on such an ambitious road-building programme if Americans wished to keep their nation great: 'Its impact on the American economy – the jobs it would produce in manufacturing and construction, the rural areas it would open up – is beyond calculation.' More ominously, Eisenhower warned that a vastly enlarged superhighway network was crucial if America was to 'meet the demands of catastrophe or defence, should an atomic war come'. The American Way of Life was equated with the car and the highway: fast new roads were essential to maintain 'the personal safety, the general prosperity, the national security of the American people'.

Eisenhower was hugely proud of his interstate programme, which he later counted as one of his administration's major achievements. As he was delighted to point out in 1956: 'The total pavement of the system would make a parking lot big enough to hold two thirds of all the automobiles of the United States. The amount of concrete poured to form

---

1 That same year, work finally began on Britain's motorway system, in the shape of the Preston bypass (later part of the M6), the London end of the M1 and, rather oddly, the Ross Spur in Herefordshire (now the M50). The initial sixty-mile stretch of the M1, from Watford to Rugby, opened in 1959.

these roadways would build eighty Hoover Dams or six sidewalks to the moon. To build them, bulldozers and shovels would move enough dirt and rock to bury all of Connecticut two feet deep. More than any single action by the government since the end of the war, this will change the face of America.'

Time later called the scheme 'the biggest public works program since the Pharaohs piled up the pyramids'. By 1965 twenty thousand miles of new interstate had opened, at an average cost per mile of $1,141,000. (Some difficult sections cost as much as $50 million per mile to build.) In 1996 the total cost so far of the new interstate system was estimated at $329 billion.

Service areas, rest areas and bridge restaurants were already a feature of American, German and Italian superhighways by 1960. Italian service areas were run by the major oil companies, German *Raststätte* by local business concerns, while in America small roadside settlements grew up by intersection retail areas. Even the British began belatedly to follow suit; on 2 November 1959 Britain's first motorway, the M1, and its first motorway service station, the romantically named Watford Gap services, were formally opened.

The private car was, inevitably, fast displacing public transport. This was particularly true in America where Detroit's car makers had given fate a little helping hand. In 1936, for example, GM had teamed up with Standard Oil of California and Firestone tyres to launch National City Lines, a bus network, using a fleet of GM buses, which aimed to convert electric train and tram lines to bus operation all over California. By 1955 NCL had largely succeeded and one of the world's best transit systems was no more. Meanwhile, GM had built Yellow Coach, later renamed Greyhound, into the nation's largest long-distance bus operator – and in the process made itself the world's largest manufacturer of buses. GM then used Greyhound to undercut the longer rail routes.

The 'motorization' of rail and streetcar lines was common in America's cities by 1950. By 1960 the final streetcar and local railway lines were ripped up in Los Angeles; Pacific Electric's last suburban railway, to

Long Beach, was closed in April 1961; and the city's last streetcar lines axed in 1963. Detroit, too, was robbed of its fine transit system, and by the end of the 1960s was completely dependent on roads.

One thing had not changed, though: the automobile world was still very much a male preserve. By 1960 women were still noticeably absent from any senior role in the car industry – as they still are today. However, women were increasingly targeted by car makers' marketing departments as a growing and important customer base. And women were being targeted by male drivers, too: the wide bench seats of American cars of the 1950s meant that in-car sex was now not only feasible, but positively encouraged.

In 1945 America's Big Three, in contrast to their war-damaged rivals across the Atlantic, were able to slide effortlessly into full-scale production of civilian automobiles. At Ford, after 'a generation of gross mismanagement', in the words of historian James J. Flink, and at a time when the company was losing about $10 million a month, Henry Ford II finally seized the reins of management from his ailing, senile grandfather. Young Henry had never been a star scholar, and had spent much of his early life driving fast cars,[1] and picking up fast women. His family connections got him into Yale, but he struggled academically; his only major achievement in New Haven was to meet and marry a stylish Long Island beauty, Anne McDonnell. But Henry II surprised most observers, and many in his own family, by rising impressively to the challenge. The departing Harry Bennett had told him: 'You are taking over a billion dollar organization here that you haven't contributed a thing to!' But Henry II knew enough to begin clearing out his grandfather's antiquated management team and substituting his own. Having sacked Bennett and closed his iniquitous Service Department, he ostentatiously brought in a clutch

---

1 His favourite was the streamlined Lincoln Zephyr in which he drove around Europe in the summer of 1938.

of six eager young Harvard Business School-trained executives from the USAAF's Office of Statistical Control. The business press soon dubbed the six the 'Whiz Kids', after the University of Illinois' highly successful Whiz Kids basketball team and the popular NBC radio show *Quiz Kids*. Two of these men, Robert McNamara and Arjay Miller, eventually became presidents of the Ford Motor Company, and subsequently McNamara was the nation's Secretary of Defense for much of the 1960s.

Henry II's other new recruit, Ernie Breech, was no Whiz Kid; he was a 49-year-old accountant and born-again Baptist who had been in the car business for twenty years. But Henry hired him as vice president to overhaul the firm's appallingly antiquated and often simply non-existent financial systems. Breech later recalled his horror at finding that Ford's 'financial statements [were] like a country grocery store'; in one department 'they figured their costs by *weighing* the pile of invoices on a scale'. Thanks to Breech's painstaking professionalism, and the Whiz Kids' energy and new ideas, the decrepit auto behemoth was completely turned around. Ford sales doubled between 1948 and 1950, as the Ford Motor Company retook second place from Chrysler in the Big Three's pecking order. By 1954 the firm had carved out a 30.83 per cent share of the US market – the best performance since the Model T years of the 1910s. That year Ford also sold its loss-making French operation to Simca, retaining a 15.2 per cent stake, which it later sold at a sizeable profit to Chrysler.

Henry II was, at least at this stage of life, a good listener, and did not interfere in Ford's day-to-day operations. Overnight, the lazy student seemed to have been transformed, like Shakespeare's dissolute Prince Hal, into a hard-working and serious leader. He seized on Walter Reuther's felicitous phrase, that 'human engineering is just as important as mechanical engineering', and tried to make the Ford factories happier and more productive places in which to work. In his first major speech, in 1946, Henry II declared that 'labour unions are here to stay', and Ford's well-earned reputation for union-bashing was now a thing of the past.

Henry II also oversaw a renaissance in product development. His Lincoln Continental of 1948, Ford's first world-class luxury car, looked good and looked fast (though it wasn't: even 90 mph was a strain). It boasted power windows, power seats, leather trim, blue-painted dials and an unusual palette of body colours, including a lurid 'pace car yellow', derived from the Continental's role as a racetrack pace car at Indianapolis. Seven years later, Henry II startled the entire motor industry when he unveiled Ford's new two-seater. Impressively styled by Frank Hershey and William T. Boyer, the Ford Thunderbird of 1955 was devised by Henry II and his chief engineer, Lewis Crusoe, as a 'personal car' and not a family transport or sports car. With its straight lines and large tail lights it looked like a Ford; but no Ford had ever been packaged like this. It looked rakish and sporty, yet never pretended to be a sports model. In America sports cars were invariably imported from Italy or, more usually, Britain. The Thunderbird was priced below these prestigious imports, initially selling at $2,695 when a Jaguar XK140 cost $3,213. It was given a gutsy V-8 engine, but also provided with the wallowing suspension typical of American family cars of the period. As historian Paul Wilson has commented: 'The complacency with which Thunderbird owners accepted handling comparable to a 1935 Packard certainly indicated that they were not closely allied with the sports car set.' Initially produced only as a two-seat, two-door convertible, in 1958 the 'T-bird' was further distanced from true European sports cars by being provided with two rows of two seats, like a normal sedan. Thunderbird sales soared, as Ford's marketing men backed their product far more wholeheartedly than GM was supporting its rival Chevrolet Corvette. In its first sales year the Thunderbird, priced similarly to its GM rival, outsold the 'Vette by an astonishing twenty-three to one.

The importance that Alfred Sloan's GM vested in styling convinced Henry II that design needed to be prioritized at Ford. In 1955 the corporation increased the size of its styling office, which was given five large new studios in which to work. (GM responded by building a $125 million Technical Center for their styling staff in Warren, complete with artificial lake and huge lawns.) Unfortunately, Ford's design chief, George Walker, was the wrong man for the job. A notorious sexual predator who made strenuous use of the casting couch and habitually sexually harassed women employees, he did not have the access to the top echelons of the corporation that his opposite numbers at GM and Chrysler enjoyed. In retrospect, George Walker was an accident waiting to happen. And in 1957 the accident occurred. The much-trumpeted Edsel range of that year – devised as a wholly new Ford Motors marque, like Mercury and Lincoln – was named after Henry Ford's late son and Henry II's father, in defiance of unambiguous research findings from advertising agency Foote, Cone and Belding (which canvassed its own employees, who picked names ranging from the 'Henry' to the 'Zoom'). The Edsel proved one of automotive history's most notorious disasters. Walker and his project stylist, Roy Brown, wanted to escape from the low-slung horizontality of American cars popularized by GM's Harley Earl, and sought to make the vehicle distinctive and individual. Conventional market research was deliberately ignored; Ford relied merely on vague motivational 'imagery studies' which addressed practical aspects of motoring, such as ease of parking and cost of maintenance, but not the car's appearance or performance. Walker and his colleagues wanted the car to have its own separate 'personality' but were not sure quite what that personality was.

Ford's marketing and public relations men pulled out all the stops for the Edsel's launch. Frank Sinatra and Bing Crosby starred in the TV campaign, singing the car's unbearably smug theme song:

> We want our friends to understand,
> When they observe our car,
> That we're as smart and successful and grand
> As we like to think we are.

Ominously, on the day of the long-awaited launch, carefully prepared news stories trumpeting the virtues of the Edsel were blown off the front pages by Soviet Russia's announcement that it now possessed an intercontinental ballistic missile that could be directed at any target within the United States. When attention was eventually focused on the new car, the Edsel failed to stand up to the media's scrutiny. The top of the range Edsel had been provided with a huge V-8 engine, making it the most powerful production car on the road. But its brakes were poor, it rode badly and its trunk was disappointingly small, despite the car's enormous length (it was as long as the largest Cadillacs). Most importantly, the Edsel looked distinctly odd. With its bulbous paired headlights and ungainly horse-collar grille ('a Mercury pushing a toilet seat', or 'an Oldsmobile sucking a lemon', in the opinion of two contemporary critics), the Edsel proved a disaster. Against projected first year sales of two hundred thousand, Ford sold just over sixty-three thousand. In 1959, the year in which the unpopular vertical grille was abandoned, just forty-five thousand Edsels were sold. The following year the model, and the division that had been created around it, were quietly laid to rest, and Ford wrote off the project's $250 million development cost. When Ford's president, Robert McNamara, left the corporation in 1961 to join John F. Kennedy's newly elected Democrat administration as Secretary of Defense, the Republican opposition constantly derided him as the man responsible for the Edsel. (In truth, McNamara thought that his greatest achievement whilst at Ford was the small, plain, no-nonsense Falcon family car of 1960.) Meanwhile, George Walker, the design chief, was quietly retired in 1961. And the wretched project designer of the 1957 Edsel, Roy Brown, was exiled to Ford's equivalent of the gulag: Dagenham in Essex.

At GM, the conglomerate's chief designer, Harley Earl, reigned supreme, his cars epitomizing the confident, masculine excesses of the automobile's Golden Age. In 1958 he was appointed a company vice president, the first designer in the car industry ever to rise to such exalted rank. He undoubtedly deserved the accolade; assisted by GM's formidable publicity machine, he had made GM's annual model upgrade into a time of national celebration and media frenzy, akin to a major public holiday. In many ways the Golden Age of the Car was also the era of Earl.

Born in 1893, Harley Earl was the son of a Californian coachbuilder, who by his mid-twenties was already designing his own cars, customizing vehicles for the likes of film stars Fatty Arbuckle and Tom Mix. (The car Earl rebuilt for western star Mix featured a real leather saddle fixed to the roof and the monogram 'TM' inscribed all over its body.) In 1919 his promising business was bought up by Cadillac, and Earl became a GM employee. Eight years later, as the first head of GM's new Art and Color Section, Earl was allowed to style GM's cars, and was soon transforming the range from a series of utilitarian-looking vehicles into objects of wonder and envy.

Success did not come overnight for Earl. While his Series 303 La Salle of 1927 borrowed its lines from contemporary Hispano-Suizas – bringing, as historian David Gartman has put it, 'the look of the hand-crafted luxury classics to the factory-produced vehicle' – his first truly radical design, unveiled two years later, was justifiably derided as 'the pregnant Buick'. The highly competitive Earl reacted by denouncing Buick for altering his section's design without his consent.

By the mid-1930s, however, Earl had succeeded in making GM's cars both distinctive and stylish. From 1937, too, he was permitted to work out his more advanced ideas using a series of one-off concept cars. The first, the Buick Y Job, was a low, two-seater sports convertible which piled on the chrome and did without customary running boards (as the Traction Avant had already done) to make the car look longer and leaner – an idiom that Earl soon applied to the whole General Motors range.

Many observers could not understand how he did it. Earl could not draw, and rarely talked to GM's engineers. Indeed, he was abysmal at almost all workplace relationships; he preferred instead to act like a Hollywood director, barking out orders rather than consulting colleagues. A quick-tempered, macho bully, who used his burly frame and great height (he was six feet five inches tall) to intimidate his colleagues, he terrified and tyrannized his immediate staff. Anyone who dared to criticize his judgement was publicly branded a 'fairy' or a 'pantywaist'. While Earl built Art and Color into a large division – in twenty years he increased its payroll from fifty to 1,400 – the section's staff turnover rates under his headship always remained alarmingly high.

The permanently tanned Earl was also very conscious of his public image. He liked to appear in freshly laundered white linen suits, and kept a large wardrobe of clothes at his office that replicated the one at home, enabling him to change into identical fresh clothes whenever he wanted. And he ensured that he always kept well away from public speaking, at which he recognized he was very poor.

The key to Earl's success was not so much his brash, intuitive genius as his excellent relationship with Alfred P. Sloan. GM's chairman treated Earl almost like a son; basking in the great man's favour, Earl was virtually unassailable. Each month he would spend a month with Sloan on his yacht, going over the latest designs. When he returned to Detroit, there was never any argument: Earl's decisions, implicitly backed by the company's president, were final.

Earl used clay, rather than the traditional wood and metal, models to design his cars, allowing him to achieve more rounded and streamlined shapes. He was also helped by US Steel's introduction in 1934 of far larger sheets of metal, which enabled him to replicate his clay models in metal, achieving a continuity of line and a unified look that had previously been impossible. His designs often used well-balanced, prominent trunks to counterbalance his increasingly long hoods, and made great play of chrome brightwork to give, as he put it, 'the look of money'. The recent introduction of unitary monocoque construction, which gave the car greater strength and stability, enabled Earl to make his cars not only longer but also lower, in the manner of Flaminio Bertoni's innovative Citroën.

Harley Earl is forever linked with the be-finned excesses of motoring's Golden Age. His first tail-finned cars appeared in 1948, as part of his long, low Futuramic range. The '48 Cadillacs consciously borrowed their pronounced fins from the twin-boom configuration of the legendary piston-engined wartime fighter, Lockheed's P-38 Lightning – whose designer, Clarence Johnson, had in turn had taken the P-38's combination of twin boom and central nacelle from Fokker's groundbreaking G1 fighter of 1937. (During the war, Earl actually visited a nearby USAAF base, Selfridge

Field, in order to examine the P-38 at close quarters.) In 1949 Earl displayed a whole range of tail-finned autos at GM's first Motorama, an in-house motor show where next year's models were displayed alongside Earl's cherished 'dream cars', the test-beds for future GM designs. Star of the first Motorama was Earl's Le Sabre XP-8 concept car, which borrowed both fins and title from the jet aircraft industry.[1] The Le Sabre was an unashamed homage to North American Aviation's contemporary swept-wing F-86 Sabre jet, with the latter's turbojet engine reflected in the Le Sabre's giant, cyclopean central headlight.

From 1949, Earl's cars became increasingly innovative, and outrageous. The vast grille he introduced to the whole GM range was soon tagged the 'dollar grin' by European motoring journalists, while his 1951 Pontiacs boasted a tripartite grille-fender that gloried in its mass of chrome. His 'hard-top convertibles', long, two-door models with no side pillars to support the roof, looked immensely sophisticated. (They were also, however, very vulnerable in the event of a rollover.) The panoramic windshields of his Cadillacs grew so large that the res-ited A-pillars created a blind spot for any driver looking sharply left. And in 1957 he ensured GM was the first car maker to fit quadruple headlights, which he introduced into the 6 litre, four-door Cadillac Eldorado.

The Eldorado carried all the hallmarks of Earl's Golden Age styling. A low-production convertible, the luxury Eldorado was first released in 1953; during the rest of the decade, the innovations that Earl introduced with the Eldorado tended to percolate down to other Cadillac models and GM divisions a year or so later. The '53 Eldorado was based on a concept car of the previous year, which had been built to Earl's specifications to mark Cadillac's fortieth anniversary. The Eldorado was available in only four colours – Aztec Red, Alpine White, Azure Blue and Artisan Ochre – and was twice as expensive as its convertible Cadillac cousins.

---

1 For the wartime US air force 'XP' denoted an experimental fighter type, but by 1949 the code was being used for 'Experimental Pursuit' jets, such as the Sabre XP-86.

With its wraparound windshield, interrupted belt-line and massive chrome fender studded with giant, shell-case projections, the Eldorado was Harley Earl's most characteristic and influential design. The fender's aggressive protrusions were soon nicknamed 'Dagmars' after a notorious TV personality of the time (played by Virginia Lewis) whose principal asset was her pronounced embonpoint. Dagmars spread from GM to all US car makers and endured for a number of years; the last car to be 'Dagmarred' was the 1961 Lincoln Continental. It is perhaps not coincidental that when the American toy maker Mattel launched its Barbie doll in 1959, her breasts appeared to be derived from the Dagmars on Earl's classic Eldorados.

The General Motors of the 1950s was not just about Dagmarred Cadillacs. When Oldsmobile's wood-panelled station wagon was introduced in 1940, station wagons were considered as ungainly, lumbering homes on wheels, and this sector accounted for a mere 1 per cent of the US car market. Car makers did not like them because the timbered construction of the rear could not be adapted easily to the assembly line, and they were consequently expensive to make. Oldsmobile's new car, however, revolutionized this dormant product category. Its six-cylinder engine guaranteed good acceleration, while its Hydra-Matic automatic suspension provided a smooth ride. Its wooden struts were applied, rather than made integral to its construction, allowing the car to be built wholly on the assembly line. (By the late 1950s station wagons' front doors were often entirely wood-free, mirroring those of a normal sedan.) Families liked them, as they seemed to be an extension of the home. Sensing an opportunity, Ford followed GM's lead, and by 1955 had snatched 47 per cent of this rapidly growing market sector – sufficient for the manufacturer to be dubbed 'the nation's wagon-master' by the motoring press. Ford even made a sporty station wagon-cum-pickup, the Ranchero, in 1957. It would be thirty more years, however, before this prescient idea was to blossom into an international phenomenon.

Far more characteristic of Harley Earl's design philosophy than Oldsmobile's station wagons was his groundbreaking Chevrolet Corvette of 1953. Named after the small naval vessel made famous in the Second World War, it was a rakish, two-seat convertible with a wraparound windscreen and a light, glass-fibre body, which Earl intended as an American rival to the British sports cars that were then taking the US by storm. Unfortunately, the first-generation Corvette failed to live up to the promise of Earl's stylish body. Neither its engine nor its transmission was suitable for a premium sports car. (For some reason, Chevrolet had fitted a two-speed Powerglide automatic gearbox instead of the manual gear change usual for sporty cars.) These factors, together with its mediocre steering and brakes, ensured that its performance proved very disappointing. It was then that the man subsequently tagged 'the Father of the Corvette', Zora Arkus-Duntov, came to the rescue.

Arkus-Duntov had had a colourful life before he arrived at GM. Born in Belgium, of Russian Jewish parents, his mother divorced his mining-engineer father when Zora was young, but then proceeded to live with her new partner (Josef Duntov, another mining engineer) and her ex-husband in an intriguing *ménage à trois*, hence Zora's double-barrelled surname. In 1927 the family moved to Berlin, where Zora, having graduated from the Charlottenburg Technological University in 1934, worked as a mechanical engineer, as well as being, in his spare time, an amateur motorcycle racer. When war broke out in 1939, the Arkus-Duntovs (who had miraculously escaped internment or execution in Germany) fled to France, where Zora joined the French air force. On France's surrender in 1940, he obtained exit visas from the Spanish consulate in Marseilles for his whole family. His new wife, Elfi, who was still living in Paris, made a dramatic dash south to join her husband in her MG, just ahead of the advancing German armies, while Zora and his brother hid in a Marseilles brothel. Zora then conducted the entire family, including his parents, to Portugal and thence by ship to New York.

Arriving in New York, the Arkus-Duntov brothers set up a factory making parts for military and civilian vehicles. This went bankrupt after the war, prompting Zora to move again, this time to Britain, where he helped the niche, Clapham-based sports car manufacturer Allard race its cars at Le Mans in 1952 and 1953. (Zora also returned to continental Europe in 1954 and 1955 to register Le Mans class victories at the wheel of a Porsche.)

Returning once more to the US, Zora saw the new Corvette prototype at 1953's Motorama. While impressed with Earl's fibreglass body, he correctly judged the car's mechanics to be underwhelming. He wrote to Chevrolet's chief engineer, Ed Cole, offering to work on the car, supplementing his offer with a relevant technical paper on motor car speed. Chevrolet was impressed and in May 1953 Zora started as an assistant staff engineer.

Arkus-Duntov made a big difference in Detroit. He upgraded the Corvette's engine, introducing a compact V-8 with a high-lift camshaft and fuel injection. His revamped Corvette soon became the class leader, able to challenge Jaguar, Ferrari and Porsche imports, commanding encouraging home sales, and performing well on the racetrack. Zora himself drove up Pikes Peak in a Corvette in 1956, in order to demonstrate its enhanced performance to the nation's media, and later that year took a Corvette to Daytona Beach and reached a record 150 mph for a flying mile. Despite GM's official prohibitions, Zora continued racing Corvettes well into the 1960s. He retired in 1975, but, aged eighty-three, still took part in the roll-out of the millionth Corvette in 1992 and drove a bulldozer at the ground-breaking ceremony for the National Corvette Museum.

The initial failure of the Corvette demonstrated that Harley Earl did not have everything his own way in the mid-fifties. And in 1955 GM's design supremo found himself beaten at his own game by a rival stylist, one whose employers had for two decades been written off as manufacturers of stodgy, old-fashioned, middle of the road automobiles.

Born in Michigan in 1909 (as Virgil Anderson) to an unmarried mother, and adopted two years later, Virgil Exner majored in fine art at Notre Dame in South Bend, Indiana, the home of Studebaker, until financial worries and his inherent impatience led him to drop out in 1928 after only two years of study. After working for a local art studio, Exner was hired by Harley Earl to work in the Pontiac division of GM, and in 1938 he got his big break, joining Raymond Loewy's already legendary industrial design firm. There, among other projects, he worked on Studebaker cars and, from 1942, on the DUKW and Weasel amphibious trucks made by GM. In 1944, though, Exner fell out with the gifted but mercurial Loewy. By then, Loewy's high-handed manner had also alienated one of his principal clients, Studebaker. As a result, the Indiana car maker promptly hired Exner as their in-house chief styling engineer, infuriating the temperamental Loewy.

Exner was no retiring genius, and could be as difficult as the notoriously short-fused Loewy. Rake-thin, but blessed with film-star good looks, he was flashy and flamboyant in the manner of Harley Earl – but, thankfully, without Earl's bullying manner. Like Earl, he sported a permanent tan, which contrasted with his habitual shiny silver suit and his grey hair – a look that inspired his staff to call him (not entirely benignly) 'the chrome-plated man'.

Exner's greatest stylistic triumph at Studebaker was the 1947 Starlight: a low, European-styled, two-door coupé, whose compact, squared-off elegance was light years ahead of its US rivals. Starlights had pillar supports for the roof, while the hard-top version was confusingly called the Starliner – an odd name for such a compact car.[1] The Starlight/ Starliner received the backhanded compliment of having its lines plagiarized by Ford in 1952 for their Crestline and smaller Lincolns, and by GM for their 1953 Oldsmobiles. Indeed, by 1954 both GM and Ford were aping Exner's squared-off body shape for all their divisional ranges. The 1957 Buick Roadmaster coupé, for example, looked just like the Starlight's stablemate. By that time, though, Exner was long gone.

The retirement in 1949 of Exner's corporate benefactor, Roy Cole, made Exner very vulnerable at the struggling Studebaker, and the designer started to look further afield. Having been promised a job as chief stylist

---

1 In 1956 Studebaker inexplicably rebranded the whole Starlight range as the Hawk, a mundane name that prevented the car maker from being able to cash in on the space craze of the post-Sputnik years.

at Ford, an offer that was then crudely withdrawn (Ford gave the job to the more malleable but more pedestrian George Walker), Exner stomped off to Chrysler. This in turn encouraged Raymond Loewy publicly to take the credit for the whole Studebaker Starlight concept, justifiably enraging Exner.

The US motor industry thought it had seen the last of Exner. Chrysler was notoriously run by engineers, not stylists or marketing men, and its cars were lumpy and old-fashioned compared with their equivalents at GM or Ford. Chrysler certainly led the field in terms of engineering innovation. The firm – now, since Chrysler's death, led by Walter Chrysler's former right-hand man, the engineer K. T. Keller – was the first to introduce disc brakes (in 1949), power steering (in 1951), hydraulic shock absorbers (1952) and the alternator (1960). But it was also, notoriously, a company run by old men; following Keller's retirement in 1950, almost all of Chrysler's senior executives were in their sixties or seventies. And most of them were still plagued by the memory of the failed Chrysler Airflow of 1934, and cited the disaster as an example of what would happen if designers were allowed to take charge (although, as we have seen, the Airflow was a product of the firm's engineers rather than its stylists). Compared with GM and even Ford, Chrysler's styling department was tiny. Everyone was therefore surprised when Exner joined Chrysler, and even more so when the designer was allowed not only to enlarge the firm's styling department but also to assume more and more responsibility for the finished models.

Exner soon showed what he was capable of with the K-310 concept car of 1952. Two-tone bodywork emphasized the long, low, lean lines of this radical design, which featured large, circular headlamps and, at the rear, 'gun-sight' (or 'microphone') tail lights, which projected on stalks. The Chrysler Special and De Soto Adventurer concept cars of 1952–4 developed Exner's vision still further, incorporating elements from contemporary Jaguars and Ferraris. And Exner's sporty, two-seater Dodge Firearrow concept series of 1953–4 prefigured the Ford Thunderbird of 1955, with plain bodywork and eccentric grilles suggesting power and speed. It was while driving a Dodge Firearrow that racing driver Betty Skelton set the women's land speed record in 1954 when she topped 143 mph at Chrysler's proving grounds.

By 1955 Exner felt confident enough to apply his design concepts to mass-production models, and in that year his Forward Look cars hit the salerooms. The Forward Look involved a complete redesign of the whole Chrysler range, from the economy Plymouths to the top of the range Imperials (now constituting a stand-alone marque). Cars were comprehensively restyled in the low, compact and distinctly European idiom Exner had pioneered with his concept cars, complete with tail fins, eyebrowed headlamps, two- and even three-tone colour schemes, and gun-sight tail lights (initially used only for the Imperials but soon applied to all the divisions' products). The Forward Look brand's 'arrow' logo (devised not by Exner himself but by Chrysler's advertising agency, McCann Erickson) was applied to all new Chrysler Corporation cars for the next six years. And it worked: Exner's Forward Look models of 1955 nearly doubled the firm's sales over the previous year.

Exner's genius helped redefine Chrysler's sclerotic divisions. The Forward Look Chrysler 300A, with its tautly styled and impossibly long hood concealing the largest engine produced by any Detroit manufacturer that year, was a great sales success. Two years later, its successor, 1957's 300C, which boasted a yawning front grille and soaring fins, was hailed as an instant classic and sold even better. The Imperials, which looked a little like Exner's old Studebakers – long, low and vaguely European, though more sculpted and chrome-laden than their transatlantic rivals – proved worthy adversaries for GM's Cadillacs and Ford's Lincolns. The 1959 Dodge Custom Royal, with its bullet-like rear lights and huge fins, rejuvenated the staid old Dodge marque. In a similar vein, Exner's Plymouth Fury of 1956 adapted the chassis and body of the nondescript Belvedere hard-top saloon to create a car that could reach 124 mph. Plymouth, previously known only for sedate, 'old lady' cars, shoehorned a 5 litre engine under the Belvedere's hood, improved the gearbox, reduced the doors from four to two, lowered the springs, widened the tyres and added police-type brake linings. The result was a very impressive car, developed at a fraction of the cost of GM's Corvette. All Furys were initially sold only in off-white with gold trim, and their success and style rejuvenated the Plymouth marque. So successful was the experiment that the Fury name was still being used for Plymouths (though with decreasing relevance to the cars' looks or performance) until the late 1970s.[1]

In 1957 Exner cranked the Forward Look up a notch and introduced more rakish lines, taller fins, massively chromed front fenders and quadruple headlights under prominent chrome eyebrows. Now it was GM's and Ford's cars that looked lumpen and old-fashioned. Two years later, as we shall see in the next chapter, Exner's cars were at their most expressive, rakish and influential. Shark-like tail fins were at their height, tail lights had never been more pronounced, headlamps were not only quadrupled but further accentuated with swooping chrome eyebrows, while grilles often stretched across the whole front end of the car. It seemed as if the party would never end.

In retrospect, however, 1959 represented the high point of Chrysler's stylistic exuberance. In 1956 Exner suffered a serious heart attack; the result was that the Chryslers for 1960 and 1961 – planned four or five years in advance – were toned-down and tepid. Exner returned to work in time to reshape the 1962 range, but his vision was derailed when Chrysler's president, 'Tex' Colbert, panicked on hearing that GM's cars for 1962 were to be significantly downsized – a Chinese whisper that turned out to be wholly wrong. Colbert demanded that Exner reduce the size and the cost of his new models late in the design process, while at the same time axeing the upmarket De Soto marque and imposing the undistinguished Valiant compact car on the revived Dodge division. Unsurprisingly, 1962's cars, which Exner derisively termed 'plucked chickens', were universally hailed with a sigh of disappointment. Chrysler had lost its design edge over its Big Three competitors, and its sales dipped alarmingly.

---

1 Stephen King cast a 1958 Fury as the star of his horror novel *Christine* of that year.

The corporation now needed a scapegoat, and Exner was it. Colbert had already gone, fired in 1961 in the midst of sales slumps, suppliers' strikes and stockholder lawsuits.[1] Now Chrysler, demonstrating a lack of business acumen that was to be a wearily familiar feature over the years to come, decided to fire Exner himself. Chrysler's time in the sun was over; the firm descended once more into a slough of mediocrity from which it is only now just emerging.

Exner devoted his remaining years to designing powerboats, while trying in vain to help revive the old luxury marques of Duesenberg, Stutz and Bugatti. His 1966 prototype Duesenberg was pre-ordered by celebrities like Elvis Presley and Frank Sinatra, but when the principal backer pulled out, the project collapsed. At least Exner's Stutz Blackhawk, bankrolled by New York investment banker James O'Donnell, did actually reach production in 1971. But while the Exner-designed steel body was made in Modena, Italy, by Carrozzeria Padana, under its skin the Blackhawk was really only a humble Pontiac – albeit a vastly expensive one, with options including such utilitarian features as mink carpeting, gold leaf, bird's-eye maple and twenty-two coats of hand-rubbed lacquer. With its vast circular headlamps, upright grille and razor-edge belt-line, the Blackhawk was very much an acquired taste for the seriously rich. Elvis bagged the first one, and later bought four more, while subsequent Blackhawk owners included Wilson Pickett, Dean Martin, Elton John, Al Pacino and Paul McCartney. But its sticker price, which stood at over $43,000 by 1973, deterred most other buyers. By the time production of the car finally ground to a halt in 1987, fewer than six hundred Blackhawks had been sold. O'Donnell's brave folly had cost him millions of dollars.

· · ·

---

1 Colbert later faced serious allegations of financial impropriety, which included profiting from his wife's shares in Chrysler suppliers.

The Golden Age in America was not just about the Big Three. In January 1954 Nash merged with (or, more properly, absorbed) Hudson to form American Motors (AMC). AMC's first president was the large and gregarious George W. Mason, Walter Chrysler's former assistant who, despite his substantial girth, was fascinated by small cars. Mason had already inaugurated the small but stylish Nash-Healey, America's first sports car since the war, and at the time of the merger was promoting European-sized 'economy cars' ('subcompacts', as they would be known by the trade today), such as the Austin-made Metropolitan.[1]

Mason died in October 1954, aged only sixty-three. In the ensuing years, however, AMC lived up to his reputation for brave innovation and astonishing prescience. A letter to AMC shareholders in 1959, the year of the Mini, claimed that the introduction of new compact and subcompact cars signalled 'the end of big-car domination in the US' – a prediction that did indeed come true, albeit a decade later. That same year, AMC announced that, as part of its research project into cars powered by alternative fuels, it would be building an electric car powered by a self-charging battery. While the Big Three concentrated on building and consolidating current market share, AMC wisely looked to the future. Unsurprisingly, when the oil crisis of the 1970s sent a seismic shock through the car industry, AMC was the first American car maker to respond with appropriate products, which had already been developed.

The formation of AMC was not the only US auto merger of 1954. That year the venerable firm of Packard acquired the equally renowned marque of Studebaker. Packard had been founded in 1900 as a manufacturer of upmarket luxury cars, and by 1929 Packards were outselling Cadillacs by three to one. Yet the firm never recovered from the Great Depression, during which time its share of the luxury car market fell from 10 per cent to 2 per cent. And after the war Packard squandered its

---

1 The Metropolitan's engine boasted only 1200cc (it was replaced by a heftier 1489cc version in 1957) and its styling was distinctly European; AMC sold ninety-seven thousand of these curious cars before production was discontinued, perhaps prematurely, in 1961.

premium heritage, and its savings, by completely failing to anticipate the market: instead, it tried to sell cheap cars, a market with which neither its engineers nor its dealers (nor, as it turned out, its customers) were familiar; it persisted with restyled 1942 models long after their sell-by date; and it tried, but failed, to break into the lucrative taxicab market, over which the Big Three had a stranglehold. By 1954 Packard had irretrievably diluted its pre-war image as a luxury car maker and found itself losing market share, profile and reputation.

Studebaker, too, had almost gone under during the Depression. The company's charismatic president, Albert R. Erskine, had assumed the recession would be brief. In 1928 he had boldly bought the bankrupt firm of Pierce-Arrow of Buffalo, best known for its luxury cars and film-star customers; and even at the height of the Depression he not only bought the struggling White Motor Company but also continued to pay out huge dividends to Studebaker shareholders. In 1933 Erskine launched a new luxury Pierce-Arrow model, the streamlined Silver Arrow, priced at an astronomical $10,000 in the year of Roosevelt's New Deal. It was hardly a surprise that only five Silver Arrows were sold – nor that the disaster would take Studebaker down with it. The firm duly went bust, and Erskine tragically committed suicide. Two years later the banks managed to refloat Studebaker's corpse, but the company was never to be quite the same again.

Studebaker did enjoy a brief respite in its fortunes during the Second World War, when it produced a range of successful military vehicles for the US Army. By 1950 the firm had also managed to carve out a niche reputation as the manufacturer of radical, 'European' cars designed by the already legendary Raymond Loewy and the rising star of auto design, Virgil Exner.

Loewy had been born in Paris in 1893 and had received the Croix de Guerre for his wartime service after 1914. In 1919 he emigrated to America, owning only the French officer's uniform he stood up in, and became a window dresser for Macy's department store in New York. In the late 1920s he moved into design; his first big break was the commission to redesign the Gestetner duplicating machine, and by 1930 he was success-ful enough to open offices in London and New York. Thereafter Loewy applied his talents to Pennsylvania Railroad locomotives, Greyhound buses, Coldspot fridges and cigarette packets (the classic Lucky Strike logo was his invention). In 1936 he also began work as a consultant for Studebaker, and designed the company's new 'lazy S' logo, as well as its new car ranges.

The much-fêted alliance between Packard and Studebaker of 1954, however, did not possess the strength of AMC. It was more a case of two castaways clinging to each other as the waters rose. Thus, as America's Big Three entered into their Golden Age, Studebaker slithered down the slipway to oblivion. The Loewy/Exner Starlight may have been the incar-nation of European sophistication, but it also helped Studebaker to a new sales low as the firm's US market share dipped below 3 per cent. The new Studebaker-Packard corporation proudly rebuffed offers of merger from AMC, but in 1959 the historic Packard marque was terminated and Studebaker-Packard became simply Studebaker. The irascible Loewy, meanwhile, was brought back to design the new Avanti. But Loewy's distinctly odd-looking, goggle-eyed car was not a success, and what lit-tle chance the model had was scuppered by serious production delays. Unveiled in 1962, the Avanti was not delivered to dealers until the fol-lowing year; even when it was picked as the pace car for the Indianapolis 500, the ultimate accolade for fast American cars, on the day of the race Studebaker could not even supply one working car and had to substitute a Lark family compact – a highly public mistake that made Studebaker the laughing stock of the motor industry. The 1964 Avantis were the last of the line, although for years cars continued to be made by enthusiasts from left-over spare parts.

Following the demise of the Avanti, Studebaker relied on the ungainly, lumpish Lark compact for most of its income, and was pre-dictably disappointed. In an effort to reverse plummeting sales, the firm also appointed a new president. Youthful, burly ex-marine Sherwood Egbert was determined to make Studebaker more competitive and called upon his friend, industrial designer Brooks Stevens, to revamp the Lark. Milwaukee-born Stevens had developed his drawing skills while stricken with polio as a child, and the home furnishings business he created in 1934 (the year in which he also became a founder member of the Industrial Designers Society of America) had already made him enough money to open his own automotive museum in Mequon, Wisconsin.

Stevens attempted to apply Alfred Sloan's concept of planned obsolescence – 'instilling in the buyer', as he put it, 'the desire to own something a little newer, a little better, a little sooner than is necessary' – to Studebaker's corporate strategy. His 1962 Lark had a less stubby body, streamlined side panels, a modernized interior and a large, Mercedes-like grille, added to what was now a far more purposeful nose – all achieved on a minuscule budget. Stevens worked the same magic again in 1964, creating a squared-off, Fiat-like car which the company rebranded in a variety of guises (Challenger, Commander, Daytona and Cruiser), having sensibly dropped the Lark badge. But not even Stevens's artifice could save the ailing company. In 1962 Egbert was diagnosed with cancer, and he resigned as president in November 1963.[1] A month after his resignation, Studebaker closed its historic plant in South Bend, Indiana; three years later it shut its one remaining factory, in Hamilton, Ontario, and Studebaker disappeared altogether.

Brooks Stevens lived until 1995. He is best known today not as the designer of the last Studebakers but of the classic Wienermobiles of the late fifties, bizarre promotional vehicles that used a conventional car chassis (in Stevens's case, the chassis of a Willys Jeep) to support a giant Oscar Mayer wiener sausage. By the 1980s, in fact, Stevens's Mequon museum site was being employed as the production centre for the entire Wienermobile fleet.

'From Studebaker to Wienermobile' could easily serve as the subtitle of a history of the car industry in the second half of the twentieth century.

---

1 Sherwood Egbert died in 1969, aged only forty-nine.

For, as we shall see, the hopes and dreams embodied in the Golden Age of the motor car turned out to be as long-lasting as yesterday's hot dog. How and why the West's motor manufacturers squandered the impressive achievements of this glittering era comprises one of the great 'what ifs' of history. But before the decline came one last outburst of outstanding achievement: the models of that *annus mirabilis,* 1959.

9

Zenith

Nineteen fifty-nine, in the words of cultural historian Fred Kaplan, was the year 'when the shockwaves of the new ripped the seams of daily life ... when categories were crossed and taboos were trampled, when everything was changing and everyone knew it – when the world as we now know it began to take form'. The Russians' Lunik 1 spacecraft became the first man-made object to break free of earth's orbit. (Later that same year, Lunik 2 managed to crash-land on the moon.) A Boeing 707 made the first non-stop air crossing of the Atlantic. Frank Lloyd Wright's revolutionary Guggenheim Museum was opened on New York's Fifth Avenue. Dave Brubeck issued his jazz album *Time Out*, whose classic track 'Take Five' came to symbolize the age. Senator John F. Kennedy launched his presidential campaign; Fidel Castro's advance prompted President Batista to flee Cuba; and Tibet rose up against Chinese rule.

It was also the year when the Golden Age of the Car reached its apogee, the zenith of the automobile. New models demonstrated an awareness of the demands of the consumer and of the primacy of engaging, contemporary styling. Superhighways were being built across the developed world. And oil had never been so cheap. Just a decade later, Western consumers were looking back to this era of plenty, confidence and innocent with nostalgia and regret.

The jet-age symbolism of the cars of America's 1959 model year was unmistakable. Chrysler's '59 De Sotos were advertised as 'personal flying machines', with 'flight-styled instrument panel', which consumers were asked to 'pilot'. The tail of the Cadillac Eldorado of that year was dominated by vast, circular finials which were shaped like jet-plane air intakes – but which actually did nothing. Buick's Electra boasted huge, canted wings which swept forward to shelter diagonally stacked head-lamps. And Harley Earl's Motorama concept car of 1959, the Firebird III, incorporated no fewer than seven wings and tail fins, substituted a joystick for the steering wheel, and featured a double bubble canopy which looked as if it were out of a jet fighter or a science-fiction movie, as well as cruise control, air conditioning, aircraft-style air-drag anti-lock brakes, an 'ultra-sonic' key which signalled the doors to open, and an automated guidance system to avoid accidents. Driving this futuristic concept vehicle was the nearest Earl would ever get to flying an aircraft.

Harley Earl's 1959's Cadillacs represented the ultimate in Golden Age confidence. The great styling race between Detroit's Big Three had reached its height, and the Cadillacs resembled futuristic rocket ships for Dan Dare or Flash Gordon, with massive rear fins which stood 42 inches above the ground. The luxury brand's flagship model, the Eldorado Brougham, was hand-made by Pininfarina in Turin and cost more than the Rolls-Royce Silver Cloud.

The biggest fan of Earl's Golden Age Cadillacs was Elvis Presley. As soon as he could afford it, Elvis bought himself a pink and white 1955 Cadillac, and soon afterwards presented a similarly coloured Cadillac Fleetwood 60 to his mother. 'I don't want anybody in Hollywood to have a better car than mine,' he declared, adding: 'A Cadillac puts the world on notice that I have arrived.' Thereafter Elvis acquired a long line of customized Cadillacs, ending with a 1977 Seville. His 1956 Eldorado was supplied with white pleated leather upholstery and purple-dyed mouton-fur carpets. Although he never seems to have bought one of the classic Cadillacs of 1959, Elvis's 1960 Series 75 Fleetwood Limousine more than made up for this omission. Gold-plated inside and out (24-carat gold leaf was applied internally to the phone, shoe buffer, refrigerator and ten-disc automatic record player, TV and tape deck, and externally to the car's hubcaps, wheel covers, headlight rims and front grille); the forty coats of exterior paintwork incorporated real pearls, diamond dust and oriental fish scales; the cabin floor was carpeted in white fur, and gold lamé drapes were used to cover the back windows and to separate the front and back seats. A Judy Holliday film of 1956 had cast the eponymous *Solid Gold Cadillac* as America's ultimate status symbol; now Elvis possessed almost exactly that. RCA Records even sent the car itself on tour, attracting huge crowds. Today Elvis's Fleetwood sits smugly in the Country Music Hall of Fame in Nashville.

The Chevrolets of 1959 looked almost as futuristic as their Cadillac cousins. At the top of the range was the full-size Impala. In many ways the quintessential Golden Age car, the '59 Impala was a resonant symbol of the era before safety concerns and the need for fuel economy encouraged the American consumer to look to smaller, more frugal and better-protected models. The Impala had been first introduced in 1958 but was completely redesigned by Earl's department for the following year. In front was a vast hood extending from a curved, wraparound windscreen; aft were vast bat-wing fins (which projected sideways rather than up), sheltering huge teardrop tail lights. The new Impala was lower and wider, and heavier, than its predecessor, with a hefty 42 foot turning circle. And there were now numerous versions to choose from; the four-door hard-top and four-door sedan were complemented by a convertible and a two-door Sport Coupe with a shortened roof-line and wrap-over back window which promised a 'virtually unlimited rear view'. The hard-top Sport Sedan had a huge, pillar-free back window under what Chevrolet described as a 'flying wing' roof-line. And under the hood, a variety of V-8 engines offered from 185 to 315 hp, assuming you had already rejected the cheaper, wimpish, six-cylinder version. Inside, Impalas were equipped with front and rear armrests, an electric clock, dual sliding sun visors, and a contoured instrument panel with deep-set gauges, positioned below hoods to prevent glare. You could even add a new Flexomatic six-way power seat. Small wonder that the Impala rapidly became America's

most popular car and helped Chevrolet back to the number one spot as
the nation's favourite automotive brand.

Priced just below the Impala was its cousin, the Chevrolet Bel Air.[1]
The Bel Air name was now six years old, but 1959's Bel Air was like nothing that had gone before – and nothing else on the road. The car's headlamps were placed as low as the law would allow, and it was longer than
ever; at 211 inches (5,400 mm) long, the Bel Air was 11 inches (280 mm)
longer than even the 1957 model. At the front, quadruple headlamps
were sited beneath huge air intakes, at either end of a wide, grinning
grille which was partitioned to look like shark's teeth. (The apex of each
vertical partition on the grille was emphasized with an aggressive cylin-
drical projection, which would have made mincemeat of any pedestrian
unlucky enough to be sandwiched against the car's front end.) Behind the
elongated hood, the Bel Air's roof swooped down in a single, graceful arc
from the wraparound windscreen to alight on the rising tail fins. At the
rear, two enormous bat wings rose up above giant teardrop lights. Never
again was car design to be so expressive or so assertive.

Over at Chrysler, Virgil Exner's Forward Look still held sway. Excess
was *de rigueur*: tail fins had never been so prominent, chromed eyebrows
never so sweeping, chrome fenders never so boldly sculpted, tail lights
never so bullet-like, and colours never so daring. Headlamp eyebrows
for the 1959 Plymouths were undulated to make the cars seem even
more anthropomorphic. Dodge's flagship car for 1959, the Custom
Royal Lancer four-door hard-top, was more bedecked with chrome
than any other Chrysler model, before or since. The Royal Lancer's vast
fins, which started at the front of the rear doors, sheltered two pairs of
giant, chrome-encased projecting tail lights, while its pillar-less glasshouse incorporated huge wraparound front and rear windshields, and
its vast front grille was topped with quadruple headlamps, shielded
under chromed eyebrows which swept majestically down to the front
wheel arches.

---

1 The model range from which the Impala had sprung the previous year.

Even Ford dipped a cautious toe into the pond of Golden Age styling. Ford's '59 Thunderbird boasted Exner-style quadruple headlamps, fins and an aggressive-looking front end, while its fender framed a large, ovoid grille. In 1959, even Ford's mid-price Mercurys looked rakish. Soon, however, the company's stylists settled down to what they did best: making unexciting but reliable, mid-size family cars. Their 1960 range largely abandoned fins and chrome, as Ford's designers scuttled back to straight lines some time before their Big Three rivals similarly rediscovered the virtues of sober modesty.

Nineteen fifty-nine in Britain was a motoring *annus mirabilis*, too: the year of the Mini, the Ford Anglia, the Triumph Herald and the impeccably styled Jaguar Mark 2 – four of the most innovative (and handsome) cars in the world. The Mini in particular broke new ground and has deservedly come to be regarded as one of the world's classic cars, one which changed the face of motoring and transformed how cars were configured.

BMC boss Leonard Lord was determined to develop a 'proper' car to trounce the Germans; in 1957 he demanded that BMC's designer Alec Issigonis 'drop everything . . . and build me something to beat the bloody bubble cars', and he championed Issigonis's Mini from the start. Yet the Mini was not the first innovative small car that BMC produced. In 1958 the combine had launched the new-look Austin A40, a revolutionary 'two-box' design which was a sharp contrast to the 'three-box' pattern of bonnet/hood, glasshouse, and boot/trunk to which most cars then conformed. The A40's snappy, angular design, commissioned from Giovanni Battista Farina's Turin-based Carrozzeria Pininfarina coach-building operation, was light years away from the comforting, rounded shapes that BMC loved. And with its rear access door, BMC had, in the A40, effectively created the world's first hatchback.

'Pinin' Farina was born in Turin in 1893 and began work for Fiat aged only seventeen. His infant nickname 'Pinin' – 'baby' in the Piedmontese dialect – stuck with him all his life; indeed, in 1961 he legally changed his name to Battista Pininfarina. Depressed by the lack of work in Mussolini's Italy, Farina, along with thousands of Italians, emigrated to America. However, he found the US little better; declining the offer of a menial job at Ford, he soon returned to Italy to work in his brother's body shop. Farina founded his own company in 1930, but it was only after the Second World War that his business really took off, when he was asked to design car bodies for Fiat, Lancia, Alfa Romeo and, after 1952, Ferrari. In 1957 BMC decided to try and enliven their products by introducing some Italian visual flair and, controversially, invited Farina to help design not only the A40 but also the new Morris Oxford and its BMC stablemates, the Austin Cambridge, the MG Magnette and the Riley 4/68. Peugeot had the same idea, and ended up with the Pinfarina-styled Peugeot 404 of 1960 – a car that looked strikingly similar to Farina's Morris Oxford.

So pleased was BMC with Pininfarina's work on the A40 that they originally added a suffix, Farina, to the car's official name. Sadly, the car's underpinnings did not live up to the promise of Pininfarina's crisply styled body. Underneath, indeed, the car was virtually identical to the old-fashioned if loveable Noddy car, the A30/A35, which had been introduced by Austin in 1951 as their answer to the Morris Minor. The A40 even shared the A35's 948cc engine and running gear; only in 1962 were these features updated. For its breakthrough model, BMC needed a wholly new concept. And for that it turned to more local talent.

Alexander Arnold Constantine Issigonis was born in 1906 in the Aegean port of Smyrna, then part of the Ottoman Empire. His father was a British citizen; this stroke of luck meant that, when Smyrna was threatened by the nationalist Turks under General Mustafa Kemal in 1922, the Issigonis family was able to find refuge first in British-owned Malta and later in Britain itself. This last move was, sadly, achieved without Alexander's father, who had died in a Maltese hospital in June 1923. Thereafter, Alec (as he now called himself) lived with his mother for the next sixty-six years.

Issigonis went to work as an engineer for Humber in Coventry.[1] Then, in 1936, he moved (along with his mother) to what was at the time the largest car factory in Europe, the Morris plant at Cowley. At the time, his favourite car was not a Morris but the 'baby car' made by Morris's bitterest rival, the Austin Seven. Issigonis's two greatest creations, the Morris Minor and the BMC Mini, were direct descendants of this influential little car.

Even his strongest admirers would not deny that Issigonis was a difficult man. As motor historian Graham Robson has written, to most observers he seemed 'a haughty, single-minded individual who was unable to accept that anyone else's ideas were equal to his own', who 'was . . . scornful of cost-cutting managers' and 'put passenger comfort way down his list of priorities'. He was, concludes Robson, a 'remote, ascetic and arrogant engineer'. Nor did Issigonis seem very impressive on paper, having only a diploma in mechanical engineering to his name. Leonard Lord accurately observed that the designer had no people skills whatsoever, and 'wasn't able to have a conversation without a pen in his hand'. Even after the phenomenal success of his Mini design, Issigonis continued to live with his mother in a modest flat on Five Mile Drive, off the Oxford ring road, commuting to Birmingham by car. He went to bed at 9 p.m. every night, appears to have been asexual in inclination, and spent most of his leisure time playing with his giant model railway in the Edgbaston bungalow he inhabited during the week. Yet unsentimental, distant and notoriously caustic as he was, he nevertheless made lasting friendships outside the car industry. Peter Ustinov, who counted himself a friend of Issigonis's, likened 'the wide-eyed innocence of the Mini's headlights, an innocence which is at once childish and highly sophisticated' to the personality of its creator.

One of Issigonis's principal ambitions was to maximize the interior space in the prototype Mini. He was determined to find space for four

---

1 The Humber marque, associated in the post-war years with solid, well-built executive saloons, was inexplicably slaughtered when Chrysler took control of Rootes in 1968.

full seats – not two barely usable back seats, as in Giacosa's Fiat 500. To do this he employed thin-sectioned sliding windows, sited the engine so it lay transversely across the car, not in line with it, and placed the transmission under, rather than alongside, the engine. The result was that, although it was over 20 per cent smaller than the Morris Minor, the Mini offered its passengers far more space.

Issigonis also saved both weight and space by starving the Mini of accessories. His ascetic nature did not comprehend the concept of customer comfort, and he fought long and hard to avoid wind-up windows (even though water collected in the runners of his sliding window panels) and more comfortable front seats (insisting that the excessively upright rake of the seats was necessary to stop the driver falling asleep). The Mini's revolutionary hydrolastic suspension, though, was the creation not of Issigonis but of his talented colleague Alex Moulton.

As we have seen, Lord had already granted a BMC styling consultancy to Pininfarina of Turin, and now he sought the Italian's advice on the Mini. Both Battista Farina and his son, Sergio, generously hailed Issigonis's design as 'unique' and told Lord 'not to change a line'. Much to his credit, the BMC chairman stood by Issigonis's revolutionary design all the way, even when senior managers preached caution.

The new Mini was smaller, lighter, more spacious, faster and far more manoeuvrable than all its rivals. It was only 10 feet long but seemed much bigger than genuinely larger cars like the Minor and the A40. It was significantly cheaper than the VW Beetle, the Renault Dauphine, the Fiat 600 and the Ford Anglia, boasted a top speed that bettered all except the Anglia,[1] and offered a rate of acceleration that was by far the best in its class.

Predictably, much of the conservative management of BMC had not wanted the radical little car in the first place, preferring the traditional certainties of the Morris Minor and the Austin Cambridge. (At the top of this long list was Lord's deputy, George Harriman, who was later to prove

---

1 Though only in 1959; the Mini soon caught up in that area, too.

an ineffectual company chairman after Lord's retirement.) Now BMC's top brass were nervous about how to badge and market the prodigy with which they found themselves saddled. Their unhappy compromise was to issue the car in two corporate guises, which both appropriated the names of tried and trusted former models. One version, made at both Cowley and Longbridge, was called the Morris Mini-Minor; while its Austin-badged twin was dubbed the Austin Seven, in memory of a car last made in 1939. In reality, the two versions differed only in the design of their front grilles. Even the Austin and Morris press offices – still, despite the merger of 1952, run entirely separately from each other, in an appalling waste of corporate resources – were uncertain how to market the new car. Austin's executives uncertainly concluded that it was aimed at the female driver. 'Women of the world rejoice,' declared Austin's advertisements, 'in a man's world, a car has been designed with women in mind.' Their opposite numbers at Morris, however, preferred to emphasize the new car's historic pedigree, bizarrely invoking Nelson, Samuel Johnson and Leonardo da Vinci in their eccentric promotional campaign. No wonder consumers were confused; indeed, it is astonishing that BMC sold any Minis at all in 1959. Before long, however, Austin's marketing department changed tack and hired the famous racing driver Stirling Moss to try out the car. (Moss liked it, although even *he* complained about the uncomfortable driving position.) And for the first time in the British car industry, a manufacturer began to personalize a car. Austin's adverts gradually began to celebrate not just the Mini but also the talented 'genius' behind its design. Issigonis found himself a lionized celebrity. Unfortunately, he came to believe all the media hype and became even more reluctant to work with his BMC colleagues.

In 1962 it was agreed, at least at Longbridge, to abandon the pretence that the Mini had been developed from past successes, and the Seven brand name was at last dropped. Cowley dragged its feet, though, and it was not until 1967 that the Morris Mini-Minor became simply the Morris Mini. Why Harriman's BMC management did not intervene long before to end these damaging inconsistencies remains a mystery. Only in 1969, after Harriman had weakly acceded to BMC's absorption into British Leyland, was the decision finally taken to abandon the now meaningless marques altogether and let the strong Mini brand stand on its own.[1]

The Mini was kept in production until October 2000, a lifespan of forty-one years. In retrospect, the barely modified model may have lived a little too long and should have been either significantly updated or else quietly put to sleep when it reached its twilight years. The Mini's sales peak of 318,475 in 1971 was never matched over the next three decades; sales dropped significantly at the end of the 1980s and by 1997 Minis were selling less than fifteen thousand per year. Altogether, though, over 5.3 million Minis were sold between 1959 and 2000.

The Mini soon became a cult. Like the Austin Seven, it was classless and gender-free, proving as popular with women as with men. It was the car of the moment. Issigonis lent a Mini to his new friend, the society photographer Anthony Armstrong-Jones, who was soon filmed bowling along in it along with his fiancée, Princess Margaret. Soon all the glitterati of the sixties – the Beatles, Twiggy, Marianne Faithfull, Peter Sellers, Christine Keeler – were being filmed or photographed driving Minis.

The Mini also became an unlikely sporting star. In 1961 Issigonis collaborated with racing car manufacturer John Cooper to produce a gutsy, racing-friendly Mini Cooper. The high-performance 997cc car was a big success, as was the even more powerful S version launched two years later. By the mid-sixties the Mini Cooper S had become the most successful competition car in Europe for road races and rallying. When a Mini won the Monte Carlo Rally in 1964, European sales of the diminutive auto soared.

In 1966 the model reached its racing peak, when Minis came first, second and third in the Monte. Yet BMC's finest were then mysteriously disqualified by the French authorities for carrying 'illegal headlamps', an arbitrary ruling that allowed the French Citroën team to claim victory.

---

1 The timeless strength of the brand was also to enable BMW to describe their up-to-date 2004 version of the old classic merely as the Mini.

(Citroën's driver was thoroughly embarrassed to receive the winner's trophy and vowed never to race for the Citroën team again.) The Mini's riposte was simply to win the Monte again in 1967. That same year the Mini Cooper proved equally adept at the new British sport of rallycross, a short-course (and therefore easily filmed) combination of track and off-road racing invented by Independent Television to fill a gap in its Saturday afternoon schedule.

Mini Coopers were also the stars of the 1967 movie *The Italian Job*, which was devised as a celebration of the Mini as much as of Swinging Britain. Once again, though, Britain's motor industry failed to rise to the occasion. As the film's star, Michael Caine, later wrote: 'We went to the British Motor Corporation, as it was then, and asked if they would donate some [Minis] in return for the publicity the Mini would receive. They were fantastically snooty about it and said they could only manage a token few. Fiat, on the other hand, completely got the idea, and offered as many cars as we wanted, including sports cars for the mafia scene. No wonder the British car industry went down the toilet . . .' The excuse for the film's eponymous 'job' was, ironically, a looming Chinese deal with Fiat. And Fiat's far-sighted management ensured that their products – and particularly the Mini's great rival, the splendid 500 – were prominently showcased in the traffic chaos of Turin which was the film's centrepiece.

In the event, BMC's negligence extended far beyond its cinematic parsimony. Incredibly, the runaway success of the Mini on both road and track never made BMC rich – and it sowed the seeds of British Leyland's ultimate collapse. Leonard Lord's typically brusque dictum was: 'If you build bloody good cars, they'll sell themselves.' Reflecting his boss's decidedly old-fashioned approach to auto manufacture, Alec Issigonis refused to let either BMC, Austin or Morris have any say in the appearance of the car, and was particularly scornful of cost accountants, whom he continued to keep at arm's length. Financial experts from other car makers across the globe puzzled how BMC could sell such a revolutionary car so cheaply. Ford calculated that each Mini cost £5 more to make than a Ford Anglia, but was priced at £30 less. And they were right: BMC had not costed the car properly. But when Ford executives generously shared their findings – Patrick Hennessey even phoned Harriman personally to inform him of his team's findings – BMC did not want to know and stuck their corporate heads in the sand. BMC preferred, like Herbert Austin, to concentrate on maximizing sales rather than ensuring profit per unit, and felt they had to make the Mini cheaper than all its rivals. Car executives across the world were soon familiar with the joke about Mini cars making mini profits, and despite the outstanding success of both the Mini and Issigonis's next project, the best-selling 1100/1300, BMC lurched into the red. As Issigonis's biographer, Gillian Bardsley, has astutely noted: 'In the final analysis men like Leonard Lord and George Harriman paid too much attention to the engineering of their products and too little attention to the efficient running of the business. They operated on instinct, barely attempting to understand the market. They paid scant attention to the pricing of their products, which were often too cheap, nor did they undertake sufficient capital investment or plan properly for the future.'

Bardsley laid much of the blame for the ultimate the collapse of the British car industry at the door of Lord and Harriman. The former exacerbated divisions within BMC by favouring Austin over the former Nuffield marques, while Harriman 'took little personal interest in what was going on at shop floor level, a sharp contrast to the days when Herbert Austin and William Morris would wander round the assembly halls making sure they kept in touch with their workforce'.

The charming Harriman always did as he was told by Lord, which is why the two managed to get on. Bardsley is surely correct when she asserts: 'Harriman turned the growing gap between the bosses and the workforce into a yawning chasm. The more the management team tried to impose its will, in an ever more arbitrary fashion, the more alienated the workers became, the more inclined to strike over the most trivial issues.'

Harriman was also guilty of allowing one of William Morris's less endearing legacies, his suspicion of graduate executives, to be perpetuated by BMC's management throughout the 1950s and 60s. The company steadfastly believed in the blinkered precepts that educated people were more trouble than they were worth, that the best route to the top was from the very bottom, and that training was a dirty word. British car makers were thus intellectually ill-equipped to deal with the difficult years following the oil crisis of the 1970s, with the result that the nation's auto industry began to implode.

Ford refused to be outmanoeuvred by the Mini. Their Anglia of 1959, while it always remained overshadowed by the appeal of the Mini (which consistently outsold the Anglia by three to two), was itself no mean achievement. Its 998cc engine delivered far more than the basic Mini's feeble power plant, its suspension was superior, and its handling was more than a match for the Mini's. Even more importantly, each Anglia made Ford a tidy profit.

Ford of Britain had been tightly managed since 1956 by its chairman, Patrick Hennessey, an Irishman who had run away from home to join first the British army and, after the First World War, Ford's new factory in Cork. In 1931 Hennessey was moved to the new Dagenham plant as purchasing manager; by 1939 he was general manager, and during the Second World War he proved so helpful to the Ministry of Aircraft Production that he was knighted in 1941. When Ford of Britain's chairman retired in 1956, the easy-going Hennessey – whose inclusive and respectful managerial style was far removed from that of his abrasive contemporary, Leonard Lord – was the obvious candidate to succeed him. Hennessey in turn promoted his young protégé Terence Beckett as styling manager, purchased the important supplier Briggs Motor Bodies, increased capacity at Dagenham, and introduced the American idea of 'product planning' – a methodical system of developing not just individual models but a whole car range, which was still a bewilderingly foreign concept to most British car makers.

Hennessey's British Fords of the 1950s, such as the Consul and the Zephyr, were still unmistakably American in their styling, although they sold respectably. Now, 1959's Ford Anglia 105E combined European and

American elements, to far greater acclaim.[1] The Anglia's wide, grinning front grille, muted tail fins and flat roof-line were distinctly American, as was the backward-slanting rear window – a feature imported, implausibly enough, from Ford's giant Lincoln Continental of 1958. But the Anglia's size and compactness were emphatically European. So, too, was its impressive, 997cc Kent engine, a vast improvement on previous wheezy power plants. While it may not have lived up to Ford's billing as 'the world's most exciting light car', it was certainly among the best.

Like the Mini, the Ford Anglia – particularly the 1198cc Anglia Super variant, introduced in September 1962 – proved an excellent rallying vehicle. It also became a frequent performer on the big and small screens, even though it never attained the film-star status of the Mini. By 1965, 105E Anglias were being used to supplement the Zephyrs and Zodiacs in BBC TV's popular police series Z-Cars, enhancing Ford's already remarkable exercise in product placement.[2] The Anglia survived endorsement by the Conservative Party's new shadow transport minister in 1969 – Margaret Thatcher declared that she drove an Anglia to demonstrate that she was 'not a car snob' – to become an iconic model thirty years later when Anglias were driven on British television by Heartbeat's Yorkshire policemen, the Young Ones' Vyvyan, the puppet Roland Rat, and on film by J. K. Rowling's character Ron Weasley in Harry Potter and the Chamber of Secrets. By the time of its Hogwarts stardom, the Anglia had not been made for thirty-five years, having been replaced by the Ford Escort in 1967.

BMC and Ford were not the only British car makers in the limelight in 1959. Standard-Triumph, too, produced something very new: the

---

1 There had actually been Ford Anglias for twenty years; the name had been invented as a patriotic gesture in 1939.
2 Ford of Britain had achieved a huge coup by providing Roy Brown's Mark III Zephyrs and Zodiacs for the BBC's new series in 1962. The programme's title implied that Ford had even dictated the series' name; in fact, the repetition of the 'Z' was coincidental. The top of the range Zodiacs, which sold well as a result of their TV exposure, were never actually used by the police.

Triumph Herald,[1] a small model designed to be easily assembled both in Britain and, in kit form, abroad. The Herald was put together in as simple a way as possible: the main body was bolted on to the chassis, and the whole front end hinged forward to allow access to the engine. As a result, different body styles – saloon, coupé, estate, van and convertible – could easily be built on the same chassis. Like the Mini and the Anglia, it also looked very different from its curvaceous predecessors. It was sharply styled by the diminutive Torinese stylist Giovanni Michelotti, who introduced American-style fins projecting above the vertical tail lights and pointed chrome headlamp hoods. The Herald's rack-and-pinion steering (similar to that of the Mini) also gave it an enviably tight turning circle, of 25 feet.

Michelotti was not only hugely gifted but also quick, turning round styling projects in as little as three months – a timescale then unheard of in Britain. His contribution to Triumph's success in the 1960s was fundamental; he gave the firm not only the sprightly Herald but also the timeless Spitfire, the later marks of the successful TR sports car, and its classic, fast executive saloon, the Triumph 2000. The 2000's sleek body style anticipated the second-generation BMW 3 Series of the 1980s and showed just what Triumph could have achieved had it not tumbled into the frigid embrace of British Leyland.

Michelotti's flexible design for the Herald worked just as he had envisaged. Soon there were, in addition to the original, two-door coupé and saloon models, a van, a convertible, an estate and, in 1962, a sports saloon version, the Vitesse, redesigned by Michelotti to incorporate raked quadruple headlamps under a dihedral bonnet. Like the Mini, the Herald was an androgynous car which appealed equally to both sexes. But the Herald was not the overnight success that the Mini and Anglia had been. While its engineering and looks were innovatory, its high price, lacklustre performance, poor reliability and poor handling meant that initial sales

---

1 The company had already decided to terminate the Standard brand, which finally disappeared in 1963.

were sluggish. Thankfully, in 1961 the ailing firm of Standard-Triumph was bought by the commercial vehicle manufacturer Leyland Motors, which shrewdly allowed the car maker comparative autonomy while providing badly needed cash to iron out the Herald's teething troubles. Quality control was tightened up, a more powerful engine was added, and the suspension improved. Sales of the Herald picked up, and by 1965 Triumph could barely keep up with demand.

The BMC Mini, the Ford Anglia and the Triumph Herald represented a new generation of radical, chic small cars. Not all of Europe's revolutionary new models for 1959 were as petite, however. In Sweden, Volvo unveiled something completely different. Having been previously known for safe, robust cars like the successful Volvo 121 saloon of 1956 – popularly known as the 'Amazon', it combined American looks with Swedish style and ruggedness – Volvo now unveiled a stylish, sporty model. The P1800 of 1959 was a low, sleek sports car of a sophistication hitherto not associated with the resilient Swedish car maker. Created by consultant engineer Helmer Petterson, it was designed by his son, Pelle, a boat designer who at the time was working for Italian stylist Pietro Frua. It suited Volvo's marketing executives at the time to attribute the car's astonishingly innovative design to the renowned Italian master Frua; only in 2009 was it publicly acknowledged that the now 77-year-old Pelle Petterson had been the car's actual stylist.

With its racy looks and sporty performance, the P1800 was a great success. Its Europe-wide appeal was, admittedly, at least partly due to its being driven by actor Roger Moore in the popular British TV series of 1962–9, The Saint. The series producer had originally wanted Moore's character, Simon Templar, to drive a Jaguar but, with typical British short-sightedness, Jaguar told him that no cars were currently available. He turned instead to Volvo, and with the free advertising provided by The Saint, P1800s soon became very popular – especially in Britain, where they were soon being assembled by Jensen at West Bromwich.

While Jaguar lost out to Volvo in providing a vehicle for Roger Moore, it did manage to produce one of the classic European cars of 1959. As we have seen, in 1955 Jaguar had launched the impressive Jaguar 2.4 litre. The fastest four-door saloon in the world, its advanced styling was the result of the firm's first foray into the world of unitary body construction, while its engine was derived from that used in its legendary series of XK racing cars. In 1959, however, the car was comprehensively updated by inserting a powerful 3.8 litre engine, creating what Jaguar confusingly called the Mark 2 (although there had never officially been a Mark 1).[1]

The Mark 2 was an instant success; beautifully proportioned, and given more chrome, tighter curves and bigger windows than its predecessor, its combination of speed, comfort and style made it one of the century's most impressive cars. Sculptor Henry Moore called his much-loved Mark 2 'sculpture in motion'. The car dominated saloon car racing from 1959, and there was nothing produced either in Europe or America that could rival it. Like the contemporary Citroën DS, the Mark 2 Jaguar was recognized even during its production lifetime as an evergreen classic. A cherry-red Mark 2 was still being driven by the TV detective Inspector Morse as late as 2000.[2]

In 1959, Jaguar had established itself as Europe's premier manufacturer of luxury and sports cars. Its models were selling well on both sides of the Atlantic, and its future as an independent car maker seemed assured. Yet in the last month of 1959 an event took place in Germany that few outside the industry remarked upon at the time, but which was to have significant repercussions for Jaguar, and indeed for all of the world's premium auto manufacturers, some twenty years later. On 9 December 1959, a general meeting of the shareholders of BMW was called in Munich to decide whether or not to liquidate the company. Pressure from Daimler-Benz's largest shareholder, Friedrich Flick, to

---

1 Naming cars was never Jaguar's strong point. The large Mark Ten saloon of the 1960s was contemporary with the E-Type and the Mark 2, the designation of which implied that the 2.4 of 1955 should be regarded in retrospect as the 'Mark 1'.

2 The car the famed inspector had driven in the original books by Colin Dexter had been a Lancia, but the actor who played Morse on television, John Thaw, insisted on driving one of the best-ever British cars. When one of the Morse/Thaw Mark 2s was auctioned in 2005, it fetched over £100,000.

dissolve BMW – then mostly known for its impressive motorcycles and comical bubble cars – seemed irresistible, with Flick apparently intent on making BMW part of his Mercedes empire. But at the last minute a white knight stepped in to rescue the ailing firm: the retiring but determined Brandenburg businessman, Herbert Quandt. That BMW would, in Quandt's hands, become an unstoppable global force in car making in less than two decades would never have occurred to anyone in 1959.

10
The Swinging Sixties

In the iconography of the sixties, the automobile always took centre stage. Cars were sexy, cars were fun. They were essential accessories – or sometimes the main attraction. They were film stars: everyone recalls Steve McQueen's Mustang in *Bullitt* of 1968 (in which McQueen drove himself, even for the most dangerous stunts); the trio of Minis, and the city full of Fiats, in *The Italian Job* of 1969; Herbie, the endearing *KdF-Wagen* of 1968's cloying but vastly successful *The Love Bug*, who was better remembered than his driver.[1] While the Triumph Spitfire of Jean-Luc Godard's scary *Week-end* of 1967 may have been forgotten, James Bond's fabulous sports cars, from the gadget-ridden Aston Martin DB5 of 1964's *Goldfinger* to the racy Toyota 2000GT of 1967's *You Only Live Twice*, are not.

Cars were also rock stars, with Cadillacs, Corvettes and Ferraris symbolizing the excess and success of a defiant new generation. Elvis's Cadillacs became almost as famous as the star himself; while the first purchase of any aspirant recording artist who wanted to demonstrate that he had arrived was inevitably a showy, top of the range auto. Famously, The Who's Keith Moon bought a Rolls-Royce and then proceeded to daub it in lilac-coloured house paint. One of the most celebrated rock vignettes of the sixties was when in 1967 Moon celebrated his twenty-first birthday

---

1 It was Disney perennial Dean Jones.

in Flint, Michigan, by driving a Lincoln Continental into the swimming pool of the Holiday Inn where the band was staying.[1]

By the end of the decade, the Motor City of Detroit was itself synonymous with pop, in the shape of the soul music assembly line of the Motown studios. One of the black families who had emigrated from the south in the 1920s in search of automotive jobs was the Gordys, who moved from Milledgeville, Georgia, to Detroit in 1922. By 1950 the Gordys' son, Berry, was working on Ford's Lincoln/Mercury assembly line. Eight years later he launched the Tamla record label in a studio on Detroit's West Grand Boulevard, which Gordy called 'Hitsville'.[2] Gordy's studio mixes were aimed specifically at the car driver and were calculated to work best within the narrow parameters of tinny car radios. And Motown's soul sound was emphatically the music of the urban working classes – a point rammed home when, in June 1965, Martha Reeves and the Vandellas filmed a promotional movie for their latest hit, 'Nowhere to Run', on the Mustang assembly line at Ford's Rouge River plant.

Two years after 'Nowhere to Run', Motown bubbled over. With its impoverished black downtown and its affluent white suburbs, Gordy's Detroit was a racial powder keg. Mayor Jerome P. Cavanagh, having won the vast majority of black votes, had supposedly converted Detroit into a city of racial harmony and world-famous music. Cavanagh appointed blacks to leading civic positions, instituted the city's first income tax, and won federal funds to make Detroit a model example of President Johnson's 'war on poverty'. In 1966 he headed both the US Conference of Mayors and the National League of Cities, and was being touted as a future Democratic president. The National Urban League called Detroit a 'demonstration city' for race relations, and the US Department of Justice hailed it as a 'racial model'. But in July 1967 it all went wrong when, after a heavy-handed police raid on an illegal downtown drinking den (which was celebrating the return of an African-American Vietnam

---

1 Moon, and the rest of The Who, were banned not just from all Holiday Inns for life but also from the city of Flint.
2 The Motown suffix was added in 1959 for a Smokey Robinson release.

veteran), a race riot erupted which left fourteen dead, three hundred injured and over $150 million of property destroyed. The Motor City was now renowned not so much for Tamla Motown's hit records as for racial problems and social deprivation. GM, Chrysler and Ford executives now arrived at their downtown offices via secure car parks and covered walkways, insulated from what had become known as 'Murder City USA'. Lured by money, and shocked by the deterioration of downtown Detroit, Berry Gordy himself left Detroit for Los Angeles in 1973, taking the Tamla Motown label with him.[1] As Motown star Mary Wilson later noted, when Berry Gordy left, 'part of Detroit died'. When in 1998 Gordy made a TV docudrama about the Motown act The Temptations, Pittsburgh stood in for Detroit; Gordy's long-time assistant, Suzanne de Passe, declared that Detroit was 'too burned out' to play itself. Motown legend Martha Reeves, though, never left, and from 2005 until 2009 served as a Detroit city councilwoman.

Britain's Detroit was Coventry. The Midlands city had tradition-ally been a centre for watch making and silk weaving, and by 1800 was renowned as the supplier of the nation's silk ribbons; however, by the 1870s French imports had almost destroyed the ribbon industry (encouraging some manufacturers to resort to producing 'Stevengraphs', pictures or bookmarks made with silk ribbon) and continental rivals were taking their toll of watch making, too. The city responded to these challenges by reinventing itself, applying its fine metalworking tradition to bicycle making. Indeed, the worldwide bicycle craze of the 1880s and 90s was largely fuelled by products made in the city; the first modern bicycle was made by a Coventry firm, J. F. Starley, in 1885, and by 1906 Coventry-based Rudge Whitworth was turning out seventy-five thousand bicycles annually. By that time, though, many of Coventry's bicycle manu-facturers had switched to car making. In 1896 the fast-talking engineer-salesman Harry Lawson established the Daimler Motor Company in a disused cotton mill, aiming to take advantage both of the city's skilled

---

1 Seven years later Gordy sold the Motown label to Boston Ventures Management.

metalworkers and of the financial support offered by Coventry cycling pioneer Henry Sturmey.[1] Daimler's success encouraged other bicycle makers to shift to car production (although some kept the bicycle business going as a standby): Humber in 1898, Swift in 1900, Lea-Francis in 1903, Rover in 1904, Singer in 1905, Hillman and Riley in 1907, and Triumph, somewhat belatedly, in 1913. Other firms started from scratch. In 1903 Reginald Maudslay started the Standard Motor Company in the city with the assistance of funding from the local machine-tool magnate Alfred Herbert.

The new automotive firms also brought Coventry a plethora of component-making concerns, names such as the Motor Radiator Manufacturing Company and Coventry Motor Fittings (both founded in 1902); Morris-Lister Magnetos (established in 1908 by two electrical engineers from Birmingham University); White and Poppe, which moved from making shell fuses for the army during the Boer War of 1899–1902 to become Britain's most famous engine-maker;[2] and, in 1903, Lee Stroyer, an engine maker which later metamorphosed into the celebrated engine and forklift manufacturer Coventry Climax, and was bought by Coventry neighbour Jaguar in 1953. By 1911, 41 per cent of Coventry's workforce was employed making cars or bicycles, and only 6 per cent in the traditional Coventry trades of silk weaving or watch making. As in Detroit, the motor industry remoulded the city, which metamorphosed into a mirror of its employers. Thus the association football team originally founded at the Singer bicycle factory was transformed into an amply funded and well-supported city club, Coventry City FC.

The future for Coventry still seemed promising in the 1950s. Workers flocked to live in the bright, modern city, which seemed to offer limitless employment possibilities. In 1948 the Labour government

---

1 Sturmey was editor of *The Cyclist* magazine and in 1895 founded the periodical *Autocar* (starting a rival publication, *Motor*, in 1903). He is nowadays perhaps better known for his three-speed Sturmey-Archer bicycle gear hub.

2 White and Poppe was bought by Guildford-based commercial vehicle manufacturer Dennis in 1919.

approved plans for over 700,000 square feet of new factories, and the city's population rose from 232,000 in 1946 to 335,000 in 1971. In 1950 a competition was launched to build a brand-new cathedral adjacent to the bombed-out ruins of the medieval church. It was won by Basil Spence, and his bold new building was opened in 1962, a fitting symbol of the city's phoenix-like rebirth and the motor industry's enduring prosperity. In 1960 (the year in which Spence was knighted) the city also unveiled the Herbert Art Gallery, built on a site just to the north of the cathedral. Appropriately, this progressive civic gesture was funded by Sir Alfred Herbert, the recently deceased machine-tool magnate whose local engineering business, then one of the world's biggest manufacturers of machine tools, was vital to Coventry's car makers. However, as early as 31 March 1959 *The Times* was warning that Coventry's economy was dangerously dependent on the car industry and allied engineering firms, cautioning that the city had failed to diversify into other industrial and manufacturing sectors.

One of the most complacent of Coventry's auto giants was Rootes. The Coventry combine thought it had the ideal car for the sixties, and aimed to capitalize on the success of the Mini with the innovatory Hillman Imp of 1963. Instead, the Imp proved the ruin of the combine. Rootes had wanted to build the new car at existing plants at Coventry or Dunstable, but in 1960 Harold Macmillan's Conservative government had insisted that the firm build a new factory at Linwood, near Glasgow, in an attempt to create jobs in an industrial black spot (to which the government had already diverted a Pressed Steel body plant). Linwood soon became notoriously strike-prone, and was closed after only eighteen years of operation. And the brave new Imp it was designed to produce proved an unreliable, rust-prone failure. The revolutionary, rear-mounted, all-aluminium Coventry Climax engine was radically new, but untested, and tended to overheat and warp, while the automatic choke rarely worked and had to be replaced with a conventional, manual device. Soon the Imp became synonymous with unreliability and breakdowns. (In contrast, GM's European mass-market offering at the time, the Opel

Kadett/Vauxhall Viva, may have been boringly conventional and tediously styled, but it was reliable – at least until rust wore away its body.) Imp sales never came anywhere near the target of 150,000 per year; in its best year, 1964, just over sixty-nine thousand were sold, but the following year Imp sales slumped to under thirty thousand, compared with ninety-six thousand Minis.

The money spent on developing the Imp, building Linwood and rectifying the mini car's myriad faults meant that Rootes had no cash to invest in other new models. This allowed Rootes, in which Chrysler had already taken a substantial stake in 1964 (the year in which Sir Billy Rootes died), to fall completely into Chrysler's hands in 1967.[1] The Imp had, true to its name, mischievously bankrupted the company, and the Rootes legacy was swiftly erased; as early as 1965 Chrysler's five-pointed star was applied to all new cars, while Rootes' prestigious Devonshire House showroom was hurriedly vacated. In 1970 the Rootes name disappeared altogether, and one by one the Rootes marques faded away, too.

Ford capitalized on the huge success of the revolutionary Anglia of 1959 with the best-selling, if pedestrian, Cortina of 1962. Rather dull-looking, the Cortina I was improbably named for the stylish Italian ski resort that had staged the 1960 Winter Olympics. Equally improbably, the plain Cortina was designed by Roy Brown, the American stylist responsible for the disastrous Edsel. Dubbed the Archbishop while in the planning stage (a Ford of Britain in-joke: Dearborn's project name for the rival, German-American Beetle-beater had been the Cardinal, named after the bird rather than the ecclesiastical hierarch[2]), the Cortina's original trade name was to have been Caprino, until Ford of Britain learned that this was Italian for goat poo. The Cortina actually smelled better than most cars, as its fresh-air ventilation combined with the heating system to give the interior a far more flexible environment than that of most family cars.

---

1 Which in turn prompted the retirement of Sir Reggie Rootes.
2 The Cardinal was launched as the Taunus 12M a week before the Cortina, on 21 September 1962. Its lines were even more unashamedly American than those of the Cortina, the sales of which it never matched.

Furthermore, a tie-up with the Grand Prix racing team of Lotus saw the appearance of 1963 of the powerful and racy Lotus-Cortina, with lowered suspension, Lotus instrumentation and a twin-cam Lotus engine. Every Lotus-Cortina was originally finished in white with a bold 'Lotus green' stripe; and, even if few people bought it, the model's halo effect gave the harmless-looking Cortina a significant edge.[1] Indeed, the model proved the mid-size sales sensation of the decade and on 7 September 1966 the millionth Cortina rolled off the assembly line at Dagenham.[2]

Over at BMC, Issigonis's Austin/Morris 1100 of 1962 – which the now-legendary designer saw as a more powerful, refined and spacious Mini – set a new standard for small family cars. Styled by Pininfarina, its compact, handsome looks, hydrolastic suspension and roomy interior ensured it sold 1.4 million cars until it was inexplicably terminated in 1973. Sadly, though, not just the Wolseley and Riley brands but even the MG marque were seriously devalued by being attached to cosmetically enhanced 1100s.

If any cars can be said to have epitomized the look of the Swinging Sixties, it was Triumph's classy 2000 and Rover's superb P6, both launched in 1963. In these two world-beating executive saloons, traditional British class was combined with modern, clean lines and sporty performance. The Triumph 2000, perhaps the most handsome of the pair, was styled by one of the greatest car designers of the century, Giovanni Michelotti, and was arguably the Italian master's most impressive creation. Developed in under two years, it was cheaper than the Rover 2000, and while the Rover was certainly more innovatory, the Triumph sold better. Properly powered and marketed, it could have taken on the BMW 3 Series of the 1970s. Indeed, had British Leyland evolved the model, Triumph could

---

1 The fabled Lotus-Cortina was the brainchild of Ford of Britain's director of public affairs, Walter Hayes, who was himself responding to Lee Iacocca's directive that Ford should get involved in motor sport in order to give the company's products a more youthful image. When the excellent Mark II Cortina was introduced, Ford took the project's direction out of the hands of the talented but unreliable Lotus boss, Colin Chapman, and rebranded the car the Cortina-Lotus.

2 A week later the millionth Anglia left Dagenham, too.

have proved a British rival to BMW during the last decades of the twentieth century. (As it was, the appearance of Michelotti's later Triumph Dolomite uncannily prefigured that of the classic, second-generation BMW 3 Series of the 1980s.[1]) The Triumph 2000's principal weakness – one that put it at a disadvantage when compared with its formidable rival from Rover – was its uninspiring engine, which it inherited from the Standard Vanguard of 1960. Not until 1968, when a petrol-injection 2.5 litre powertrain was introduced, was the Triumph 2000 given the engine it deserved. And by then it was too late: Triumph had fallen into the maw of British Leyland, and within a decade its name was being used to re-badge Japanese imports.

The Rover 2000 (or P6, as it was known in the trade) was, unlike its Triumph rival, all new. One of the most remarkable cars of the century, it was a substantial departure from the familiar old Rovers of the 1950s. (Not for nothing was the dignified P4 series, launched as the Rover 75 in 1949, affectionately labelled the 'Auntie' by its loyal drivers.) Its unashamedly contemporary body, styled by Rover's David Bache, looked rangy, stylish and fast, and recalled the lines of the fabled Citroën DS. (Indeed, it borrowed the DS concept of a unitary body fitted with large, stressed-steel panels.) It had tube suspension at the rear, giving an extremely comfortable ride, and disc brakes on all four wheels – the first mass-produced European model to include such an advanced feature. It was the first large saloon car to add Cortina-style fresh-air vents. And by the standards of the day it was extremely safe, carrying a collapsible steering wheel six years before this feature was made mandatory in the US.

David Bache was born in Mannheim, in Germany, but brought up in the heart of the Britain's motor country, the West Midlands. The son of Aston Villa footballer Joe Bache, he studied at Birmingham College of Art (now part of Birmingham City University), joined Austin in 1948, and six years later was headhunted by Rover at Solihull. Bache's first

---

1 Michelotti's 'Ajax' project of 1962 gave birth to the front-wheel-drive Triumph 1300 of 1965 and its progeny, the Triumph 1500, Toledo and Dolomite.

complete design for Rover was inspired; his classic, owlish Rover P5 of 1958 became the sturdy, reliable favourite of government ministers and senior executives.[1] However, following the problems encountered with the P6's much-troubled successor, Bache retired from British Leyland to found his own design consultancy in 1981. He died in 1994.

Lauded across the globe, Bache's Rover 2000 became the media's first-ever Car of the Year, a designation invented by the Dutch magazine *Autovisie* in 1963. It was bought by executives, by families, and by young and old alike. It was even bought by celebrities; Princess Grace of Monaco was tragically killed at the wheel of a P6 in 1982 after suffering a stroke. And it was coveted by police forces across the UK, particularly in its 3500 guise of 1968. (The compact, lightweight but powerful 3.5 litre engine had been adapted from an American V-8 originally developed by Buick. Rover's managing director, William Martin-Hirst, came across the engine by accident during a visit to Detroit.)

The Rover 2000/3500's international success was paralleled by British car makers' domination of the worldwide sports car market. Serious customers bought ACs, Lotuses and Jaguars. (Those with deep pockets might even have looked at the Jensen FF of 1968 which introduced four-wheel control to the sports car, but was also hideously expensive.) For those drivers who wanted sports car styling allied to a more manageable engine – and price – there was the perky Sunbeam Alpine, the classic Austin Healey, the evergreen MG range, Triumph's traditionally styled TR series, the Michelotti-styled Triumph Spitfire, and the beautiful E-Type from Jaguar. And after 1964, the year of *Goldfinger's* gilded DB5, the Bond-inspired phenomenon of Aston Martin, too, conquered the world.

MG's Midget of 1961 was a tiny but classless, affordable, non-gendered sports car derived from the Austin-Healey Sprite Mark II and produced at MG's Abingdon factory. It sold moderately well; 226,000

---

1 And monarchs, too: Queen Elizabeth II loved her personal P5, which can still be seen at the Heritage Motor Centre at Gaydon, Warwickshire.

had been produced by the time the model was axed (without a replacement) in 1979. But MG's international breakthrough came with the MGB of 1962, BMC's first unitary sports car. Fast and nippy yet safe – it was one of the first cars to offer crumple zones – it proved a huge success in the US; over half a million MGBs were produced before the model, together with MG's Abingdon works, was terminated in 1980, and most of those were exported to America.

The failure of British Leyland and its successors to plan for the replacement of the Midget and the MGB effectively handed the sports car market, which in the sixties had been a largely British preserve, to the Germans and Japanese. One famous sporting marque of the 1960s, however, did manage to survive the vicissitudes of the late twentieth century. That it is still with us today is partly due to its illustrious movie heritage, as the transport of Britain's most celebrated fictional spy.

In 1963 Aston Martin[1] released its DB5 luxury sports car. Developed from the DB4 of 1958 and powered by a new, aluminium, 4 litre engine, it offered reclining seats, wool pile carpets, electric windows, twin fuel tanks, chrome wire wheels, an oil cooler, full leather trim and even a fire extinguisher, and was the first car to have an alternator as standard. It was already selling relatively well when it was chosen to star in the 1964 Bond film *Goldfinger*, in which it was tricked out with weaponry, a bullet-proof rear plate and an ejector seat.[2] Bond's DB5 was so successful that it returned for 1964's follow-up movie, *Thunderball* – and again for 2012's *Skyfall*. Aston continued to produce the DB5 and its similarly styled successor, the DB6, until 1971. The following year, even the Bond effect could not prevent the overstretched car maker's bankruptcy; but after a troubled few years, Aston Martin recovered, renegotiated a link to the Bond film franchise, and today remains perhaps the world's best-known independent sports car manufacturer.

---

1 The company name derives from the company's founder, Lionel Martin, and the Aston Hill hill-climb in Buckinghamshire, which Martin adored.
2 Ian Fleming's novel of 1959 had described Bond driving a DB Mark III, but Fleming agreed with the producers' request to substitute Aston's latest model.

  While the DB5 was the decade's most famous sports model, perhaps
the most accessible small sports car of the sixties was the Triumph Spitfire.
Triumph had not originally wanted another sports car to sit beside the
successful TR4/TR5, first introduced in 1961. But Triumph's quicksilver
Italian designer, Giovanni Michelotti had, unbidden, already designed
one, based around the Triumph Herald's 1147cc engine. Triumph boss
Alick Dick later recalled: 'Michelotti was always reeling off new designs;
you just couldn't stop him. If you took him out to dinner he'd practically
get every menu card in the place, design cars and leave them as souvenirs
for the waiters! He could design a car in four or five minutes, and the nice
thing was that he would do it to *our* ideas, not just his own.' Michelotti's
new design was clean, handsome and racy.[1] And it was an instant hit,
in Europe and particularly in America – so much so that the same basic
model, with minor changes, was produced until 1980, when its Canley
factory was closed.

  Even more successful in 1960s America than MG and Triumph was
the British car maker Jaguar which, in the E-Type, created of one of the
most beautiful and iconic cars of the era. Jaguar had started life in 1922 as
the Swallow Sidecar Company, making motorcycle sidecars. The driving
force behind Swallow was William Lyons, who was a rare animal in the
British motor industry: an automotive entrepreneur who could not only
run a company but also design cars. His wide-ranging talents put most
of his industry rivals in the shade and were to prove crucial to Jaguar's
post-war success. Born in Blackpool in 1901, he was set to join the Barrow
shipyards after the First World War when a friend recommended the
motor business. There he learned both engineering (with Crossley of
Manchester) and salesmanship (with the Sunbeam dealers Brown and
Mallalieu of Blackpool). By 1922 he was making motorcycles and sidecars
with William Walmsley, and six years later he took the firm, now known
as Swallow Sidecars, to Coventry, in order to be closer to his suppliers. In

---

1 In contrast to the rugged appearance of his TR4, which was dominated by its vast
headlamps.

1931 Lyons unveiled his first models under the SS Cars brand: sleek, low-slung, two-door coupés, designated the SS1 and SS2. Their immediate success, even at the height of the Great Depression, was due to Lyons's unique qualities: as his own designer, he ensured that the cars looked good, giving them long bonnets and sinuous, curving lines; while the salesman in him ensured that they were all fully road-tested before their launch and, crucially, were heavily marketed. (The 1933 SS1 even graced the cover of *Autocar* magazine.)

The Jaguar name first surfaced in 1935, when it was applied to a four-door variant of the SS1. This carried a distinctive, lozenge-like radiator which Lyons (using the example of Rolls-Royce) subsequently applied to all his Jaguars. In February 1945 the Jaguar brand was applied to the company's entire product range, since SS Cars had become a somewhat inappropriate name following the atrocities of the Second World War.

As we have seen, Jaguar's big breakthrough came in 1949 with the XK120 sports car. Available as an open roadster or a closed coupé, it took America by storm, helped by a spectacular series of motor racing victories. (All the three premier racing drivers – Giuseppe Farina, Juan Manuel Fangio and Alberto Ascari – at one time drove Jaguars. Lyons's own son, John, also drove for the Jaguar racing team.) In the early 1950s, the British motor industry's the only real US export successes were Jaguar and MG. With Britain still immersed in a world of rationing and currency controls, few of its citizens could afford an XK120 – but the wealthy denizens of Eisenhower's America certainly could. Even so, by 1952, twenty British police forces were using Jaguars, and were, moreover, sending their officers to Jaguar's in-house mechanics' training school. As Britain's highway system expanded, the police were determined that they should be able to catch anything on the road and opted to buy the best sports car available.

At a time when most British motor executives were opting for safety over innovation, Lyons cleverly built on the XK120's success by venturing into a different market segment – while taking care that the XK120's core brand values of looks, performance and luxury (or, as the Jaguar sales slogan of the time had it, 'Grace, Space, Pace') were just as relevant to this new sector. The Jaguar 2.4 and 3.4 fast executive saloons of 1955, which in turn metamorphosed into the splendid Mark 2s we have already seen in debuting in 1959, were beautiful to look at, exciting to drive, and luxuriously well-appointed. And as the fastest four-door saloons in the world, they, too, were swiftly snapped up by Britain's lucky police forces.

In 1960 Sir William Lyons'[1] took advantage of his firm's spectacular US sales to create the Jaguar Group of Companies. He took Jaguar out of motor racing (now proving prohibitively expensive) and concentrated instead on building a modest automotive empire. Over two years he bought the bankrupt operation of Daimler of Coventry – then producing very few cars and absorbed with their new, rear-engined bus, the Fleetline – along with BSA (Birmingham Small Arms), bus and truck makers Guy Motors and, in 1963, Coventry Climax engines. The purchase of both Daimler and Guy gave Lyons badly needed factory space, which in turn allowed him to make more cars; thus while around thirty thousand XKs had been made between 1947 and 1959, during the next twelve years over seventy thousand E-Types were produced.

The E-Type was launched to a rapturous reception in 1961. It was a beautiful, two-seater touring car that looked like a racing car – but wasn't. The fact that it rarely ever reached its advertised top speed of 150 mph rather missed the point; like the Ford Thunderbird, it was devised as a personal style accessory and not as a performance car. Its 3.8 litre engine was buoyed by a new suspension system, and in later models the narrow and small wheels were enlarged to give better grip and cornering.

The E-Type's classic curves, devised partly by Lyons himself, instantly won over motoring critics and customers on both sides of the Atlantic. To many, then and now, the E-Type – along perhaps with the Mini, the Aston Martin DB5, Bill Mitchell's '63 Corvette and the 1964 Mustang – embodies sixties style. Even Enzo Ferrari called it 'the most beautiful car ever made'. Less reverently, American journalist Henry Manney, demonstrating an

---

1 He had been knighted four years previously.

impressive knowledge of British slang, termed the E-type 'the Greatest Crumpet-Catcher Known to Man'.

In twelve years Sir William Lyons had designed, produced and sold three of the greatest and most characterful cars of the twentieth century. His innate business acumen also ensured that they were outstanding commercial successes. In 1968 he added yet another global hit to this impressive roster: the XJ6 large executive saloon. If his British contemporaries and successors had followed Lyons's example, the British motor industry might well have weathered the vagaries of the 1970s and 80s. As it was, his vision and daring were inherited not by the bosses of British Leyland but by the managers of BMW, Mercedes and Toyota.

Inevitably, as he grew older, even Lyons's vision began to become clouded. In 1966 Sir William made perhaps his biggest mistake, agreeing to merge the Jaguar Group with BMC and its Pressed Steel body making subsidiary to form British Motor Holdings (BMH). Lyons was nearing retirement, had no obvious successor within the firm (his only son, racing driver John Lyons, had been killed in a car accident in 1955), and thought BMH offered Jaguar its best bet for future investment. Two years later, and much against Lyons's wishes, BMH merged with Leyland, now owners of both Triumph and Rover, to form the giant conglomerate British Leyland.[1] Jaguar's reputation and standards plummeted and took almost two decades to recover.

Aside from the Porsche 911 of 1963, there were few direct equivalents to the E-Type Jaguar (and the DB5 and TR4) made in continental Europe during the Swinging Sixties.[2] This is not to say that continental car

---

1 Technically, British Leyland was formed as the British Leyland Motor Company (BLMC) in 1968 and only became British Leyland in 1975. In 1978 its official name was changed again, to BL Ltd (BL plc after 1978) and in 1986 BL was renamed the Rover Group. However, the term British Leyland and the acronym BL are used throughout this book in order to avoid confusion.

2 Ferrari's splendid models remained beyond the pockets of most drivers. Even the Porsche 911, and its stablemate the 912 of 1965, initially sold in relatively low numbers.

makers were only making lacklustre cars at this time. During this decade Renault, for example, introduced a series of impressive cars. The Renault 4 of 1961 was a very belated response to Citroën's 2CV, but its tardiness did not prevent its spacious, hatchback design generating wide appeal in Europe, and it continued in production for thirty-one years. The Renault 8 small family car of 1962, with its distinctive, dihedral bonnet, borrowed from the Triumph Vitesse, was moderately successful, but was eclipsed by the innovative Renault 16 of 1965. The 16 invented a whole new car form: it was a large family car that was also a hatchback. It was stylish, too; its 'bird-beak' grille and pugnacious snout were balanced by the vast, gently tapering rear 'fastback' roof, which also constituted the 'fifth door'.

In 1968 Peugeot unveiled its response to the Renault 16 in the form of the four-door 504. More conventionally styled than the 16 (as Peugeot customers had come to expect), its taut, Pininfarina lines nevertheless earned it public and critical acclaim; declared European Car of the Year for 1969, it remained a familiar sight on French roads until well into the 1980s and continued in production under licence in China, Africa and South America until 2004.

Citroën's incomparable DS and its quirky, adaptable 2CV had long been in full production. In 1961, though, Flaminio Bertoni, Citroën's legendary designer, launched an 'upmarket' version of the 2CV, the Ami 6. With its bizarre, bug-like nose, tiny tail lights, windswept roof and exaggerated, reverse-rake rear pillars (C-pillars), the Ami qualifies as one of the ugliest cars ever made. Nevertheless, the '3CV', as it was popularly known, was cheap and frugal, and accordingly sold well in France and southern Europe until axed in 1978.

Under the rule of company president Dr Vittorio Valletta, and with its distinctive cars still styled by chief designer Dante Giacosa, Fiat had by the sixties become synonymous with Italy's post-war recovery. Indeed, in many ways industrial Italy of the 1960s *was* Fiat. Valletta had steered the company to success after 1945 and continued to rule it with a rod of iron, firing any workers who were suspected of leftist leanings and sacking managers who disagreed with him. But in 1966 the grandson of the firm's founder, Giovanni Agnelli, quietly took the helm of the automotive giant from the 83-year-old Valletta. The succession was seamless and painless (at least to everyone except Valletta, who did not want to go), and demonstrated to the rest of the world that corporate Italy had come of age.

Gianni Agnelli (he was generally called by the diminutive in order to distinguish him from Fiat's founder) was a very different person from his revered grandfather. His father, Eduardo, had been killed in a bizarre aircraft accident when he was only fourteen.[1] Freed from the control of his father, young Gianni developed a reputation firstly as a war hero after 1940 (he was wounded once in North Africa, where he was serving in a Fiat-built armoured car division, and twice on the Russian front) and secondly as a playboy, whose mistresses ranged from American socialite Pamela Harriman to Swedish film star Anita Ekberg. Gianni seemed to display more enthusiasm for the progress of Juventus (the Fiat-owned, Turin-based football team) than for Fiat's product strategy. As a result, Valletta became increasingly nervous about the prospect of grooming Gianni for the succession, preferring instead to promote his assistant, Gaudenzio Bono, as Fiat's future boss. Agnelli appeared to agree with the tyrannical doctor's judgement; he publicly declared, 'I haven't the slightest idea how to build a car' and that 'Fiat is a machine which needs a chief who is an expert in all phases of its operations, like Bono'. But when the ailing Valletta was forced by the Italian government to retire, the high-living Prince Hal of Italy's premier motoring dynasty unhesitatingly seized the reins. Valletta naively asked Agnelli whom he believed would be his successor as chairman, assuming the notorious playboy would suggest Bono, but Agnelli stunned the ageing technocrat by succinctly

---

1 As Eduardo was climbing down from his seaplane as it rode on the water, the aircraft hit a floating log, which in turn caused his head to hit the still-revolving propeller.

announcing: 'I believe I shall do it myself.' ('I decided,' Agnelli later commented, 'that I was the best person.') Almost overnight, the former lounge lizard became an active and committed leader of, and advocate for, Fiat, which he ran for thirty years.[1]

Agnelli's energy and flair for the automotive business were soon evident. In 1969 he bought Fiat a controlling interest in Ferrari and Lancia.[2] Vincenzo Lancia, a big man who barely squeezed into the cars he loved to race, had started his career as Fiat's chief test driver. In 1906 he founded his own automobile company, which soon became famous for unconventional, racy models. Like Citroën, though, Lancia found by the late 1960s that it could no longer afford the development costs of innovative cars.

In 1969 Agnelli also unveiled the firm's first mass-produced mid-size car. The Fiat 128 combined economic performance with front-wheel drive and good handling, and became an instant classic. Its mundane, box-like body, which made it easy to assemble, concealed a gutsy new power plant designed by the famous Ferrari racing-engine designer, Aurelio Lampredi. Soon Agnelli had set up factories in Russia, Yugoslavia and Poland to make derivatives of the 128, models that were still being produced by some Eastern Bloc countries when the Iron Curtain came down twenty years later.

Fiat was keen to expand eastwards. In 1966 the firm collaborated with the Russian government to create AvtoVAZ (*Avtomobilniy Volzhsky Avtomobilny Zavod*, or 'Automobile Volga Automobile Plant'), a car maker based in the new city of Tolyatti (named after the legendary Italian communist leader, Palmiro Togliatti, who had died two years before) on the Volga river. The company made its name with the VAZ-2101 of 1970, a rugged adaptation of the uninspiring but reliable and widely acclaimed Fiat 124 saloon of 1966. The VAZ-2101 was sold under the brand name of Lada abroad, but as Zhiguli in Russia (where Lada was already well

---

1 And this despite a tragic personal life: Gianni Agnelli's son and heir, Eduardo, was an introverted, disturbed and obsessively religious man who committed suicide in 2000.
2 Alfa Romeo was added to the Fiat empire in 1986 and Maserati in 1993.

known as a type of cheese). The Lada/Zhiguli's steel body panels were 30 per cent thicker than the 124's, and the Fiat's suspension, steering and gearbox were all strengthened to survive the bumpy Soviet roads and atrocious Russian winters. Although they handled very poorly, and their fuel economy was atrocious, Ladas could take a lot of punishment and accordingly sold well in Europe and South America – particularly after 1973, when consumers were looking for cheap alternatives to local car marques. Soon Russian trawler-men visiting Britain and Iceland were buying up export Ladas, which were made to a better specification than the home-market Zhigulis, and taking them back to Russia to be cannibalized for badly needed spare parts.[1]

The appeal of the Lada for Western consumers was rather hard to define. Academic Peter Hamilton recalls the 'strangely brittle plastic, lumpy foam and clingingly uncomfortable fabric, hideously inadequate fittings, parts that came off in your hand when using them – such as handbrakes. Erratic gauges, either wildly optimistic or non-functioning. Keys that broke in the locks. Seats that listed drunkenly. Paintwork whose surface recalled the bark of a tree rather than the peel of an orange.' But Ladas were cheap, they were hardy, and they won an affectionate following across the world.

At the same time as the Russian Lada was becoming a byword for ugliness, the Germans were quietly creating one of motor history's classic designs. One of the best-looking European cars of the 1960s, the NSU Ro80 was also one of the most innovatory. Unfortunately, however, its radical engineering proved a bridge too far. NSU had begun life in 1873 as a knitting-machine manufacturer in Württemberg in southern Germany. It diversified into bicycles and (for a few years) cars, and by 1955 had

---

1 Russian fishermen did the same with the Moskvich 2140 of 1976, which was loosely based on the Simca 1307 of the previous year. Moskvich had prospered after the Second World War, making poor copies of the pre-war Opel Kadett, with machinery bodily transplanted from the ruined Opel works to Russia.

become the biggest motorcycle manufacturer in the world. In 1957 the firm restarted automobile production, and a decade later launched, to worldwide surprise, the astonishing Ro80 car.

The Ro80 was beautifully designed by NSU's Claus Luthe. Its sleek, subtle, aerodynamic wedge shape and quadruple headlights echoed those of Michelotti's Triumph 2000 and anticipated the executive saloons of the subsequent two decades. It had disc brakes, power-assisted rack-and-pinion steering, front-wheel drive and independent suspension. It was extremely quiet and possessed almost-unknown extras such as a heated rear window and a rear ski hatch. Most importantly, it was powered by a revolutionary rotary engine devised by German engineer Felix Wankel. The Wankel engine worked by a system of rotors rather than pistons, which made it far more compact than its conventional predecessors, while at the same time enviably powerful. (The Ro80's original engine produced what was then a highly impressive 128 bhp.) However, the Wankel's development was rushed and in the Ro80 it proved highly unreliable. While many European motor magazines hailed the Ro80 as their Car of the Year for 1967, by 1968 they were acknowledging that it was plagued with faults and failures. The numerous manufacturers who had expressed interest in the rotary concept now melted away; only Mazda stayed the course, developing the rotary engine (at great cost) into a viable power plant by the mid-1970s. Today, the Wankel engine is once more the subject of widespread interest, as its compact size and quiet operation make it an ideal candidate to partner with electric motors in hybrid cars.

The Ro80's failure, allied to the vast cost of developing the car, led to NSU's collapse and in 1969 the bankrupt firm was absorbed into Volkswagen. The Ro80 itself limped on in production until 1977, but by then mechanics were used to substituting Ford's far cruder Essex engine (the engine that powered the rough and ready Ford Transit van) for the delicate Wankel rotary.

Following the 1969 takeover, NSU's gifted designer, Claus Luthe, worked for a time for VW's Audi division, where he helped create the

Audi 50 (the parent of the VW Polo) and revised the brilliant Audi 100. In 1976 he moved to BMW as chief designer; there he created many of the iconic 3, 5 and 7 Series BMW saloons of the 1980s. Luthe's 7 Series of 1986 (known internally as the E32) actually bore a distinct resemblance to his classic Ro80 of almost twenty years before. Luthe's career evaporated in tragic circumstances, however, when in 1990 he was convicted of fatally stabbing his drug-dependent, 33-year-old son.

The executive saloon market that the Ro80 had sought to conquer was by the end of the 1960s captured (outside Britain, France and North America, at least) by Mercedes. Not only did Mercedes have an impressive range of four-door saloons in their 190, 200 and 300 series, but in 1964 Daimler-Benz also launched a top of the range limousine which offered Rolls-Royce and Cadillac quality at a far cheaper price. The Mercedes 600 was lengthy, heavy and powered by a massive 6.3 litre engine. Its long-wheelbase version could be supplied as a four- or six-door limousine, both of which could be adapted as chauffeured vehicles; in this latter guise it proved the quintessential car for heads of state who preferred to avoid the colonial baggage of vehicles from the former imperial powers, such as Britain and France, or the capitalist excesses implied by a Cadillac or a Lincoln. As a result, presidents, monarchs, tycoons and celebrities the world over flocked to buy 600s. Russia's Leonid Brezhnev bought one, as did Albania's ludicrous tyrant Enver Hoxha, Uganda's despotic 'President-for-Life' Idi Amin, Korean dictator Kim Il Sung, Kenya's Jomo Kenyatta, the Philippines' long-serving strongman Ferdinand Marcos, Cambodia's Prince Sihanouk, the Shah of Iran (who ordered a whole fleet of 600s), and Iraq's Saddam Hussein. Production of the 600 ended in 1981, but today they are still highly sought after by collectors.

For Britain and the more anglophile Commonwealth countries, the Mercedes 600, no matter how far it could be stretched, could never hope to compete with a Rolls-Royce. In order to tackle the challenge of Mercedes' new limousines in the rest of the world, in 1965 Rolls-Royce boldly introduced something very different: the compact and boxy Silver Shadow. This ultra-luxury flagship model, which was also available with a Bentley badge,[1] was subsequently adapted as a convertible (called the Corniche) and, more improbably, as a coupé (the Pininfarina-styled Camargue). The Silver Shadow was the first Rolls-Royce to be built in one piece, as a monocoque; thus, even though the car was shorter and narrower than its predecessor, the stately Silver Cloud, its interior was more spacious. The Silver Shadow's hydraulic, self-levelling suspension system, licensed from Citroën, represented a major departure in both technological and styling terms for the luxury car maker, but the risk paid off and the car sold very well in both the US and other overseas markets. Thankfully, the model's original name of 'Silver Mist' was vetoed when Rolls discovered that 'Mist' was German for 'manure'.

America remained a good market for British exports in the sixties, from the Silver Shadow to the MGB.[2] But Americans did not rely solely on British imports to satisfy their apparently insatiable demand for racy autos. By the mid-1960s America had its own contender in the small sports car market.

In 1961 GM's chief stylist Bill Mitchell (who had succeeded his patron, Harley Earl, as vice president and corporate styling chief in 1958) bought a Jaguar E-Type.[3] He soon fell in love with its graceful curves and wondered why GM did not produce something along the same lines. Using the E-Type as his starting point, and working with fellow stylist Larry Shinoda, he comprehensively restyled Earl's open-topped Corvette as a sleek, hard-topped coupé. This second-generation (C2) Corvette of 1963, called the Sting Ray to distinguish it from Earl's 1953 original

---

1 Two years earlier, Rolls had established commonality of parts between all Rolls and Bentley cars, thus effectively extinguishing Bentley as an individual marque.

2 Other European imports, aside from the best-selling Volkswagen – by far the biggest foreign seller in the US during the decade – generally fared less well.

3 Sold in the US as the XK-E.

(now retrospectively termed the C1), was reinterpreted as a compact, powerful, curvaceous racer and provided with hidden headlights and independent rear suspension. Its gently sloping rear roof mirrored that of its exact contemporary, the Porsche 911 (although its split rear windscreen, which Mitchell adored, severely reduced visibility, and was removed for 1964). And like the 911, its basic form lasted for decades.[1] In contrast to the American-made 'pony' and 'muscle' cars which followed later, the Corvette Sting Ray was a genuine American sports car – a rare commodity in the 1960s. Chevrolet also recognized the importance of retaining a Corvette family resemblance, much as Porsche was to do with its evergreen 911. While the Ford Mustang changed out of all recognition during the 1970s, becoming a bloated, sagging parody of its taut 1964 namesake, the Corvettes of the early twenty-first century still bore a strong family resemblance to Mitchell and Shinoda's masterly original.

The new Ford Mustang was a conundrum. Its performance was decidedly inferior to that of the Sting Ray; it was effectively little more than an old Ford family car, cleverly repackaged. But this gas-guzzling sports-family crossover still managed to become a runaway success – largely thanks to its fabulous styling, which created one of the signature cars of the decade. The brainchild of Ford's ambitious young vice president Lee Iacocca, and styled by the talented Eugene Bordinat, the Mustang was launched in 1964 to great acclaim. Indeed, in later years almost everyone at Ford appeared to have had a hand in its development, demonstrating how success can spawn many fathers. Few of these men, interestingly, queued up to accept responsibility for the Ford Pinto.

Lido 'Lee' Iacocca came from humble beginnings. The son of the owner of the Orpheum Wiener House in working-class Allentown, Pennsylvania, he studied engineering at the local university, Lehigh, and went straight into a trainee engineering spot at Ford on his graduation in

---

1 The C4 version of the car of 1984 eliminated the brand's unique, cat-like curves, which were thankfully reinstated in the C5 of 1997.

1946. Initially shy and awkward, Iacocca's dealings with regional dealers made him tougher and sharper. Recognizing an up and coming executive, in 1956 the Ford Motor Company sent him to that mecca of self-improvement, the Dale Carnegie Institute, to hone his public-speaking skills. Thereafter, Iacocca became increasingly confident. When the Mustang concept surfaced, Iacocca not only recognized it as a winner but also as the means of muscling his way to the top. On the way up, both he and Ford forgot many others who had been equally responsible for the car's gestation and birth.

The Mustang, even more than the Thunderbird, was aimed squarely at the younger driver. It seemed to encapsulate the spirit of the sixties with its racy bodywork and suggestion of raw power. Henry Ford II wanted the car to be called the 'Thunderbird II', while Ford car division executives originally tagged it the 'Torino' (a name hastily withdrawn when it was pointed out that this Italian name might draw unwelcome attention to Henry Ford II's Italian mistress). Yet Mustang – a name coined by Ford's advertising agency, J. Walter Thompson, after both the horse and the legendary wartime P-51 fighter – was the clear winner in market research.

In truth, the Mustang was not a new car. Iacocca's department had merely put Bordinat's body on to the conventional underpinnings of that most mundane of family sedans, the mid-size Ford Falcon, and had borrowed the engine from the run of the mill Ford Fairlane. The Mustang's lengthy bonnet did not conceal, as it implied, an enormous power train in the manner of the pre-war Bentleys, Bugattis and Cords; much of the forward space was actually empty. The interminable hood was all just for show, all style and no content. Iacocca later admitted that he had merely taken a Falcon and 'put a youth wrapper around it' – and this, he boasted, 'was done for less than $50 million'. In contrast to the family-friendly Falcon, the Mustang's rear seats were all but useless – only fit for 'legless children', as one critic wrote – while its trunk was tiny. Consumer campaigner Ralph Nader later categorized the Mustang as 'a hoked-up Falcon with inadequate brakes, poor handling and marvellous promotion'. 'Like most American cars,' he concluded, 'the Mustang abounds with new and startling engineering features carried over from 1910.' Nor was Nader alone. *Road Test* magazine found that the Mustang was unstable at high speed, while *Car Life* derided the car's 'teen-age rear suspension'.

Yet in spite of the critics' warnings, the Mustang was a winner. This was due not only to Bordinat's inspired and flexible design, which offered sleek fastback, coupé and convertible options, but also to Iacocca's energetic marketing. Iacocca ensured that two hundred of America's leading disc jockeys – opinion formers for the crucial market segment of sixteen to twenty-five year-olds – were each provided with a free Mustang. This helped garner the car very favourable publicity from the youth-oriented radio stations, if not from the motoring press. Four hundred and eighteen thousand Mustangs were sold in the first year, and an astonishing total of over one million in the first eighteen months.[1]

Ford's Thunderbird found itself outflanked and outpaced by its young cousin. The stylish, youthful 'personal car' of 1955 now looked dated and middle-aged. Sales had already been slipping fast in the early sixties; the 1961 redesign, giving the T-bird a more futuristic, space-age look and a pointed nose, did little to affect the slide. In 1967 the car was distanced from the Mustang by more conservative styling and a four-door option, and ended up resembling a small Lincoln. The 1971 sixth generation Thunderbird proved to be the model's nadir; the provision of a large V-8 engine was more than offset by the car's heaviness, making the new Thunderbird's performance no more than modest, while its body style was that of a middle-aged Mercury. Harley Earl's original concept was belatedly revived in the 1983 T-bird, but the magic was gone and in 1997 the model was finally discontinued. A retro-styled coupé/convertible of 2002, powered by a Jaguar V-8, was similarly unsuccessful and was terminated in 2005.

---

1 In 1967 a Mercury equivalent, the hard-top Cougar, was introduced, with distinctive front grille panels hiding the headlamps.

Chrysler reacted to the news of the Mustang's imminent launch in an over-hasty and slapdash manner, fitting a crisply styled fastback roof with a giant rear windscreen to the undistinguished Plymouth Valiant compact to make the Plymouth Barracuda. A V-8 engine option was available, but otherwise the engines that Plymouth offered for the Barracuda were the same as for the Valiant. The Barracuda did beat the Mustang's public release by two weeks, but was widely recognized as a decidedly inferior product; in its best year, 1966, only thirty-eight thousand Barracudas were sold – a fraction of the Mustang's astronomical sales. The car lost its Valiant nomenclature for 1965, and in 1967, in a belated attempt to endow it with more youthful appeal than its staid parent,[1] it was furnished with flared hips, curved body panels and a more determined nose. In the late sixties Barracudas were even offered with 'Mod Top' vinyl roofs finished in flower-power motifs, trying to associate what was still basically a Valiant family car with the hippies of Haight-Ashbury.

Meanwhile, Chrysler's Dodge division, envious of the runaway success of the Mustang and jealous of Plymouth's early start, slapped a fastback rear and a V-8 engine into the 1966 Dodge Coronet to create the Dodge Charger. With its tapered lines and hidden headlamps, the '68 Charger was a huge success and, much to Dodge's delight, the model soon eclipsed its Barracuda cousin. AMC, too, responded quickly to the Mustang, but their new Tarpon was even less thought out than the Plymouth Barracuda, being little more than a Rambler Classic compact fitted with a fastback roof, and sales were accordingly dismal. In 1965 the unfortunately named Tarpon was rebranded as the Marlin, and quietly withdrawn in 1967.

GM, meanwhile, spent more than two years deliberating its response to the Mustang. When the result appeared in September 1966, the Chevrolet Camaro[2] used the same basic formula as the Mustang: a short,

---

1 By 1970 the Valiant family resemblance was wholly severed.
2 Together with its Pontiac clone, the Firebird, which sported a now-traditional Pontiac split-front grille.

109 inch wheelbase (short for America, if not the rest of the world) and distinctive, racy styling. As the Mustang was adapted from the Falcon, so the Camaro was in essence a remodelled Chevette. Like the Mustang, the Camaro incorporated fake louvres and air scoops, which did not actually do anything but did look suitably impressive and fast. And, like the Mustang, it scored a palpable hit.

In 1964 GM's Pontiac division also got in on the act when their chief engineer, John Z. DeLorean, re-engined an existing Pontiac compact to create a Mustang rival. DeLorean had joined GM's Pontiac division from the ailing Packard in 1956, initially as a senior engineer in charge of advance planning. Encouraged by his boss at Pontiac, Semon 'Bunkie' Knudsen, DeLorean began to widen the model range at Pontiac, previously associated merely with staid and stolid cars. Pontiacs, asserted DeLorean, should compete at both ends of the market, and to that end he tested his new 'muscle car', the Pontiac Tempest of 1959, at racetrack meetings. The subsequent new strategy for the division treated Pontiac almost as a separate company from its GM partners, and drove a coach and horses through Durant's much-vaunted and time-honoured policy of market sector equivalence. It was also ultimately to lead to confusion in consumers' minds – a confusion that had serious consequences when GM began to falter in the 1970s.

In 1961 Knudsen was moved to head GM's mass-market division, Chevrolet, and DeLorean became chief engineer at Pontiac. Here he was partly responsible for the crude new Tempest, a car that *Road Test* magazine branded 'probably the worst riding, worst all-round handling car available to the American public'. De Lorean then shoehorned a five-litre V-8 power plant into a Tempest to create 1962's gutsy Pontiac GTO, which he named in homage to Ferrari's outstandingly potent 250 GTO coupé of the same year.[1] Designed by Bill Porter, the car did not look as special or attractive as the Corvette and the Mustang, while its unresponsive

---

1 The Italian acronym GTO (*Gran Turismo Omologato* means, literally, 'registered to race in the GT category') had hitherto been used only for Ferraris. Its adoption by Pontiac prompted a howl of protest from the Ferrari *tifosi*.

steering and antiquated drum brakes were poor. It also sported the raised waist that was to become such a tedious and unsightly stylistic cliché of the late 1960s and the 1970s.¹ But the GTO was undoubtedly fast and, marketed as a 'factory hot-rod', sold well. (In 1967 Chrysler confirmed the GTO's triumph by impersonating it with its equally formidable Plymouth Belvedere GTX 'gentleman's muscle car'.) Meanwhile, the incorrigibly self-promoting DeLorean took sole credit for the GTO's achievements – though, in truth, he was only one element of a larger team. Perhaps a larger share in the GTO's success should be assigned to Ronny and the Daytonas' million-selling single, 'G.T.O.', which, while little more than an extended commercial for the car, actually reached number three in the pop charts in 1964.

Not every classic sports car of the sixties came from Europe or America. Toyota responded to the E-Type, the Sting Ray and the Mustang with the remarkably advanced 2000GT of 1967. Manufactured by Yamaha, as Toyota then did not have the plant for such an unusual job, the 2000GT brought Japan to the attention of the world's car buyers for the first time, demonstrating to even the most sceptical motorist that the Japanese could produce a sports car that could rival the best of Coventry, Stuttgart and Detroit. Toyota's rear-drive, hard-top coupé was designed in-house by Satoru Nozaki, whose flowing contours and low-slung body made the car an instant classic. In 1967 America's *Road and Track* magazine described the 2000GT as 'one of the most exciting and enjoyable cars we've driven', and declared it equal, and in some respects even superior, to the legendary Porsche 911.

Even Toyota was surprised by the car's success. Only 351 production 2000GTs were built,² and as early as 1970 second-hand models were selling for vast sums. Toyota also neglected to capitalize on the car's film-star status – earned when, instead of using another Aston Martin as the featured car in the 1967 Bond film *You Only Live Twice* (partly shot in

1 And which was subsequently compared to the styling of a Coke bottle, an analogy that never seems to tire of repetition.
2 Most were painted red or white.

Japan), the producers chose a Toyota 2000GT[1] as the car owned by Bond's girlfriend, Aki.[2]

The year after the 2000GT appeared to great acclaim, Ferrari demonstrated that it could still make world-class cars with the Ferrari 365 GTB/4 of 1968. The 365 was soon known popularly as the Daytona, after Ferrari's 1-2-3 finish in the 24-hour Daytona race of 1967 (though the 365 itself was not actually racing that day). Sharply designed by Pininfarina, the Daytona was, like the Toyota 2000GT, hailed as an instant classic. But, again like the 2000GT, the model's popularity caught the manufacturer unawares. Only 1,284 Daytonas had been manufactured when production was stopped in 1973. Ironically, in the subsequent years the Daytona gained a reputation as one of the finest sports cars of all time, which in turn prompted film and television appearances in productions as varied as *Gone in 60 Seconds, The Rookie* and *Miami Vice*. The principal beneficiary of these star turns was not the Maranello factory, which had long stopped making the Daytona, but the dealers who traded in used Ferraris. Once more, the motor industry found itself surprised by success.

Unhappily, the failure to exploit market opportunities was a trait with which the world's auto manufacturers were to become increasingly identified over the next two decades. By the time the industry had started planning ahead and was properly responding to customers' demands, for many firms – some as illustrious as Ferrari – it was simply too late.

---

1 The film's 2000GT was a fake convertible not then commercially available.

2 During shooting, the actress playing Aki, Akiko Wakabayashi, proved unable to drive the GT2000 fast enough to realize the key scene in which she rescues Bond from Osato's headquarters. The 'Aki' we see in this scene is actually film runner Mick Messenger, dressed in a long black wig. He pulled off the scene adeptly in the first (printed) take, only to crash the car in the second.

11

Heroes and Villains

The mid-1960s marked a watershed in the public perception of the motor car. As early as 1911 the editor of the magazine *Living Age* suggested: 'From being the plaything of society [the car] has come to dominate society. It is now our tyrant, so that at last we have turned in revolt against it, and begun to protest against its arrogant ways.' Fifty years later these words finally came true and the automobile switched from being a national hero to society's villain. In 1965, Congress passed the first serious attempt by the US government to curb car emissions, the Motor Vehicle Air Pollution Act.[1] But there was no initial response on the part of the complacent and conservative US manufacturers. As a result, the first car maker to offer the American public a reliable, clean, fuel-efficient small car was Japanese.[2]

In the 1950s the car had symbolized material success and consumer confidence. Now it was pilloried as an enemy of society and a potential coffin. In 1973 J. G. Ballard published his searing novel *Crash*, whose characters' relationships were defined by the charge of crashed and crashing automobiles. The following year, the American artists of the Ant Farm Collective buried a line of ten old Cadillacs in the ground near Amarillo, Texas, to create the prescient *Cadillac Ranch*, in which the baleful, interred

---

1 Two years later its provisions were stiffened by the tougher Air Quality Act, and in 1970 by the Federal Clean Air Act. Concern about urban car emissions and excessive consumption also prompted New York and California's Clean Air Acts of 1968 and 1970.
2 The car was the Honda Civic.

rear ends of GM's finest formed a line of tombstones for the Golden Age of the motor car.[1]

Safety gradually inched its way up legislators' lists of priorities. The world's first car to feature three-point seat belts, in 1959, had predictably been a Volvo; eight years later, the British government made front seat belts mandatory. Yet it was another decade before the US followed suit; even then, during the 1980s the Reagan administration consistently delayed the introduction of seat belts. Meanwhile, as early as 1967 America had become, for the first time in sixty years, a net *importer* of automotive products.

Sensing a change in consumer priorities, American car styling became more apologetic. By 1962 Dagmars has disappeared, and fins had vanished from all but the luxury marques of Imperial and Cadillac. For 1963, even Chrysler's Imperials, restyled by ex-Ford stylist Elwood Engel, were shorn of their decorative excesses, although modest fins (puny things when compared with the soaring appendages devised by Harley Earl and Virgil Exner) lingered on at Cadillac until 1964. In place of the bright hues of the cars of the 1950s and early 1960s, brown, bronze and beige tones now became all the rage, while tacky black or brown 'vinyl roofs' implied a convertible configuration which could not in fact be delivered.

Ford's refreshed Lincoln Continental – extremely long and low, yet also soberly plain and rectilinear – heralded the direction of things to come. The last version of the Continental II had been, in critic Paul Wilson's words, 'a nineteen-foot monster with sides creased and wrinkled like the hide of a rhino'. The Continental III of 1961 matched the Kennedy era: sleek, smooth and quietly confident, with no flashy or unnecessary ornamentation. Chrome was kept to a bare minimum and there were no fins at all. It was a classic model which was bought by corporate fat cats and heads of state alike.[2]

---

1 In 1975 the Collective followed this up with *Media Burn*, a video showing a classic 1959 Cadillac being driven through a wall of forty-two blazing television sets.

2 Meanwhile, in Soviet Russia, vast ZiL limousines (made by *Zavod imeni Likhacheva*,

The Continental III came to reflect an age in more ways than one. Just before 12.30 p.m. on 22 November 1963, an open-top Continental III carrying John F. Kennedy, thirty-fifth president of the United States, slowly turned left directly in front of the old Book Depository in Dallas, Texas. This particular Continental was 21 feet long, covered in armour plating, and weighed in at a hefty 7,822 pounds. It also had two removable roofs – neither of which was in use that day; Kennedy had ordered that the detachable glasshouse should be taken off since the weather was fine. As the car passed the Book Depository and continued down Elm Street, shots were fired at the president. As Kennedy waved to the crowds on his right a bullet entered his upper back, penetrated his neck, and exited from his throat. As Jackie Kennedy climbed on to the capacious trunk rear of the Continental (she later had no recollection of doing so), a secret serviceman jumped on to the back of the car, pushed her back into her seat, and clung to the vehicle as it sped to Parkland Memorial Hospital. Shortly after the Lincoln arrived, doctors pronounced the president dead. Vice President Johnson – who had been riding two cars behind Kennedy in the motorcade, in a closed saloon – took the oath of office as thirty-sixth president on board Air Force One, just before it departed from Dallas's inappropriately named Love Field.

American confidence in the automobile's invulnerability, wavering in the wake of Kennedy's death, received a further blow with the publication of Ralph Nader's 1965 polemic *Unsafe at Any Speed*. Nader damned the US car industry's pursuit of profit, blatant disregard for safety and indifference to increasing concerns about pollution with a vehemence that no critic of the American auto had ever employed before. Nader's text unequivocally pointed the finger at the automobile as one of the principal delinquents of the age, declaiming: 'For over half a century the automobile has brought death, injury, and the most inestimable sorrow

___

named after the plant's director, Ivan Likhachev) plied up and down Moscow's boulevards carrying senior communist officials in a style reminiscent of 1940s America. The ZiL 41047, which was still being made as late as 2001, weighed an astronomical 4.2 tonnes and was powered by a 7.7 litre V-8 engine.

and deprivation to millions of people'. He cited the US Department of Commerce's 1959 estimate that fifty-one thousand Americans would be killed on the road by 1975 – suggesting that this target was liable to be reached ten years early – and calculated that US highway accidents now cost the nation $8 billion in property damage each year. He was also way ahead of his time in denouncing the car's 'power to pollute'. His principal complaint, though, was that the powerful vested interests of Detroit had made the automobile immune from criticism. Nader alleged that the car 'has remained the only transportation vehicle to escape being called to meaningful public account', and derided the motoring media as craven and subservient to the manufacturers.

Nader's principal target was one unfortunate model: GM's Chervolet Corvair. Developed hurriedly as a response to the huge success of the VW Beetle in America, the Corvair's poor handling (partly caused by the omission of a $15 stabilizing bar) resulted in a tendency to flip over when turning sharply at speed. Nader's book called Corvairs 'one-car accidents', and by the time it appeared GM was facing 103 lawsuits from Corvair owners. Even Chevrolet chief 'Bunkie' Knudsen demanded that the car be redesigned after his niece was seriously injured in one. (As early as 1959 Ford had come to the same conclusion when its test driver lost control of an early Corvair at the company's track.) Yet Nader noted that GM had to date done nothing about these apparent failings: 'bureaucratic rigidness and the abject worship of that bitch-goddess, cost reduction', had encouraged them just to sit tight. This seemed to support his theory that modern car makers 'put appearance above safety' – a clear dig at the fifties cult of the omnipotent car stylist.

GM responded to Nader's accusations not by remodelling the car but by attempting to muffle the messenger. The company commissioned private detectives to try to uncover evidence of his presumed (but actually non-existent) communist or homosexual leanings. But the cat was out of the bag. At the annual GM shareholders meeting of May 1965, Nader ally Dr Seymour Charles publicly demanded recalls of all 1960–3 Corvairs. (GM officers tried to stifle the debate by asking Dr Charles to talk to them privately after the meeting.) In the subsequent senatorial hearings, GM's top executives showed a worrying lack of knowledge about their own products, and had no answer to Senator Robert Kennedy's telling comparison of the GM safety budget for 1964, of $1.25 million, with that year's corporate profits of $1.7 billion. Eventually, GM president James Roche, a colourless accountant who had none of the vision or presence of Alfred Sloan, was forced to apologize to Nader before a Senate subcommittee, and to pay him $425,000 in damages. In 1969 the Corvair itself was finally withdrawn. Sloan's successors had successfully disposed of much of his carefully wrought business philosophy, eroding the much-vaunted ladder system of market segmentation and making a nonsense of GM's internal demarcations. The result was, as evidenced in Roche's lacklustre response to Congress, a lack of corporate leadership and conviction about how to react to the changing marketplace.

Nader's assault on Motor City unleashed a torrent of criticism of the unsafe nature and ecological irresponsibility of the modern American car. As Stephen Bayley has observed: 'Nader made American cars appear both dangerous and ridiculous.' Now everyone felt able to voice their concerns. The visual pyrotechnics of designers such as Earl, Exner and Mitchell only served, observers now dared to suggest, as increasingly irrelevant facades for the Big Three's complacency and indifference. Historian Lewis Mumford, the first part of whose magisterial *Myth of the Machine* appeared in 1967, declared that the American auto was 'the result of a secret collaboration between the beautician and the mortician', and that 'according to sales and accident statistics both have reason to be satisfied'.

Nader, Mumford and their likes destroyed the confidence of the US auto industry – so much so that, in the opinion of many motor critics, the Big Three never made another great car during the next thirty years. An indication of the muddled thinking of the late sixties can be seen by comparing Bill Mitchell's taut, compact Corvette Sting Ray of 1963 with the fate of his Buick Riviera. The 1963 Riviera was a sleek, low, stylish, hard-top, two-door coupé, which changed the Buick division's reputation for stodgy family cars almost overnight. Its pronounced side fenders and flared waist were the look of things to come; indeed, designer Sergio Pininfarina called the Riviera 'one of the most beautiful American cars ever built'. However, three years later not only did GM consign Alfred Sloan's corporate philosophy to the wastebasket by allowing the Pontiac division to launch a downmarket rival to the Riviera, the Pontiac Grand Prix hard-top. The Riviera itself was pumped up to ludicrous proportions, with Mitchell and his team now converted to the belief that bloated was invariably better. Longer, wider and more distended, the Riviera was soon more powerful, too; in 1967 it was provided with Buick's impressive new V-8 engine. Four years later, Bill Mitchell's redesign completely sacrificed the car's sporty image and by the end of the 1970s the Riviera, like the Ford Thunderbird, was almost indistinguishable from its more commonplace rivals.

Even more overblown than the later Rivieras was the Oldsmobile Toronado of 1966. A 'full-size personal car', equipped with hidden headlights and a Camaro-like fastback roof, aimed squarely at the Thunderbird market, the Toronado was, like the original Mustang, a two-door coupé. But there resemblances ended. With vast overhangs at front and rear, and projecting, potentially lethal, side 'guards' either side of the front grille, the Toronado measured an astonishing 17½ feet and weighed almost 2 tonnes. It shared a platform and some parts with the 1966 Riviera but was far heftier – so much so that Oldsmobile soon had to install a 'built-in assist mechanism' to enable less sprightly owners to open the all-too-solid doors. Passenger space was, ironically, minimal – partly in order to make space for the gigantic, 7 litre Super Rocket V-8 engine (which was enlarged to a whopping 7.4 litres in 1968). But, aside from its sheer straight-line speed, the car's overall performance was dismal. Its braking was inadequate (it was only fitted with feeble drum brakes), its fuel consumption was astronomical, its transmission was unreliable, and its inability to take corners gave a new meaning to understeer.[1] Even GM

---

1 The technical term for the inability to cope with corners: the car prefers to head

admitted it may have gone too far. Sales of the model fell by 50 per cent in its second year, and in 1970 the Toronado – which Oldsmobile was now boasting was the largest front-wheel-drive car in the world – was repackaged as a cut-price Cadillac.

The Toronado was not the only swollen disappointment of the period. Ford's sleek, spare Mustang 'pony car' of a decade earlier had now become, as Lee Iacocca himself later lamented, 'a fat pig'. Iacocca, by now president of the Ford Motor Company, had ordered a smaller, more fuel-efficient Mustang for 1974. But this new Mustang II was based on the platform of the discredited Ford Pinto in order to pitch it against smaller, imported sports coupés such as Japan's Toyota Celica and the Anglo-German Ford Capri (itself a derivative of the first Mustang). And although the new Mustang was smaller than its illustrious predecessor, it weighed 600 pounds more than the original. Moreover, its performance was barely mediocre, while its body styling was decidedly uninspired. With the brand seriously devalued, sales plummeted. It was not until 2005 that an attempt was made to recapture the stylistic clues of Eugene Bordinat's classic original.

In the year in which the stylistically stunted Mustang II was launched, Ford also thoughtlessly disposed of their best styling asset. In 1974 the motor giant closed the Vignale styling workshop of Ghia, in which they had bought a controlling stake as recently as 1970. Ford continued to exploit the Ghia name (suggesting that this had been the only reason they had bought the company), but gradually whittled down the number of Ghia staff on the payroll; by 2001 there were only five.

The failure to exploit Ghia's potential indicated that all was not well at Ford. Much of this was due to the increasingly erratic behaviour of its president – a familiar story to anyone acquainted with the firm's history. Had Henry Ford II retired in 1970, he would have been hailed as the man who saved the company in the post-war era. As it was, his last decades were mired in personal and corporate wrangling.

---

straight on rather than follow the curve.

By 1960, when he casually disposed of his financial wizard, Ernie Breech, Henry Ford II had already begun to resemble his autocratic grandfather. He now preferred to run the Ford Motor Company, as Henry Ford himslef had done, more as a personal fiefdom than as a vast corporate enterprise. The legacy of his careful nurturing of the media during the late 1940s and 1950s was carelessly squandered when he abandoned his wife, Anne, to conduct a very public affair with the lively, outspoken Italian divorcée Cristina Vettore (whom he finally married in 1965). Notoriously touchy about any reference to his grandfather, he also sought to impose his own imprint on Detroit and, by implication, to eclipse the achievement of Henry Ford I. In 1971 he commissioned downtown Detroit's biggest-ever building project: John Portman's Renaissance Center, consisting of shops, offices and what was at the time the tallest hotel in the world. Finally completed in 1977, the Center's five giant towers dominated the heart of Motor City. By the early 1980s, however, many of the Renaissance Center's shops lay eerily empty, while Ford was defaulting on the interest on the loans negotiated to build the site. In 1996 Ford cheerfully sold the complex to GM, which, in 2004, optimistically moved its world headquarters to the site. Meanwhile, Henry II had tired of his combative Italian wife and begun an affair with photographic model Kathy DuRoss, who was one of the attractive young women the company employed to help market cars in showrooms and at conventions. DuRoss and Ford were finally married in Nevada, away from the prying eyes of Detroit's motor executives, in 1980.

With the national media were more interested in Henry II's colourful private life than in the company's new model line-up, Ford took its eyes off the ball. As a result, the firm whose fortunes had been founded on the small, durable, no-nonsense Model T found itself outmanoeuvred by a far smaller rival whose presence it had barely acknowledged.

With the American public increasingly preoccupied with the need to cut car emissions and reduce fuel consumption, it was clear that a new generation of economy cars – which by the mid-1970s were being referred to as 'subcompacts' or 'superminis' – was required. But the first American subcompact did not come from any of the Big Three. The AMC Gremlin of 1970 looked like a bug whose rear end had been sawn off; but it was economical, cheap and practical. AMC called it its 'bold and innovative approach' to the dual threat of increasing gas prices and fuel-efficient Japanese and German imports. The company did not even seem worried about the negative connotations of the car's brand name. *Time* magazine noted that, while *Webster's Dictionary* defined a gremlin as 'a small gnome held to be responsible for malfunction of equipment', American Motors preferred to describe it as 'a pal to its friends and an ogre to its enemies'. Released six months ahead of its domestic competitors, AMC's 'import-fighter' outperformed its adversaries even when they did appear. It rode, accelerated, and handled better, and offered more space than all its rivals, including the Volkswagen, and was more frugal with fuel than all but the VW. It also suffered far fewer recalls than its US challengers. In 1973 *Automobile Quarterly* judged that 'the Gremlin offers outstanding performance for an economy car and excellent fuel mileage'. And, like the Volkswagen, it certainly looked distinctive. AMC's chief designer, Richard Teague, was so proud of his creation that he told *Motor Trend* magazine that to compare the Gremlin to the Beetle was like 'comparing a Ford GT40 to the Hindenburg'.

Richard Teague started his working life as a child star in film comedy shorts, usually playing the role of a girl, 'Dixie Duval'. However, when he was only six his mother's car was hit by a drunk driver, leaving young Richard without the sight of one eye and his mother an invalid. A year later, his father was killed in another automobile crash – also caused by an inebriated driver. Shrugging off his traumatic childhood, Richard became a technical illustrator for Northrop and then Kaiser, before joining GM in 1948 and Packard in 1951. Having been made chief stylist at Packard, on the firm's forced merger with Studebaker he and his entire staff were recruited by Exner at Chrysler. Two years later the restive Teague left for AMC, where he achieved wonders on minuscule budgets. His last work for the corporation was the splendid 1984 Jeep Cherokee XJ, which *Automobile* magazine later lauded as one of the '20 greatest cars of all time'.

Given General Motors' immense resources, its answer to Teague's diminutive Gremlin, the Chevrolet Vega of 1971, should have been far superior to AMC's subcompact. But it wasn't. Styled like a sports car with a fastback roof, it looked suspiciously like a Fiat. Even its name sounded Italian. But its reputation for poor reliability, rusting bodywork and perpetual recalls dogged it throughout its brief, six-year lifespan. Engines stalled, brakes failed, gear-shift levers fell off, exhausts set fire to the petrol tank, and water leaks were legion. In July 1972 GM recalled 95 per cent of Vegas because their rear axles were, astonishingly, 'too short'.[1] Part of the problem was that the factory where the Vega was made, GM's brand-new plant at Lordstown, Pennsylvania, was plagued with strikes. By early 1972, when Chevrolet management was claiming that Lordstown workers were deliberately sabotaging Vegas, the workforce (97 per cent of whom had just voted for an all-out strike) replied that they didn't have to: the car fell apart without their help. Lordstown had been touted as the 'fastest assembly line in the world', but its staff conditions were little better than those at Ford's Rouge River plant in 1913: penalties for transgressing rules were severe, a table showing workers' 'demerits' was publicly displayed, and there was still no worker participation at senior level. The factory did boast the latest Unimate robotic painting technology; unfortunately, the untested robots often lost control and spray-painted the wrong bits. In 1977 GM finally put the Vega out of its misery.

Even more notorious than the Vega was Ford's response to the Gremlin, the Pinto. Lee Iacocca had been involved in the Pinto's development as vice president (a fact that he conveniently airbrushed out of his self-serving memoir of 1985), and in his original brief for the project he demanded a car that weighed no more than 2,000 pounds and cost no more than $2,000. However, the search for savings encouraged the

---

1 This was the Vega's third total recall.

Pinto's designers to cut some dangerous corners. To save weight, the rear was shortened, exposing the fuel tank to the possibility of explosion in the event of a rear-end collision. The Pinto's first, highly publicized, victim was Mrs Lilian Gray, a Californian housewife who was burned to death in a fuel tank fire in May 1972 when her Pinto was rear-ended by another car. Her passenger, teenager Richard Grimshaw, survived but was horrifically scarred by extensive burns. Motor critics were soon cruelly dubbing the Pinto 'the barbecue that seats four'.

In 1974 Ralph Nader's Center for Auto Safety urged a recall of all Ford Pintos. But both Henry Ford II and Lee Iacocca refused to acknowledge the car's fatal flaw, and Henry II even lobbied vigorously in Washington against new safety legislation. Ford's considered response to Nader's allegations was that 'he's full of crap', adding: 'The American people want good cars, good-looking cars, fast cars, cars with power and styling, and that's the kind of cars we build. We spend a hell of a lot of time trying to make them better and safer, and then some pipsqueak who doesn't know a thing about the industry comes along and tries to tell us how to do what we've dedicated our lives and billions of dollars to doing.'

However, in 1977 *Mother Jones* magazine revealed how the Ford Motor Company had conducted its own crash tests, and had indeed been aware of the Pinto's shortcomings well before 1972. Damningly, the publication estimated that as many as nine hundred drivers had died since then in Pinto fuel-tank fires. The magazine article, written by Mark Dowie, also revealed how Ford's cost-benefit analysis had chillingly calculated that the cost of each fatality (assessed at an implausibly precise $200,725, which included a mere $10,000 for the 'victim's pain and suffering') and of serious burns (estimated at $67,000) was less than the cost of making each Pinto safer. Ford had no answer to this devastating assault and agreed to withdraw 1.5 million Pintos. Meanwhile, Pinto victim Richard Grimshaw won a record $125 million in damages from a Californian court.[1]

---

1 Following appeals this sum was massively reduced, but Grimshaw still eventually received well over $6 million.

After Ford had been charged with reckless homicide, had been forced to recall yet more Pintos, and had belatedly improved protection for the fuel tank, only to find that the car was now far too unwieldy to drive, the Pinto was finally withdrawn in 1980.

The disasters of the Vega and Pinto, however, appeared almost trivial when compared with the industrial implosion currently occurring on the other side of the Atlantic, where, as the 1970s progressed, large chunks of Britain's and France's motor industries appeared to be blithely heading towards meltdown.

Both Citroën and its owners, Michelin, were struggling by 1970. Citroën was still producing two of the most iconic and impressive cars of the century, the 2CV and the DS. But its engineers and stylists simply could not leave well alone. Designating the classic DS for replacement well before its time, the firm had spent far too much on developing its mediocre substitute, the CX, which never quite delivered what it promised. At the same time, Michelin's dependence on oil-derived carbon black (then the basis for all synthetic rubber products) in an age of escalating oil prices severely weakened its finances.

In the midst of all this, Citroën made one of the most bizarre purchases of the automotive era when it bought the legendary Italian niche sports car manufacturer Maserati in 1968. The principal fruit of this strange alliance, the Citroën SM, was a massively oversized two-door coupé which Citroën launched in 1970. Powered by a Maserati V-6 engine, it was packed with innovations typical of Citroën's progressive past: hydraulic, self-levelling suspension even more sophisticated than that used on the DS; an all-glass nose; self-centred power steering; self-levelling headlamps; disc brakes at all corners; and rain-sensitive windscreen wipers. Yet the SM failed to find much of a market in a world in which its splendid performance and advanced technology were fatally undermined by its voracious fuel consumption.

Having spent enormous sums of money on the disappointing CX

and the exotic SM, by 1973 Citroën was close to collapse. An alliance with Fiat foundered when the Italians withdrew, worried by the French firm's mounting debts. The SM predictably proved a sales disaster, and even the CX – which, despite its cutting-edge engineering, still looked cheap and plasticky – was selling poorly. Fortunately for Citroën, France's government was in no mood to let such a large and prestigious national car maker go to the wall. In 1974 Georges Pompidou's administration saved the firm from collapse by arranging a shotgun marriage with its old rival Peugeot – the tortoise to Citroën's hare. Peugeot's first actions was to sell Maserati, stop production of the SM and close Citroën's historic Quai de Javel factory in the centre of Paris. There was no place for romance in the stark economic context of the oil crisis.

That year, 1974, was also the year in which the British government stepped in to save the country's largest car maker from ruin. At the beginning of the 1970s British motor manufacturing was still dangerously fragmented. While it remained a key part of the country's economy – as late as 1975 vehicle manufacture still accounted for 11 per cent of industrial output – the car industry's practices were sadly outmoded, its workforce increasingly unreliable, and its management palpably inadequate. As early as 1962, business analyst Samuel Saul had accused the British car industry of a lack of commercial acumen and a 'passion for technical perfection and individuality for its own sake'. A decade later, Saul's astute warnings had come true.

Much of the problem stemmed from poor senior management. BMC boss George Harriman's laissez-faire approach to the combine meant that little was done to rationalize its overlapping product lines and multiplicity of plants. Harriman's principal concern was merely that his shareholders should always get a generous dividend – a philosophy that he dutifully followed until 1967, when there was simply no money left for any sort of dividend at all, because BMC, despite its best-selling Minis and 1100s, stood on the verge of bankruptcy. Weakness at the top infected the whole company; morale on the shop floor was perilously low, and a 1971 *Which?* report damned the former BMC's dealers as the worst in the country.

The British auto industry's decline and fall makes for grim reading. In 1950 Britain was the largest car exporter in the world, but by 1970 the UK's auto exports had been surpassed by France, Italy and Japan. Most revealingly, by 1976 the productivity of Germany's car makers was 40 per cent higher than their UK equivalents. Between 1973 and 1977 Ford was the only British car maker to post a consistent profit: in 1975 British Leyland lost £23.6 million, Rootes (now owned by Chrysler) £35.5 million and GM's Vauxhall £2.5 million – while Ford made a £40.8 million profit. By 1974, 25 per cent of car-making capacity in the UK was being lost to strikes. Small wonder that in that year Cowley workers' wives demonstrated at the plant gates *against* their husbands' 'perpetual strikes' and in support of the beleaguered BL management.

The consolidation of most of Britain's mass car makers at the end of the sixties was not just promoted by Harold Wilson's Labour government. Prudential Assurance, the largest shareholder in both BMC and Leyland-Triumph, also urged the merger. Together, the government and the insurers forced the ailing BMC into a series of alliances, first with Jaguar and Pressed Steel in 1966 and two years later with Leyland Motors, which had itself already absorbed Triumph and Rover.

Leyland was a truck and bus maker with little experience of car production. In the 1920s the firm had produced just two models of car: a large Straight Eight, designed to compete with Rolls-Royce (which it signally failed to do); and, from 1925, the Trojan, a solid-wheeled 'utility car' with a wheelspan that exactly matched that of most of Britain tramlines, triggering a number of horrific accidents and unintended diversions. Leyland built the Cromwell tank during the Second World War (and the magnificent Centurion tank afterwards), and in 1951 embarked on a spending spree that, in sixteen years, procured such household names as Scammell, Triumph, AEC, Bristol and Rover.

The new British Leyland combine of 1968, headed by Leyland's former boss, Donald Stokes, seemed unable to offer anything new. Even the marriage had been unhappy: George Harriman had found himself railroaded by stronger characters such as Wilson and Stokes, and subsequently complained to Alec Issigonis that, having arrived at the prime minister's country residence of Chequers in October 1967, supposedly to discuss the proposed merger between Leyland and BMC,[1] he found Stokes already there and the deal secured. Thereafter, Harriman fell conveniently ill and took little part in the negotiations. Thus, just as the creation of BMC in 1952 was in reality a takeover of Morris by Austin, so the creation of British Leyland – which industry minister Tony Benn hailed as 'a fantastic achievement' – actually represented a takeover by Leyland-Triumph of BMC, which was now haemorrhaging money at an alarming rate.

British Leyland served no one well. Austin and Morris still retained their separate dealerships, which needed to be supplied with a range of appropriately badged cars. In 1968 BL had forty-eight factories, many of which were ponderously old-fashioned and operated with antiquated piecework contracts – complex agreements that differed from department to department. Most tragically, two of BL's world-beating models, the Rover 2000/3500 (P6) and the Triumph 2000/2500, now not only competed with each other but also with the executive-market Jaguars from elsewhere in the conglomerate. The powerful Sir William Lyons (who had cannily shoehorned himself into the deputy chairman's role at BL) ensured that Triumph's impressive executive range was killed off prematurely and that the marque was forbidden to develop any further products in that area. Lyons also ensured that Rover's planned Jaguar-sized replacement for the P6, the four-door P8, was axed in 1971 because it might conceivably have competed with Jaguar's own models. The chance to compete with BMW and Mercedes (and the design for the P8 did look very much like the BMWs of the late 1970s and early 80s) was thus heedlessly tossed away. Rover and Triumph were instead chained together in a 'Special Division'

---

1 Which, since its incorporation of Jaguar and Pressed Steel the previous year, was officially known by the unimaginative title of British Motor Holdings.

whose single product, the Rover SD1, did not appear until 1976. Over at Austin Morris, the racy Mini Cooper was discontinued in 1971 because BL did not want to pay John Cooper his miserly royalties – which worked out at roughly £5 per car – and the charismatic Austin Healey was killed off for much the same reason. Thus were two splendid brands flushed away for myopic, short-term gains.

Even Sir Alec Issigonis[1] seemed mysteriously to have mislaid his talent. The celebrated designer of the Minor and the Mini had been promoted by Harriman into senior management positions for which his prickly temperament and pronounced opinions made him ill-suited. His Austin/Morris 1100 of 1962 had proved Britain's best-selling car through the 1960s, but his subsequent models – the Austin 1800 of 1964 (which Issigonis saw only as 'a giant Mini'); its bloated cousins the Austin 2200, Wolseley Six and Austin 3-Litre; and the much-derided Maxi of 1969 – were all squat, overweight, oversized and poorly built. Issigonis simply applied the principle of the Mini to ever-larger cars, maximizing internal space but providing little in the way of boot area or interior sophistication. Issigonis's inherent parsimony also meant that the interiors of these ungainly 'land crabs', as the models were unaffectionately known in the trade, were very sparsely furnished. The genius of the Mini did, after all, have feet of clay.

Stokes later admitted of the Austin Maxi: 'It was ghastly . . . It looked wrong; you couldn't change gear on it; it just wasn't developed.' BL's desperate advertising agency was reduced to promoting the Maxi as a double bed on wheels; certainly, there was nothing to brag about in its poor performance, fault-prone gearbox and excruciating build. Once again, a British car maker had released a new model far too early, just at the time when the Germans, and particularly the Japanese, were ensuring that all of their new models were rigorously tested *before*, and not after, their launch. Thus all of Issgonis's new cars, from the 1800 to the Maxi, were plagued with wholly avoidable post-production faults. At the same

---

1 He was knighted in 1969.

time, the successful models that Issigonis had previously designed for BMC were never properly updated. While European manufacturers stole a march on the British – the highly successful 'superminis' of 1972, the Renault 5 and the Fiat 127, suddenly made the original Mini look old – BL had nothing to offer in response. Stokes's British Leyland actually abandoned the Mini replacement project, ADO74, just in time for the oil crisis of 1973 – after which superminis were massively in demand. It took BMW to recognize what Austin and its successors should have acknowledged decades before: that the marvellous Mini could be adapted to contemporary parameters and still retain its innate charm and uniqueness, and sales appeal.

BL's supremo, Donald Stokes,[1] was hardly the ideal figure to lead the British car industry out of its slough of despond. The Plymouth-born engineer had joined Leyland's sales department in 1930 and had demonstrated great flair when, twenty years later, he both expanded Leyland's bus range and won the company new export markets. But Stokes always remained at heart a bus enthusiast and seemed ill at ease in the world of mass car production. He was an excellent salesman and a good communicator. But he failed to comprehend the scale, complexity and internal fissures within British Leyland, and often shied away from making difficult decisions. In short, he seemed unable to grasp the big picture. He was the man, after all, who had described the unfortunate overlap between two of the most promising British cars of the post-war era, the Rover P6 and the Triumph 2000, as merely 'friendly competition'. Most revealingly, when in 1968 Harold Wilson asked Stokes for BL's long-term plan, he simply did not have one. Highly embarrassed by his failure, he asked his financial director, John Barber (formerly of Ford), to concoct something in a day. Barber merely copied out Ford's five-car strategy – which, depressingly, seems to have satisfied both Stokes and Wilson. Stokes later admitted: 'I think I was probably good at selling', but 'I was not and have never pretended to be a manufacturing expert.' John Barber

---

1 Or Lord Stokes, as he became in 1969.

was the only member of the new BL board who had any experience of mass-market car production.

Stokes's new empire went from bad to worse. BL's production rate was about half that of Ford of Britain, while its naive 'no search' policy on which the unions had insisted meant that bootfuls of car parts – even whole engines – regularly disappeared out of the factory gates. In addition, the continued application of antediluvian piecework agreements meant that many British Leyland factories were half deserted by mid-afternoon. (Ford of Britain, in contrast, paid its workers a fixed daily rate.) Strikes, too, became more frequent; in 1969–70 BL lost 5 million man-hours to stoppages, and the next financial year the figure doubled to an appalling 10 million man-hours. On top of all this, the model development BL had inherited from BMC was shambolic. Issigonis's 'land crabs' proved a stylistic and technological dead end, and little real effort had been put into updating either the Mini or the Austin/Morris 1300. The 'new' Morris Marina of 1971, the last car to use the Morris name, was supposed to be BL's answer to the Vauxhall Viva and Ford Cortina (Cowley dubbed it the 'Cortina Beater'). Yet it was created mostly by cannibalizing existing models and ended up as little more than a re-skinned Morris Minor, likened by critics at the time to 'a skip on wheels'. While European saloon cars were increasingly being built with front-wheel drive, the Marina retained the Minor's ancient and unresponsive rear-wheel drive. Worse still, the Cowley plant where the Marina was made had been expanded in such a cack-handed, stopgap way that the conveyor belt taking half-built cars over the Oxford bypass was left open to the elements, ensuring that parts were corroding even before they left the factory. Marinas arrived at the showrooms with their paintwork already bubbling with rust, and quickly sprung leaks. (One Cowley worker, Bill Roche, blamed the 'gate-line' assembly process, by which the two sides of a car were each built in a jig and then put together at the end of the line, a demoralizingly imprecise manufacturing method which Renault, Fiat and the Japanese had already dismissed as obsolete.)

Against Ford's Cortina – and, after 1974, VW's immensely superior Golf – the Marina never stood a chance, and the export sales on which British Leyland had based its over-optimistic forecasts never materialized. The Marina did, in Stokes's Panglossian phrase, 'quite well' in sales terms. But, as historian Martin Adeney has noted, 'quite well' was 'not sufficient for a company which was striving to push up its profits in the face of increasing . . . industrial disruption'. America was less forgiving: the Marina was soon placed on *Consumer Reports'* notorious 'Cars to Avoid' list.

British Leyland's second new mass-market car of the 1970s, the Austin Allegro of 1973 ('our Song for Europe', in the words of Longbridge supremo George Turnbull), was a dumpy disaster whose curious, lumpy shape found few admirers. Turnbull had promised that the car would appeal to customers 'from the Arctic Circle to the toe of Italy' because of the way 'the eye is beguiled by its excellent proportions'. It was intended as a replacement for the bestselling 1100/1300; yet, as critic James Ruppert has observed, 'strike-torn and terrorist-threatened Britain got the car it deserved'. The Allegro's blobby styling – light years away from the razor-sharp edges of Giorgetto Giugiaro's groundbreaking VW Golf – earned it the nickname of 'the Flying Pig'. And its 'revolutionary' square (or, rather, 'quartic') steering wheel was dismissed as an eccentric joke; even skilled police drivers had trouble steering their Allegro panda cars. The Allegro had a boot, whereas its rival, the Golf, was an easy-to-access hatchback;[1] the car's hydragas suspension (introduced by BL just as Citroën was thinking of abandoning the system) proved highly unreliable on the road; there was actually less room inside an Allegro than there had been in a 1300; and, once again, build quality was very poor, with leaks being commonplace. As a result, the car sold significantly less than the successful and much-loved models it was designed to replace. In its best sales year, 1975, only 63,339 Allegros

---

1 BMC had, of course, pioneered the hatchback with the Farina-styled Austin A40 of 1958, but this valuable legacy appeared to have been forgotten by the brave new British Leyland of the mid-1970s.

The most beautiful car in the world? The Citroën DS mobbed at the 1955 Paris Motor Show.

The Jaguar XK120 proved to the world that 'Britain Could Make It', and won the nation valuable dollar income in the postwar years of austerity. Here British racing driver Stirling Moss drives an export model down the ramp.

Ferdinand Porsche with an early Porsche 356.

The notorious Ford Edsel of 1957, with its ungainly 'horse-collar' grille. The late Edsel Ford's three sons perch inside: from left to right, William Clay Ford, Benson Ford and company president Henry Ford II.

One of Virgil Exner's 'New Look' Chryslers for 1957: a Dodge Custom Royal.

The zenith of Baroque car design: the taillights of a 1959 Cadillac Eldorado.

This 1959 promotion optimistically suggested that all of this could be packed into a Mini. A revolutionary car, the Mini was initially handicapped by the timid BMC's insistence on recycling inappropriate, pre-war brand names.

Stylishly confident: an Aston Martin DB5 of 1963, entirely at home in the English Cotswolds.

were sold (very few of them overseas); in contrast, the 1100/1300 had regularly sold over 100,000 per year. The car was hardly improved when, in 1974, the venerable, premium coach-making marque of Vanden Plas was inappropriately harnessed to an upmarket Allegro variant equipped with a uniquely hideous, pig-like nose. In that bleak year, British Leyland's best-selling model was not the Allegro, nor the Maxi, but the ageing Mini.

BL's other, much-vaunted, new products of the early seventies fared little better. The Triumph Stag of 1970 certainly looked the part. It was designed by Giovanni Michelotti, author of the Stag's handsome cousin, the Triumph 2000. But the stylish Stag turned out to be badly built, unreliably powered and hugely rust-prone. Instead of using Rover's trusty, lightweight V-8 engine, Triumph's management refused to employ their erstwhile rival's power train and instead bolted together two four-cylinder Dolomite engines to create their own 3 litre V-8. Unsurprisingly, this engine proved far too heavy and unreliable. The Stag's bodywork leaked and its 'removable' hard top took at least two people to manhandle it. As journalist Tony Davis commented: 'When an owner stands by his Triumph Stag, it's usually because he can't get the door open'.'

The Stag did nothing to help sustain Triumph's reputation. Nor did Triumph's other sporty offering, the latest in the famed TR series. When in 1974 *Motor* magazine reviewed the new Triumph TR7 – a good-looking sports car of the sort at which British manufacturers in general, and Triumph in particular, had excelled during the sixties – its journalists were sadly unimpressed. By the end of the test they had had to rebuild the engine, and noted 'disfiguring rust', 'unbearable' noise and 'a sluggish power train'. Unsurprisingly, *Motor* judged the car to be 'a particularly nasty lemon'. The car's scallop-sided styling and tartan upholstery looked plain daft, while visibility from both front and rear windows was appalling. The TR7 successfully garrotted the international market for Triumph

---

1 In 1977 the British guide *Making Money from Collectable Cars* declared that 'if you are a mechanical masochist, this is your car'.

sports cars, wiping fond memories of the TR4 and the Spitfire from its erstwhile customers' minds.

When different parts of British Leyland did actually try to work together, the result was often farcical. In 1968 Stokes lamely agreed that the firm's quality marques of Jaguar, Rover and Triumph would not share plans or designs with the volume car division, Austin Morris, and that the two corporate halves would maintain entirely separate dealer networks. But when, in 1970, some daring souls at Austin Morris dared to challenge this *ukase* and lent their Cowley-made gearbox to Canley for its Triumph Toledo, it was found that it did not fit.

There was one occasion for modified rapture at BL. The new Range Rover of 1970, an upmarket, David Bache-designed, V-8 engined version of that hardy perennial, the Land Rover, was a qualified success. The concept had been suggested as far back as 1954, but Rover had lacked the financial backing to develop both this and the P6. Now BL finally realized Rover's vision. But while the car was excellent in theory, its execution was predictably flawed. The initial build quality, like most British Leyland products of the 1970s, was abysmal. And BL was slow to respond to the model's popularity, only investing in new plant for the Range Rover at Solihull in 1978.[1]

British Leyland, however, was not the only floundering British automotive giant of the early 1970s. Most British-based manufacturers preferred to milk established successes well past their sell-by dates rather respond to consumers who now demanded fuel efficiency, reliability and technological advance. Top of the list was Chrysler Europe, which tried to sell in the US the lacklustre model range it had inherited from Rootes[2] as the Chrysler Hunter and Dodge Husky.

By 1966 the Sunbeam marque had been so devalued that it was used to badge the upmarket version of the dismal Hillman Imp, the car

---

1 The widening gap between the basic Land Rover and the increasingly luxurious Range Rover later encouraged the Rover Group (as BL had by then become) to launch the Land Rover Discovery in 1989 and the more downmarket Freelander in 1997.

2 The boxy Arrow range of cars: the Hillman Minx, Hillman Hunter and Singer Vogue.

that was to break the fragile Rootes empire. The Sunbeam name was given a last hurrah by Rootes with the Arrow range's Sunbeam Rapier coupé of 1968, a car whose sloping, fastback rear made it look more like a Plymouth Barracuda than the Hillman it really was. Having seemingly perished along with Rootes, the Sunbeam name was exhumed as a meaningless designation by Chrysler and Peugeot in the late 1970s.

Rootes' multi-brand policy had proved that badge engineering could seriously devalue prestigious marques. Once these brands had been cheapened, it was almost impossible to upgrade them again – something that Alfred Sloan and Walter Chrysler had clearly recognized, but which Billy Rootes had failed to grasp. This was a lesson that BMC (in the 1960s), British Leyland and Rover (after 1968) and even the mighty GM (after 1981) also subsequently ignored, to the detriment of their businesses. The collapse of Rover at the turn of the twenty-first century, and the near ruin of GM in 2009, can be partly attributed to the careless squandering of their once-valuable brand heritages.

Chrysler's odd-looking and mechanically conventional new British model, the ungainly Hillman Avenger of 1970,[1] sold tolerably well in the UK – or at least, well enough to compensate for the lack of investment in any other new models. But Chrysler Europe's American management was paralysed by indecision and seemed unable to do anything to prevent the strikes that were increasingly crippling factory production. To many observers, the only thing keeping the company afloat appeared to be the income from the 1967 agreement with the Iranian government, whereby Rootes had agreed to supply Hillman Hunters in kit form to be assembled in Iran under the name 'Paykan'. This lucrative deal ultimately lasted for twenty years.

Even GM seemed to have lost the plot in Britain. Vauxhall's performance in the 1970s was little better than Chrysler's as it continued to rely on an outdated model range based on the uninspiring, American-looking Victor FD/FE and its smaller sister, the mediocre Viva. Ominously for

---

1 Which Chrysler also attempted to sell in America, as the Plymouth Cricket.

Britain, the Vauxhall Victor was the last car to be developed in the UK independently of GM's larger, German subsidiary, Opel. From 1979 Britain's Vauxhalls were little more than re-badged Opels.

While the British public were not unduly distressed by the troubles of British Leyland, Chrysler Europe and Vauxhall in the early 1970s, one automotive failure, at the ultra-premium end of the market, caused many to realize just how precarious the nation's industrial base had become. The collapse of Rolls-Royce in 1971 was biggest shock yet to those who still believed in the global superiority of the British car industry. In truth, Rolls-Royce's downfall was not due to any serious problems with the car division but was caused by the bankruptcy of the much larger aircraft engine business, following the enormous cost of developing the advanced RB211 jet engine.[1] However, the ruin of a car maker that most Britons regarded as the best in the world came as an unpleasant awakening. If Rolls-Royce could fail, what might be next?

---

1 Edward Heath's Conservative government saved the company by immediately nationalizing it. In 1973 the car division was sold separately as Rolls-Royce Motors.

12

Crisis? What Crisis?

On 6 October 1973, the Jewish public holiday of Yom Kippur, cheap oil and cheap motoring suddenly became a thing of the past as 222 Egyptian jets and three thousand guns attacked Israeli positions in the Sinai and on the eastern bank of the Suez Canal, while Syrian aircraft, artillery and tanks stormed across Israel's northern border. Egypt and Syria were seeking retribution for the territory they had lost in the Six Day War, which Israel had unleashed on its unsuspecting neighbours six years before. And for a time it seemed as if they would succeed; the Israeli army initially fell back as American intelligence dismissed Arab military activity as seasonal manoeuvres. By 15 October, however, Israeli counter-offensives had forced Egyptian units in the Sinai to retreat. By the 25th, when Israeli forces were only thirty miles from Damascus and seventy miles from Cairo, all parties agreed to a UN-brokered ceasefire.

The Arab states' previous attempt to use the 'oil weapon' against Israel's Western supporters, in 1967, had failed. This time, however, the Arab-dominated Organization of Petroleum Exporting Countries (OPEC) was better prepared, and more ruthless. In the midst of the fighting of 16 October, and two days after US planes had been spotted bringing military supplies into Israel in broad daylight, OPEC announced that the price of oil was rising by 70 per cent, with immediate effect. OPEC's Arab members then both cut oil production and simultaneously announced that they would halt all oil exports to those countries that had not supported

UN resolution 242, which demanded that Israel be forced to return to its 1967 borders. That meant those countries that were actively supporting Israel, and America in particular. President Richard Nixon, already mired in the Watergate scandal which was to end in his ignominious resignation, retaliated by brazenly proposing a $2.2 billion military aid package for Israel. This unhelpful gesture merely served to harden OPEC's resolve to impose an oil embargo on America and other prominent friends of Israel, notably the Netherlands, Portugal and South Africa. The rest of the world would have to endure the after-effects of the draconian rise in oil prices.

In 1973 world economies were enormously dependent on oil and consequently very vulnerable to any sharp rise in the value of this essential commodity. The Japanese were especially reliant on imported oil, with 77 per cent of their energy was created from oil, compared with 46 per cent in the US. Accordingly, in 1974 Japanese GNP fell for the first time since the Second World War. Many Japanese now began to think the unthinkable: that their post-war economic miracle was over. As a result, the government rushed into energy diversification, investigating alternative fuel sources for industry, homes and automobiles. Japan was also the first country to introduce catalytic converters into car engines in order to reduce emissions, leading to a noticeable improvement in air quality (air pollutants dropped by one third in Japan in the decade after 1972). Toyota initially dragged its corporate feet, but the car maker was ultimately forced to apologize to the Japanese parliament for its recalcitrance and was soon joining its competitors in fitting converters to its vehicles.

Across the Pacific, the fundamental tenet of American consumerism, that resources were endless and abundant, was shaken to its core. Alfred Sloan had built GM on the principle of planned obsolescence; now GM's customers wanted durability and fuel economy, not stylistic or technological novelty. Western pump prices quickly rose by 40 per cent and kept rising – often daily. Service stations across the globe were beset by vast queues of impatient and exasperated drivers. In the US emergency measures, such as a blanket national speed limit of 55 mph and tougher

standards for fuel consumption for new cars, (including the compulsory
fitting of catalytic converters to reduce toxic emissions) were formalized
in the Energy Policy and Conservation Act of 1975. The act also set quixotic new fuel-efficiency standards, designed to double the fuel efficiency
of an average new car from 13 mpg, as it currently stood, to 27.5 mpg.
(Even in the mid-1950s the vast, befinned Cadillacs and Lincolns had
managed a vaguely respectable 20 mpg.) Yet progress in this direction
was still painfully slow.

An uneasy peace came to the Middle East in 1974. But this did not
see the end of the crisis; prices may have initially calmed after the panics
of 1973–4, but American support for the beleaguered Shah of Iran during
the country's Islamic Revolution of December 1978–January 1979 led to
a second oil shock' in 1979, instigated by the nationalization of Iran's oil
extraction and a consequent steep rise in the price of petrol. Oil prices
were increased still further when two of the world's biggest oil producers,
Iran and Iraq, engaged in all-out war in September 1980. The age of
cheap gasoline was emphatically over.

With the seemingly unending rises in the cost of fuel during the
1970s, the gas-guzzling behemoths manufactured by American car makers since the Second World War – vehicles previously regarded as the
embodiment of automotive ambition – suddenly started to be viewed not
as powerful, handsome beasts but as lumbering dinosaurs whose fuel
consumption was placing an intolerable burden on the planet. The world
now belonged to small mammals such as the Honda Civic, the Renault
5 and the VW Golf, and America's Big Three were wrong-footed. The
introduction of new subcompact models at the beginning of the decade
had not, as we have seen, proved a great success, and US producers found
themselves making the wrong kinds of cars when consumers were looking for small, frugal models. And as America's automotive giants stumbled, European and Japanese car makers were happy to fill the gap.

One of the Big Three, indeed, seemed to have reached the end of
the road. In 1975 free-market champions Chrysler, unable to compete
with the European and Japanese onslaught, let alone the products of Ford

and GM, shut five of its six US plants. Chrysler Europe collapsed and its UK factories were sold in 1978 to the protectionist French. When, in November 1978, Lee Iacocca joined Chrysler as president, he found few financial controls and no consistent planning.

Since the late 1950s, Chrysler had expanded globally as well as domestically. But the foreign companies it bought – Simca in France, Rootes in Britain and Barrieros in Spain, together with a bewildering range of components factories from Turkey to Brazil – were all too small or too troubled to enhance Chrysler's worldwide status. Chrysler president Lynn Townsend, an accountant by training, was suspicious of automotive experts and preferred to promote men like his protégé, former Touche Ross accountant John Riccardo, who ultimately succeeded him as company president. The conglomerate accordingly lacked vision and drive. By the mid-1970s the firm had virtually given up on its European investment; even promising cars like Roy Axe's classy Sunbeam Rapier were given paltry marketing support and then inexplicably discontinued. In America, Chrysler was faced with an avalanche of complaints about poor build. In 1977 Ralph Nader's Center for Auto Safety publicly named the Dodge Aspen luxury compact its 'Lemon of the Year'.

Lacking inspiring new models for the US market, the desperate Chrysler management attempted to foist Mitsubishi Colts and mediocre Hillmans on an unsuspecting American public, rebranding them unconvincingly as Plymouths and Dodges. Chrysler persevered with its dull Plymouth Valiant compact for far too long and did not introduce a post-oil crisis subcompact, the Simca-derived Dodge Omni/Plymouth Horizon, until 1978; even then, the Omni's engine was borrowed from Volkswagen. Despite initial optimism, *Consumer Reports* was soon labelling the subcompact 'unpredictable and dangerous'. Meanwhile, the company discontinued production of its Dodge Charger 'muscle car', despite the fact that management was fully aware that the Charger was to be featured prominently (as 'General Lee') in an upcoming CBS TV series, *The Dukes of Hazzard*. Chrysler thus failed to take advantage of a potentially lucrative TV tie-in. Instead, the series' producers were forced to raid Chrysler showrooms for hundreds of the last Chargers; by series six of the show they were reduced to using scale models for some shots because all of their original stock of Chargers had been destroyed or damaged during shooting.

In 1975, as Lynn Townsend stepped down from the global presidency, Chrysler's American market share fell to a dismal 12 per cent and the firm announced a record $259 million loss. Simultaneously, Chrysler Europe announced that it was bankrupt. Chrysler subsequently received over £30 million to bail out its British factories from Harold Wilson's Labour government, provided that the firm lost eight thousand workers and that production of the new Alpine was moved from France to Ryton in Coventry.[1] Chrysler also closed its loss-making Linwood plant in Scotland, where the Hillman Imp was born and died, making thirteen thousand workers redundant and giving the Renfrewshire area one of the UK's highest unemployment rates.

Three years later Chrysler – to the understandable chagrin of the British government – sold the former Rootes plants it still owned to Peugeot for $1. Peugeot also agreed to shoulder £400 million of accumulated debt, and sold the Barrieros truck and bus operation in Spain to Renault. Chrysler went back to being just another American car maker.

America's fourth-largest auto manufacturer, AMC, which had only been created twenty years earlier, was also in serious financial trouble by the mid-1970s. Like Chrysler, it also found its ultimate salvation in French ownership. AMC had begun the decade by buying the Jeep marque from Kaiser, a venerable firm that had decided to quit the motor industry. (Jeep was to prove an enduringly successful brand for both AMC and Chrysler.) Yet while AMC's reaction to the oil crisis, the Pacer subcompact of 1975, may have been radically designed – its massive glasshouse led *Car and Driver* magazine to dub it 'the flying fishbowl', while others likened it to

---

1 In truth, the Ryton factory just assembled French-made kits, while the Alpine itself was merely a re-badging of a model from Chrysler's Simca subsidiary – the successful but mundane Simca 1307, a large, lumpish, four-door hatchback which bore no relation whatsoever to the illustrious Alpine sports cars of the 1960s.

a frog – it was also poorly built, overweight and underpowered. It was a curious response from a car maker that, unlike the Big Three, had long been accustomed to building small autos for the US market and had done well with the Pacer's predecessor, the Gremlin. It came as no surprise when, in February 1977, *Time* magazine reported not only that AMC's stockholders had received no dividends since 1974 but also that Pacer sales had fallen well below expectations.

Things simply got worse for American Motors. In May 1978 the Environmental Protection Agency ordered the recall of all of AMC's 1976 cars, a total of some three hundred thousand vehicles, to correct a fault in the pollution control system. The cost of this recall was estimated at around $3 million – more than AMC had earned the previous quarter. Strong Jeep sales enabled the firm to make a small profit in 1978–80, but new emissions directives due to come into force for four-wheel-drive vehicles in 1981, which necessitated costly engineering work on all new and existing Jeeps, prompted another nosedive in profitability. America wanted small cars, but AMC had the wrong product line and, in its ageing plant at Kenosha in Wisconsin (then the oldest continuously operating car factory in the world), an out-of-date and inefficient production line. In early 1980 the banks refused AMC further credit and, as its US market share dipped below 2 per cent (kept afloat only through healthy Jeep sales), AMC decided to throw in the towel. In 1981 the firm sold Renault a 22.5 per cent interest in the firm, in return for a $150 million cash injection and the rights to start building the Renault 5 in the US. This was effectively a Renault takeover: the new AMC president of January 1982, José Dedeurwaerder, was a Renault executive, and by 1983 Renault owned 49 per cent of the firm. New, Renault-designed, front-wheel-drive cars began to be produced at a modernized Kenosha; the first, the AMC/ Renault Alliance, was merely a re-skinned Renault 9. On 14 December 1987 the last AMC-badged car, an Eagle crossover SUV, left Kenosha.

By then, even Renault had withdrawn from the fray. Many at the French car giant had been sceptical about the AMC acquisition, seeing the loss-making American firm simply as an everlasting money pit – although

Renault chairman Georges Besse insisted that profitability was not far away. However, on 17 November 1986, Besse was assassinated by members of the communist terrorist group Action Directe, which cited the tens of thousands of workers Besse had sacked in France (redundancies partly made necessary by the poor performance of Renault's loss-making AMC division) as one of the reasons for the murder. After this tragedy, Besse's dispirited colleagues gave up and, in March 1987, sold AMC to Chrysler.

At Chrysler, Lee Iacocca was only really interested in acquiring the Jeep brand; in 1992 Chrysler finally unveiled the Jeep Grand Cherokee, the flagship SUV that AMC and Renault had been developing. Yet, once again, Chrysler made the mistake of believing that the cut-price purchase of a flagging car maker would lead to increasing sales rather than haemorrhaging profits. Despite the exciting new Jeeps, Chrysler's market share continued to decline until, in 1998, Chrysler itself was taken over by Daimler-Benz of Germany, in what was initially billed as a 'merger of equals' but which, it was quickly apparent, was really a straightforward acquisition. Daimler-Benz was determined to emulate its great rival, BMW, which had recently bought the loss-making Rover Group in Britain. However, much as BMW regretted buying Rover, soon Daimler-Benz was lamenting its purchase of Chrysler. In August 2010, much to the horror of the local population and the sadness of the motoring press, Chrysler's German management announced the closure of the historic former AMC plant at Kenosha.

Across the Atlantic, the effects of the oil crisis hit the British car industry like a tsunami. Aside from outstanding models such as the Mini, British family cars found little favour outside traditional Commonwealth markets – and even these were turning increasingly to German and Japanese rivals. British car makers were also winning a reputation for poor build quality and strike-prone factories. Industrial relations at most UK plants were abysmal, as unrealistic union demands met head-on with blinkered management. By 1975 Toyota was producing thirty-six cars per employee per year, and Honda nearly twenty-three, while Ford UK was able to make only seven and BL's factories a dismal four.

Much of the blame for this decline can be assigned to inadequate management. Whereas in France, Germany, Japan and America, top-flight graduates – not just from engineering but from a wide variety of disciplines – were encouraged to enter the motor industry, in Britain there had been a long-standing prejudice against graduate talent and, accordingly, far too few of Britain's bright young graduates chose auto manufacturing. Men like Morris, Austin and Lord, engineers who had worked their way up from repair shops or the factory floor, distrusted men from dissimilar backgrounds and despised what they viewed as peripheral functions such as product planning, marketing and financial forecasting – operations that were increasingly essential to the automotive world. The result was that mediocre British management was unable to cope with the changing circumstances, and workers' restlessness, of the post-war years. John Barber, who had joined BMC from Ford, later recalled of British Leyland: 'I think my worst shock was the quality of the Midlands management. The management had been so bad since 1946 that labour had got out of control; the unions had taken control and the thing was getting chaotic.' Barber was also astonished at the insularity of BMC and British Leyland – a quality that, again, probably derived from the poor education of many of its senior managers: 'Everyone in Ford lived cars; they couldn't help it. You were always watching what the customer wanted and looking forward to market requirements, whereas in BMC they didn't seem particularly interested in cars. They weren't interested in competitors. I remember asking a BMC director who had a problem . . . "What do they do at Volkswagen in Wolfsburg?" He said, "I don't know; this is what we do at Longbridge."'

Nor were BL's workers' representatives much more impressive. Geoffrey Whalen, who had started out at the National Coal Board prior to joining British Leyland (and who was subsequently to lead Peugeot's British operation as its managing director after Peugeot's buyout of

Chrysler UK), was appalled at the inadequacy of Cowley's union bosses, particularly when compared to the professional negotiators of the National Union of Mineworkers (NUM): 'I was surprised at the relatively poor standard of union officials; they were neither so dedicated nor so professional [as those of the NUM]. On the whole they were of poor quality though there were obvious exceptions.'

It did not help that British Leyland's model programme was also a shambles. While German and Japanese car makers concentrated on one or two principal products, their British equivalents were selling too many models made by too many factories, and had not invested sufficiently in future planning. BL failed to spot the growing market for fleet cars, which Ford of Europe and GM's Vauxhall quickly cornered. And while Ford was refreshing models such as the highly successful Cortina every few years, BL still resorted merely to badge engineering, reissuing the same basic model under a different marque. John Barber later asserted: 'What was needed was a really ruthless rationalization – models, people, the lot.'

The fate of Rover's new large model, which was supposed to compete with BMW's growing executive range, was a sorry tale that exemplified the almost insurmountable problems that beset British Leyland. Rather than adapt the formula of the splendid Rover P6 (as BMW was to do with its 3 Series from 1975), and having been prevented by BL management from developing its exciting P8, Rover introduced a wholly new body design in the form of the SDI or P10, which was effectively an oversized hatchback. The new car's unmistakably seventies curves and lack of a boot were by no means to everyone's taste – particularly the fleet buyers, who generally insisted on capacious boots for their corporate clients. (The P10's designer, David Bache, had an Issigonis moment when he refused to incorporate a rear wiper on to the 'lift-back' rear, declaring that the car's aerodynamics would keep it clean. He was wrong and Rover had to fit rear wipers retrospectively.) Rover also used antiquated drum brakes at the rear, while the cheap-looking interior detailing was a retrograde step back from the impressive 2000 of 1962. Crucially, as had become commonplace in the British car industry, BL's senior managers insisted that the car be mass-produced before it had been properly tested and all its faults ironed out, while at the same time saddling the untested model with wildly over-optimistic sales forecasts. The end result was thus a car the up-to-date styling of which belied its appalling build quality, and which was plagued by faults after its launch (initially as the Rover 3500) in 1976.

While the 3500 was, at first, received well by the press, strikes meant that BL could not fulfil the demand generated by this coverage. There were not even enough cars available to display them properly at the Geneva Motor Show of 1977. And by the time Rover was able to clear the backlog of orders, the car's ever-lengthening menu of faults had earned it a reputation as an unreliable lemon. *Autocar* noted the 'gap between windscreen and pillars, which allowed in rain and draughts', and concluded that the 'general fit and finish was . . . poor'. The 2300 and 2600 versions of 1978 were underpowered and noisy; export sales were appalling and production targets were never met. On top of all this, the fuel shock of 1979 led to hundreds of unsold, fuel-hungry SD1's rusting away in BL parking lots. The model was finally laid to rest in 1986, its place in the line-up being taken by a re-badged Honda.

Triumph fared little better under BL's aegis. The car being developing to replace the Dolomite range, a four-door vehicle tagged the SD2, which looked a bit like the idiosyncratic Citroën BX, was axed in 1976 because BL's management feared it would steal sales from the dismal Marina and its planned successor, the Maestro. To its eternal shame, BL also squandered the legacy of Triumph's globally successful sports cars of the 1960s. The new Triumph TR7 of 1974 featured an ungainly wedge shape, a heavy tail, a pointed snout and an inexplicable 'go-faster' crease along the side. Performance was poor and build quality – as was typical of BL in the 1970s – was appalling. Road testers complained of 'unbearable' road noise at a miserly 78 mph. Most importantly, the TR7 was built as a fifties-style two-seater just when Datsun's groundbreaking 240Z had introduced a 'two-plus-two' layout which allowed children or midgets to ride in the rear. American customers, whose parents had bought Triumph sports cars in droves in the 1960s, complained, with some justification, that they were being used as guinea pigs for a car that was launched before thorough testing had been undertaken. In 1982 the brand-new Solihull plant that made the SD1 and the TR7 was closed; production of the former went to Cowley, and of the TR7 to Speke. In the same year the old Vitesse brand name, which Triumph had once prized, was applied to an upmarket version of the ailing SD1.

Even Jaguar's sure touch seemed to disappear. When British Leyland was created, Jaguar found itself chained to a patient on life-support. Submerged in a flailing combine principally geared to high-volume small-car production, both development and standards plunged. The classic E-Type was in 1975 replaced with the ungainly XJS, whose notorious unreliability earned it a wholly different reputation. Jaguar dealers found they were making more money on repairs than on sales. Even more disappointingly, heavy investment in the E-Type's replacement meant that Jaguar could not afford to retire the model until 1996.

By 1974 British Leyland was broke. With the company headed for a £24 million loss, and its market share down to 32 per cent (from 41 per cent in 1971), the banks refused to extend its overdraft. Fearful of the mass unemployment that would result, the British government felt that it could not allow British Leyland to go under; Harold Wilson's new Labour administration bought 90 per cent of the company and commissioned a report on the debacle from Lord Ryder, Wilson's favourite businessman.

In 1974 Sydney Thomas Franklin Ryder, head of the Reed International paper and printing combine and known to his friends as 'Don', saw himself as Wilson's industrial right-hand man. In November 1974, a month after winning the second election of the year, the premier had proposed Ryder as chairman of the new National Enterprise Board (NEB),[1] a post he accepted the following year. At first, Tony Benn,

---

1 The NEB was designed to be a 'catalyst for British industry' and eventually acquired stakes in up to seventy British companies.

the industry minister, welcomed the appointment, finding Ryder 'very energetic and . . . sympathetic'; but soon Benn was labelling him 'very managerial, rather conceited, and thinks he is the cat's whiskers'.

Ryder's background was in printing and he knew nothing of the motor industry. None of this would have mattered if his report had been realistic and had sought to match BL's future planning to its resources. But instead it was naively optimistic, presenting Wilson with what he wanted to hear, rather than the stark facts. The increasingly self-important Ryder believed that he could turn the company round in just a few years. He proposed that there should be no redundancies, that none of BL's fifty-five factories should be closed, and that the government should inject £1 billion into the firm in return for a two thirds stake in it – in effect, a nationalization.

For the next two years Ryder took a far closer interest in British Leyland than he did in any of the NEB's other basket cases. Yet his constant interference proved futile. Stokes (kicked upstairs, as a result of Ryder's reforms, to the non-executive role of president) later said that he thought Ryder's team 'were an incompetent lot': 'They published a report which was bland and innocuous itself and then mysteriously added that there were certain pages which were not for publication – and they were equally bland and innocuous'. Management was demoralized, strikes continued, and the Ryder plan, which had put all its eggs in the quixotic basket of a new Mini project, got nowhere. No new car at all appeared from any of BL's plants for four years after the launch of the SD1 in 1976. There were some positive signs: union officials such as Bill Roche and Derek Robinson were invited to discussions between BL and the NEB – the first time the British car industry had ever dared experiment with German-style worker participation. But in 1976 Harold Wilson resigned as prime minister, and this proved a fatal blow to Ryder's ambitions. Ryder resigned from the NEB, and from his involvement in British Leyland, a few months later, when only halfway through a five-year contract. His mission had visibly failed: BL's market share in the UK had fallen from 32 per cent four years earlier to a dismal 23 per cent.

Harold Wilson's successor as prime minister, James 'Sunny Jim' Callaghan, held no torch for political animals such as Ryder and happily waved him goodbye. Instead, in 1977 he appointed a far tougher industrialist, Michael Edwardes, a confrontational South African, as the new chief of British Leyland, throwing in a knighthood for good measure.

The combative Edwardes was not a motor man either. He had read law at Grahamstown University and had risen through the ranks of the Chloride Corporation, the battery manufacturer, to become chairman by 1974. Chloride was only a fraction of the size of mighty British Leyland, but he seemed to know the answers – decisive action rather than the bland, Panglossian palliatives prescribed by Ryder. Edwardes was single-minded in pursuing his ends – and he was convinced that his way was the right way. His attitude was remarkably similar to that of Margaret Thatcher, who replaced Callaghan after her party's comprehensive victory in the 1979 general election, and his combative style won him many enemies in government as well as in the motor industry. Derek Robinson's tart description of Edwardes as 'ruthless and cynical' was something with which most of Edwardes's colleagues and acquaintances would have agreed. Admirers called him 'the Mighty Mini'; critics within BL – of which there were far more – christened him 'the poison dwarf'. And, like many aggressive managers, Edwardes was curiously sensitive to criticism. Accordingly, when his five-year contract expired in 1982, he abruptly left British Leyland for IT manufacturer ICL.

Michael Edwardes began by insisting his role be that of an executive chairman ('I couldn't accept less than the combined role of chairman and chief executive', he later declared), dismissing the Ryder report as a 'charade', earning more subsidies from the Callaghan government, and making brutal job cuts of the kind from which the more politicized Ryder had recoiled. On his very first day, Edwardes dismissed all but three BL directors. The point was made. Two thirds of BL's senior staff were culled and twelve thousand shop-floor staff lost via natural wastage. (A month after he joined, the NEB claimed back its promised bail-out because

BL's accountants had 'misplaced' their claim.) By 1982 Sir Michael Edwardes had sold off nineteen of the fifty-five British Leyland businesses he had inherited five years earlier, and almost halved the workforce – cutting it from 196,000 to 104,000. One of the closures was the strike-plagued Speke No. 2 factory, where the Triumph TR7 was built between stoppages and which was only nine years old. Edwardes also scrapped the Stag's planned replacement sports car, the impressive Triumph Lynx, and shut the old Abingdon MG works (which had enjoyed the best labour relations of any BL factory) in 1980. In effect, BL had already signed MG's death warrant by designating the TR7 as BL's only sports car. A year after Abingdon, the TR7 was itself axed.

In retrospect, Edwardes's euthanasia of MG and Abingdon, while it may have made economic sense at the time, was a serious error. Edwardes also made another key mistake: having originally separated BL's monolithic and unhelpful cars division into two parts, Jaguar-Rover-Triumph and Austin-Morris, after only two years he separated Jaguar completely and threw Rover and Triumph back in with the mass-market marques. While the decision was a good result for Jaguar, which began to recover under the new management of John Egan, it was disastrous for Rover and Triumph. Over the next few years, these two famous, resonant brand names were applied inappropriately downmarket cars (Rover) or simply as a badge for Japanese imports (Triumph).

Coventry-born Egan was, unlike Edwardes, steeped in engineering and familiar with the shop floor. The son of a garage owner, he had studied petroleum engineering at Imperial College and then worked for Shell, GM's A C Delco and Canadian tractor maker Massey Ferguson (then controlled by Conrad Black, later notorious as the media mogul imprisoned for fraud in 2007), before joining BL. His arrival at Jaguar, on 27 April 1980, ended a long strike, as Egan gave workers his personal commitment to the company and its workforce. Jaguar, which had lacked any sort of chief executive or leadership between 1975 and 1980, now had a new heart and a sense of independent purpose. Egan hired racing guru Tom Walkinshaw to guide Jaguar back into the racing world for the first time in over twenty years. (In 1984 Walkinshaw ended a string of BMW victories by winning the European Touring Car Championship in a Jaguar.) At the other end of the spectrum, Egan was appalled by the poor quality of many of the cars Jaguar was then building and by the abysmal productivity of the workforce. He was particularly disgusted by the rock-bottom standards of many of his suppliers: 'There were tyres that weren't round; radio aerials which wouldn't go up and down; switches that failed.' He instituted a black museum of badly made car parts to show visiting suppliers, and instituted a new series of standards for supplies. At the same time, he reduced the workforce – while improving productivity.

In 1984, to Egan's delight, the firm was privatized by the Thatcher government, now seemingly invulnerable after victory in the Falklands War and its success in 1983's general election. Jaguar was back to impressive profits, and Egan was knighted in 1986. In the 1980s and 90s the venerable XJ6, originally unveiled in 1968, was continually revamped and reinvented, appearing in its final guise as a lightweight, aluminium-bodied, long-wheelbase variant, simply called the XJ, in 2003. Meanwhile, the firm was made an offer it couldn't refuse by Ford, which promised large-scale investment (and a Formula 1 racing team). Ford bought the company in 1990 – just in time for the recession of the early 1990s, which saw luxury car sales decimated. Egan, who had turned Jaguar's fortunes around so spectacularly in the 1980s, sensibly decided to bow out of the new, Ford-owned Jaguar, and joined the British Airports Authority as chief executive.

Both John Egan and Michael Edwardes were adept at manipulating the media – far better, indeed, than contemporaries such as Lee Iacocca of Chrysler or Roger Smith of GM. Edwardes carefully limited his appearances on television to times when he could announce good news, and staged 'impromptu' interviews while apparently getting in or out of his car, uttering carefully rehearsed statements that he believed would influence the workforce and union negotiators. He also ensured that his view of events – which, in true Thatcherite fashion, he firmly believed would be vindicated by history – was set down in an 'autobiography' published only a year after he stepped down as chairman.[1]

Edwardes's no-prisoners approach to labour relations also seemed to show immediate results. He culled a large tranche of the combine's underperforming management; and, on 1 February 1978, followed a meeting with 720 union representatives with a snap vote on his restructuring plan – which only five stunned shop stewards voted against. Yet notorious strike-brokers such as Longbridge's Derek 'Red Robbo' Robinson continued to exercise huge influence over the workforce, while the ancient piecework system, whereby workers could leave the plant once they had performed their strictly measured, pre-agreed tasks, was still in place. Accordingly, Edwardes confronted the unions head-on, sacking Robinson on 27 November 1979 and replacing the piecework agreements with day-work rosters. Robinson's dismissal prompted an immediate walkout at Longbridge, but the majority of BL's workers realized that the days of guaranteed jobs were long past and that BL was now in serious trouble. To Robinson's horror, in February 1980 a union vote rejected strike action. 'On yer bike, Red Robbo' read one worker's placard.

However, while Edwardes succeeded in cowing the unions and in launching some viable new cars – the Metro was the first successful mass-market model that British car makers had introduced in over twenty years – the development of new products at BL continued only at snail's pace. Work on the Metro, Maestro and Montego was already well advanced when Edwardes arrived, and his only real innovation was to re-badge existing Hondas as Triumphs; this got BL nowhere, while handily giving Honda a leg-up in Europe. The disposal of Triumph's brand-new factory at Speke (the first closure of a British car factory since 1945) was also hardly a model example of the sustainable adaptation of resources. (Edwardes's brief flirtation in the early 1980s with GM, which would have permitted the US giant to make use of BL's underused plants, would surely have been a sensible option for this facility.) The extinguishing

---

1 This strategy would be mimicked by Iacocca in 1984.

of the Vanden Plas and Park Royal factories, and the mothballing and subsequent closure of the new Rover plant at Solihull, were similarly controversial. And the abandonment of MG production was, in hindsight, a serious mistake; Edwardes had effectively ceded the sports car market to the Germans and Japanese, and trashed fifty years' worth of accumulated brand value.[1] Typically, the historic and evocative octagonal MG badge was pressed into service to decorate upmarket versions of family cars, motors that had precious little in common with the famed MGB or Midget.

In many ways, Edwardes's tenure at BL was a false dawn. Altogether the firm lost £1 billion between 1979 and 1982, the year in which Edwardes departed, leaving someone else to clean up the mess. More days had been lost to strikes in British car factories in 1979–81 than ever before. And BL simply had no new models up its sleeve; thus the outdated and outclassed Allegro and Marina were simply relaunched as the Allegro 2 and Ital, in 1979 and 1980, respectively. The popular but boxy Austin Metro of 1980, hailed as the 'Car for the 1980s' (and the first British car to be made largely by robots, using technology borrowed from Fiat), was soon eclipsed by Ford's Fiesta; the much-vaunted replacement for the Mini never appeared; the Austin Maestro of 1983, while innovative and good value, gained a well-deserved reputation for poor build and unreliability; and the Austin Montego's only distinction was that it was the last car to bear the Austin name. While foreign manufacturers made huge inroads into the UK market with reliable and modern small models such as the VW Golf, Renault 5 and Datsun Cherry, BL's own export market collapsed spectacularly. In 1984 BL, which ten years earlier had sold thousands of cars to America, sold precisely four.

British Leyland and Chrysler were not the only automotive giants with problems in of post-oil crisis Britain. Ford was not immune from the scourge of poor industrial relations either. In 1970 the newly launched Cortina III was plagued by build problems, reliability issues

---

1 At the time of writing, the MG name is the only element to have resurfaced from the wreck of British Leyland.

and a nine-week strike at Dagenham; virtually all the 'launch' cars were so poorly made they were subsequently scrapped. Reg Birch, the Maoist-inclined Amalgamated Engineering Union representative responsible for negotiations with Ford at Dagenham, was deliberately provocative (though personally charming) and did nothing to improve relations with the management or, when a Commons committee came to see for themselves, the government. Nevertheless, in the early 1970s there were indications that the Ford workforce was tired of being manipulated by a handful of extremist representatives. In February 1973 workers at Dagenham voted against their union convenors' recommendation of a strike and overtime ban, prompting even Henry Ford II to send his personal congratulations.

Ford was fortunate in that, unlike BL's overlapping line-up, its model range was simple and sound. Rather than replace the best-selling Cortina, as British Leyland had done with the 1100/1300, Ford re-bodied and updated it in 1966 as the compact and handsome Mark II, in 1970 as the larger Mark III, and in 1976 as the sleek and stylish Mark IV. While the Mark III's large scale, raised waist, protruding bumper and cheap interior looked more Dearborn than Dagenham – indeed, for many the Mark III epitomizes the ungainly style and brash, misplaced confidence of the crisis-ridden seventies – it still sold well, becoming Britain's best-selling car in 1972. The Mark IV Cortina, while hardly Ford's first Anglo-German collaboration,[1] helped to weld together the constituent parts of Ford Europe. Previously, the German equivalent of the Cortina had been the Taunus, which had been differently styled and equipped, and which competed with the Cortina in international markets; even the Mark III, while developed by Ford of Europe as the TC (the Taunus Cortina), looked very different in Britain and Germany. But the crisp, angular Mark IV, which did away with the outmoded Americanisms of the Mark III,

---

1 In 1968 Ford replaced the old Anglia with the Anglo-German Escort; touted as 'the small car that isn't', it was built in both Britain and Germany, and sold well across Europe for thirty-five years.

was designed in Germany by Uwe Bahnsen, already the author of Ford Europe's answer to the Mustang, the Capri.[1]

In 1976, the small car that Ford had been promising for Europe finally arrived, four years after Henry Ford II had sanctioned the project. The multilingual name for the new subcompact, Fiesta, lacked charisma, but was not up for discussion. Henry Ford II had personally picked the title – having rejected the market research winner, Bravo, and despite the fact that the brand name had, in the UK, been previously used for a packet dessert and a type of condom. (Other unsuccessful names in this exercise, such as Sierra and Tempo, were later used for other Ford models.) Moreover, the engine was intrinsically the same Kent power plant that had been used for the 1959 Anglia. But the Fiesta proved an enduring success. Its sharp, distinctly European boxiness was devised by stylist Tom Tjaarda in Detroit, who borrowed freely from the Fiat 127 and the VW Golf. Its pleasing looks, allied to its reliability and excellent handling (its front-wheel drive was a novelty for post-war Fords) won many admirers. In two years it was the UK's best-selling supermini, and even made inroads into the US market. In 1981 a successful hot-hatch version, the XR2, was unveiled. At the time of writing, the Fiesta is still being made, and is still massively successful. It is no trend-setter – the sixth generation of the Fiesta was widely criticized for plagiarizing the styling of the Peugeot 207 – but continues to garner awards. And it remains a truly global car, being currently made in Germany, Spain, Mexico, Thailand and China.

It is many years, however, since the Fiesta was made in Britain. By 1979 productivity in Ford's UK factories had fallen alarmingly and stood at thirteen cars per employee per year, compared with thirty-one in Germany. Ford's US bosses were not impressed, and began a slow withdrawal from Britain. At the same time, GM began to prioritize car

---

1 The Mustang was adapted (and made 19 inches shorter) for the British and German markets as the Capri in 1969. The lean, taut styling of the Capri's Mark II version of 1974–8 echoed Iacocca's Mustang Mark I, and the car was available with engines up to 3.3 litres. Britain's strike-prone factories, however, encouraged Ford to pull production out of Halewood in 1976 and concentrate production of the Capri in Köln.

production at Opel in Germany, with its UK Vauxhall factories becoming little more than assembly plants for foreign-made parts. In 2002 Ford's Dagenham factory produced its last car, a Fiesta. From 2004 GM owned only one car factory in Britain: the Vauxhall plant at Ellesmere Port on the Wirral, which made Astras.

While Britain's foreign-owned auto manufacturers failed to impress their American and German paymasters during the 1970s, Italy's leading car maker continued to plough a proudly independent furrow. In 1970, the year in which the Fiat 128 was named European Car of the Year by the motoring press, Fiat was the world's largest automobile manufacturer outside the US, outperforming even the mighty Volkswagen. In 1974, Gianni Agnelli was elected president of Confindustria, the national employer's association. And in 1975, at a time when most car makers were retrenching, Agnelli created a successful bus and truck division, Iveco, which ultimately absorbed Ford's European commercial vehicle operation. Agnelli simultaneously agreed an astute deal with union leader Luciano Lama to establish an inflation-linked wage system (the *scala mobile*, or 'sliding stair'), which would eliminate some of the crippling strikes that Fiat, along with most of the car makers of the Western world, had recently suffered. Subsequent devaluations of the Italian lira, while crippling the national economy, were greeted with private relief by Agnelli, who found his cars becoming even more competitive in foreign markets.

In 1971 Agnelli's Fiat again showed itself to be ahead of the game, launching the first of what would be called superminis – or, in America, subcompacts – the Fiat 127. This perky, square little car, effectively a replacement for the firm's old 850, sold well across Europe and South America, and was additionally built in Brazil, Argentina and Colombia. But it failed to gain much of a foothold in North America; that market was instead conquered by the second of the modern superminis, the Renault 5, which was advertised in Canada and the US simply as 'Le Car'. Michel

Boué's crisp styling, which masked the fact that most of its mechanical elements came from the venerable Renault 4, gave the 5 a distinct edge over the routine lines of the Fiat 127. As a result, the Renault 5 swiftly gained cult status comparable to the Mini and became one of Europe's best-selling cars.[1]

In the midst of these automotive successes, Agnelli still found time to maintain his reputation as one of the most elegantly clad men of his era. Milanese fashion designer Nino Cerruti cited Agnelli as one of his principal inspirations, alongside James Bond and John F. Kennedy, while *Esquire* magazine named Agnelli one of five best-dressed men in the history of the world. Agnelli's personal fashion eccentricities, such as wearing his watch over his cuff, pulling his tie askew or sporting high brown hiking boots under a bespoke suit – were all carefully chosen in a spirit of *sprezzatura*, the Italian art of making the difficult look easy.

By the end of the seventies, though, Fiat found itself at risk from an unexpected and very dangerous quarter. When Agnelli became head of Confindustria, he and his firm immediately became prime targets for the murderous activities of the Red Brigades, Italy's communist terrorist organization. Agnelli himself was safe behind his barricade of security measures, but over the next five years the Brigate Rosse murdered four Fiat managers and seriously wounded twenty-seven others. Productivity plummeted as terrorist sympathizers sabotaged production lines and encouraged go-slows, and by 1975 Fiat was producing only eleven cars per worker per year, to Toyota's forty-three.[2] In 1978, in an atrocity that shocked the whole world, the Red Brigades kidnapped and killed Italy's former prime minister, Aldo Moro, as he was seeking to reach a compromise with the country's powerful communist party. Then, on 21 September 1979, a 51-year-old senior manager at Fiat, Carlo Ghiglieno, was shot dead in a Turin street as he went to buy his early morning espresso. This cowardly murder finally galvanized Agnelli into action. Resolving to take the

---

1 In 1976 Renault added a powerful Alpine version – sold in Britain as the Gordini, since Chrysler still owned the rights to Sunbeam's old Alpine name.
2 Further north, though, strike-prone British Leyland could only manage four.

terrorists and their fellow travellers head-on, he fired sixty-one workers suspected of connections to the Brigate Rosse. As trade unions turned firmly against the Red Brigades, a slew of arrests severely weakened the movement, which collapsed altogether in 1984.

Preoccupied with the terrorist threat and with labour relations, forward planning at Fiat had suffered and by 1980 the company's sales and market share were both falling. But Agnelli had an answer for that, too, ruthlessly replacing his brother, Umberto, as the firm's day-to-day head with the brusque but highly efficient Cesare Romiti. ('I believe the age of the family firm is over,' Umberto Agnelli grimly told waiting reporters on 31 July 1980.¹) Cesare Romiti had joined Fiat as finance director in 1974, having previously been managing director of the national airline, Alitalia. Arrogant and overbearing, he was nevertheless given absolute authority by Agnelli, who saw his Romiti's harsh medicine as the only way to keep the company independent. It was Romiti who cut back the Fiat workforce in the early 1980s, making thirteen thousand workers redundant, and temporarily suspending another twenty-four thousand, in September 1980. The result was a vast and seemingly endless strike, ostentatiously supported by the veteran communist leader Enrico Berlinguer. But on the thirty-fourth day of the strike, forty thousand Fiat workers, including many from middle management, took to the streets of Turin demanding an end to the stoppage. The union was discredited and swiftly backed away – agreeing, just four days later, to the redundancy of a further 22,884 metalworkers. In the months that followed, union membership at Fiat fell dramatically. Romiti, and Fiat, had won.

In 1981 Fiat successfully launched its new supermini replacement for the 127, the Uno, which the European media also hailed as the Car of the Year. In the ensuing years Fiat pioneered assembly-line robotics, and by

---

1 Umberto was to have his revenge, albeit over twenty years later. On Gianni Agnelli's retirement in 1996, Romiti's power base evaporated, and in 2002 Umberto was elected chairman of Fiat. Sadly, he was able to enjoy his success for only two years before his death from lung cancer in 2004.

1984 was making very healthy profits. Today the firm created by Giovanni Agnelli and shaped by his grandson, Gianni, is one of the world's leading car makers, one that not only owns most of Italy's most prestigious auto marques, from Ferrari to Maserati, but also controls Chrysler.[1]

The most successful new small car of the 1970s did not come from Italy, however, but from Germany. The Volkswagen Golf of 1974 blended a revolutionary shape with a reliable build, strong residual values, fuel efficiency, impressive handling and striking performance.[2] Giorgetto Giugiaro's design was sharp, angular and compact – in short, nothing like Nordhoff's cherished Beetle, let alone rivals such as Britain's blobby Allegro.

In 1967 a reluctant Heinz Nordhoff had been forced to retire from Volkswagen, ostensibly due to ill health, after a clumsy campaign by the West German government to force him to step down. (Parted from his cherished Wolfsburg office, Nordhoff deteriorated rapidly and died the following year.) With Nordhoff gone, Volkswagen found itself liberated from his obsessional one-model policy. From 1973 VW launched the Passat executive saloon, drastically reduced the range of Beetle options (something Nordhoff would never have allowed) and introduced a smaller version of the Golf, the Polo.[3]

The Golf proved as successful as the Beetle; the first million Golfs sold in only thirty-one months. Innovative, witty advertising campaigns by DDB targeted the Golf successfully at younger consumers and small families, leaving their rivals looking staid or complacent. In 1975 the Golf was launched in the US as the Rabbit, and the following year production began at an American plant at Westmoreland, Pennsylvania. In 1987, as

---

1 In 2009 Fiat even made a bid for GM's Opel division.
2 Early Golfs were also, it has to be said, spartan and uncomfortable; however, customers were less interested in luxury and more sensitive about performance and economy in the years after the oil crisis.
3 Developed from the short-lived Audi 50.

worldwide sales reached 15 million, the Golf overtook the Ford Model T to become the second best-selling car ever, after the Beetle.

The Golf's designer, Giorgetto Giugiaro, had studied design in Turin in the 1950s, and by 1965 had become chief executive of Torinese coachbuilders Ghia. In 1968 he set up on his own, wisely baling out just before Ghia's sale to Ford. His new company, ItalDesign, was asked to worked for Alfa, Ferrari, Daewoo, Fiat (for which Guigiaro created the Uno in 1983), BMW (for which he created the M1 sports car), Hyundai, Saab, SEAT (for which he created the Toledo and Ibiza in 1991 and 1993), Lancia, Maserati, Renault, Ford and Lotus.[1] In 1999 the motoring press dubbed Giugiaro the Car Designer of the Century. His greatest achievements were surely the Volkswagen Golf and its VAG relatives of 1973–4: the Passat, the Scirocco and the Audi 80.

While Wolfsburg was revolutionizing the automobile world in the 1970s, Stuttgart was resting on its laurels. Second-hand Mercedes 200s[2] had conquered the global taxi market, while 600s were still popular with film stars and totalitarian rulers alike. But Mercedes had no answer to Jaguar's excellent XJ6 large executive saloon of 1968, which made Mercedes' highly confusing model range (still classified by engine size, a byzantine numerical system which Daimler-Benz only dropped in the mid-1990s) seem staid and dull. Even more worryingly, only in 1982 did Mercedes belatedly launch an answer to BMW's 3 Series – a compact four-door saloon sold under the old 190 label. While undoubtedly a fine car, which sold respectably in Europe, the new 190 reached the market later than its rivals, while its dull styling and average performance failed to ignite the US market. It was withdrawn after only eleven years.

In sharp contrast, BMW, like Volkswagen, got it absolutely right in the 1970s. BMW had been a minor player in the motor industry until the 1960s, when it was unexpectedly revived by white knight Dr Herbert

---

1 Unsurprisingly, ItalDesign's peripheral involvement in the forlorn attempt to update the Morris Marina, the Ital of 1980, to which British Leyland was desperate lend Italian chic, does not appear on Giugiaro's CV.

2 In 1993 the 200 series became the E-Class.

Quandt, who bought up lots of cheap BMW stock to emerge as the firm's largest shareholder. Quandt, who had already bought 10 per cent of Daimler-Benz,[1] was on the point of agreeing to BMW's sale to its Stuttgart rival when, noting the strong union opposition to the deal, he changed his mind and, against the advice of his cautious bankers, increased his share in BMW to 50 per cent. Quandt was right and the bankers wrong, and BMW never looked back.

Herbert Quandt was born in 1910 in Pritzwalk, near Berlin. His ancestors were Dutch rope makers who had diversified into other textiles and relocated to Germany. During the First World War, the family firm supplied the German army with uniforms, amassing a fortune it would use after the war to acquire battery manufacturer Accumulatorenfabrik AG (AFA), a potash mine and various metal fabricators. Young Herbert was nearly blind from the age of nine, and was educated at home – both in academic subjects and, most importantly, in the Quandt business. After extensive training at Quandt companies at home and abroad, he became a member of the executive board of AFA in 1940. He was never tried or questioned after the war (although his father, Günther, was interned until 1948), yet a TV documentary made by the German public broadcaster ARD in October 2007, examining the role of the Quandt businesses before 1945,[2] did belatedly prompt a muted apology from what had become a notoriously reclusive family, which now announced that it would fund academic research into AFA's wartime activities.

From 1945, Herbert was effectively in charge of AFA, and by the time of Günther's death in 1954 he had built the Quandt group into a conglomerate of about two hundred businesses. In sharp contrast to the class-ridden attitudes of many British car executives, and the greed and suspicion displayed by many of their American equivalents, Quandt happily involved the workforce in the day-to-day management of his empire,

---

1 A stake astutely sold in 1974 to the oil-rich Kuwaiti government.
2 The documentary uncovered evidence showing that female slave labourers, transferred from Auschwitz, had been used at many of the Quandt factories during the Second World War, and that conditions at some of the Quandt plants were brutally harsh.

decentralizing the organization, giving his executives considerable autonomy, and allowing all employees to participate in company decisions.
BMW's biographer later attributed to Quandt 'the gift of always putting
the right men in the right place'. Thus, when many other European car
makers were paralysed by industrial action during the 1970s, BMW's
apparently contented workforce was building a new generation of executive saloons.

Quandt astutely avoided the mistakes of his fellow automotive magnates. He ensured that his private life did not become a major corporate
issue, as Henry Ford II's had done. His first two marriages lasted seven
and nine years, respectively, and in 1960 he married his personal assistant, Johanna Bruhn. But there he stopped, and BMW was never riven
by the dynastic squabbles that characterized Ford's board in the 1960s
and 1970s. Quandt also ensured that the shares in his companies were
not thinly spread, avoiding the sort of intra-family disputes that wrecked
Henry Ford II's last years in charge.

Quandt's vision for BMW was of a range of solid, dependable family
and executive saloons based on traditional German qualities, cars that
were engineered to a high standard, were built well, and that boasted the
high performance and reliability that had made Mercedes and Auto Union
famous before the war. He began with the 1962 launch of the boxy but
unapologetically modern 'new generation' 1500, the first of what became
known as BMW's New Class (*Neue Klasse*). A decade later Quandt's resurgent BMW launched the first model range aimed squarely at the executive market, the 5 Series. Designed by Frenchman Paul Bracq, who had
already designed the fabulous, high-speed TGV trains for the SNCF, the 5
Series established the design characteristics that BMW has followed ever
since: purposeful, compact lines; a squared body; quadruple headlamps,
between which still lay the familiar double-kidney grille;[1] and a tidy and
understated rear. The equally impressive 3 Series of compact executive
cars followed in 1975, after Quandt had completed an impressive new

---

1 Introduced on the BMW 303 of 1933.

corporate headquarters outside Munich, in the form of Austrian architect Karl Schwanzer's cloverleaf-shaped Four-Cylinder Building. The 3 Series became one of the iconic cars of the age. Its trim size appealed to customers dealing with the legacy of the oil crisis and mindful of the need to limit fuel consumption and restrict emissions, while its performance could compete with the best from Jaguar and Mercedes. Its success encouraged BMW to take Mercedes head-on; accordingly, in 1977 it launched the hefty 7 Series as the firm's full-size executive flagship. The Bavarians had taken on the world – and they appeared to be winning.

While Quandt successfully restructured BMW into a world-beating concern, governments and manufacturers in Britain and the US were desperately flailing around for solutions in an age of rising oil prices and growing environmental concerns, losing vast sums of taxpayers' money in pursuit of the golden fleece of automotive success. Perhaps the most notorious and colourful of these car-making disasters revolved around the controversial figure of Lee Iacocca's former protégé John DeLorean.

John Zachary DeLorean had risen meteorically through the ranks of GM. In 1965, when he was promoted to the post of general manager at Pontiac, he became the youngest-ever vice president at the company, aged only forty. By then, though, GM was losing its way. Frederic G. Donner, chairman of the giant conglomerate from 1958 to 1967, was not a car man and preferred to promote solid, cautious financial heads rather than individuals with engineering or marketing expertise. After 1967 the GM chairmanship passed to two of Donner's financial protégés: James M. Roche (1967–71) and Richard C. Gerstenberg (1971–4). Numbers was the only game in town, creating an environment in which maverick creatives such as DeLorean were looked upon with benevolent, if mystified, indulgence.

By 1974 DeLorean was already showing signs of megalomania. The hard-working young executive had turned into a corporate glutton, devouring all possible perks and options. Scores of cars were given away free to friends and associates (a practice that only came to light after DeLorean's departure). Never a comfortable socializer, DeLorean scandalized audiences with his unfunny, off-colour jokes and inveterate name-dropping. His management style was chaotic; he centralized all responsibility within a tight-knit coterie whose principal qualifications were an avid enthusiasm for racing cars and bedding women, rather than any noted ability at making autos. DeLorean coloured his hair, lost weight and hired a plastic surgeon to elongate his chin. He bought stakes in the New York Yankees baseball team and the San Diego Chargers football club, and spent much of his time lavishly entertaining his friends at games. He also changed his wife for a younger model, the gorgeous Kelly Harmon – a marriage that appalled Harmon's conservative relatives. To the media, though, he still appeared the incarnation of the bright, youthful future of the car industry, a refreshingly sharp contrast to grey old men like James Roche or Henry Ford II. Unfortunately, DeLorean came to believe the hype.

DeLorean's father-figure and original patron, Semon 'Bunkie' Knudsen, had expected to go all the way to the top at GM – and DeLorean had expected to follow him up the ladder. But in 1968 Knudsen found himself elbowed out, and a week later he joined Ford as its new president. Delorean's sure touch suddenly appeared to be fallible. Promoted to Chevrolet, and touted as a future company president, he announced that Chevrolet's headquarters would be relocating to suburban Detroit from its current downtown site – only to have his message flatly repudiated by GM's exasperated public relations staff a few hours later. DeLorean also found that his neglect of administration was beginning to erode his mystique. In 1970 he publicly had to cancel the relaunch of the Camaro and Corvette, having ordered too many last-minute design changes. He also began spending much of his time in California rather than Detroit, and diverting funds to pet projects – or simply to his own bank accounts. (Investigative journalists Ivan Fallon and James Srodes estimate that, during his years at the helm of the DeLorean Motor Company, John DeLorean siphoned off $17.8 million of taxpayers' and investors' money for his own private use, and a further £7 million for business, art and property investments.) Meanwhile, he kept the gossip columnists busy by trading in his young wife Kelly for movie starlet Cristina Ferrare.

The great white hope of the car industry seemed to be self-destructing. When, in 1973, senior GM executives saw a draft speech by DeLorean alleging that the company was deliberately selling mediocre models and possessed little design talent, and learned that he was responsible for a number of embarrassing leaks to the media, their patience with the maverick engineer finally ran out. On 18 April GM announced that DeLorean was leaving the company to 'pursue his dream'. 'I want to do things in the social area,' he told reporters, unconvincingly.

DeLorean's self-belief carried him serenely through the next nine turbulent years. He set up his own company to build an 'ethical' sports car, and hired world-renowned designer Giorgetto Giugiaro to shape it. By February 1975 Giugiaro had produced the wedge-shaped body that was to characterize the production model. It was three years, however, before DeLorean was able to persuade the British government to part with £55 million to produce his cars at Dunmurry, in strife-torn Northern Ireland. Unemployment was high in the province and DeLorean's factory would, the government hoped, provide badly needed new jobs. Unfortunately, none of the Dunmurry workers had any previous experience in car manufacture, let alone in the assembly of an incredibly complex, high-performance sports car like the gull-winged DMC-12. The launch date kept being put back, while DeLorean threatened the British government that he would pull out of Dunmurry if there were no additional investment. As a result, the new British premier, Margaret Thatcher, gave DeLorean another £30 million.

The DMC-12 finally appeared in April 1981. The car, though, was a disaster. Appallingly built and far too heavy, it was certainly not the supercar that had been promised. The windows leaked and often fell out of their tracks. The cumbersome gull-winged doors frequently jammed. (A man who climbed into a DMC-12 at a Cleveland museum found he couldn't open the doors again and was only extricated by mechanics many hours later.) The underpowered batteries failed, and the unpainted steel body was far from 'stainless'. Those few customers who did buy examples quickly demanded refunds. The DMC-12 owned by TV chat-show host Johnny Carson (an investor in DeLorean's enterprise) broke down after only a few miles on the road; when a replacement distributor was rushed out to the stranded Carson, that failed, too. On top of all this, in November 1981 DeLorean was forced to recall all 2,200 DMC-12s to rebuild the front suspension.

Despite DeLorean's crude attempts at blackmail, such as ham-fistedly attempting to enlist the support of the IRA and insisting that the British government owed him millions in unpaid subsidies, Thatcher's administration finally decided enough was enough and refused to proffer him any more money. His company was put into the hands of administrators, who soon discovered that a sizeable chunk of the government's investment had found its way into DeLorean's private bank accounts in Switzerland and Panama.¹ The Dunmurry workforce of 2,400, who had entertained such high hopes of long-term employment, were laid off, and DeLorean was arrested on charges of drug-trafficking (which he ducked by using a defence of entrapment).

The DMC-12 did enjoy a brief moment in the sun. The unlikely star of Steven Spielberg's *Back to the Future* trilogy of 1985–90 thankfully did not have to rely on its atrocious visibility and abysmal reliability in order to travel the few hundred yards required for filming. Thanks to the popularity of Spielberg's engaging franchise, today the DMC-12 is remembered not as the failed centrepiece of a fraudulent industrial scam but as a central character in one of cinema's most enduringly successful film series. Thus one of the biggest disasters in automotive history passed from tragedy, to farce, to movie stardom. Few of its failed successors were given a similar reprieve.

---

1 Not all the losses were the British government's; private investors who had counted themselves among DeLorean's intimate friends lost heavily, too. Celebrity singer Sammy Davis junior invested $150,000, as did Johnny Carson; both lost their entire stake, while the Texan oil tycoon Gary Laughlin lost $500,000.

13

Eastern Promise

Few visiting Japan in 1960 would have guessed that the nation's lead-ing car makers would, in as little as twenty years, be challenging the world's established automotive giants, and that in thirty years they would have conquered almost every global market. The Japanese had, after all, never seemed that interested in cars. The first automobile had only been imported into Japan (from France) in 1904; seven years later there were just eighty-two cars in Tokyo – alongside 22,403 rickshaws, 12,547 bicy-cles and 156 horse-drawn carriages.

It was not until the post-war American occupation of 1945–52 that the Japanese seemed to take the motor car seriously. Even then, Japan spent most of the post-war era building poor-quality copies of Austins, Hillmans and Renaults. (Between 1953 and 1959 Nissan produced 20,855 Austins, and it continued to use Austin and Rootes models as the basis of its own range well into the 1960s.) In 1956 the Japanese auto indus-try produced a mere thirty-two thousand cars, mostly pallid parodies of European originals – many of which were no great shakes themselves. Grandly named products such as the Prince Skyline Deluxe and the Toyopet Crown Deluxe were, in the words of auto historian Jonathan Mantle, 'a perplexing amalgam of the worst in Western styling, in a size the Japanese government allowed'. In 1952 Nissan's Datsun brand began assembling the British Austin A40 Somerset, a lacklustre, 'Transatlantic'-styled model, powered by a feeble pre-war engine; while the 1957 Isuzu

Minx was even heavier and slower than Rootes' bland original. In 1960 Nissan began production of its own, even heavier version of Austin's over-sized and underpowered A60 Cambridge, improbably called the Cedric. The model lingered on until the early 1970s, but the Cedric brand, pre-sumably intended as a backhanded tribute to British tradition, is still – incredibly – in use today. (Mitsubishi's rival to the Cedric, incidentally, rejoiced in the name of the Debonair Exceed.)

As late as 1954 the steel needed to make Japanese cars still had to be imported from the US. And when the Japanese did venture to make their own cars, the results were often disastrous. The tiny, appallingly built Subaru 360 of 1958, for example, was marketed by Malcolm Bricklin in the US under the refreshingly honest slogan 'Cheap and Ugly Does It'; but the few Americans who were attracted by Bricklin's campaign were soon dissuaded by *Consumer Reports* magazine's verdict that the 360 was 'the most unsafe car in America'.

It was not until the late 1960s that Japanese car makers were able to export reliable and popular cars to the rest of the world on a signifi-cant scale. The first Toyotas reached Britain in 1965; the first Hondas and Datsuns three years later. Under pressure from the Americans, the Japanese government liberalized their protectionist trade arrangements, raising the quota for imported engines and automotive parts, and lower-ing the punitive tariffs on imported cars. By 1973 it was even theoretically possible for a foreign company to own a Japanese car maker. (GM had already bought a 34.2 per cent interest in commercial vehicle manufac-turer Isuzu in 1971.) But in return for these concessions, Japanese car makers won invaluable toeholds in the world's most lucrative market, the United States. In 1968 the Toyota Corolla became the first Japanese car to be manufactured in the US.

Western car makers were suddenly apprised of a major challenge on their doorstep, and were painfully aware that Japan's car makers enjoyed several important advantages. Wages were lower and productivity levels higher in Japan (most Japanese workers still worked a six-day week in the 1970s). And the highly efficient, just-in-time, Japanese supply system, which avoided stockpiling vast numbers of components and finished cars, meant that firms did not have a large proportion of their assets tied up in parts or unsold stock.¹ It also meant that suppliers, and not car makers, were responsible for much of the quality control. This abdication of responsibility was to rebound on Toyota during the recall scandals of 2009, while the downside of the just-in-time philosophy was dramatically revealed after the earthquake and tsunami of May 2011, when many Japanese plants worldwide were forced to close.

Japanese cars were also thoroughly tested before they were unveiled to the public, and were not, as was becoming increasingly the case in America and Britain, hurriedly released to customers in a misguided effort to maximize sales before faults had been properly identified and ironed out. Japanese automotive workers were also more flexible than their Western equivalents – able and happy to undertake a variety of tasks, rather than sticking to just one. The result was that manning levels at Japanese plants were far lower than in America and Europe. However, it is a myth that these hard-working car workers were better represented at senior management level than their Western counterparts. Workers were routinely represented on senior boards in Germany and Sweden; in Japan, however, their place was definitely on the shop floor.

The first Japanese car maker to make significant inroads into Western markets was Nissan, which first marketed its cars under the Datsun marque. The car maker was effectively born in 1914 as DAT, an acronym derived from the three partners: Kenijiro Den, Rokura Aoyama and Meitaro Takeuchi.

In 1931, DAT produced a small car, shamelessly plagiarized from the Austin Seven (already made under licence from Austin), which was given the anglophone name of Datson – 'Son of DAT'. Two years later, the last syllable was changed to 'sun', as DAT's management belatedly realized that 'son' in Japanese meant 'loss'.² But by the time the first Datson rolled

1 John DeLorean later recalled that the Chevrolet parts manual was 1½ feet thick and contained 165,000 different specifications.
2 The Datsun brand survived until 1986.

out, DAT's founders had been bought out. In 1931 the industrial entrepreneur Yoshisuke Aikawa, head of Japanese Industries – Nippon Sangyo, soon shortened to Nissan – took advantage of the Depression by buying up DAT and subsuming it into his huge industrial combine, or *zaibatsu*.

Yoshisuke Aikawa was born in Yamaguchi City in Japan in 1880. He graduated from Tokyo Imperial University in 1903 and went to study cast-iron technology in America. Hugely impressed with what he had seen there – America was then the world's largest producer of iron and steel – on his return to Japan he established a company, which he named Hitachi Metals. By 1931 this single firm had become a giant *zaibatsu*, with constituent companies ranging from DAT cars and Isuzu trucks to mining concerns and marine and life insurance providers.

Aikawa, like most of the great car makers of the period, also began to dabble in right-wing politics. He was accordingly very well placed when, in 1937, the Japanese government sought to industrialize the fake client state, Manchukuo, which Japan had carved out by force following its invasion of northern China.[1] Aikawa became Manchukuo's industrial supremo and de facto ruler. The wily industrialist even managed to secure American bank loans to support the fledgling economy of Manchukuo, a state the US government refused to recognize.

Aikawa was quick to acknowledge American expertise in the auto industry. On incorporating Kubota tractors into his vast *zaibatsu*, he found he had also acquired Kubota's influential chief designer, American expatriate William R. Gorham. Aikawa soon transferred the talented Gorham to the far larger enterprise at DAT and, under Gorham's direction, all of Dastun's machinery and vehicle designs were bought from America. Shortly before the Japanese bombing of Pearl Harbor in 1941, Gorham took Japanese nationality; unsurprisingly, he remained in Japan after the war's conclusion, being regarded in the US as a rank traitor. He died in 1949, revered by the Japanese and reviled in the country of his birth.

---

1 And over which the 'Last Emperor', Pu Yi, notionally presided.

While Gorham escaped retribution from the occupying Americans in 1945, Aikawa did not. The industrial magnate was arrested by the American military government and imprisoned for twenty months as a Class A war crimes suspect, largely due to his leading role in the rapacious Manchukuo administration. Aikawa was freed before his case came to trial, but not before his Nissan *zaibatsu* had been forcibly dissolved. In later years he successfully resurrected his business career, but preferred to concentrate on oil rather than automobiles, serving as president of Teikoku Oil and the Japan Petroleum Exploration Company. Yet he lived long enough to see his creation finally come of age. In the year of his death, 1967, Nissan took its first independent step and introduced its first viable home-grown car, the Datsun 510 saloon, powered by Nissan's own, highly advanced, four-cylinder L engine. Two years later Nissan used the L engine as the basis for its first international success, the 240Z sports car.[1]

The late 1960s saw phenomenal growth in Japanese car production. By 1968 Japan was manufacturing over four million cars per year, and exporting six hundred thousand. In that year American imports of Japanese cars more than doubled, from 82,035 in 1967 to 182,547 in 1968. The Datsun 510 was partly responsible for this outstanding success in America; badged as the Bluebird, and redesigned to a more crisp silhouette by the Pininfarina studio (although Nissan insisted that the Italians had to remain silent about their role), the 510 made substantial inroads into the compact car market, a sector that Detroit's Big Three were still not taking seriously. In 1969 Nissan also introduced the 240Z to the US market, to great acclaim; the model was even voted Sports Car of the Year by America's *Road Test* magazine. By 1970 Toyota was America's second-largest importer of foreign cars (after Volkswagen) and Datsun the third-largest.

As we have seen, Japanese car makers responded to the oil crisis of 1973 with a series of small, economic models which, while they lacked

---

1 Sold in Japan as the bizarrely named Fairlady Z.

excitement and originality, offered what the customer wanted: compact build, guaranteed reliability, fuel efficiency, and fewer emissions. As a result, Japanese car exports to Western Europe and, particularly, America soared. By 1975 both Nissan and Toyota had overtaken Volkswagen to become, respectively, the largest and second-largest exporters of cars to the US. Japanese compact and mid-size cars such as Toyota's Corolla and Camry were soon serving as the default option for families and taxi fleets alike. Nor was Japanese success limited to America and Europe; Japanese car makers also penetrated worldwide markets that had previously been regarded as the preserve of the Big Three. As historian Daniel Yergin has observed, in the later 1970s, 'The proliferation of Datsun pickup trucks in Saudi Arabia was a sign of the times' – the Fords and Chevrolets that the Saudis had previously preferred having suddenly disappeared following America's overt support for Israel.

Japanese marques came to dominate the small sports car market which British manufacturers had so abjectly ceded. Nissan's Z cars, descended from 1969's groundbreaking 240Z, went from strength to strength; while the Toyota MR2[1] of 1984 was a clever composite of European and American forms and systems which not only freely borrowed elements from the Lancia Beta, Pontiac Fiero and Fiat X1/9 but also officially enlisted assistance from the men at Lotus, whose engineer Roger Becker helped design the MR2's suspension and handling. Mazda responded to the MR2 with the MX5 of 1989,[2] which Mazda publicly acknowledged was based on the Lotuses of the 1960s, and later built on this success with a more affordable sports model called (confusingly) the MX3. Where Jaguar, Lotus and MG once reigned supreme, Nissan, Toyota and Mazda now ruled the roost.

In 1981 Japan became the world's largest producer of automobiles, overtaking the US only thirty-six years after the country's wartime defeat. Yet the initial response of the American automotive industry's top brass

---

1 In France this was called merely the MR, as the French pronunciation of MR2 sounded uncannily like the French noun *merde*.

2 Known as the Roadster, or *miata*, in Japan .

was dismissive and condescending. The combative, arrogant and pasty-faced CEO of General Motors, Roger Smith – a name that was, as we shall see, to become synonymous with the appalling mismanagement of the US car industry in the 1980s – derided the Japanese as myopic mimics. 'What did the Japanese invent in cars?' he mocked. 'The only thing I can think of is that little coin holder.' But Smith stopped laughing when the Japanese manufacturers began making substantial inroads into GM's market share. In response, the Americans tried to forge a series of quick alliances with a variety of Japanese companies. Chrysler started marketing Mitsubishi products under the Dodge name, while Smith's GM agreed to a partnership with Toyota. GM even began to make assembly-line robots in association with the Japanese robot manufacturer Fujitsu-Fanuc. Unfortunately, the robots malfunctioned and the project proved a disaster; the vast amount of money wasted on the robot venture could, GM's finance director later admitted, have been used to buy both Toyota and Nissan outright.

European manufacturers were similarly forced to swallow their pride and cosy up to Japanese partners – firms that, a mere decade or two before, they had dismissed as imitative parvenus. As early as 1979 Honda entered into a partnership with British Leyland, which proceeded to sell re-badged Hondas as Triumphs and Rovers. By the end of the 1980s even the Germans were bowing to the inevitable; in 1989 Toyota entered into a partnership with Volkswagen to build a small pickup truck in Germany.

Japanese car makers subscribed to a very different business ethos from their new Western partners. Each Honda employee, for example, carried a credit card-sized summary of the company philosophy – centred on principles of equality, teamwork and personal initiative – as enshrined in what the company's founder, Soichiro Honda, termed 'the Three Joys': the joy of buying (i.e. of owning), the joy of selling, and the joy of creating. Toyota's corporate creed was explained to its employees in a similar vein via the five principles of the Toyota Way: challenge, improvement (*kaizen*), *genchi genbutsu* (literally, 'go and see'), respect and teamwork. And unlike many Western car makers, Japanese auto manufacturers concentrated on building the overall brand or marque as a reliable and trusted entity, rather than spending millions on promoting individual models. While the names that Japanese companies applied to their cars were often (quite rightly) criticized in the West as unmemorable or arbitrary, such censure missed the point. The Japanese preferred to foster the reputation of the overall manufacturer – Nissan, Toyota, Honda or Mazda – in order to create a guarantee of reliability and quality that could be extended to any model the customer bought, rather than to nurture the brand value of a model that would only have a limited lifespan. In the long term, their policy was to be proved right.

While Nissan established the first foothold in Western markets, and Toyota grew to become the world's largest auto manufacturer, it was their smaller but nimbler rival, Honda, that became the first Japanese car maker to make major inroads into the West. In 1979 Honda opened the first Japanese-owned motor plant in the US, at Marysville, Ohio.[1] Marysville initially focused on making motorcycles, but in 1982 Honda took the plunge and began to produce mid-size Accord cars there. Following Honda's lead, Nissan erected an American plant at Smyrna, Tennessee, to build trucks; while Toyota not only opened a joint venture with GM in Fremont, California, early in 1984 but soon began work on a new factory in Georgetown, Kentucky. As journalist Paul Ingrassia has commented, in the 1980s: 'It was the Japanese . . . who showed that American workers could build quality automobiles, and thus stripped away Detroit's excuses.'

From 1990 until 1993 the Honda Accord was America's best-selling car, relegating Dearborn's Ford Taurus to second place. (This was the first time a Japanese car had earned that accolade, but it was not to be the last.) By 2002 the Marysville plant where the Accord was made – and which Honda had originally promised would hire one thousand people – boasted

---

1 Honda was also, interestingly, the first car maker to comply with America's Clean Air Act of 1975.

a workforce of fourteen thousand. In that same year, Honda, which had just opened a second US plant outside Birmingham, Alabama, and had become America's biggest importer of foreign cars,[1] earned more money than GM, Ford and Chrysler combined.

Honda was a latecomer to automobile manufacture. Famous for its motorcycles, the firm only started making cars in 1962. But it soon sought to outpace its larger rivals, Nissan and Toyota, by pioneering new technology and promoting international partnerships. As a result it was Honda, not Nissan or Toyota, that built the first Japanese plant in Europe, erecting a factory outside Swindon in 1985. (Once again, Honda's rivals followed in its wake: Nissan opened a factory in Sunderland, the first single-union car plant in Britain, in 1986; while Toyota's Burnaston complex, near Derby, opened in 1992.[2]) Honda's new-look, fourth-generation Accord saloon of 1989, along with the refreshed V30 Toyota Camry, dominated the mid-size car market in America during the ensuing decade. In 1998, too, the Honda Odyssey compact minivan[3] became the first product to challenge Chrysler's early lead in this valuable new sector. Soon even Honda's bilingual robot mascot, Asimo,[4] had become as familiar in America as in his homeland.

The Toyota Motor Corporation sprang from an unlikely parent, the Toyoda Loom Works, established by Sakichi Toyoda in 1926 to make automatic textile looms. In 1933 Sakichi's son, Kiichiro, set up a subsidiary to manufacture automobiles, which became formally independent of the main company (although still part of the Toyoda *zaibatsu*) four years later. At the same time, the decision was taken to change one letter of the brand name, to Toyota. This was not just easier to pronounce than the family

---

1 Although Toyota later retook the top spot.
2 The erection of the Burnaston plant controversially involved the demolition of the listed Regency mansion of Burnaston House.
3 A 'compact minivan' in America, a 'small MPV' (multi-purpose vehicle) in Europe.
4 From 2002 Asimo officially spoke English as well as Japanese.

name; 'Toyoda' is Japanese for 'fertile rice paddies', which was hardly an auspicious brand name for a would-be car maker.

During the Second World War, Toyota made trucks for the Japanese army, but it found the transition to peacetime production difficult. Virtually bankrupt by 1950, the firm was only saved from disaster by the outbreak of the Korean War which prompted a timely order for five thousand military vehicles from the US Army. In 1957 the Toyota Crown became the first Japanese car to be exported to America, and in 1963 the firm established a factory in Melbourne, Australia. Yet it was not until the 1970s that the company began to witness rapid growth, as its small, reliable, if bland, cars found ready export markets abroad. The small four-door compacts of 1970 – the Carina, the Celica, the second-generation Corolla and the fourth-generation Corona – had a worldwide appeal, and did increasingly well in America after the oil crisis of 1973.

In 1980 Toyota felt confident enough to replace the Corona in America with the larger and more powerful Camry, the first car the firm had specifically targeted at the American market. The Camry earned its curious name from an anglicization of the Japanese word for 'crown', *kanmuri*, variations on which had been used for most of Toyota's previous models. The company's ever-cautious American dealers had wanted the new model to be called the Crown, too; but there was already a car of that name in Toyota's line-up, so Camry was chosen as an easily pronounce-able compromise. The Camry was, like most of its stablemates, tame and dull – a 'vanilla' car, its Western critics asserted. But it was also reliable and well equipped, and held its residual value well, unlike most of its Big Three competitors. Since 1997 the Camry (which, like the Honda Accord, grew from a compact to a mid-size vehicle) has been the best-selling car in the US and American manufacturers have been left floundering in its wake.

. . .

Japan was not the only nation to emerge as a global force in the car industry in the 1970s and 80s. In the aftermath of the Second World War, mechanic Chung Ju-yung set up Hyundai Engineering (*hyundai* simply means 'modern') in the sleepy Korean fishing village of Ulsan. In 1967 he moved into car manufacture, assembling British Ford Cortinas supplied in kit form. As yet, no one outside Korea (or Dagenham) took much notice.

The scene now moves to Britain in 1973. In that year the former Ford executive John Barber was appointed Lord Stokes's deputy, and effective successor, at British Leyland. Barber was a man who, like Stokes himself, believed strongly in the need to keep British Leyland much as it was: a centralized conglomerate with a diverse product line, ranging from the Mini to the Jaguar XJ6. In contrast, Barber's principal boardroom rival, George Turnbull, wanted to break up British Leyland so that its constituent parts could flourish separately in the market. Subsequent events suggest that Turnbull was right and Barber wrong; but it was Barber who reflected his master's voice and won promotion. Turnbull thereupon surprised the British motor industry not just by resigning from BL but by moving to the other side of the world, to South Korea. There the ambitious and shrewd Chung Ju-yung made Turnbull vice president of Hyundai, responsible for manufacturing the firm's first locally made car.

Turnbull was a large, bluff Midlander, with little formal education, an individual who cut a bizarre figure in Ulsan. Born in Coventry, the son of a works manager at Standard Motors' Canley factory, he joined Standard at the age of just fourteen. Remaining at the firm throughout the 1950s and 60s, in 1968 he found himself in charge of the Austin-Morris division at British Leyland and, at forty-one, the youngest member of the new BL board. Translated to South Korea, Turnbull, a former Coventry Rugby Club forward and Warwickshire county cricketer, found himself several sizes bigger than most of his Korean staff. He also encountered a workplace ethos markedly at odds with the environment at Canley, Cowley or Longbridge, plants that were still mired in myriad outdated working practices. On his first day at the Hyundai factory, in the midst of a bitterly cold Korean winter, Turnbull is supposed to have asked what had happened to the factory's heating. 'When we make profits', replied Chung, 'they get heating.' As Chung had hoped, Turnbull immediately put his years of experience in British mass car making to excellent use. He hired five top British car engineers, imported British Leyland and Ford cars as his benchmarks, consulted world-famous auto stylist Giorgetto Giugiaro, bought an excellent engine from Mitsubishi – and within a year of his arrival launched the first truly Korean car, the four-door Hyundai Pony saloon. The Pony was available in Britain as early as 1976, and by 1978 was selling across Europe. The Korean invasion had begun.

Meanwhile, the restless Turnbull himself had moved on – to equally exotic pastures. In 1977 he left Hyundai for Iran National, where he supervised the transformation of Chrysler's mundane British workhorse, the Hillman Hunter, into the evergreen, Iranian-built Paykan, which continued to be produced until 2005. George Turnbull (Sir George, as he later became) was thus responsible for establishing a native car industry for two of the worlds' most strategically important emerging nations.

One major East Asian country, however, did not rush to join the automotive world in the 1970s. The largest potential market in the world stood idly by, its political masters preferring to promote the bicycle over the automobile and communist doctrine over car ownership.

The first motor car did not appear on China's streets until 1901, when a French model was imported into Shanghai by a wealthy foreign doctor; but by 1912 there were 1,400 motor cars registered in the city of Shanghai alone. Following the abdication of the last Qing emperor in 1911, the new president, Yuan Shikai, created a new road (the Avenue of Eternal Peace) simply in order to allow his personal limousine a smooth passage into the city. The first car factory on Chinese soil was built by the Japanese in Changchun (then called Hsinking), which they had established as the capital of Manchukuo following their invasion of Manchuria in 1931. In 1945 this plant fell into the hands of the invading Soviet army, and after

Mao's communist victory it was renamed the Number One Automobile Plant. From 1953 Number One began to make copies of Soviet trucks and, after 1958 (the year in which Mao Zedong imposed his disastrous 'Great Leap Forward' on an unsuspecting nation), passenger cars under the Red Flag ('Hong Qi') label. Senior party cadres, however, continued to be provided with Soviet ZiLs or Volgas until China's rift with Russia of 1965, after which they had to make do with whatever 'limousines' Red Flag could devise.

The rest of the Chinese population had to wait for the car to arrive. When it did, in the 1990s, the effect would be astonishing.

14

Big Beasts

The 'me' decade of the 1980s was a time of conspicuous consumption and brazen display. It was an era when bigger was invariably better. And it was an age of careless contradiction: what was ostensibly a time of growing ecological concern simultaneously spawned a motoring revolution which dismissed increasing unease about the pillaging of the planet's resources and instead positively gloried in the size and unsustainability of a wholly new species of large, fuel-hungry vehicles.

From the early 1980s, oversized, gas-guzzling, high-riding, 'off-road', four-wheel-drive 4×4s – or, as they were known in America, sports utility vehicles (SUVs)[1] – began to populate the world's highways. The off-road experience of the majority of these vehicles was confined to occasionally mounting the pavement. But consumers were attracted by their roomy interiors and the high ride height, which gave their occupants the illusion of greater safety. (Ironically, the exaggerated ride height of SUVs actually caused *more* accidents, because drivers failed to see what was happening at ground level.) SUVs could also tow all manner of objects, from caravans to boats, and were expedient in colder climates where their high ground clearance helped carry them over banks of snow. Women loved them, finding their luxury, space, strength and security (partly because

---

1 Technically, an SUV has less off-road capability than a true 4×4, but in practice the terms are often interchangeable. In Australia and New Zealand the term 4WD (for 'four-wheel drive') is preferred. In France, a 4×4 is simply a *quatre-quatre*.

they were so remote from the everyday dramas of the road) highly appealing; in the US in 2011 over 50 per cent of SUV drivers were women. And while car makers could extract far more profit from an SUV than from a regular saloon, buyers also found them a good investment; classified in America as 'light trucks', which helped them circumvent emission and consumption regulations, their gluttony for fuel seemed less of an issue as oil prices continued to fall during the 1990s.

Technically, the world's first luxury 4×4s were Kaiser's Jeep Wagoneer of 1963 (which never won the popularity it deserved, owing to Kaiser's slender resources) and the Range Rover of 1970. These bold, far-sighted initiatives were, by the mid-1970s, being widely imitated by Chevrolet, Nissan and Toyota. However, the modern SUV market was effectively created in 1980 by a far more affordable product, Toyota's Land Cruiser – a luxury, yet compact, off-roader which made the august Land Rover look like a spartan dinosaur and the Range Rover seem brusquely utilitarian. The Land Cruiser actually dated back to 1951 and was derived from the classic US Jeep.[1] By the 1970s it had evolved into a rugged station wagon – a market sector soon to be almost obliterated by the all-conquering SUVs. However, the 60 Series Land Cruiser of 1980, which borrowed many elements from the Range Rover (but not its high price), introduced far more cabin refinements, together with a higher driving position. The result was a success, particularly in America. Today, its successors, the bulky 200 Series Land Cruiser and its more lavish Lexus sibling, the LX570, still sell very well in the US – although, revealingly, it is the more luxurious Lexus that commands most of the range's sales.

The success of the Land Cruiser stung American car makers into action.[2] The Jeep Cherokee,[3] which AMC and Renault had been working

---

1 Its wartime predecessor, the AK of 1941–2, had been adapted from an American Jeep captured in the Philippines by the invading Japanese army.

2 Typically, though, it was not until 1994 that the Range Rover itself was overhauled and upgraded.

3 Initially badged the Wagoneer in the US in order to emphasize the continuity with the established Jeep wagon.

on since 1978, finally appeared in 1984 as the first American-made SUV, and was enthusiastically promoted by Chrysler after its purchase of AMC in 1987. Made both in Toledo, Ohio, and in China, the Cherokee proved a genuine world-beater. GM and Ford were slower off the mark, and initially preferred just to adapt existing light trucks[1] into two-door SUVs. By the end of the 1980s, however, everyone was getting in on the act, and manufacturers across the globe were producing four-door SUVs[2] of varying shapes and sizes. Indeed, so marked was the enthusiasm for SUVs that saloons began to be forgotten. Thus, while GM converted its Arlington, Texas, plant from the manufacture of Chevrolets, Buicks and Cadillac sedans to the production of SUVs, it forgot to update existing more conventional models such as the Buick Century and the Pontiac Grand Prix, which as a consequence began to fall behind their Japanese and German competitors in terms of specification and styling.

Back in the world of everyday saloons, it was the Germans who now set the standard for family and executive cars. The Audi 80 of 1978 was the first distinctive Audi that Volkswagen had produced since it had bought the car maker in 1965, while the Audi 100 of 1982 set new benchmarks for comfort and performance. Created by Audi boss Ferdinand Piëch (the grandson of Ferdinand Porsche) and designed by Giugiaro, the 80 was based on the same platform as the VW Passat but, for the first time in Audi's history, it was a car that did not look like a Volkswagen. Trim, streamlined and tight, it looked fast – and it was. When it was updated in 1986, Audi's anglophone advertising agency, BBH, ingeniously harnessed perceived German brand values, using the same '*Vorsprung durch Technik*' tag line it had already coined for Germany. American and British manufacturers found they had little with which to challenge either the new Audis or even the revamped and improved VW Passat.

---

1 GM's Chevrolet Blazer/Jimmy, which originally appeared in 1969, and Ford's Bronco, originally introduced in 1966.

2 In the 1990s the two-door SUV fell out of favour, as consumers rushed to big ever-bigger vehicles. The advent of the Range Rover Evoque of 2011 possibly signals a return to more modestly scaled, two-door 4×4s.

BMW also went from strength to strength. During the 1980s the 3, 5 and 7 Series were all updated, yet the BMW family resemblance, which traced its ancestry back to the 1500 of 1962, always remained very apparent. The 3 Series became the symbol of Western capitalism in the 1980s, the transport of choice for the newly enriched 'yuppie' who had profited from the laissez-faire economies of the Reagan, Thatcher and Kohl years. A 6 Series (coupé versions of the 5s) and an 8 Series (a rather heavy coupé development of the 7s) were subsequently added, and in 1986 BMW introduced a sports version of the best-selling 3 Series, the M3, a more aggressively designed and highly tuned version of the basic saloon. Meanwhile, the civilian 3 Series became ever larger, prompting the Bavarian car maker to issue a truncated, 'compact' version in 1994.

Like BMW, Mercedes was in 1980 widely regarded as one of the world's principal automotive beasts. Yet the company's apparent strength, confidence and success belied numerous internal corporate tensions. These finally surfaced in 1986 when the televised celebration of Daimler-Benz's centennial was ruined by avoidable technical problems, prompting Europe's TV stations to pull the plug on the event halfway through. Daimler-Benz executives were horrified, forced the resignation of the company's chairman and CEO, Werner Breitschwerdt, and indulged in an orgy of soul-searching.

The centennial debacle was a watershed for Daimler-Benz. The company realized it could not continue to prosper by complacently relying on the legacy of the 1960s while Audi and BMW surged further ahead. It started by abandoning the unfathomable classification system traditionally used for Mercedes cars. Accordingly, in 1993 the mid-size Mercedes 220 range became known as the E-Class; the label S-Class began to be used more prominently for top of the range *Sonderklasse* ('special class') luxury saloons; and Mercedes extended its range downwards with a new C-Class, effectively a replacement for the discontinued 190 series.

The repackaged S-Class was designed to challenge the supremacy of the BMW 7 Series and, while it only achieved moderate success in this regard, it sold tolerably well and acquired an enviable reputation for build, reliability and safety.[1] Nevertheless, while the S-Class cars still recognizably resembled the Mercedes of old, they also looked overweight, oversized and old-fashioned when compared with the latest products emerging from their Munich-based rivals. The S-Class had, BMW's Wolfgang Reitzle cheerfully told reporters, 'not one innovative thing about it'.

While the British and the Americans can be said to have invented the off-road SUV, and the Germans perfected the executive saloon during the 1980s, it was the French who pioneered one of the era's signature vehicles. In 1984 France's state-owned auto manufacturer launched the world's first full-size personnel carrier – also known as a people carrier, multi-purpose vehicle (MPV) or, in the US, minivan.[2]

The Renault Espace was a car that, like the Jeep Cherokee and the BMW 5 Series, flagrantly disregarded contemporary anxieties about fuel economy. But it changed the face of family motoring forever. To the chagrin of the French, the concept of the Espace actually originated in the imagination of a Briton. In the mid-1970s British designer Fergus Pollock drafted a design for a large family transport for Chrysler UK at their design centre at Whitley in Coventry.[3] Thereafter, his idea was passed from pillar to post; with Chrysler's British subsidiary in meltdown, the design was swiftly forwarded to Chrysler's French division, Simca, which in turn presented it to its affiliate Matra. This seemed to be an eccentric choice, given that Matra was then best known for its niche sports models. However, it proved the right decision. Matra designer Antonis Volanis (who later helped create Citroën's popular compact MPV of 1999,

---

1 It is grimly ironic, then, that it was while riding in an S-Class Mercedes that Diana, Princess of Wales died in a Paris underpass on 30 August 1997.

2 Although L. J. K. Setright stoutly maintained that the personnel carrier had first been introduced in 1950 in the shape of the Bedford Dormobile, 'a slab-sided soggy horror that began as a smart resource for lively families and ended as a scruffy transport for builders' labourers'.

3 Today the Jaguar Design Centre. In 1978 Giorgetto Giugiaro came up with a similar idea for ItalDesign in the form of the boxy Lancia Megagamma concept car, which Lancia's parent, Fiat, rejected as too radical and risky to qualify for mass production.

the Xsara Picasso) successfully adapted Pollock's concept for assembly as an Anglo-French Talbot product. Then, in 1978, Simca found itself sold to Peugeot-Citroën, which recoiled from the novelty of Pollock and Volanis's concept. Instead, Matra took the idea to Renault, which recognized it as the key to a whole new market sector, and renamed it the Espace. With its fibreglass body and vast, single-floor cabin, Renault's roomy MPV was a dramatic new departure in auto design. Too extreme for some at first, it would seem: only nine Espaces were sold in the car's first sales month. But the vehicle soon caught on with families and taxi operators alike, and by 1986 was selling in impressive numbers across the world.

While Renault broke new ground with the Espace, its principal French rival faced some difficult years. Citroën's characterful and unmistakably French BX family car of 1982 used the same pneumatic suspension as the classic, and much larger, DS. But after launching the BX, Citroën appeared to retreat from its reputation for innovation and instead took refuge in a series of bland, unremarkable cars. In addition, Peugeot-Citroën's factories, with their highly unionized and restive workforces, also endured crippling stoppages; as a result, the combine descended ever deeper into the red. In 1983, facing bankruptcy due to the huge losses incurred by Chrysler Europe's toxic legacy, Peugeot-Citroën announced a 10 per cent cut in the workforce at Poissy and announced that its new supermini, the 205 (later hailed by Europe's motoring journalists as the Car of the Decade) was to be built not at Poissy but at Sochaux. The unions naturally objected, and demanded that the whole company be nationalized, as Renault had been in 1945. Peugeot-Citroën simply retaliated by threatening to close the whole plant. Talks broke down and rioting broke out; the violence became so serious that even the unions asked Peugeot-Citroën to call in the feared CRS riot police. Poissy was shut, and then reopened with a drastically pruned workforce. At the same time, Citroën's old, cramped factory at Levallois, now surrounded by prime middle-class real estate, was permanently closed. With it died one of the world's most famous cars, the Citroën 2CV.

Even Renault found it was not immune from violence. In 1985 the new chairman, Georges Besse, followed in the footsteps of his rivals at Peugeot-Citroën and initiated a dramatic cost-cutting programme. A few months later, however, Besse was assassinated by terrorists from the revolutionary group Action Directe. Stoically, Renault's management persevered with Besse's restructuring plans, and in 1989 shut the venerable Billancourt factory for good. The unions protested vociferously, but after Besse's murder the initiative passed to the management. Five years later Renault was privatized with barely a whimper.

Privatization was also the name of the game in Margaret Thatcher's free-market Britain. At British Leyland, however, Michael Edwardes's initial replacement could by no stretch of the imagination have been called a Thatcherite sword-bearer. In an astonishingly myopic attempt to turn the clock back several decades (and to present the departing and little-loved Edwardes with a public raspberry), right under the noses of Thatcher's struggling government[1] BL promoted a long-serving motor executive, with no proven track record of leadership or decision-making, to become the auto giant's new CEO. Harold Musgrove was a former Austin apprentice who had risen to become chief of the Longbridge factory, but his tenure at the summit of BL definitely proved a bridge too far. Musgrove's unguarded and inappropriate comments alienated the workforce, while his senior staff were exasperated by mistakes such as his secretive attempts to kill off the Mini, his supine accession to the government's privatization of Jaguar in 1984, and his termination of the contract of the gifted designer David Bache, who had been responsible for the Rover P6 and the Range Rover. Under Musgrove's tenure, BL's export market dissolved. In 1978 foreign exports had stood at around 40 per cent of BL's output; by 1984 (admittedly now without Jaguar) they were down to 20 per cent. The American market, in particular, had vaporized; as critic James Ruppert has recorded, 'from a buoyant

---

1 Early in 1982, Thatcher had yet to reap the electoral benefits of the imminent Falklands War, and her government was increasingly unpopular.

75,291 cars in 1976, BL cars in America managed to export just the one in 1984'.

In 1986, with BL's market share in the UK down to a dismal 17 per cent, Musgrove was finally shunted aside to make way for a completely different animal, the disciplined Canadian business lawyer Graham Day. A man who had made his name in the shipbuilding industry, Day began by publicly admitting he had no idea how to make cars. But he did recognize that BL needed to concentrate on profits rather than on market share – a sound philosophy, albeit one that was applied thirty years too late. He also created a proper marketing department for the automotive giant, almost twenty years after British Leyland had been formed and almost forty since the creation of BMC. Knighted in 1989 (an honour ostentatiously denied to Musgrove), Day sought to take his new charge upmarket by renaming British Leyland the Rover Group and remodelling it as a serious rival to BMW. The problem was, Day had neither the right models nor the requisite finance to realize this plucky ambition. The tired and still notoriously unreliable Rover SD1 was the only premium model available to pit against BMW's effortlessly superior 5 and 7 Series, and the SD1 was due for the axe without any replacement having being developed. In response to this dilemma, Day resorted to the same gambit Edwardes had adopted a few years earlier, selling off bits of the auto group piecemeal with no thought for the long-term future. Unipart was sold to its management, as was Leyland Buses, while Freight Rover went to the Dutch firm Daf. Just two marques were left standing, Rover and MG (and no true MG sports cars had been made since Abingdon closed in 1980). Day felt he had no choice but to settle into an ever-closer relationship with Honda – hardly the way, perhaps, to take on BMW. Since the new Rover Group seemed as bereft of ideas as British Leyland had been, that meant pretending that Honda products were as British as the Spitfire fighter and Stilton cheese.

Michael Edwardes had begun BL's brand devaluation in 1981, ruining the venerable Triumph marque, formerly associated with inexpensive but stylish sports cars and fast executive saloons, by re-badging the Honda

Ballade, a four-door version of the best-selling Civic, as the Triumph Acclaim. This uninspiring model sold fairly well in the three brief years it was on the market; but no one was deceived by its name, and the car was soon popularly nicknamed the 'Ronda'. In 1984 Musgrove launched the 200 series – which, once again, was merely a re-skinned version of Honda's Ballade, with a few more British parts. But this time Honda struck a tough deal. In 1981 Edwardes had insisted that no Ballade should be available in Britain during the Acclaim years; now Musgrove cheerfully gave way, severely handicapping the new 200 both at home and abroad by allowing a Japanese equivalent to be made at Honda's new British plant at Swindon. After 1986 Day continued the Honda alliance, replacing the SD1 with the Honda-derived Rover 800 and launching a Honda-based 400 series. He also reprieved the ageing Mini, which Musgrove had marked out for euthanasia in 1988. But neither Edwardes, Musgrove nor Day ever gave much thought to updating the Mini in the manner of Ford's Fiesta or VW's Golf.

As the 1980s wore on, British car manufacturing became an increasingly pallid and pathetic reflection of German and Japanese successes. Day's new model numbering system – from 200 to 400 and 800 – was a feebly disguised attempt to trump BMW's numerical nomenclature, a strategy that was as obvious as it was laughable. The 400, though made at Longbridge, was basically a Honda Concerto, while the Cowley-made 800 was little more than a repackaged Honda Legend. At least the petrol versions of the 400 used a British engine (although Rover imported their diesel powertrains from Peugeot). But the range's flagship, the Honda-powered Rover 800, fared particularly poorly. Ambitiously marketed in the US as the Sterling, serious quality and reliability problems, publicly highlighted by J. D. Power's highly regarded customer surveys, soon made the 800/Sterling an American laughing stock – just at a time when its Japanese-made sister, the Acura Legend, was beginning to sell rather well. In 1992 the 800 was superficially Roverized by being provided with a Rover grille. But worldwide sales continued to be disappointing; even in its best year, 1987, only 54,000 cars were sold, and by 1998 a mere 6,500 were being made. The following year the 800 was axed to make way for what turned out to be Rover's last hurrah, the aspiring, handsome, yet ill-fated Rover 75. Meanwhile, the old MG badge was trundled out to give the faster Rondas a spuriously sporty image, a fabrication that fooled no one either at home or abroad.

Despite Day's brave assurances of future success, Margaret Thatcher's Conservative administration preferred to wash its hands of the whole business. When the government began negotiations to sell Rover to General Motors, Day countered with an eccentric proposal to sell the group to aircraft manufacturer British Aerospace (BAe). Day's patriotic concept won the approbation of MPs, although many within BL and the motor industry were baffled, and Rover was duly delivered to BAe in 1988. But the industry experts had been right to be mystified. BAe had little idea of how to run a car maker, and had only been tempted by the government's offer to write off Rover's debts of £1 billion and provide BAe with £800 million in new investment and £500 million in tax credits. BAe's single achievement was to add yet another Ronda, the Accord-clone 600, to the Anglo-Japanese Rover line-up. When it realized it had no further ideas, BAe sold the ailing car maker for £800 million in 1994, thus realizing a tidy profit. To everyone's astonishment, the unlucky buyer was BMW.

Not all British car makers found themselves in a downward spiral during the 1980s. By the end of the decade, Jaguar had emerged from its malaise and had recovered some of the jaunty confidence of the Lyons years. The much-vaunted replacement for the Jaguar XJ6, code-named (with typical Jaguar irrationality) the XJ40, had been in development throughout the 1970s, but nothing had appeared by the time Jaguar was spun off from the rest of BL as an autonomous division in 1980. Jaguar's new boss, John Egan, believed in testing cars thoroughly before launch, as the Germans and Japanese had always done. Accordingly, the XJ40 became the most tested car Jaguar had ever produced, completing 1.24 million miles in Arizona's summer heat, 1.1 million miles in Canada's arctic winter, and 1.8 million miles in Australia's unforgiving outback.

When the car was finally released in October 1986, however, it did not look enormously different from the Series III XJ6 it was supposed to be replacing. Its front end was squared off and provided with rectangular headlamps, features that made it resemble a 1970s Ford. And shortly after the XJ40's launch, it found itself eclipsed by the appearance of BMW's revamped 7 Series. Jaguar would need something far more appealing and novel to take on BMW and Mercedes, and win.

While Egan was reigniting a sense of corporate enthusiasm at newly privatized Jaguar, across the city of Coventry Rootes' new French owners were losing heart. In 1986 Peugeot replaced the old Simca/Chrysler/Talbot Horizon with the Peugeot 309. The French had originally intended to anglicize the model by selling it as the Talbot Arizona in Britain, but now they simply could not be bothered. Instead, they ended the pretence that Ryton's cars were as English as roast beef, badging all their UK-built models as Peugeots, and simultaneously sold their Whitley design centre to Jaguar.[1] The only Talbot-badged product to survive the cull was the Talbot Express van, which lasted until 1992. Many now questioned how long Peugeot would commit to car production in Britain.

While British Leyland and Peugeot-Talbot agonized over their lacklustre product range, Ford's Fiesta wrestled with Peugeot's French-made 205 for domination of the European supermini market. Further up the Ford range, in 1982 Ford took the decision to abandon the name and replace the legendary if unspectacular Cortina, along with Germany's evergreen Taunus, with something completely different, the all-European Sierra. The company's new family car originated as the pet project of Ford of Europe's Bob Lutz. Alongside fabled figures such as Iacocca and DeLorean, Lutz was one of the glamorous, colourful, tough guys who burst into the higher ranks of the auto industry at the end of the 1970s. The Swiss-born Lutz was an imposing, charismatic figure who had served as a Marine fighter

---

1 The Centre was sited just outside Coventry, on a famous old wartime base, adjacent to the factory where the eccentric Whitley bomber had been built.

pilot in the US. He cultivated an old-fashioned macho image, flying his own private jet fighters and collecting sports cars, and derided contemporary ecological concerns, such as global warming, which he famously labelled 'a total crock of shit'. Yet in 1982 Lutz stumbled, showing that even mighty Ford could still sometimes get it wrong. The Sierra's aerodynamic, 'jelly-mould' external styling was devised by Ford's German stylist, Uwe Bahnsen (the author of the Capris and Taunuses of the 1970s), and the design department's rising French star, Patrick le Quément, to provide a dramatic contrast with the familiar contours of generations of Cortinas and Taunuses. But instead of winning new customers for Ford, the highly controversial styling proved a major stumbling block for potential buyers. Moreover, the Sierra's cheap interior plastics looked outdated and tacky, the car's old-fashioned rear-wheel drive seemed to be a backward step, and the model's hatchback format implied that the boot would be too small for family or executive use. More seriously, the car's erratic behaviour in crosswinds prompted Dagenham and Köln to add rear spoilers to keep it straight and stable. Ford belatedly attempted to make amends for the lack of a boot by issuing a traditional saloon version, the Sierra Sapphire, in 1987, but by then the damage had been done. Although Sierra sales had become quite respectable by the end of the 1980s, in 1993 the model was quietly dropped to make way for Ford's much-vaunted 'world car', the Mondeo, whose all-round qualities (and capacious boot) helped Ford of Europe to recapture the fleet sales it had lost with the Sierra.

Ford's rivals were quick to scent that the American giant had tripped. The big corporate fleet orders of the 1980s went not to the Sierra but to more orthodox rivals, notably GM's conservatively styled and well-packaged second-generation Vauxhall Cavalier/Opel Ascona/Opel Vectra, which was one of Europe's best-selling models throughout the decade. Uwe Bahnsen's reputation never recovered. Having adapted the Sierra format for the upmarket Ford Scorpio, which aimed to challenge the mid-range BMWs and Mercedes but which failed to make any impact in the executive market,[1] Bahnsen left Ford for academia in 1986. Le Quément was luckier. Leaving Ford for Volkswagen in 1985, two years later he joined Renault as vice president in charge of corporate design – on the understanding that he would answer only to the firm's chairman, that he would sit on the main board, that all Renault's external design consultants would be dismissed, and that his design team would be doubled to more than 350 people. The Renault board agreed, and strapped themselves in for a rollercoaster twenty-two years with le Quément, during which he gave the firm some audacious and successful new models, such as the anthropomorphic Twingo, the Espace II, the Mégane II, the Scénic 'compact MPV' and the idiosyncratic Kangoo 'leisure activity vehicle', and some courageous failures, such as the angular Vel Satis executive car and the Matra-made Avantime crossover.

Thanks to le Quément's boldness, Renault entered the twenty-first century with a reputation for cutting-edge design and technological advance, and – along with Volkswagen, BMW, Mercedes, Fiat, Toyota, Nissan and Honda – as one of the world's premier auto manufacturers. The fact that Renault and its European and Japanese rivals were able to expand their global sales, however, was due not just to the excellence of their products but also to the failures of America's Big Three. During the 1980s General Motors fell from its lofty position as the manufacturer of almost half of America's cars to a dismal 35 per cent domestic market share. In 1979 Chrysler boss Lee Iacocca had acknowledged that 'imports and GM cracked 70 per cent of the [US] market'; by 1990 GM had not only lost this pre-eminence but was dangerously deep in debt. And as GM faltered, the gates opened for the rest of the world.

In 1980 General Motors had seemed by far the healthiest of the Big Three. In that year Ford reported a $1.5 billion loss, while Chrysler, which had recently been bailed out by the federal government, declared an annual loss of $1.7 billion. GM, though, announced only a very modest

---

1 The Scorpio's failure also ruined the prospects for Ford's new American import brand, Merkur (German for 'Mercury'), under which label the car was promoted in the US.

annual deficit, of $762 million, and continued to pay quarterly dividends to its shareholders. Moreover, in 1981 GM's new chairman appeared to have found the right solution: rather than demand government subsidies, as Chrysler had done, or insist that Washington limit imports of Japanese cars, as Iacocca was doing, GM's boss announced: 'The answer is to become competitive.' Over the next nine years, however, GM did exactly the opposite, squandering its impressive heritage through a series of elementary errors.

The erosion of GM's position in the 1980s can in part be attributed to a single individual. The new chairman, Roger Bonham Smith, was the definitive insider. He had begun his career at GM in 1949 as an accounting clerk, having graduated from the University of Michigan as a business major. Twenty-one years later he found himself GM's company treasurer, and the following year became a vice president. In 1974 he was promoted still further, to become executive vice president in charge of finance, government relations and public relations. Seven years later this former accountant was elevated to the head of the company.

A man whose character the *Detroit News* later described as 'brilliance unimpeded by humanity', and whom CNBC voted 'one of the worst CEOs of all time', Roger Smith was a short, pink, bespectacled figure, with few social graces ('He long ago lost "please" and "thank you" from his active vocabulary,' commented one GM vice president), a very short fuse (he often stormed out of meetings, and was notoriously unaware of others' sensibilities) and, famously, no sense of humour. Smith was also uneasy in social situations, rarely making eye contact with others when he spoke, and was an appalling public speaker, reading in a monotone from his script in a high, squeaky voice. He scolded his senior executives like children, and issued a stream of diktats from his office without consulting anyone. By the end of his tenure he had destroyed morale at GM ('No one believes he gives a damn about anyone but himself and his bonus buddies,' noted one Flint foreman) and brought the once-proud giant to its knees through a series of abysmal business decisions. Yet in the early 1980s he was hailed as a 'visionary' and 'the innovator of the age'. Smith, the motoring press suggested in 1981, was just the man to take on, and beat, the Japanese and Germans.

Smith's first big mistake came in 1984, when he destroyed Sloan's painstakingly assembled divisional ladder in one fell swoop. All GM's divisions, including Fisher bodies (which ceased to exist as a separate entity), were combined into two huge combines: Chevrolet-Pontiac-Canada (CPC)[1] and Buick-Oldsmobile-Cadillac (BOC). The result was chaos. Nothing new was launched or developed for almost two years, while workers' divisional loyalties disappeared at a stroke. Smith's seemingly random binary split also made no sense when applied to the various GM plants; thus CPC ended up building Cadillacs while BOC found itself making Pontiacs. New layers of management were added just at the time when GM's rivals were streamlining, and existing staff were duplicated (CPC alone added eight thousand new staff). Crucially, the new GM10 range of mid-size cars was seriously delayed; approved by Smith in 1981, GM10's first tangible results – the new Pontiac Grand Prix, Buick Regal and Oldsmobile Cutlass Supreme – were not available until 1988. By 1989, the year before the last of the GM10s was launched, General Motors was losing $2,000 on every one of these cars. When asked by *Fortune* magazine why the project had been such a catastrophe, Smith replied: 'I don't know.' ('It's a mysterious thing,' he later added inarticulately. 'I've said I'll take my share of the blame on all those things.') One of the first decisions taken after Smith's departure was to undo his corporate structure and group all of the car brands into one single division.

Roger Smith's method of dealing with the increasing threat of Japanese imports was similarly planned – and similarly flawed. Ignoring, once more, GM's proud and valuable brand heritage, to say nothing of the allegiance of both consumers and dealers, he established wholly separate, stand-alone ventures outside GM's existing brand structure. Turning his back on GM's own historic marques, he made common cause with the Japanese manufacturers he had so recently and bitterly denounced,

---

1 GM's Canadian operation was thrown into the mix merely to make up the numbers.

thereby providing GM's rivals with the ideal Trojan horse with which to penetrate the American market.

In 1984 GM and Toyota launched New United Motors Manufacturing Inc. (NUMMI) at an old plant at Fremont, California, which had actually been closed by GM two year earlier. Fremont had been a notoriously badly run factory, with appallingly high rates of absenteeism, stoppages, drunkenness, assembly-line sabotage, and even fist fights. It was the Wild West of American automobile production. ('When GM locked the plant,' said one reporter, 'the greatest surprise was that they bothered to save the keys.') Now NUMMI proposed to make Chevrolet Novas and Toyota Corollas at Fremont with many of the same workers – but with a largely Japanese management. The result was predictably embarrassing for America's floundering car makers: NUMMI's Japanese or Japanese-trained management was soon able to produce 25 per cent more cars per hour than its GM parent, using one third of the floor space and with minimal absenteeism and shop-floor disruption. Boundaries between workers and management were dismantled; there were no executive washrooms or cafeterias, and not even any assigned parking spaces. Revealingly, too, NUMMI's cars had far fewer defects than their American rivals.[1]

Smith's ostensible reason for creating NUMMI was to enable him to export Japanese management to other GM plants. Yet the lessons of Fremont were never applied elsewhere; instead, Smith launched a brand-new subsidiary in Toyota's image. Saturn Corporation was a £5 billion autonomous concern which, Smith declared, would be 'a different kind of car company', one that completely distanced itself from GM and which overtly aped the Japanese. Even its sinuously enigmatic logo looked Asian rather than American. But the Saturn initiative, too, was delayed by Smith's complex restructuring plans; first devised in 1982, the new company was not launched until 1985, and the first Saturn car (driven off the assembly line by Smith himself) did not appear until July

---

1 By 2008 the two NUMMI partners had predictably fallen out. GM pulled out of the deal in June 2009, and on 1 April 2010 Toyota produced its last Corolla at Fremont, transferring production to Canada.

1990 – just in time for the recession. Saturn had little to do with the rest of GM: its Spring Hill, Tennessee, plant was entirely new; its models were distinct from those of its GM cousins and incorporated no existing GM parts; and there was even a separate Saturn dealer network. Yet Smith had not thought the idea through properly. While the faux-Japanese Saturns, when they finally appeared, were initially popular (largely because they were cheap), they were never quite good enough to compete head-on with Japanese cars, many of which were by now being made in American plants. At the same time, Saturn sales tended to cannibalize GM's existing market share; over 40 per cent of Saturn buyers already owned a GM car. When these factors were added to the recession of the early 1990s, it is not surprising that Saturn never reached its optimistic sales targets. Meanwhile, the rest of GM was seething with jealousy at the £5 billion that Smith used to launch Saturn – money that they believed, rightly, should have been invested in existing brands and plants. After Smith's departure, Saturn was run down as an expensive irrelevance. In 1994 Saturn was merged into the rest of GM's operations; the last Saturn cars were made in 2009; and the Saturn Corporation itself was finally dissolved on 31 October 2010.

Casting the old GM brands aside, Smith eroded differences between divisional ranges while failing to address complex differences in the engineering of each model – the exact opposite of the strategy then being adopted by car makers such as Volkswagen, BMW and Ford. GM cars thus began to look more alike outside, while still remaining bewilderingly (and expensively) different inside. In 1982, for example, the once-prized Cadillac badge was applied to a top of the range model from the inexpensive J-car platform, the Chevrolet Cavalier, to create the Cadillac Cimarron, a crude sleight of hand that lost GM thousands of customers. In a similar vein, the Chevrolet Citation, the most basic version of 1981's front-wheel-drive X-car platform,[1] cost only $100 less than its supposedly

---

1 The 'X' range soon won a reputation for abysmal quality, with thousands of cars were being recalled.

The Ford Mustang of 1964. Its exciting and innovative styling belied the old Ford mechanics under the hood.

The languid Jaguar E-Type of 1961.

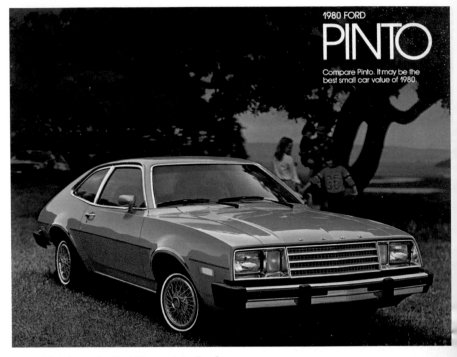

False dawn: the Ford Pinto, originally of 1971.

New dawn: the VW Golf of 1974.

Epitome of the Eighties: the BMW E30 of 1983–6.

Built on the sand: John DeLorean, his third wife Christina Ferrare, and the disastrous DMC-12.

Retro rides: new BMW-made Minis in 2001 (*left*), and the stylish new Fiat 500 with a potential customer at its 2007 launch (*below*).

The way ahead? The plug-in hybrid Chevrolet Volt, sold in Europe as the Vauxhall/Opel Ampera, at the 2012 Geneva Motor Show

more upmarket sister compacts, the Pontiac Phoenix, Oldsmobile Omega and Buick Skylark. What was the point of buying a Chevrolet if you could have a Buick for almost the same price? For a man with a prestigious MBA and years of accountancy training, Roger Smith seemed to have a surprisingly poor grasp of pricing strategy.

Smith's irreversible erosion of Sloan's brand ladder was eagerly seized upon by his competitors – most notoriously in Young & Rubicam's notorious 'Valet' television advertisement for Ford's Lincoln division of 1985. Y&R's film featured a parking valet who, when asked by a well-heeled couple to produce their black Cadillac, kept bringing out other GM products, Buicks and Oldsmobiles, by mistake; but, when asked by another couple for their Lincoln Town Car, had no problem identifying the model. The ad worked: Lincoln-Mercury sales soared, while Cadillac dealers complained strongly (though in vain) to Ford's exultant management.

Roger Smith was particularly fascinated by new technology and placed a naive, boyish faith in its ability to transform GM's prospects. During the 1980s he spent more than $90 billion on robots and other automated short cuts. His vision was of 'the light-out factory of the future', in which only a handful of employees supervised the automatic robots – a cost-effective dream, certainly, but one that did little to endear him to the unions. And while he may have been right in the long term, Smith, like many pioneers, was bound to make mistakes from which others were later able to profit. His joint venture with the Japanese robot manufacturer Fujitsu-Fanuc, GM Robotics, created the largest manufacturer of robotic machines in the world. But his early robots were, inevitably, somewhat unreliable, and often malfunctioned hilariously – painting each other instead of the cars, or welding car doors shut.[1] Thus they

---

1 As Smith's biographer Albert Lee (formerly a GM speech-writer) noted, the new robots 'frequently gave cockeyed instructions, ordering up the wrong bumpers, the wrong trim, the wrong welds, or the wrong paint, sending instructions to the next robot, which was too simple-minded to notice the errors. The paint robots were particularly cantankerous, slopping gobs of paint on one car, then not enough on the next.'

were never able to achieve the efficiencies that Smith imagined. As a result, GM's hi-tech, $600 million Hamtramck, Michigan, plant rarely operated at more than half capacity, while the Buicks and Cadillacs it produced were so poorly made that the factory's luxury car contract was soon cancelled.

Smith's spending spree did not stop with robots. Once again ignoring the need to invest in GM's core brands, he made two disastrous investments. Both were in cutting-edge technology. Both were bought at a high price, and both were intended by Smith to diversify out of GM's manufacturing base and into technology and services. In 1984 Smith bought Electronic Data Systems (EDS) for $2.55 billion from its billionaire founder, Ross Perot. Now best known for his quixotic campaigns for the US presidency in 1992 and 1996, the prickly, opinionated Perot had founded EDS in 1962 and had since made millions of dollars. Smith saw the acquisition of EDS as a means of absorbing advanced technology easily; Perot – who had become GM's largest single shareholder and had recently joined its board of directors – saw it as a way of reorienting America's largest corporation. After 1984 Perot became a constant critic of the hapless chairman, publicly censuring everything from factory overmanning to the opulence of Smith's offices.[1] As Perot told *Fortune* magazine: 'I come from an environment where, if you see a snake, you kill it. At GM, if you see a snake, the first thing you do is go hire a consultant on snakes. Then you get a committee on snakes, and then you discuss it for a couple of years. The most likely course of action is – nothing. You figure, the snake hasn't bitten anybody yet, so you just let him crawl around on the factory floor. We need to build an environment where the first guy who sees the snake kills it.'

As early as September 1985, the notoriously volatile Smith raged at Perot at a major GM meeting. EDS's chief financial officer subsequently recorded: 'People in the room later would remember Smith's angry

---

1 Perot kept returning to the GM chairman's opulent lifestyle, declaring of the twenty-fifth floor of the GM offices in New York, where Smith was based: 'An entire teak forest must have been decimated for that floor.'

explosion as being wondrous and terrifying at the same time: wondrous for the extreme colors and sounds it brought to the room, terrifying because none of them had ever seen someone lose his temper so completely in a business meeting. The EDS officers stared in disbelief as the chairman of the world's biggest and most powerful company lost it.'

Only two years after buying EDS, Smith's patience snapped, and he bought out Perot's stock for $743 million – a sum considerably above the market rate and one that Perot, while cheerfully accepting the cash, publicly denounced as an outrageous purchase at a time when GM was closing plants and laying off hundreds of thousands of workers.¹ Meanwhile, the EDS acquisition had proved an administrative disaster. EDS had been run almost on military lines, with strict dress and moral codes; employees were, for example, forbidden to live together. Thus it naturally proved difficult to blend EDS personnel into GM's elephantine bureaucracy, let alone to ensure that the two worked harmoniously together. In 1996, Smith's successor sold off EDS.

The money Roger Smith spent on EDS, however, was dwarfed by the expenditure necessitated by his 1985 purchase of Hughes Aircraft for an astronomical $5.2 billion – a price tag that many analysts calculated was five times what Hughes' assets were actually worth. On New Year's Day 1986, Smith paid over $2.5 million to rent Disneyland for an ostentatious away-day for Hughes employees. But Hughes never made a profit for its new owner, and in 1997 was broken up and unloaded.

As GM's financial reserves evaporated and its plants atrophied from lack of investment, Smith seemed unaware of the mounting criticism. In 1986, the year in which he paid way over the odds to buy out Perot, he spent yet another big chunk of money, $20 million, on British niche sports car manufacturer Lotus, a tiny outfit whose production methods seemed wholly at variance with those of the Detroit auto giant. Smith declared

---

1 A policy that was highlighted by Michael Moore's unexpectedly successful film documentary *Roger and Me* of 1989, in which Smith unwittingly played the part of Moore's tragi-comic stooge. Smith laid off two hundred thousand GM workers in the first two years of his tenure as chairman.

that the purchase was designed to acquire Lotus's computer-based performance engineering. But to GM's workers, and the international motoring press, it looked more like an old man's selfish indulgence – buying a sports car in order to satisfy a mid-life crisis. And it was an indulgence that GM patently could not afford; at the same time as buying Lotus, Smith coolly announced the closure of thirteen plants and the loss of forty thousand additional jobs.[1]

Smith compounded his business disasters with some appalling public relations blunders. While spending billions of dollars on puzzling new acquisitions, he pressured the unions to cut both jobs and wages, aiming to replicate Japan's labour costs (which in 1981 were $8 per car less than GM's) while conveniently forgetting that Japanese car makers generously subsidized their workers' housing and food. In order to cut costs, he imposed a wage cut for every GM executive of $135 per month, a tiny drop in the ocean for senior management but a hefty blow for junior grades. To make things worse, Smith gave himself and his senior staff a whopping 18.8 per cent pay rise. The vehement protests that this astonishing own-goal elicited at 1982's meeting of GM shareholders failed to persuade Smith to rethink his plans; he merely announced that he would limit shareholders to two minutes of podium time each and would in future conduct half the day in private and accept only written questions. The outcry that greeted this proposal forced Smith, for once, to back down; but, typically, he then publicly blamed the media for making something out of nothing, with the result that relations between GM and the press were permanently soured. (Smith also publicly condemned his Chrysler rival, Lee Iacocca, whom he accused of undermining US car making. In 1981 Smith had earned $56,250 per month, while the publicity-savvy Chrysler boss had ostentatiously taken only a $1 annual salary from his company.)

Smith seemed to learn nothing. Over the next two years, with an astonishing disregard for his own employees and for public opinion, he

---

1 In 1993 Lotus, too, was quietly disposed of.

openly pursued a policy of closing plants in the US while creating new GM jobs south of the border in Mexico, where labour was far less expensive.[1] By 1990 Roger Smith had become the leading hate figure for the unions of America.

Ford, led by its low-profile president, Donald Petersen,[2] fared much better than GM during the 1980s. The profits from Ford of Europe kept the firm in the black, while in America the new Ford Taurus offered a way forward. Introduced for the 1986 model year, the Taurus's aerodynamic body was based on that of the European Sierra, but was sensibly provided with a pronounced trunk. It introduced flush front headlights and a flush rear fender to the US, and abandoned the classic American front grille in favour of a 'bottom breather' nose – innovations that helped cast the car as the futuristic police transport in the 1987 film *Robocop*. But not everything in the Ford garden was rosy. The Taurus was launched far too soon; only a week after the model's official launch, 4,500 Tauruses and Sables[3] were recalled to amend defective ignition switches. Two months later, back they went again to have their substandard window glass replaced. And it took Ford months to remedy the car's pollution-control system, which emitted a distinct odour of rotten eggs. Nevertheless, the Taurus/ Sable survived these mishaps to notch up impressive sales figures, helping Ford to achieve record profits in 1986–8. In July 1988, Standard & Poor's elevated Ford's credit rating above that of General Motors for the first time in history.

Meanwhile, on the other side of Detroit, Ford's former president was making Chrysler a viable entity once more. In November 1978 Lee Iacocca had been ruthlessly fired from the summit of Ford by an increasingly imperious and out-of-touch Henry Ford II, who effectively replaced him with his own brother, William Clay Ford. ('It's personal,' Henry II

---

1 Mexican workers were about $20 per hour cheaper than their American equivalents.
2 Petersen may have seemed far quieter than his more celebrated contemporaries, Smith and Iacocca, but he had an explosive temper, being notorious for shouting at his staff and for throwing his Rolex watches against the wall when crossed.
3 The Taurus's Mercury-badged twin.

had blurted out incoherently, 'and I just can't tell you any more. It's just one of those things.') Iacocca soon made Ford regret its decision.

Lee Iacocca was perhaps the greatest of the automotive big beasts of the 1980s. The son of Italian immigrants who ran hot-dog restaurants, movie theatres and car rental businesses in working-class Allentown, Pennsylvania, he graduated as an engineer and joined Ford in 1946. There he gradually worked his way up the company's ranks, in the process metamorphosing from a shy, introverted engineer to a bullish, aggressive salesman.

The Chrysler that Iacocca joined was in a bad way. There seemed to be no financial controls (odd for a company that had been largely run by former accountants since the war) and no forward planning. Volkswagen had looked at purchasing the ailing giant but had swiftly walked away from its administrative and financial chaos. As Iacocca harshly but truthfully put it in his autobiography: 'Chrysler executives had a better reputation for their golfing abilities than for any expertise with cars.'

Iacocca was understandably livid at being so abruptly discarded by Ford, and immediately set about rejuvenating Chrysler in order to hit back at his former employers. Typically, he began by promoting himself as the star of his own TV commercials. Despite his wooden delivery and over-rehearsed one-liners, let alone the cringingly embarrassing guest slots filled by pals such as Frank Sinatra ('I'm a man of business myself'), Iacocca gave America a corporate face and projected candid honesty. He also emphasized the home-grown origin of Chrysler's products – 'Made in the USA' became a ubiquitous Chrysler marketing tag line – in an attempt to undermine Japanese imports. It was an image that seemed light years away from the corporate fat cats of GM and Ford, and it worked. In 1981, in a commercial promoting the Chrysler LeBaron, Iacocca stumbled across his archetypal message: 'If you can find a better car, buy it.' It was a slogan he proceeded to milk for the next eleven years.

Buoyed by his televisual success, Iacocca began to foster his own personality cult – even conniving at an 'Iacocca for President' campaign.

But Iacocca's chutzpah could work wonders for Chrysler. He secured an aid package of $1.5 million from the federal government – a deal that had been denied his predecessor. He also appointed UAW president Douglas Fraser to the Chrysler board. (This strategy, while common in Germany, caused enormous controversy in conservative Detroit; but it helped bring Chrysler to the attention of the nation.) He launched safe, dependable new models, such as the insipid but reliable Dodge Aries/ Plymouth Reliant compact and America's first minivan, the Dodge Caravan/Plymouth Voyager. He exhumed the luxury Imperial marque, and persuaded the equally venerable Frank Sinatra to extol its virtues on TV. And in 1983, having announced that the company had repaid the last of its federal loans, early, he opened exciting new Chrysler Design Centers in California and Arizona.

If Iacocca had stepped down in 1984 (the year in which his ghost-written autobiography was published), he would have departed with a stratospheric reputation as The Man Who Had Saved Chrysler. After 1985, however, it all started to go wrong. Just like Henry Ford II in the 1970s, Iacocca's growing paranoia about possible rivals to his Olympian throne seemed to dominate his thoughts and adversely affected his ability to manage effectively.

In 1986 Iacocca hired a disgruntled Bob Lutz from Ford – largely so as to discomfit his former employers. Lutz's recent and highly public ridiculing of Ford's increasingly impenetrable business-speak had made him a marked man at Dearborn. Even when Lutz came up with such signal successes as the superb Dodge Viper sports car of 1991 – an instant classic based on the iconic Anglo-American AC Cobra of the 1960s – Iacocca still seemed determined to ensure that Lutz never succeeded him.

Iacocca's behaviour, moulded by his messianic self-belief, was growing increasingly eccentric. He embarked on a bizarre spending spree that almost matched that of GM. In 1985 Chrysler acquired Gulfstream Aerospace, makers of corporate jets (Iacocca, naturally, nabbed a top of the range Gulfstream G4 for himself). He also tried to buy Hughes Aircraft, which went instead to GM. Iacocca even tried to emulate his Detroit rival by announcing the Liberty project, a misguided attempt to set up a new division in the mould of GM's costly, Japanese-style Saturn project. (Thankfully, Chrysler executives managed to bury this concept before too much money had been spent, and before any cars had been made.) Iacocca then spent $500 million of Chrysler's money on acquiring a large stake in Maserati, then owned by his Argentinian friend Alessandro de Tomaso (who in turn had bought the niche sports car maker from Citroën in 1975). In order to validate this deal to his board, Iacocca sought to develop a fantasy Maserati-Chrysler, the Chrysler Turbo Convertible. This particular TC, however, was no Top Cat. When it finally reached US showrooms in 1988, it bombed. Only seven thousand TCs were sold before the model was terminated, in 1991.

Iacocca was not deterred by this failure, despite the fact that virtually all of Chrysler's multi-million dollar investment in the Maserati project had to be written off. In 1987 (the year he embarked on a messy and very public divorce from his second wife, Peggy), he bought Lamborghini, another world-famous Italian sports car manufacturer. Chrysler's top brass were delighted, as they were each able to acquire a free Lambo. But despite the fame of the marque, the legendary Italian car maker rarely made more than four hundred cars per year. Moreover, Lamborghini was mired in debt, having recently gone bust and having, over the past decade, endured more changes in ownership than there had been Italian governments. Moreover, neither Iacocca nor Chrysler really had any idea what to do with their new toys. After Iacocca's departure, Lamborghini was sold to a cartel of Indonesian businessmen (who in turn sold it to Volkswagen in 1998), while Maserati was offloaded to Fiat.

One Iacocca purchase of the late 1980s did make business sense. In 1987 Chrysler bought AMC, largely for its Jeep marque. The Jeep Grand Cherokee, which had been developed by AMC at Kenosha and which was launched by Chrysler in 1992 as America's first mid-size SUV, proved a great success with both critics and public. However, Iacocca's interference in the sedan market was less helpful. He insisted on boxy styling for the 1987 Chrysler range, just when Ford's Taurus had popularized a rounded, organic look. As a result, in 1987 as in 1947, Chrysler's cars looked distinctly more old-fashioned than those of its rivals. Bob Lutz publicly commented that Chrysler was now offering only 'yestertech'.

Iacocca's reaction to the economic downturn of 1987–8 was equally maladroit. When he proposed closing the former AMC factory at Kenosha, Wisconsin, and transferring production of the new Chrysler LeBaron and its K-car platform clones from Detroit to Mexico – a flagrant betrayal of his own, much-vaunted 'Buy American' campaigns – the media revealed that the Chrysler president's previous year's pay had totalled $17.9 million. In the furore that followed, Kenosha was reprieved, for a while. But in 1989 the Jefferson Avenue plant in Detroit was demolished, and the following year Kenosha was finally axed, along with the firm's St Louis factory. Iacocca's shopping spree had finally caught up with him.

Faced with a corporate meltdown, Iacocca's response was to put pressure on his senior staff – many of whom, as a result, abruptly left the company.[1] In 1990 Iacocca attempted to sell a big stake in Chrysler to Fiat and, astonishingly, to Ford, but got nowhere. At the same time, and despite the firm's mounting losses (Chrysler's 1991 deficit was almost $800 million), Iacocca's lifestyle became increasingly presidential. Whisked from meeting to meeting in a fleet of limousines or his personal Gulfstream (he refused to fly commercially, as the wiser chairmen of Ford and GM were now doing), his New York apartment was extensively renovated at great expense just as he was announcing a new round of cuts. He also seemed to have lost his gift for public relations. In 1986, interviewed on NBC television about the safety of Chrysler's new minivans, he came across as rude, patronizing, complacent and sexist. In 1988, as his executives announced the closure of the Kenosha plant – and Wisconsin state officials accused him of breaking his word – Iacocca awarded himself yet another huge pay rise. By 1992 he was earning over $14 million per year in salary, bonuses and stock options.

---

1 The most serious loss was that of Chrysler's number two, Jerry Greenwald, who left to run United Airlines.

Lee Iacocca was sixty-five in 1989, at the summit of Chrysler long after contemporaries such as Roger Smith and Donald Petersen had gone. As historian Paul Ingrassia has observed: 'Lee Iacocca had many talents, but knowing when to quit was not one of them.' GM veteran Bob Eaton was suggested by Chrysler's directors as a potential replacement; but while Iacocca liked him, and was prepared to install him as CEO, he still refused to vacate the presidency. It took subtle but relentless pressure from key Chrysler shareholders to persuade him to agree that Eaton should be nominated as his successor.

On 1 January 1993 Lee Iacocca was finally ushered out of the door. Even then, he tried to hang on to his corporate Gulfstream and his two Chrysler-owned homes, and insisted that his already sizeable pension pot be topped up yet further and that he be given a two-year, $500,000 consultancy contract. The following August he sold some of his Chrysler shares for an astronomical $53.3 million. Despite this windfall, he showed precious little loyalty to the company that had made his name and his fortune. In 1995 he persuaded his friend, financier Kirk Kerkorian, to make a hostile bid for Chrysler. (It failed.) Two years later, he condemned Chrysler's merger with Daimler, appearing to forget that many of the problems that now beset the firm were of his own making. Even in retirement, it seemed, the largest automotive animals were unable to let go.

15

Merge In Turn

The last decade of the twentieth century, and the first decade of the twenty-first, saw a worldwide realignment of the car industry. This tragi-comical game of corporate musical chairs dramatically brought to a conclusion issues and problems that had been simmering away for thirty years; the resulting cull of famous names, and the disposal of hundreds of thousands of jobs, was necessarily (and possibly overly) brutal. By 2010 – after worldwide recession had hastened the collapse of those walking wounded that still remained – it seemed that the sun was finally setting on some of the most distinguished American marques of the past fifty years, as well as on almost all of the famous British auto manufacturers of the preceding century. German and Japanese reliability, quality and market-awareness had, apparently, triumphed. Or had they? At the dawn of the twenty-first century, even the very largest car makers could not afford to be complacent.

By the 1990s there was certainly little to be smug about in British auto manufacture. Like a punch-drunk boxer, Britain's sole-surviving indigenous mass car maker, the Rover Group, staggered from disaster to disaster. BMW, which bought the sickly combine in 1994, initially seemed unsure exactly why it had made the purchase. When asked how he viewed Rover cars, BMW boss Bernd Pischetsrieder, the man behind the acquisition (and who was actually the great-nephew of Alec Issigonis), merely replied that he saw them 'as cheap Jaguars' – hardly an adequate description, for example, of the Honda-based 200 series of hatchbacks. Subsequently, a contrite Pischetsrieder declared that he also saw a market for the smaller Rovers, which he suggested might fill a notional gap beneath BMW's 3 Series. But in 1994 Rover was barely equipped to fulfil either role. Aside from Land Rover's impressive and expanding range, there was not much to boast about in the firm's current portfolio. As we have seen, the supposedly upmarket Rover marque had become completely devalued since the 1976 withdrawal of the last Rover that could look Jaguar in the eye, the P6. By the mid-1990s Rover's small cars were either ageing standbys like the old Mini and the Metro (farcically re-badged as the Rover 100 in 1994) or poor man's Hondas. Many observers, puzzled as to why BMW had bought Rover in the first place, assumed that the Bavarians had acquired the conglomerate simply to get their hands on the profitable Land Rover business – which, in retrospect, seems to have been largely correct. Some critics were even more cynical. Motor journalist James Ruppert later wrote that 'at a stroke, or rather £800 million, BMW had removed their largest single competitor in the UK car market'.

Under BMW's ownership, Rover did at least launch a genuinely new model. The MG brand was exhumed in the shape of the MGF, an attractive, lightweight two-seater, neatly designed by Rover's Gerry McGovern. The first genuine MG for fifteen years, it proved, despite some predictable reliability problems, to be a hit. In 2002 it was replaced with a more conventional version, the TF (named after MG's TF Midget of 1953). This, too, earned respectable sales – particularly encouraging in a market crowded with outstanding, sporty world-beaters such as the Audi TT, the BMW ZX and the Mazda's MX-5 (a model that the F and TF strongly resembled). The TF even survived the final collapse of Rover, being disinterred by the Chinese after 2007.

Three years later, BMW also introduced a wholly new, executive Rover: the 75. The original idea was simply to re-skin the 600, but braver souls at BMW decided on a completely new model. The 75 was a serious upmarket contender, handsomely styled by Richard Woolley both to reflect contemporary mores and to acknowledge Rover's illustrious past. It was also a genuinely British product: both the platform and the petrol engines were entirely Rover's, and only the diesel power train came from BMW. The model won plaudits across the globe. It won the *What Car?* 'Car of the Year' accolade in 1999, the Italian 'World's Most Beautiful High Class Saloon' award in 1999, Japan's 'Import Car of the Year' prize in 1999 (and again in 2000), and the top European slot in J. D. Power's revered customer satisfaction survey in 2001. Sadly, though, the impressive 75 was soon eclipsed by BMW's hasty exit from Britain. Pischetsrieder used the occasion of the model's unveiling at the Birmingham Motor Show not to celebrate the rebirth of Rover or to celebrate the 75's qualities, but to lambast the British company's senior management and to demand hefty government subsidies – without which, he threatened, BMW would pull out of Britain, closing its plants and throwing its British workforce on the dole. In the event, Pischetsrieder's outburst was ill-timed. Tony Blair's New Labour government was adamant that the 1970s had not come again and that it would not intervene either to prop up Rover or to subsidize BMW. The Bavarians, meanwhile, used the episode to force the unlamented Pischetsrieder to fall on his sword; he left BMW to join Volkswagen, whose chairman he became in 2002. (His tenure there lasted only four years, after which the mighty boss of the Volkswagen Group, Ferdinand Piëch, ousted him in a clash of titans.)

But Pischetsrieder's message had been essentially correct, and before too long the BMW board was demanding that the company get rid of Rover. When BMW announced it was walking away from the loss-making Rover operation, all it took with it was the new Mini (or, rather, MINI), along with the Cowley plant in which to build the new car, and the Land Rover know-how which it had in order exploited to plan its own SUV.[1] The American-built BMW X5, manufactured initially only in Greer,

---

1 Somewhat mysteriously, BMW also retained the rights to the Triumph and Riley names.

South Carolina,[1] and called by BMW a sports activity vehicle, rather than an SUV, proved a huge hit.[2] Unsurprisingly, the first, E53, version of the X5 shared many parts with the Range Rover, but it still looked very much like a BMW with its quadruple headlights and double-kidney grille. The X5 proved such a success that in 2003 BMW added a X3 version, based on the smaller 3 Series platform.

As they departed from Rover, BMW shrewdly bought the rights to Rolls-Royce Motors when Vickers, which had owned the luxury car maker since 1980, put both Rolls and Bentley up for sale.[3] Volkswagen had recently bought both marques from Vickers – or at least it thought it had – but soon discovered that, while it now owned the rights to the trademark portico radiator and Charles Sykes's classic Spirit of Ecstasy bonnet mascot, it did not actually have the legal right to build Rolls-Royce cars. Vickers itself had never owned all the rights to the Rolls-Royce name; Rolls-Royce plc, the aircraft engine manufacturer, still owned the right to license key trademarks, including the Rolls-Royce name and logo, to the company of its choice. And now it chose not VW but BMW, with which it had recently worked on a number of aircraft projects. Wolfsburg eventually agreed to license the flying lady and the grille to BMW for £40 million – an absurdly low price for such a valuable commodity – and held on to the Bentley brand, which it was able to develop as a recognizably separate entity for the first time in seventy years. Volkswagen subsequently (if unconvincingly) claimed it had only wanted Bentley all along. BMW's management, meanwhile, licked their lips and counted their winnings.

For British observers, it was all highly unedifying and depressing, as the Germans fought over British household names in a manner that would have been unthinkable in 1945 or even 1965. As James Ruppert

---

1 It was subsequently also built in Toluca, Mexico, and, from 2009, in Kaliningrad in Russia.

2 Although it did horrify some diehard BMW fans, who thought that this extension of the BMW brand was a betrayal of the firm's racing and motorcycling heritage.

3 Bentley then accounted for a miserly 5 per cent of Rolls-Royce's car production.

observed, 'the heads of Germany's industrial giants [were] carving up the spoils of their victory like a couple of bickering Wehrmacht generals'. The rights to the Rover name, however, went not to the Germans but to Tata Motors, who in 2007 bought Land Rover and Jaguar from Ford, along with the Rover, Daimler and Lanchester marques. Tata paid BMW £1.8 billion for this – £1 billion more than BMW had paid for the whole of the Rover Group in 1994. Once again, the Germans had won.

Now in German hands, both Rolls-Royce and Bentley prospered. In 2003 BMW opened a new Rolls-Royce factory at Goodwood, in Sussex, and launched the new Rolls-Royce Phantom which shared parts with and was powered by an engine taken from the new BMW 7 Series. Volkswagen, meanwhile, spent £500 million revamping the old Rolls-Royce factory at Crewe and revitalizing the Bentley line-up. The result was staggeringly successful. Demand for the new Bentley Continental GT and its four-door variant, the Flying Spur, so overwhelmed the Crewe works that for a few years the Flying Spur was made at VW's prestigious 'Transparent Factory' in Dresden, a glass-walled, maple-floored plant built by architect Gunter Henn, which had originally been intended merely to assemble VW's top of the range Phaeton.

Meanwhile, what remained of the Rover Group collapsed in ignominious circumstances. At first it seemed as if the Rover business could survive and prosper in the hands of the four British white knights who offered themselves as the company's saviours and called themselves the Phoenix Consortium. Phoenix's actions, though, soon showed that such optimism was sadly misplaced.

The first of the Phoenix Four, John Towers, had joined Rover from Massey Ferguson tractors and had risen to become managing director of the Rover Group by 2000. None of his colleagues, however, had ever been a major figure in the car industry. Nick Stephenson was an engineer; Peter Beale was an accountant and former car dealer; and John Edwards had run a network of twenty dealers. Nevertheless, in May 2000 the Phoenix Four succeeded in convincing an obscure bank in North Carolina, First

National, to lend them £200 million.[1] Despite their brave talk of a renaissance, the partners themselves only invested a miserly £60,000 each in the business. BMW agreed to pay them £500 million to help pay for mass redundancies and restructuring.

The Phoenix Four were like a gaggle of little boys with a new toy. They uprated the existing 25, 45 and 75 models, adding revamped engines and tauter suspension to create the boy-racer Z range (the MG ZR, ZS and ZT, respectively). As a sign of their desperation, they added a union flag on the bonnet for good measure. The Z cars actually drove rather well, though the pimping of the sedate Rover 75 into the 'full-fat' MG ZT looked rather like watching an embarrassing old uncle don student clothes. Inexplicably, the Phoenix Four then travelled to Italy, bought an ailing sports car manufacturer, Qvale, and, using BMW's severance money, attempted to adapt Qvale's last foray into the motor business, the famously unconventional Mangusta, to American tastes. Next, they accompanied racing car experts Lola (for whom Stephenson had once worked) to Le Mans, blowing thousands of pounds on entertainment without anything to show for it. They also bought the massive nineteenth-century pile of Studley Castle in Warwickshire as a conference centre, at the same time selling off the Longbridge site for a housing development and leasing back only the footprint of the car plant.

The Phoenix Four were not just naive, they were also greedy. In 2002, the year MG Rover (as it was now called) made a pre-tax loss of over £77 million, they set up a £13 million trust for themselves and their families, and on top of that paid themselves £15.1 million in salaries. In that year, too, the realization belatedly dawned on them that they would need to work with a proper automotive partner if they were to produce any sort of mass-market car. Honda, Fiat and others turned them down flat as a liability, but Tata Motors agreed to supply them with a cheap, budget car, the Indica, which MG Rover would re-badge as the CityRover. While they

---

1 First National soon merged with Wachovia. In December 2008, thanks to inadvisable loans like that proffered to the Phoenix Four, Wachovia went spectacularly bankrupt. Its assets were then absorbed into Wells Fargo.

bought each Indica for £3,000, they sold them on – after a bit of modest redesign (which included sticking another union flag on the bonnet in a vain attempt to conjure some patriotic sentiment) – for £7,000 a pop, at which price the CityRover could not hope to compete with better-built and more sophisticated models like Fiat's Panda, Toyota's Yaris, Vauxhall's Corsa or Ford's Fiesta. Poorly designed, unreliable and with high running costs, the CityRover was a disaster from the start. Even the Phoenix Four implicitly acknowledged as much when they refused to make one available for the BBC's hugely popular and influential *Top Gear* TV series. The producers borrowed one anyway, and presenter James May declared it to be the worst car he had ever driven on the show.

The Phoenix Four were clearly ill at ease in the world of the supermini and soon retreated back into the fantasy land of the supercar – a market with which MG Rover had little in common. They finally succeeded in converting the Qvale Mangusta into a British racer, which in 2004 they launched as the MG XPower SV (SV stood for Sport Veloce). The name sounded like a gag from *The Simpsons* and the vehicle itself – partly styled by Peter Stevens, who had previously worked on the ultimate supercar, the McLaren F1 – looked like a teenager's wet dream. The ostensibly British XPower was actually built in Italy from British-made body parts and bits of old Fiats; the headlights, for example, were culled from the Fiat Punto. And hardly anyone actually bought an XPower; aside from the prototypes, only eighty-two cars were ever made.

Barely had the first XPowers rolled out of the factory than it was announced that the Phoenix Four's fantasy was over. On 8 April 2005 John Towers placed MG Rover into receivership in the face of debts of over £1.4 billion. The Shanghai Automotive Industry Corporation (SAIC) had been interested in saving the firm but, given the scale of MG Rover's losses, the Chinese government doubted that SIAC could fashion a success where BMW had failed. Finally, in July 2005 China's Nanjing Automobile Group bought MG Rover's remaining assets. (SAIC won the right to make both stretched and shortened versions of the Rover 75, but was forced to call these cars the Roewe 750 and 550, as it had not purchased the rights to the

Rover name.)[1] On 15 September 2005, in the ultimate humiliation for the British car industry, key ex-workers were contracted to begin to dismantle the machinery at Longbridge for shipping to China.

Occasionally the embers of Rover's funeral pyre stirred. In 2008 a man called William Riley, who claimed descent from the Riley motor dynasty (a claim that was challenged in the *Financial Times* in January 2010), announced that he would be making MG XPowers in Worcestershire. Before full-scale production could be started, Riley was arrested for theft, sued by two ex-employees for non-payment of wages, and, in February 2010, legally prevented by Nanjing from using the MG name.

Meanwhile, in August 2008, SAIC, which had bought up Nanjing Automobile and restarted production of the MG TF, hired back two hundred and fifty workers to begin assembling TFs at the Longbridge plant – where they were to be made, mortifyingly, from Chinese kits. After a mere 550 TFs had been assembled, the recession intervened, and the experiment was terminated in October 2009. SAIC then unveiled an entirely new MG, made in China but assembled back at Longbridge and sold through a growing network of UK dealers. Yet neither the four-door MG6 nor its subsequent, two-door sibling, the MG3 (known in China as the Roewe 150), looked anything like their sporty MG ancestors. Dull and anodyne externally, and cheaply appointed internally, neither seemed likely to make much of a dent in the crowded European marketplace. To its credit, SAIC persisted with the concept, and in 2011 launched a hatchback version, the MG6 GT, and a sportier saloon which exhumed the old MG name Magnette, last used in 1968. What had started as an attempt to conquer the European market had ended as a tawdry exercise in grave-robbing.

In September 2009 the British government's investigation into the collapse of MG Rover was finally published. The report sharply criticized the Phoenix Four, charging that they had taken £42 million in pay and

---

1 The ongoing bickering between Shanghai and Nanjing was resolved in December 2007, when SIAC absorbed Nanjing Automobile.

pensions from the troubled firm as it collapsed, that Nick Stephenson had paid a friend more than £1.6 million to act as a consultant in 2005–6, that 'evidence eliminator' software installed by Peter Beale had deleted documents that would have provided useful evidence to the investigation, and that all four partners had been 'untruthful' to the report's authors. The opposition's veteran business spokesman, Kenneth Clarke, called the Phoenix Four's behaviour 'disgraceful', while business secretary Lord Mandelson denounced them for failing to show even an 'ounce of humility' regarding the firm's demise and the massive job losses that had ensued. Thanks to Beale's software, the Serious Fraud Office declined to investigate further, but Mandelson instructed lawyers to prepare a case to disqualify the Phoenix Four from future company directorships.

With the collapse of MG Rover, Britain, once the pioneer of vehicle mass manufacture in Europe, no longer boasted a British-owned mass-market car maker. In the same year as the production of Rovers at Longbridge ceased, Jaguar shut its Browns Lane plant in Coventry and sold its Formula 1 racing team. A year later, Peugeot finally closed its Ryton and Stoke factories, having moved all car production to Poland, Spain and France. Even before the onset of recession in 2008, Coventry's unemployment rate was vastly in excess of the rest of the UK.

Even the Americans were leaving. Ford had closed its Langley factory in 1997 and its vast Dagenham plant in 2002, while Vauxhall ended car production at Luton in 2002 and cut the workforce at Ellesmere Port. (The British operation only just managed to survive the near-death experience of its parent, General Motors, in 2009.) By 2010 Vauxhall and Ford's British operations had both been reduced by their American masters to become mere assemblers of parts for cars designed and made in continental Europe.

Large car factories did survive in Britain – but they were all owned by the Japanese or Germans: Nissan in Sunderland, Toyota in Derby, Honda in Swindon and BMW's Mini plant in Oxford. The success of the Japanese seemed to disprove the charge that British workers were not suited to the rigours of large-scale mass production. Nissan's Sunderland plant boasted that it had not lost a minute of production to industrial disputes since it opened in 1985. By 2000 it was making the Micra, Primera and Almera; and by 2006 it had, analysts agreed, become the most efficient car plant in Europe – being awarded Nissan's new Qashqai SUV as a reward for this good behaviour. In 2010 the Sunderland factory, now the jewel in Nissan's global crown, was also selected to produce the Qashqai's smaller sibling, the frog-like crossover Juke; and in 2013 it became the European manufacturing centre for the all-electric Leaf and the Leaf's bespoke lithium batteries.

Under Indian ownership, the prospects for Jaguar Land Rover (as the combine was now called) improved considerably. Jaguar, in particular, shook off its Ford legacy like a dog emerging from a pond. When Ford bought Jaguar, it had used the chassis of the ubiquitous and highly successful Mondeo as the basis for a new 'baby Jag', the X-Type. While in many ways this was a very successful car, which garnered numerous awards, it could never shake off the Ford aura and the widespread belief that the X-Type was actually a descendant of the Cortina rather than of the E-Type. In 2008 it was declared that production of the X-Type and the S-Type, both of which had been derived from Ford platforms (from the Mondeo and the Lincoln LS, respectively), would end in 2008–9. In 2009 Jaguar launched its new executive car, the XF, which won plaudits and honours across the globe; and in 2010 it added both the XKR high-performance sports car and the top of the range XJ. The latter, designed as the heir to the classic XJs of the 1960s, 70s and 80s, was styled by Jaguar's Ian Callum in a manner that looked more to its contemporary competitors than to its illustrious predecessors. Gone was the traditional veneered dashboard, the XJ6's flat, horizontal emphasis, the slender nineties grille and the conventional, clustered rear lights; in their place came a shiny new dash with LCD displays, a swoopingly curved roof, a tapering body, a larger, squarer grille (actually borrowed from the original XJ6 of 1968), and swooping, boot-hugging 'cat's claws' tail lights. By the beginning of 2010 Jaguar was back in the black, the wisdom of developing its own models seemingly vindicated.

Underlining this success, on 11 May 2010 British prime minister David Cameron took delivery of a long-wheelbase armoured XJ as the nation's official state car. Two years later, Jaguar announced it was building a factory in China.

Jaguar's German rival Mercedes had, like BMW and Volkswagen, steered a crafty course through the minefields of the late twentieth century. Mercedes limousines, like the larger BMWs, remained lighter, faster, safer and far more economical than their US counterparts from Cadillac and Lincoln. The build of Mercedes cars was exemplary and far out-classed products from America, Britain or France. Equally importantly, a Mercedes continued to look like a Mercedes, and nothing else. Mercedes, BMW and Porsche adhered firmly to the hereditary principle, evolving their new models organically rather than reinventing their brands every few years.

As we have seen, in the early 1990s Mercedes resolved to shake off its staid, traditional image by relaunching and relabelling its various model ranges. Daimler-Benz simultaneously launched a series of spectacular sports cars – led by the coupé/convertible CLK and the smaller Roadster of 1996 – and began to expand into markets it had previously scorned. Thus in 1997 the firm unveiled its first mini MPV, the A-Class, and in 1998 introduced its first mid-size SUV, the M-Class. (There was much *Schadenfreude* when a prototype of Mercedes A-class tipped over during an 'elk' evasion test staged by the Swedish motoring magazine *Teknikens Värld* in 1997. However, this well-publicized episode did not appear to dent subsequent sales of the new model.) In 2005 the A-Class in turn spawned a B-Class of more conventional, four-door compact sports tour-ers, aimed particularly at the young and at women. And in 2006 came Mercedes' first full-size MPV, the R-Class.

Mercedes, however, made the same fundamental mistake as its Bavarian rival. Four years after BMW had bought the stumbling Rover Group, Stuttgart emulated Munich by purchasing the ailing American

giant Chrysler. What was initially billed as a merger was very evidently little more than a takeover, planned by Daimler-Benz's ambitious, ruthless
CEO, Jürgen Schrempp. In 1992, when Schremp was head of Daimler-
Benz's aerospace division, he had persuaded his fellow directors to buy
the famous Dutch aircraft firm of Fokker – only to dump it in 1996 when
bankruptcy seemed imminent for the Dutch company. Now the assertive
and aggressive Schrempp sought to get it absolutely right. Most senior
American executives at Chrysler – even the everlasting survivor, Bob
Lutz – were fired or retired; Germans were swiftly installed in all of the
key posts at DaimlerChrysler, as the conglomerate was now known; and
twenty-six thousand American job losses were announced.

Schrempp's newly installed president of DaimlerChrysler, Dieter
Zetsche, was an old-fashioned automobile man. Having studied electrical
engineering at the University of Karlsruhe, he had joined Daimler-Benz
in 1976 and gradually worked his way up the firm. A solid and dependable
figure, his trademark large grey moustache inspired the firm's advertising agencies to use his face, Iacocca-style, to advertise Mercedes in both
Germany and the US. (Sadly, the campaign backfired in America, where
many viewers had trouble deciphering Zetsche's heavy German accent.)
But even with Zetsche on board, the acquisition of a firm the prosperity
of which had, since Walther Chrysler's death, ebbed and flowed like the
tide, was still fraught with risk. The staid, influential German newspaper,
Frankfurter Allgemeine Zeitung, labelled Daimler-Benz's acquisition 'an
adventure with an uncertain outcome'. Chrysler appeared to be far too
big – and, in the US, had far too high an employment profile – to be
hastily unloaded at the first sign of trouble, as Fokker had been.

Initially the auguries appeared to be propitious – as, indeed, they
had originally been with BMW's purchase of Rover. Chrysler added the
German-built Crossfire to its line-up, and made encouraging noises
about future investment. But soon the Germans realized that financing
Chrysler's return to health would be too much even for their deep pockets.
Zetsche axed the historic Plymouth marque and began cutting production in the US. Soon most senior managers at Daimler-Benz realized that

Schrempp had, once again, made a serious error of judgement. And, while he had successfully evaded blame for the Fokker debacle, this time he was unable to avoid the inevitable fallout. On 1 January 2006 Zetsche replaced Schrempp as CEO of Daimler-Benz, and in May 2007 DaimlerChrysler announced the sale of Chrysler to private equity firm Cerberus Capital Management.[1] What was left of the former American colossus collapsed in April 2009 as Cerberus itself declared bankruptcy, forcing the US government to bail out the insolvent car maker with $6.6 billion of taxpayers' money. Federal negotiators subsequently sold Chrysler to Fiat, which was allowed to buy a 25 per cent stake in the new, slimmed-down company when it emerged from the legal protection of chapter 11 bankruptcy in June 2010. When the government's loans were paid off, in June 2011, Fiat was then able to buy a controlling stake of 53 per cent. Fiat installed Olivier Francois, Lancia's CEO, as the new Chrysler boss. Francois rid the firm of most of its centrally owned dealerships and concentrated on just five areas of operation: Chrysler-badged cars and minivans, a brand that Fiat aimed to take upmarket (and now advertised, somewhat ironically, as 'Imported from Detroit'); Dodge cars; Ram trucks (a division spun off in 2009 from the successful Dodge Ram light truck); Jeep; and Global Electric hybrid and electric projects. Fiat had originally intended to co-develop future Chrysler models alongside its planned Lancias; by 2011, however, Fiat appeared to have given up on the historic Lancia marque, and new Lancias, such as the impressive Delta of 2011, were hastily re-badged as Chryslers.

Meanwhile, Mercedes itself enlarged its US operation by building a plant at Vance, outside Birmingham, Alabama, an area of the country by then known to motor journalists as 'Detroit South'. Birmingham, formerly notorious as the capital of segregation and the epicentre of the civil rights struggles of the 1960s, was on its knees by the 1970s as the steel industry that had created the state's largest conurbation contracted

---

1 Meanwhile, the German parent company retitled itself simply Daimler AG, losing the Benz name after eighty years.

and collapsed. By 2010, though, Birmingham had become home to a growing number of motor businesses: not just Mercedes, but also Honda (whose Lincoln, Alabama, plant was built only twenty miles from downtown Birmingham), Toyota (which based an engine plant in Huntsville, Alabama), and Hyundai (which built its principal American plant outside Alabama's state capital, Montgomery).[1] Alabama had pressed hard for these plants – and particularly for the Mercedes contract – in the face of stiff competition from thirty other, mainly Southern and Midwestern, states. The state's governor, Jim Folsom, had personally led the campaign to entice the Germans. In return for Mercedes' $300 million investment, Alabama pledged $253 million in tax breaks and subsidies, and agreed to buy 2,500 Mercedes vehicles for state agencies. It was highly generous, but other states were offering just as much, if not more. Folsom's victory helped to pull Alabama out of its economic torpor and back into the front rank for the first time in over fifty years.

A new American influence also began to be discernible back in Germany. For almost two decades, Chris Bangle, BMW's eccentric, Ohio-born head of design, had shaped BMW's distinctive cars. Bangle was the product of an odd assortment of influences: having considered becoming a Methodist minister, he instead studied fine art at Center College in Pasadena, California, and then earned a master's degree in industrial design at the University of Wisconsin. Moving to Europe, he worked first at Opel and then at Fiat, where he married a Swiss woman. Then, in 1992, he was appointed as the Munich car maker's first American chief of design – the first American head stylist of any German auto manufacturer. Bangle's design ethos soon spread across the whole BMW range; his philosophy was evident not just in the existing 3, 5 and 7 Series but also in the compact 1 Series of 2004, the new X5, X3 and X6 (the latter a mid-size luxury crossover of 2008) and, most famously, the 'Boy's Own' Z4 sports car of 2002. He was able to exploit BMW's new metal-pressing

---

1 In 2009, too, Hyundai-owned Kia built its first American plant just over the Alabama/Georgia state line, at West Point.

technology, which was able to create complex, compound curves in one action rather than by multiple pressings, to create a convoluted and at times bewildering interplay of creases and curves reminiscent of Frank Gehry's architectural designs (which Bangle readily acknowledged as a key inspiration for his work). But Bangle's swooping styling did not please everyone. Potential customers occasionally baulked at cars they considered to be over-designed, while Bangle's fellow automotive designers criticized his cars as 'origami'. Ford's Martin Smith derided the 'surface entertainment' of Bangle's BMWs, while *Time* magazine dubbed the new 7 Series of 2002 one of the fifty 'Worst Cars of All Time'. However, during Bangle's time at BMW, the Bavarian car maker overtook its Württemberger rivals, Daimler-Benz, to become the world's biggest seller of premium cars. In 2009 Bangle, tired of the constant disparagement, left BMW to set up his own design consultancy.

At the close of the century, Volkswagen was pursuing a corporate strategy that was almost as expansive as those adopted by BMW and Mercedes. Back in 1982, the Spanish state-owned car maker Seat (Sociedad Española de Automóviles de Turismo) had agreed to act as VW's agent in Spain. Four years later Seat was bought outright by Wolfsburg and its model range, while still retaining its autonomous identity, was adapted and revamped on the basis of VW platforms and, where appropriate, VW parts. In 1990 Volkswagen followed this purchase with an even more daring coup, buying the newly liberated Czech Republic's flagship car maker, Škoda.

When car production restarted again at Škoda after the war, only small numbers of pre-war Populars were made. Gradually the Russians allowed Škoda to increase car production and, from 1959, to return to the use of names, rather than numbers, to delineate its models. Yet there was little that was original or inspiring about these Škoda cars. The series of Octavia saloons of the 1960s were simply plainer versions of the Volvos and Standard Vanguards of the previous decade, while the Škoda 100/110 range of 1966 was a duller, four-door version of the Renault Dauphine. Škoda soon fell well behind its Western competitors in terms of innovation and quality; styling became unimaginative and boxy, and only the Rapid sporty saloon (tagged by some as 'the poor man's Porsche') found many admirers in Western Europe. Škoda cars, along with the Soviet-built Ladas and East Germany's smoke-spewing Wartburgs and Trabants, had become the laughing stock of Europe.

The Velvet Revolution of 1989 brought about the fall of communism in Czechoslovakia, liberating the Czechs twenty-one years after the false dawn of the Prague Spring. But it also left Škoda, previously protected from the ravages of free-market capitalism and international competition, dangerously exposed to imports of far superior cars from Volkswagen, Fiat, Renault and Peugeot. Škoda, like its Eastern Bloc equivalents, was soon on the verge of bankruptcy. The new Czech government accordingly made the revitalization of the fortunes of the nation's principal auto manufacturer one of its top priorities. In 1990 the government invited Volkswagen – which had previously won a beauty contest in competition with Renault – to take a controlling stake in Škoda, and by 2000 the Prague car maker was wholly owned by VAG. Nevertheless, Volkswagen took care to preserve Škoda's autonomy, exactly as it had done with Spain's Seat, merely ensuring that all new Škoda models used standard VW floor plans and were, in the best Volkswagen tradition, well built and well equipped. Soon Škoda cars boasted far more kit, and more room, than their VW equivalents.

Volkswagen also invested much time, effort and money in giving back the Škoda marque some of the style and panache it had lost in 1939. VW assigned its star designer, the Belgian stylist Dirk van Braeckl,[1] to design the handsome new Octavia saloon for Škoda. The results were stunningly successful; the Octavia helped Škoda shed its image as a maker of plain, old-fashioned bathtubs, and made Škoda cars desirable

---

1 Van Braeckl later created the exciting new Continental for VW's recently acquired Bentley division.

again. In Britain, Škoda's advertising agency employed a high-risk marketing strategy, acknowledging the car maker's recent abysmal reputation by using the strapline 'It's a Škoda, honest'. But the risk paid off: by 2005 the waiting lists for Škoda cars in the UK were full.

Built atop the Golf's chassis, the new Octavia was, thanks to van Braeckel, bigger, roomier and cheaper than its Wolfsburg cousin. Soon taxi firms across Britain and the Continent were changing to the new Octavia, which was not only unusually well appointed but also boasted a cavernous boot. Meanwhile, the Octavia's 'hot' vRS variant, which offered the Golf GTi's performance at a fraction of the price, won Europe-wide critical acclaim and droves of enthusiastic buyers. By 2001 Škoda felt confident enough not only to make the vRS more widely available but also to give the old Superb name the exposure it was denied in 1939. The new Škoda Superb, based on the platform of the VW Passat but, in the mould of the Octavia, more spacious and better equipped than its VW parent, sold slowly at first, but by 2010 was doing surprisingly well across Europe and finally coming to the attention of critics who had dismissed it as merely a cut-price Passat.

Volkswagen's successful management of Seat and Škoda had not gone unnoticed by its rivals. In October 2005 Mercedes bought an 18.53 per cent stake in VW, which was countered the following year by Porsche, which bought a 25.1 per cent 'blocking minority' stake. In 2007 Porsche increased its stake to 30.9 per cent, while assuring the world's media that it did not intend to absorb Volkswagen and was merely protecting the fabled car maker from hostile bids. But Porsche was, of course, bluffing; by January 2009 the sports car manufacturer had acquired a 50.76 per cent holding in Volkswagen AG and the following May the two companies merged.[1] Subsequently, it turned out that Porsche had bitten off more than it could chew. With the recession of 2008–10 decimating worldwide sales of sports cars and premium SUVs, Porsche found itself in financial

---

1 The combine was, however, to be dominated by the far larger VW operation. Later in 2009, VW bought a 49.9 per cent stake in Porsche.

trouble. The tables were turned, and in the event it was Volkswagen that acquired Porsche, rather than the other way round.

Volkswagen, newly secure after its merger, now declared that it aimed to become the world's number one car maker by 2018. Bolstered by the addition of Porsche's upmarket products, VW also affirmed that it sought to achieve goal that by competing in all market sectors. The group built two new factories in China and began to collaborate with the Chinese government on research and development projects. It also began to think more about the needs of its American customers, offering modified versions of its cars through its US dealers.[1] (Thus the new American Passat of 2011, made at Chattanooga in Tennessee, was both longer and wider than its European sister.)

At the same time, the German giant resolved to pursue a bolder model strategy. VW redesigned the retro New Beetle, ensuring that the revamped 2011 version was far less cute and feminine than its 1998 predecessor, and introduced the Up! to replace the mediocre Lupo/Fox city car in the market that BMW's new Mini had astutely exploited. The Up!, as its novel name suggested, was aimed at the younger market. Its flexible platform could be adapted to make a mini-MPV; an Up! Lite diesel-electric hybrid was planned; a longer Blue variant was developed, which could incorporate a smorgasbord of alternative fuels (its glass roof carried a solar cell, lithium batteries lay beneath the floor, and there was even space to stash a hydrogen fuel cell); and VW also planned an all-electric E-Up![2]

The Up! was designed by another of VW's new acquisitions, styling chief Walter de'Silva, celebrated for the beautiful, award-winning series of Seat saloons he had created from 1999. On arriving at Wolfsburg in 2007, de'Silva announced that he would henceforth ban the 'excessive decoration and over-design of models' (hardly the design qualities with which VW had been historically associated) and would concentrate on

---

1 The VW-owned Seat and Škoda marques, however, are not sold in America.
2 A model presumably aimed at customers in the north of England.

a 'clean and precise' brand look. 'VW design has to be distinctive,' he said, 'because VWs are world cars that everybody understands and recognizes as VWs.' Yet while de'Silva focused on revamping the Volkswagen model range, the VW group's jewel in the crown continued to be the Audi marque, which by 2010 was contributing nearly 50 per cent of its profits, even though it sold only a quarter of the vehicles of VW's car division. It is an established axiom of motor manufacture that luxury models, if they sell well, make far more profit per unit than economy cars; thus Lexus, Acura and Audi all contribute a disproportionately large proportion of the profits of their Toyota, Honda and VW parents. In all three cases, the lessons learned from the mass production of smaller cars have been applied to their premium ranges. By 2011 VW's Audi division was making more profit per car than either BMW or Mercedes.

Volkswagen was not the only European car maker that began to harbour dreams of world domination. In 1999 Renault, privatized by the French government three years earlier, took a 44.4 per cent stake in Nissan to create the world's fourth-largest car maker. In 2006 Renault-Nissan even proposed to absorb GM, but the affronted Americans turned the project down – only to stare bankruptcy in the face two years later.

The driving force behind the new, intensely ambitious, combine had, by 2005, become CEO of both Renault and Nissan. Carlos Ghosn's career path was far removed from the traditional engineering or accountancy route followed by most motor executives, while his multinational ancestry neatly reflected the global business that car making had become. Born in Brazil in 1954 to a French mother and Lebanese father, Ghosn was educated at a Jesuit school in Beirut, a lycée in Paris, and the illustrious École Polytechnique at Palaiseau, graduating from the last with an engineering degree in 1978. He spoke six languages fluently, including English, Arabic and Japanese, and became as familiar in Japan, where he became the hero of a manga comic book series, as in Lebanon, where he was hailed as a potential presidential candidate. Having spent eighteen years with Michelin, where he ended up as CEO of Michelin North America, based in Greenville, South Carolina (where he still has a home), he joined Renault as executive vice president in 1996 and, three years later, was parachuted into Nissan.

Not all of Ghosn's new Renaults were a success. Encouraged by his CEO to be radically original, Patrick le Quément developed two bold new models for 2002, the Avantime and the Vel Satis. The Avantime was a bizarre, coupé MPV which featured four huge seats (the rear two raked higher than those in front), massive doors and a bizarre, inverted tail. But its unorthodox looks were also accompanied by unreliable performance, and production was stopped after only two years. The bizarrely named Vel Satis was slightly more successful – but only just. Intended as Renault's new flagship saloon, it sat unusually high and combined a bland front end with an inverted, Avantime-style stern. The Vel Satis not only looked ugly (Renault later alleged that it had intended to attract 'less conformist' customers who 'distanced themselves from the conventional saloon'), but also rode poorly and handled clumsily. Sales were accordingly dismal. Facelifted to look more conventional in 2006, the Vel Satis was finally axed in 2009.

Renault's traditional rival, Citroën, was safe from the merger wars of the 1990s, having been bought by Peugeot in 1974. But it seemed to lose its way during those years, failing either to build on its historic reputation for daring innovation or to rival the sales of impressive Peugeot models such as the 205 and 207 superminis. The Citroën BX of 1983 was the last vehicle to incorporate the firm's celebrated pneumatic suspension, and subsequent Citroën models became ever more bland and mediocre. The large XM saloon of 1989, intended to rekindle the magic of the DS, was unreliable and performed disappointingly, while its oversized, wedge design was neither attractive nor advanced. In 2009 Citroën announced it would apply the renowned DS label to a series of high-specification variants of existing models, which would themselves be developed from recent concept cars. The DS3, launched in March 2010, was based on the new C3, and the DS4 and DS5, both of 2011, were intended as premium, high-spec versions of the C4 and C5 ranges, respectively. Many critics, though, accused Citroën of tomb-raiding, and overpriced and over-styled models such as the DS3 received decidedly mixed reviews at their launch. Knowing references to past successes are all very well, but attempting to appropriate the celebrity of classic cars such as the Citroën DS is an exercise that is inevitably fraught with danger. BMW and Fiat have proved you can get it right, with the Mini and the Fiat 500, but many other car makers have fallen disappointingly short.

At least Citroën survived. Other, equally famous but less fortunate, motoring names became sorry victims of the era's mania for acquisition and merger. Top of the list was the historic Swedish car maker Saab, which in 1989 entered into a partnership with GM, but by 2000 found itself wholly owned by the American leviathan. GM never seemed to formulate any real plan for Saab other than the desire to incorporate the Swedish firm into its Opel subsidiary. New Saab models were built on Opel platforms, and Saab production was gradually shifted away from Trollhättan to Opel's Rüsselsheim factory. In America, a half-hearted attempt in 2005–6 to sell re-badged Subarus and Chevrolets as Saabs failed disastrously.[1]

When GM itself hit the rocks late in 2008, one of its first announcements was that the Saab marque was 'under review'. The only buyer GM could find by the target date of December 2009 was the Dutch niche car maker Spyker, led by the dashing Dutch lawyer and entrepreneur Victor Muller. Unsurprisingly, neither Muller nor his Spyker colleagues possessed the financial resources to make a success of Saab, let alone to expand into China and build a new US headquarters, as were optimistically promised. Muller's recruitment of Russian banker Vladimir Antonov as his principal backer merely added to his woes; in July 2011

---

1 The Saab 9-2X, which was built in Japan and was little more than a re-skinned Subaru Impreza, was being called a 'Saabaru' even before its launch.

the European Investment Bank rejected Antonov's bid to become part-owner of Saab following allegations that he was involved with organized crime.[1] Meanwhile, Saab's new cars of 2010 (which still bore a marked resemblance to the classic, wedge-shaped Saab 99 that Sixten Sason had designed in 1967) were underwhelming; while the GM-designed platform of the much-vaunted 9-4X of 2011, Saab's first-ever SUV crossover,[2] would not, Saab belatedly discovered, be able to carry a diesel engine, thus making European sales almost impossible. Early in 2011, the overstretched and beleaguered Victor Muller announced he had agreed to sell his sports car operation to 'focus on Saab'.[3] But the Saab operation continued to unravel. In April 2011 several suppliers halted shipment of components to the Trollhättan plant because of unpaid invoices and Saab had to stop vehicle production. In May 2011 it was reported that the Dutch owners, lacking the money to invest in a new range of cars, were being forced to sell 29.9 per cent of Saab to Chinese SUV manufacturer Hawtai, in return for a cash injection of 150 million euros. Yet Hawtai never signed the deal, and Muller was forced to hawk the company around China like a used pram. He approached both Great Wall Motors, a company hitherto known for its suspiciously Fiat-like city cars, and Pang Da, China's largest dealership network; and on 16 May announced that he had signed a memorandum of understanding with Pang Da which would give Saab the financing it needed to restart manufacture. On 27 May Trollhättan's assembly line restarted – only to stop again a few weeks later when spare parts ran out and the firm admitted it could not meet its monthly wage bill.[4] On 19 December 2011 Saab filed for bankruptcy with the Swedish

---

1 The EIB's stance did not, however, prevent Antonov from buying English football club Portsmouth FC that summer.

2 The car was based on the platform of the Cadillac SRX and built at a GM plant in Mexico.

3 Spyker had already moved its sports car production base from Holland to Britain's beleaguered motor city, Coventry, in 2009.

4 Ultimately paid only when Antonov's Gemini Fund generously footed the bill on 5 August.

government. A long and illustrious corporate history had limped to an ignominious and humiliating conclusion.[1]

General Motors' shabby treatment of Saab deserved all the worldwide condemnation it earned. But by 2008 the car giant's own status was almost as precarious as that of its Swedish subsidiary. In 2001 GM had recruited veteran motor executive Bob Lutz to rescue the ailing firm. When Lutz arrived, GM was producing bland cars, cutting corners wherever possible, and consistently losing market share and sales to the Japanese and Germans. Lutz now prioritized design, for the first time since the 1960s. His restyled Chevrolet Camaro consistently outsold the Ford Mustang, while his Saturn Aura and Malibu won North American Car of the Year awards in 2007 and 2008, respectively. Lutz also lobbied against government fuel economy rules and rubbished hybrid-electric cars – until he saw the sales and public acclaim that Toyota was generating with its Prius. Thereafter he gave his full backing to GM's electric car programme, an initiative that saw the launch of the Chevrolet Volt hybrid in 2010.

On his retirement from GM in May 2010, at the age of seventy-eight, Lutz buzzed downtown Detroit in one of his own decommissioned military jets, provoking a dramatic response from the emergency services and garnering media headlines the next day. Even his biggest fans thought that this typical act of macho bravado was sadly inappropriate and served only to demonstrate how out of touch GM's senior executives were with their customer base. For just eleven months earlier, on 1 June 2009, General Motors had filed for bankruptcy. The company that had dominated the global car industry since the mid-1920s was finally on its knees.

---

1 In June 2012 a Sino-Japanese consortium calling itself National Electric Vehicles Sweden (NEVS) announced it had bought Saab and its plant, and that it intended to use the latter to build an electric version of the former Saab 9-3 model. However, Saab AB, the aerospace firm that was Saab Automotive's original parent, still owned the rights to the Saab name and declared that it would block any attempt to restart production of 'Saab' cars outside Sweden.

General Motors was, as its management hoped, saved by the US government. The incoming administration of President Barack Obama decided that it could not face the enormous job losses that the wholesale collapse of GM would entail, and accordingly bought a 61 per cent slice of the humbled auto goliath on behalf of the American taxpayer. But the federal authorities also forced GM to disgorge many of the marques that had made it famous, including Pontiac and Buick, as well as many of its recent acquisitions, such as Saab. At the same time, GM announced it would be closing a number of plants, among them the historic Willow Run complex in Detroit, which the company had owned since 1953. Most humiliatingly of all, GM's Hummer brand, so redolent of American military might and machismo, was offered to the Chinese – who, on closer inspection, turned the proposal down flat.

GM's Hummer had been derived from a hefty, armoured military transport, the Hum-Vee, for which AMC had been contracted in 1983. According to one (possibly apocryphal) story, the film star Arnold Schwarzenegger had seen a convoy of US Army Hum-Vees while shooting a film and asked for a civilian version to be made for him, with air conditioning, a modern sound system and comfortable seats. In 1990 two civilian Hummers, as they were popularly known, were driven from London to Beijing, while the original Hum-Vee served prominently in Operation Desert Storm – the allied invasion of Kuwait – a few months later. Fortified by this incomparable publicity, a civilian Hummer became generally available from 1992, and from 1999 was marketed and developed by GM. However, rising oil prices put an end to this absurd fad; by 2005 even movie stars were abandoning their Hummers for Priuses or, at the very least, eco-friendly SUVs. When no buyers could be found, the Hummer marque was dissolved in April 2010.

Like GM and Chrysler, Ford was also tried to amass a global empire in the 1990s. Alongside the many parts manufacturers and repair businesses it bought (including Europe's high-profile Kwik-Fit chain), Ford acquired

Jaguar in 1989, Aston Martin in 1994, Volvo in 1999 and Land Rover, from BMW, in 2000. Just one man was responsible for most of these purchases: the Lebanese-born Australian Jacques Nasser. Emphatically not one of the Ford clan, nor one of the colourless accountants who had dominated the company since Henry Ford II stepped down, Nasser was keen to establish Ford as the world's dominant force in motor manufacture. By 2002, however, almost all of his empire had been dismantled and the company's ambitious international strategy lay in ruins.

Jacques Nasser was chairman of Ford Europe at only forty-one, and president and CEO of the whole Ford Motor Company by 1999. He was particularly identified with the Premier Automotive Group (PAG), the new division that he created to manage the new, upmarket brands he had recently bought. But PAG never reached its ambitious sales targets and, as Jaguar and Aston Martin failed to recoup Ford's massive investment, PAG was increasingly viewed by Nasser's colleagues as a costly mistake. Jaguar, in particular, was clumsily handled, with millions of dollars being spent on extending the Jaguar brand to a Formula 1 racing team, which then proceeded to haemorrhage money without earning its sponsor regular podium places. Meanwhile, the exciting new Ford Thunderbird, introduced by Nasser himself to dealers in a fanfare of publicity in 1999, did not reach Ford showrooms as a production model until 2001.

Nasser also faltered on what was regarded as Ford's home ground. The Ford Mondeo, launched worldwide in 1993, had been touted by Dearborn as the world's first genuinely global car. Developed on both sides of the Atlantic, and made in Belgium for the European market, it replaced the Sierra in Europe and the Telstar (a Sierra equivalent) in Asia, and revived Ford in Europe at a time when fleet sales were regularly being lost to Vauxhall/Opel.[1] But in North America, the Mondeo's equivalent, the Ford Contour/Mercury Mystique, shared only a few elements with the Mondeo, such as its windscreen, front doors and rear. Marketed as a

---

1 Nasser's Mark 2 Mondeo of 1996, however, was a retrograde step, its reduced specification and cheap-looking interior enabling the highly successful Opel/Vauxhall Vectra to regain lost territory.

family car in Europe, the Mondeo was still judged by American customers to be too small; America (and Australia, too) preferred the larger Ford Taurus or Falcon, and thus the Contour/Mystique sold disappointingly there. (Interestingly, the BMW 3 Series, which was the same size as the Contour/Mystique, sold well in the US.) In 2000 Nasser accepted the inevitable and abandoned the pretence that the Mondeo was a world car. A sharply styled and much larger Mark 3 Mondeo was offered to Europe, but North America and Australia were presented with the even bigger Fusion.[1]

Nasser's exciting new initiatives were now starting to look more like unpardonable mistakes, and his power base within the company was gradually eroding. Having refused to testify in a congressional hearing to investigate the tendency of the new Ford Explorer SUV crossovers[2] to roll over in the event of a tyre failure, Nasser soon regretted his decision and attended, but then caused serious offence in the Ford family when he heaped blame not on Ford's car but on the Firestone tyres with which the Explorer was fitted.[3] The two companies had been dynastically intertwined for decades, and the mother of William Clay Ford, the senior family member then in the firm, was a Firestone. In 2001, with Ford facing huge annual losses of almost £2 billion, Nasser was removed from the summit of the Ford Motor Company and replaced as chairman by Bill Ford.

William Clay Ford junior, the great-grandson of the firm's founder, had always wanted to run what he still saw as the family business. He had worked for Ford since 1979 and felt that, in contrast to the cosmopolitan arriviste Nasser, his interests were the company's interests.

---

1 Not to be confused with the European Ford Fusion, a larger and taller version of the Fiesta supermini. In the BBC's *Top Gear* 2002 awards, the European Fusion won the 'Most Pointless Car' accolade – presenter Richard Hammond memorably describing it as 'a Ford Fiesta in a hat'. Even more confusingly, Fusion was the original name for the car that was finally launched in the US in 2000 as the Ford Focus compact.

2 Together with its corporate clones, the Mercury Mountaineer and Mazda Navajo.

3 Few believed Nasser's charges; in 2003 U-Haul, the US rental giant, refused to allow Ford Explorers to pull its trailers – a prohibition that still stands.

A keen ice-hockey player, enthusiastic folk singer, and vice chairman of Ford-sponsored American football team the Detroit Lions, he seemed to embody the same timeless American virtues as the firm's products. He also encouraged new sustainability projects, steering Ford towards a greener vehicle development programme and speeding up the introduction of flexible-fuel hybrids. In April 2006, feeling that things were finally going his way, he added the roles of president and CEO to his tally of company posts. But his triumph did not last long. Hampered by the appalling relationship between his two British vice presidents, Sir Nick Scheele and David Thursfield, who could not bear to talk to each other, Bill Ford's senior management team became seriously dysfunctional. Five months later, Bill Ford himself was kicked upstairs to a non-executive chairmanship, and his place at the helm of the company was taken by a complete outsider, Alan Mulally, who had no connection whatsoever with the Ford family but had been headhunted from aircraft colossus Boeing.

The outspoken Mulally was a controversial choice as president of Ford. Leading figures in the motor industry had already turned down the job, regarding it as a poisoned chalice. And Mulally, who knew little about the industry (his original degree had been in aeronautical engineering), almost torpedoed his appointment before he had officially started by publicly praising his Lexus LS430 as 'the finest car in the world'. He was certainly not sentimental about automotive history, as his rapid disposal of the premium British marques showed.[1] Declaring that he 'had no regrets' about selling Jaguar and Land Rover to Tata, in 2008 he also sold Aston Martin to a private Anglo-Kuwaiti consortium (though the famous marque kept its German CEO, the former Porsche, BMW and Daewoo executive Ulrich Bez). Three months after selling Jaguar, Ford also finally completed the sale of Volvo to Zhejiang Geely Automobile of China.

Sweden's famed manufacturer of reliable and safe cars could seemingly do no wrong until, at the height of the merger mania of the 1990s,

---

1 Kwik-Fit, which Nasser had bought at the top of the market, was also sold at a huge loss.

it was forced into a shotgun marriage by Pehr Gyllenhammar. Although he had no background in the car industry,[1] Gyllenhammar had effortlessly risen to become CEO of Volvo by virtue of being the son-in-law of the previous chairman. In 1993 the Francophile Gyllenhammar had announced a merger with the French state-owned car maker, Renault. But on closer inspection, this was not a merger but a takeover by the French. The French government now held 46 per cent of Volvo's shares; Renault controlled 65 per cent of the company; and it was formally announced that the new combine's headquarters would be based in Paris. Even the French industry minister acknowledged that Renault would be the 'driving force' in the partnership, with Volvo the 'minority partner'. Furious at being duped, Volvo's board demanded, and received, the resignation of Gyllenhammar and his allies. Proud Swedes, for whom Volvo had always been a key ingredient in defining their national identity, now regarded Gyllenhammar as an unprincipled pariah. Renault turned instead to a partnership with Mercedes, and the subsequent merger with Nissan. But Gyllenhammar's policy had fatally weakened the previously rock-solid Swedish auto maker, which was now globally perceived as being vulnerable to takeover. In 1999 Ford helped itself to Volvo's car operation, leaving the rump of the company to concentrate on trucks.[2]

Whilst Volvo Group, as the trucking business was known, went from strength to strength, Ford seemed to have no forward strategy for the car division after Nasser's departure in 2001 – much as GM had seemed to have little idea what to do with its new Swedish subsidiary, Saab. However, following its sale by Ford, Volvo fortunately avoided Saab's fate. Having passed into Chinese ownership – with a Chinese chairman, Li Shufu, and a former VW executive, Stefan Jacoby, installed as new its president

1 Both Gyllenhammar and his father-in-law came from an insurance and banking background, and their insurance company, Scandia, was one of Volvo's largest shareholders.
2 Ironically, following Volvo's merger with Renault's truck operation in 2001, to create Europe's largest heavy truck manufacturer, Renault now finally does have a stake in Volvo.

and CEO,[1] respectively – Volvo survived the recession in good shape and by 2010 possessed an impressive model range spanning almost all major market sectors.

Ford's rapid disposal of Volvo demonstrated how serious Mulally was about ensuring that the company concentrate on its traditional core business. But his strategy was not just about disposals. At the same time as selling most of Nasser's acquisitions, Mulally resurrected the Taunus brand in Germany, believing that it still had some life in it. He also instilled a sense of commercial reality into the corporation, repeatedly telling groups of Ford workers that 'we have been going out of business for forty years', while making 47 per cent of the workforce redundant between 2006 and 2010. Robots, Ford had discovered, could now do the job of thousands of human workers.

Mulally also learned from his mistakes. Widely criticized, along with other motor industry leaders, for flying to bail-out talks with the US government in 2008 in an expensive corporate jet, Mulally, despite his aircraft industry background, subsequently sold all but one of Ford's aircraft fleet and travelled to his next meeting in Washington in a hybrid Ford Fusion. Clearly, Alan Mulally was no Lee Iacocca. And in the years that followed, Ford's impressive performance seemed to justify his appointment. During the recession of 2008–10, Ford was the only one of America's former Big Three that did not have to rely on federal loans to survive. Indeed, when the federal government demanded the dramatic downsizing of both GM and Chrysler as the price of its subsidies, Ford emerged briefly as the nation's biggest car maker – a claim it had not been able to make since the early 1920s.[2] As William Clay Ford candidly admitted in 2009: 'Alan was the right choice, and it gets more right every day.'

· · ·

1 Volvo's Swedish former president and CEO, Hans-Olov Olsson, survived only as a member of the new board.

2 By the end of 2010 it had reverted to a still highly creditable fifth, behind Toyota, a rejuvenated GM, Volkswagen and Hyundai.

While Detroit's Big Three may have stumbled in the years following the demolition of the Iron Curtain in 1989–91, their counterparts in former Soviet Russia, now exposed to foreign competition for the first time, completely collapsed. By the end of the century, indeed, the communist era's major car makers were virtually unrecognizable. Many of them had been rescued by Western rivals; others had simply disappeared.

The most celebrated Russian victim was Lada. After the worthy VAZ-2101 ceased production in 1984, Lada failed to follow up its success with anything similar. The much-heralded (and surprisingly large) VAZ-2110 of 1996, for example, was a mechanical disaster which had to be repeatedly recalled. The following year Lada threw in the towel and withdrew from Western Europe, though it continued to sell cars to Eastern Europe and South America. The buoyancy of these latter markets helped Lada to survive near-bankruptcy and to subsist long enough to make common cause (in 2001) with General Motors – an organization that had, before 1990, been reviled in Soviet Russia as an incarnation of Western capitalism at its worst. In 2008, with GM facing its own domestic difficulties, Renault stepped in and bought a 25 per cent stake in AvtoVAZ. In the economic crisis that then engulfed the globe, and which once more brought the maker of Lada cars to its knees, Russian prime minister Vladimir Putin made a televised public statement expressing his personal determination to save the firm. His public declaration saw the value of AvtoVAZ's shares leap by 30 per cent and saved the company from insolvency.

Other venerable Russian marques were not so fortunate. Moskvitch of Moscow went bankrupt in 2002 and was formally dissolved in 2006, while in 2007 GAZ ceased production of Volga cars, using the brand thereafter merely to re-badge mid-range Chryslers. Global economics had arrived in Russia with a vengeance.

Further east, even the biggest Japanese manufacturers were turning to global alliances to offset the economic and ecological demands of the new century. Nissan had performed so well in the 1980s that in 1991 the company dared to open its new technical centre in the suburbs of Detroit, right under the noses of the Big Three. But by 1999 Nissan's stake in the export and international markets was eroding under pressure from Toyota and Honda, and the firm was $20 million in debt. Its models looked uninspiring when compared with Honda's and Toyota's new products, while its new luxury marque, Infiniti, was wallowing in Lexus's wake.

It was Carlos Ghosn who came to Nissan's rescue. Renault bought a 43.4 per cent stake in Nissan, and Ghosn, having installed himself as boss, turned the company round, investing abroad (in 2003, for example, a new Nissan factory opened in Canton, Mississippi) and completely rethinking the company's ageing model range. In 2002 Ghosn launched a new version of Nissan's legendary Z series sports cars, the 350Z – styled not in the retrospective idiom that his designers favoured but devised as a forward-looking, clean-limbed car with distinctly American lines. In 2004 Ghosn also launched the company's first light pickup truck aimed specifically at the American market (and made in Mississippi), the Titan. More controversially, Ghosn also cut thousands of jobs, shut outmoded car plants and sold off underperforming parts of the Nissan empire, such as Nissan Aerospace. In 2006 he even contemplated acquiring a 20 per cent Renault-Nissan stake in General Motors. His success earned him celebrity status in Japan, where the comic book series *The True Story of Carlos Ghosn* was first serialized in 2002. By 2010 Nissan announced it could do without Toyota's technological know-how in developing hybrid cars and launched its own all-electric, lithium-powered Nissan Leaf to international acclaim.

In 1989 Toyota felt strong enough to enter the lucrative but perilous luxury car market, then dominated by BMW, Mercedes, Volkswagen's Audi and Jaguar (which was shortly to be bought by Ford). Once again, though, Toyota had not been the pioneer. Honda had, predictably, led the way with its upmarket export brand, Acura, in 1986 – an initiative it supported with the creation of sixty new American dealerships. However, Acura's marketing strategy closely tied the new marque to the established

Honda brand, then closely identified with small family cars. The result was that the Acura marque failed to seize consumers' imagination, and sales of the first model, the Legend, were disappointing. Nissan's launch of its upmarket Infiniti brand in North America in 1989 was similarly cautious, and that marque, too, stalled. Toyota, learning from its rivals' mistakes, ensured that its new premium range, Lexus, was properly distanced from the existing Toyota brand, then popularly associated in America with small pickups and small cars like the Camry.[1]

Toyota never pretended to be innovative in the fields of styling or engineering. Critics pointed out that the first Lexus, the LS 400, bore a marked resemblance to its European rivals and railed at its 'derivative styling'. Its profile did indeed resemble that of the Mercedes 300E, while its rear end recalled that of the BMW 735. Toyota did not bother to deny the comparisons; the firm was merely keen to avoid undue risk, given the vast investment it had made in developing this new brand over the last six years. After a predictably shaky start (in December 1989 Toyota had to recall eight thousand LS 400s due to a wiring problem), Lexus sales in the US soared – largely because they were so much cheaper than their German rivals from Mercedes and BMW. To Detroit's horror, over a third of new Lexus buyers were found to be part-exchanging Lincolns or Cadillacs, while Lexus's highly competitive pricing even prompted the German manufacturers to accuse Toyota of dumping Lexuses in America as loss-leaders. Realizing that Lexus was here to stay, the Germans launched their counter-attack: Mercedes slashed the prices of their E- and S-Class models, while BMW unveiled revamped 3 and 5 Series saloons (the hugely successful E36 and E39, respectively). But it was too late: Lexus had already won a firm toehold in the American luxury market. By 1998 Lexus had introduced a sports saloon, the ES; a mid-size sports sedan, the GS; an SUV, the LX; and a crossover SUV, the RX. In 1999 the millionth Lexus was sold in America, and in 2001 the firm introduced a

---

1 The new brand was emphatically an American initiative; Lexus cars were not sold in the Japanese home market until 2005.

luxury compact, the IS. In 2004 Lexus launched the world's first luxury hybrid SUV, the RX 400h; and in 2006 the firm launched its F series as a reply to new high-performance models from Mercedes' AMG marque and BMW's M division.

By 2008 Toyota was the world's biggest car maker. It had achieved a 17 per cent share of the US market and had overtaken all of Detroit's Big Three in terms of both size and global sales. Toyota had also carved out a dominant market share in Japan, accounting for 44.3 per cent of Japanese car production in 2010. It had built a new plant at Valenciennes in France, doubled the size of its British plant in Derby, and opened new American factories at Princeton in Indiana (in 1991), Huntsville in Alabama (in 2001) and San Antonio in Texas (in 2006). Toyota also opened a technical centre in Ann Arbor, Michigan, helpfully adjacent to the academic expertise of the University of Michigan and squarely in the back yard of America's Big Three. J. D. Power named Lexus as the most reliable brand in the US fourteen times between 1995 and 2009, while Interbrand ranked Lexus as Japan's seventh-largest worldwide brand by sales, just below Panasonic but ahead of Nissan. Significantly, the Lexus marque was contributing a large proportion – perhaps as much as half – of the Toyota group's profits.

Yet cracks had started to appear in the edifice. In November 2008, Toyota reported its first operating loss in decades. Analysts attributed this downturn to the fact that management was focusing too much on the US market, where Lexus seemed to be doing so well, at the expense of the rest of the world, where innovative car makers such as VW and Hyundai were making big inroads. Then two big shocks hit the company: the after-effects of the recession of 2008, which caused luxury car sales to slump; and the disastrous recalls of 2009–10, from which both the Lexus and Toyota brands suffered badly.

In September 2009, recently made Lexus ES, Lexus IS and Toyota Camry models were recalled, ostensibly because the driver's floor mat could conceivably jam the accelerator pedal open. Toyota insisted it could rectify the fault easily and that there was no structural fault in the cars.

But this obstinate denial merely gave rise to intense speculation in the US media. The *New York Times* castigated Toyota for failing to provide proper answers to the growing number of complaints about out-of-control cars, and soon declared that it had found more federal reports of unrestrained acceleration. Things then went from bad to worse. On 22 January 2010, eight Toyota and Lexus models, totalling 2.3 million cars, were recalled – supposedly because their accelerator pedals were now sticking when 'warmed by the car's heater'. On 27 January, another 1.1 million vehicles were recalled, again because of 'jamming floor mats'. Toyota still insisted that nothing was intrinsically wrong with their vehicles' pedals or brakes. On 13 April, the influential US magazine *Consumer Reports* issued a rare 'Don't Buy' bulletin for the new Lexus GS 460 SUV, claiming that the slow response of the vehicle's electronic stability control system meant there was a possible rollover risk if the car was turning at high speed. Lexus sales plummeted and the marque's reputation for reliability nosedived.

Toyota's nightmare did not end there. On 25 June, the firm was forced to recall its seventeen thousand Lexus HS 250h luxury hybrids because of a risk of fuel spilling following a crash – an oddly old-fashioned fault for such a supposedly sophisticated car. And on 2 July 2010, around 270,000 Lexus vehicles worldwide were recalled for faulty valve springs – a problem that shamefaced Toyota executives admitted they had been alerted to as early as March 2007. Lexus and Toyota tumbled down J. D. Power's initial quality study and sales plunged still further.

American car bosses, caught in the depths of the recession and fighting for their corporate lives, could not believe their luck. GM's vice chairman Bob Lutz, never a shrinking violet, crowed to the press: 'Toyota's god-like status will never be reclaimed . . . I don't think they'll ever reach the exalted status of the world's best auto company.' Toyota was subsequently forced to pay a humiliating $16.4 million fine to the US government for hiding car defects, while the company's president, Akio Toyoda, was summoned before Congress and forced to make a public apology, during which he declared repeatedly that he was 'deeply sorry'.

The end of Toyota's reign as the world's largest car maker seemed nigh, and its rivals indulged in an orgy of *Schadenfreude*.

Toyota's board had been dominated by Toyoda family members since 1937. Kiichrio's son, Shoichiro, was president between 1982 and 1992, and when the next president, Katsuaki Watanabe, retired in 2009, it was Shoichiro's son, Akio, who took his place. The American-educated Akio was a jovial, candid entrepreneur, with a passion for racing cars, who had made his name as an international banker-playboy in the early 1980s after earning his MBA from Boston's prestigious Babson College. He took the reins at Toyota just in time to face the biggest challenge to the company's reputation since the Second World War.

Akio Toyoda's strategy for coping with seeming disaster was to fall back on the corporate ethos of 'continuous improvement', which had long been enshrined in the fabled Toyota production system. While many now believed this philosophy to have been terminally undermined, Toyoda saw it as a way of reminding customers of the car maker's former reputation for reliability. More pragmatically, and far less subtly, Akio also resorted to an age-old sales technique: a determined campaign of price-cutting. As a result of these initiatives, Toyota swiftly bounced back. In March 2010 sales were reported to be 7.7 per cent down; but twelve months later Toyota announced that profits for 2010–11 were up by 40 per cent on the previous financial year, with Lexus sales up 31 per cent. And this had been achieved while the US market was actually shrinking; American auto sales had fallen by nearly 40 per cent in 2009, to their lowest level since 1970. Toyota had survived the storm.

Toyota was not the only Asian manufacturer to falter in the modern era. Notwithstanding its astonishing success during the 1980s, by the mid-1990s the poor quality of many of Hyundai's exports had made the brand a joke in the US, where they were derided on national TV in the same breath as Lada and Yugo cars. It took a corporate lawyer, Finbarr O'Neill, Hyundai's general counsel since the company's American launch in 1985, to turn the Korean car maker around in America. In 1998 O'Neill, who had no background at all in the car industry, was appointed the head of Hyundai's US operation at a time when the firm was desperate for someone to improve its tarnished image.[1] O'Neill's solution to Hyundai's woes was a traditional one: an eye-catching offer which he called 'America's best warranty', which offered ten years' coverage on every engine and transmission, the areas that had been the most prone to failure. At the same time, O'Neill cut forecourt prices, ensuring that his cars were priced below their Japanese counterparts and well below their US rivals. These old-fashioned ploys worked: sales soared, and the reputation of Hyundai cars leapt. Though Hyundai cars were still cheap, they were no longer publicly perceived as shoddily built.

In 2002 Hyundai had its best sales year ever, selling over 360,000 cars to the United States. Having absorbed South Korea's second-largest car maker, Kia, Hyundai hired German design wizard Peter Schreyer to revitalize Kia's downmarket products. As head of design for Audi after 1994, Shreyer had been responsible for the A2, the A3 and, most notably, for that instant design classic, the Audi TT of 1999, before he was lured to Kia in 2006. A self-conscious design guru, who wore only black and was often seen behind Philippe Starck sunglasses, in 2003 he won the German government's prestigious design award, and followed that in 2007 with an honorary doctorate from the Royal College of Art in London, where he had studied as a student in 1979–80. (He was only the third car designer to receive this honour, after Sergio Pininfarina and Giorgetto Giugiaro.)

In 2004 Hyundai opened a new factory in Alabama and a testing centre in the California desert. Five years later the Hyundai Genesis executive saloon – an upmarket model light years from Turnbull's cheap and cheerful Pony – was acclaimed North American Car of the Year. The following year Hyundai was ranked as the world's fourth-biggest

---

1 An image that was not improved by the 1999 conviction and imprisonment of Chung Ju-yung's son, Chung Mong-koo, for embezzling over $100 million from Hyundai.

car manufacturer, behind Toyota, General Motors and Volkswagen – but ahead of every other European and American car maker, manufacturers that had barely registered the Pony's arrival thirty-four years before.

Not all Korean car makers fared as well as Hyundai. In 1967 the rich, young and ambitious industrialist Kim Woo-jung founded the Daewoo Group, which he soon made into the fourth-biggest industrial conglomerate (*chaebol*) in South Korea. In 1982 Kim moved into car manufacture, buying a well-established car maker, Saehan, which had long made GM models under licence. When an economic crisis hit the Far East in 1998, Kim thought he could brazen it out by expanding rather than contracting, aiming to rely on the easy credit and cheap labour that had allowed him to expand his *chaebol* so spectacularly over the previous thirty years. But his credit evaporated, while Korean labour costs spiralled. In 1999 Daewoo – by now the second-largest *chaebol* in South Korea, and with interests in almost a hundred other countries – declared bankruptcy with debts of 80 billion won. Chairman Kim fled to France, prompting former Daewoo factory workers to distribute 'Wanted' posters decorated with his face. Kim finally returned to South Korea in June 2005, and was promptly arrested. He was subsequently charged with masterminding an accounting fraud worth 41 trillion won ($43.4 billion), illegally borrowing 9.8 trillion won ($10.3 billion) and smuggling $3.2 billion won out of the country. After an exhaustingly long trial, on 30 May 2006 Kim – who tearfully told the court, 'I cannot dodge my responsibility of wrongly buttoning up the final button of fate' – was sentenced to ten years in prison.

Motor mania also spread to Southern Asia in the 1980s. For decades India's car makers had contented themselves with making licensed copies of mediocre old British models. Indeed, the Hindustan Ambassador, based on the 1954 Morris Oxford, has been in continuous production since 1958 (although its original BMC engines have now been replaced by smoother power plants from Isuzu).[1] However, from the 1980s onwards, many Japanese and European manufacturers began to be attracted to India by its strong engineering base and low wages. By 2010 Volkswagen, Nissan, Toyota and Hyundai had all established factories there. The biggest Indian car maker, Maruti, was bought by Suzuki; and following a 1994 deal with General Motors, Hindustan began to make Opel Astras and Bedford trucks under licence, alongside a range of cars made in association with Mitsubishi and a line of trucks built in partnership with Isuzu and OKA of Australia. Astonishingly, though, the Hindustan Ambassador – the much-loved 'Amby' – remains an Indian national treasure which is driven by film stars and politicians alike.[2]

Underlining India's new status as an automotive world power, in 2008 – sixty years after the end of the British Raj – an Indian company bought some of the most illustrious marques in British motoring history. In March of that year the Tata Group of India, led by colourful entrepreneur Ratan Tata, bought the rights to the Rover name and the remaining Land Rover and Jaguar factories from Ford. The former British colony may have acquired some of its former imperial master's most cherished automotive brands, but Ratan Tata was not motivated by sentimentality. In 2010 he made it clear that Tata would be closing one of the group's two remaining factories, Castle Bromwich in Birmingham and Halewood in Liverpool. In the event, a £27 million government grant earned Halewood (due for disposal after it ceased making the Jaguar X-Type in 2009) a reprieve, and in 2011 the Liverpool plant rolled out the first examples of the radical new Range Rover Evoque.

While Hindustan Motors was still debating how to update the Ambassador, in 1985 Malaysian prime minister, Dr Mahathir Mohamad,

---

1 The Ambassador was actually offered for sale in Britain in 1993 as the Fullbore Mark 10. Indian Ambassadors were imported into Southampton and fitted with such luxuries such as seat belts, electric wipers (the Ambassador's wipers were foot-operated) and mirrors, while all the liquid was drained from the car in case any water-borne diseases made it into the country. Predictably, the venture was a disaster, and Fullbore went into liquidation in 1998.

2 Even Sonia Ghandi owned one.

opened the brand-new Proton car factory at Shah Alam. The new company's name was an acronym for *PeRusahaan OTOmobil Nasional*, or 'National Automobile Enterprise'. But the plant was effectively owned and run by Mitsubishi, whose first Proton car, the economical, if spartan, Saga, was a thinly disguised Mitsubishi Lancer. Malaysians eccentrically voted the Saga 'Man of the Year' for 1985; yet this public acclaim was not reflected in model sales and by 1986 Proton was losing $15,000 on each car sold. The project was turning into a very sorry Saga indeed. Attempts to enter the US market via the good offices of the ubiquitous American automotive entrepreneur Malcolm Bricklin failed dismally. However, Proton refused to give up. In 1989 it made its cars available in the UK; in 1993 the Malaysian government took control of the company from Mitsubishi; and in 1996, to the astonishment of motoring critics and petrol-heads the world over, government-owned Proton bought the legendary British sports and racing car manufacturer Lotus Cars, and even returned Lotus to the Formula 1 grid in 2009.

By 2010, however, it was not America or Japan that constituted the world's biggest automobile market, but the sleeping giant of China.

Following the political thaw of the 1980s, China's government-owned auto maker Number One – or First Automobile Works (FAW), as it was now called – began to look for Western partners to help update its drab and old-fashioned products. A link with Volkswagen was established in 1990, and in 1998 the Red Flag marque was reborn in a new Chinese executive model, a thinly disguised Audi A6,[1] branded somewhat clumsily as an Audi-Chrysler-Red-Flag. In 2003 FAW did a deal with Toyota, and in 2009, at the height of the recession, linked up with the troubled US giant General Motors. By 2009 FAW was the largest Chinese auto maker, ahead of its four big rivals: Dongfen, closely allied to both Nissan and Honda; Shanghai Automotive Industry Corporation (SAIC), which

---

1 The old Audi 100 had been renamed the Audi A6 in 1994.

owned the rights to many of the former BMC/British Leyland/Rover Group models and marques; Chang'an Motors, which had worked closely with Ford since 2001, and which in 2010 agreed to make Peugeot and Citroën cars in China under licence; and Chery, which became notorious in the motoring world for copying GM cars *without* a licence. In 2010 these five car makers were joined by a sixth Chinese manufacturer, as the previously little-known Geely Automobile Holdings of Hangzhou bought the illustrious Swedish car maker Volvo from Ford. A year later two smaller Chinese auto firms, Youngman and Pang Da, announced that they were buying Volvo's renowned but ailing Swedish rival, Saab, although their attempts to salvage the moribund firm were in vain.

Conscious of their new status as the world's biggest car-making nation, from 2003 the Chinese built up the Jiading suburb of Shanghai as China's motor city – the Detroit of the twenty-first century. In 2004 the newly completed Jiading racetrack hosted China's first Formula 1 motor race, and work subsequently began on a vast new centre for automotive research and development, developed as a joint venture between SAIC and Volkswagen.

Two million cars were sold in China in 2000; four years later the figure had soared to five million, and by 2010 it was nearer eight million. In 2010 Chinese factories produced a staggering 18.2 million vehicles, compared with Japan's 9.6 million, America's 7.7 million and Germany's 5.9 million.[1] Admittedly, the majority of these cars were built by foreign-owned firms. (Honda, for example, launched a Chinese brand, Li Nian, in 2011; its models were sold under the Everus name in the West and its first product, the S1, was based on the platform of the Honda Jazz.) However, the sheer size of China's untapped market and its vast resources of cheap labour suggest that the nation will soon become a major force in the global auto industry. The future of car making in the twenty-first century seems to lie not in Europe, the Americas nor even in Japan, but in China.

---

1 Korea was the fifth-largest producer, at 4.2 million cars. France and Britain lay a distant tenth and fifteenth, respectively, at 2.2 and 1.4 million.

16

Futureworld

Today the world seems to be as in thrall to the gasoline-powered car as it was seventy years ago. In 2003 the number of cars Americans owned surpassed the number of Americans with driving licences; nine out of ten US households now owns a car, and 65 per cent have a second car. (At the same time, in some of the poorer areas of America, 90 per cent of motorists are estimated to be uninsured.) Cars continue to drive the expansion of the developed world's suburbs; thus Nashville is expanding south down Interstate 65 at a phenomenal rate, while Atlanta races west down Interstate 20 towards the massive new Kia plant. As Catherine Lutz and Anne Lutz Fernandez have pointed out, in America (aside from Alaska and the Louisiana swamps), 'no spot [is] more than 22 miles from the nearest road'. As a result, urban areas are ever more choked with dangerous vehicle emissions. A Denver study of 2000 showed that children living in corridors of heavy traffic use – which can be up to a mile each side of the highway – were six times more likely to develop cancer than those living further away. In 2007 Phoenix, Arizona, had ninety-four days on which, in the opinion the Environmental Protection Agency, it was unhealthy to go outside. To combat this, increasing numbers of cities are seeking to emulate London and introduce congestion charges, designed to force commuters out of their cars and back on to public transport. But such palliatives cannot hope to hold back the tide on their own. The launch of the London congestion charge in 2003 was initially very successful, but by 2008 impossible levels of traffic were back choking the capital's roads.

While the world becomes increasingly clogged with vehicle emissions, the vehicles themselves get ever more sophisticated. Electronic 'active systems' help cars to brake and park. Stop-start engines save fuel when the car is stationary. Voice-activated controls are now common, responding to everyday speech patterns rather than just to pre-set commands. Electronic stability controls prevent rollovers, and crash-imminent braking systems lessen the likelihood of rear-end collisions. Radar technology 'reads' road markings for the driver – though perhaps its introduction has been a little premature, since the general state of the world's poorly maintained roads means that it only functions properly on pristine superhighways.

On the highway, the SUV continues to reign as the world's capital car. Even in the recession-hit 2010s, the craze for SUVs shows no signs of abating. Cars like the Audi Q7, BMW X5 and Volvo XC90 continue, for example, to sell far more than their conventional saloon cousins. And SUV drivers, since they are seated higher than their saloon equivalents, feel safer and so often drive faster. But, as we have seen, the sense of safety that SUVs provide is often illusory. Some SUV bumpers are now higher than many highway guard rails.

In more affluent households, the SUV is not the only vehicle on the drive. Many families in the West are now buying two or even three cars in order to fulfil different motoring tasks. Households that own an electric, hybrid or petrol-powered city car for short, local journeys are also tending to purchase larger, more powerful models for long-distance trips. Similarly, sports car users need a more practical runabout for weekday use. In 2011 Toyota launched the tiny Cygnet, a premium, two-door, city car-cum-hot-hatch, developed in conjunction with Aston Martin. In possibly the most unlikely auto partnership to date, Aston chief Ulrich Bez declared the Cygnet had been created to provide 'our customers [with] a small car for urban use'. Toyota and Aston expected initial demand to be limited to those who already owned an Aston Martin sports car.

The trademark Aston badge and grille were accordingly applied, rather uncomfortably, to the Cygnet's front end; the interior was given a once-over by Aston's designers; and the result was launched in 2011 at a sticker price of around £30,000 – a lot of money for a tiny car. In the event, the Cygnet's minuscule boot couldn't really accommodate much more shopping than an Aston Martin Vantage sports car.

As the world's largest car maker, Toyota can afford a few eccentric experiments. As we have seen, the automotive industry at the dawn of the twenty-first century is dominated and directed by the Japanese, the Chinese, the Germans and the French – with the Koreans of Hyundai Kia close behind. Moreover, Japanese cars continue to outshine their American and European rivals in terms of reliability. In *What Car?* magazine's reliability survey of 2011, the top eleven manufacturers were Japanese or Korean: in descending order, Honda (top in 2010, too), Toyota, Lexus, Mitsubishi, Suzuki, Mazda, Subaru, Hyundai, Kia, Nissan and (now defunct) Daewoo. The highest-ranked European marque, Škoda, came twelfth, while historic European car makers Renault, Alfa and Land Rover propped up the table – as indeed they had the previous year. Of the ten most reliable small hatchbacks, all but two were Japanese (the *gaijins* were Volvo's A40 and Peugeot's 207). Nine out of the ten best SUVs were Japanese, with the Land Rover Freelander the highest Western entry, at number five.

The fate of America's Motor City mirrors the predicament of those American and European car makers struggling to meet the Asian challenge. Detroit is still the home of America's Big Three. But the inner-city suburbs that once housed their workers have disappeared – leaving, as architectural historian Joe Kerr has noted, 'one of the most distressed urban landscapes in the Western world'. Downtown Detroit is littered with empty skyscrapers; its once-famed department store, Hudson's (which had been America's second-largest department store, after Macy's in New York), closed in 1983 and the building was demolished fifteen years later. The Michigan Theater is now a parking garage; the big hotels are largely empty, and the supermarket chains have deserted the downtown area altogether. The few houses that remain in desolated sections of the inner city (one in five inner-city homes currently stand empty) are being demolished and their inhabitants forcibly rehoused in order to return vast swathes of land to cultivation or grassland. By January 2010, 40 square miles – almost a third of the historic inner city – had been reclaimed by nature. A wry website now promotes tours of 'The Fabulous Ruins of Detroit', equating the scarred urban landscape with the remains of Ancient Rome. Journalist Julien Temple wrote in the *Guardian* in March 2010 that driving down the 'eerily empty ghost freeways into the ruins of inner-city Detroit [was] an Alice-like journey into a severely dystopian future'. Temple noted 'the giant rubber tyre that dwarfs the non-existent traffic in ironic testament to the busted hubris of Motown's auto makers', and 'the vast, rusted hulks of abandoned car plants [in] the derelict shell of Downtown Detroit'. Property prices, he observed, had fallen by 80 per cent between 2007 and 2010. Unemployment had reached 30 per cent; 33.8 per cent of Detroit's population and 48.5 per cent of its children lived below the poverty line; and 47 per cent of adults were functionally illiterate.

Temple noted 'the blind belief of the Big Three in the automobile as an inexhaustible golden goose, guaranteeing endless streams of cash, resulted in [Detroit] becoming reliant on a single industry'. African-American author, critic and film-maker Nelson George was of the same mind. Detroit, he observed, 'once a city of long cars and high hopes, is a place where prosperity, optimism and jobs have disappeared or moved away. Unemployment and crime haunt this city like a death in the family . . . There is a hole in Detroit's soul . . . and there is nothing on the horizon ready to fill it.'

. . .

While Detroit's Big Three continued to contract, shedding historic marques and models, Asian and European car makers chose to stretch successful brands as far as they could feasibly go. While Aston Martin unveiled the Cygnet, its Warwickshire neighbour, Land Rover, launched a hot-hatch coupé which also doubled as an SUV, and stablemate Jaguar planned a crossover SUV. By 2012, indeed, the crossover SUV (which was ostensibly more environmentally responsible than its full-sized cousins) was all the rage, as astute car makers sought to conjure up yet another lucrative new market. Nissan, having in 2007 introduced the absurdly named but reasonably successful Qashqai compact crossover[1] (styled not in Japan but at the firm's Milan design centre), followed this with the even smaller mini-crossover Juke in 2011. The Juke was cheap and nippy, but the ride was choppy and its exterior looked like a mutant frog fresh from the animal hospital. Nevertheless, the fun-size crossover concept triumphed over the car's styling and performance, and sales greatly exceeded expectations.

As the world's car makers rushed to emulate Nissan, many of the new SUV crossovers they produced sported some unlikely badges. In 2012 Fiat launched a Maserati-branded SUV, the Kubang, targeted at the US market; yet while the Kubang was designed by Fiat's Ferrari subsidiary, it was effectively little more than a Jeep Grand Cherokee (now the flagship of Fiat's Chrysler operation) and was built alongside the Jeep in Detroit. Even Porsche, which for decades had confined its model range to sports cars, introduced a crossover SUV, the Cayenne, in 2002, and a decade later partnered this with a smaller, two-door version, the Cajun. Porsche also created a four-door luxury sedan,[2] the Panamera, for 2009. However, critical reaction was mixed. To many, the Panamera was awkward and ugly – a bloated and distended 911. *Top Gear's* indefatigable presenter Jeremy Clarkson (writing in *The Times* in 2008), declared that the car 'made Quasimodo look like George Clooney'. The Panamera was

---

1 Known, more conservatively, as the Dualis in Japan and Australia.
2 Officially, a five-door luxury liftback.

also undeniably overpriced, costing far more than superior competitors such as the Jaguar XFR. Nevertheless, by 2010 the Panamera had, despite its critical reception, become Porsche's best-selling model, proving particularly popular in America, where Porsche's traditional sports cars were often perceived as being both too small and too 'European'. Not every cross-genre model proved a sales success, however. Ford's Lincoln Blackwood luxury pickup of 2001 proved to be a crossover too far, and production was halted after just one year.

While eager to develop new markets and product types, prescient car makers such as Porsche were also careful to stress the continuity of their ranges, recognizing the invaluable role that the corporate DNA plays in reassuring both current owners and potential customers. Thus even the newest Porsches, Mercedes and BMWs still bear a family resemblance to their illustrious predecessors. In addition, by the mid-1990s some auto manufacturers were not only acknowledging the evolutionary design of their current models, but were beginning to disinter much-loved models from automotive history.

Early attempts at raiding the past were essentially conjectural exercises in nostalgia rather than revivals of particular classics. Perhaps for that reason they were not entirely successful. The Nissan Figaro, a cartoon parody of the Renault Dauphine, was launched with the inevitable slogan 'Back to the Future' in 1990. Its nervous manufacturer marketed the little car without the Nissan badge; underneath, though, it was little more than a Nissan Micra. Initially intended just for Japan, the Figaro established a niche market in Britain, where it featured on television as the mount for the fictional character Sarah Jane Smith and for the BBC political commentator Andrew Marr. However, it remains very much an acquired taste, its styling hovering uneasily between retro and caricature.

Equally awkward was the Chrysler PT Cruiser of 2000, designed by Bryan Nesbitt for Chrysler design boss Thomas Gale. This unashamedly old-fashioned model sought to recapture the glory days of Chrysler's postwar heyday by combining an MPV's space with the looks of a streamlined saloon of the late 1930s. The result, though, was a graceless and ungainly car which, like the Figaro, seemed more of a mocking satire than an affectionate tribute. From 2007 production of the PT Cruiser was wound down, and it ceased altogether in 2010.

In 1994 Volkswagen entered the retro market with the first real attempt to exhume a past masterpiece, unveiling its prototype New Beetle compact at the Detroit Motor Show. It was another four years, however, before the New Beetle appeared in American showrooms, while the car's European launch was not until 1999. The production model was based on the Polo platform and featured an engine at the front – not at the rear, as in Ferdinand Porsche's *KdF-Wagen*. Yet the parabola curve of the New Beetle's roof, together with the distinctive styling of front and rear, undoubtedly recalled the ancient *Käfer*.

VW soon found that the retro design hampered maintenance. At the same time, the car's reputation was damaged by a series of reliability problems and its appeal hindered by its over-identification with young female buyers. VW's New Beetle was just too cutesy – and, unusually for Volkswagen, too fault-prone – for the mainstream market. In 2011 VW, acknowledging its faults, launched a comprehensive redesign. The new-new Beetle[1] was larger (based on the platform of the Jetta rather than the smaller Polo) and more purposeful, having had its sweeping roof brusquely flattened.

While Volkswagen initially floundered with its daring retro concept, BMW got it right first time. The Munich giant, having acquired one of the most iconic models of the twentieth century (and one frequently cited as the most influential car after the Model T Ford), adapted it for a demanding new audience. BMW's new Mini[2] had its fair share of problems on its launch – even a recall or two, reminiscent of the bad old days of British Leyland. It also had a tiny boot and precious little legroom in the rear. But it proved to be a huge hit. Like its 1959 predecessor (and unlike the New Beetle), it was both classless and gender-free. Designed by BMW's Frank

---

1 In fact, in 2011 VW dropped the New prefix.
2 Officially described in capitals – MINI – in order to distinguish it from its BMC predecessor.

Stephenson – who told *Autocar* he wanted everyone's first impression to be 'it could only be a Mini' – its appeal seemed limitless. And, as BMW had hoped, it particularly fascinated American consumers. By 2002 over 260,000 Minis were being sold annually in the US, and over a million worldwide. At Cowley, BMW expanded the highly successful Mini range into the Cooper S, a convertible, a coupé, the Clubman, the Countryman and the lower, sleeker Paceman sports activity coupé of 2012. It has to be said, though, that the further BMW departed from Stephenson's original concept, the less visually successful were the results. The Cooper SD coupé of 2011, in particular, looked as if it had lost its rear in a nasty accident.

Where BMW led, Fiat followed with its immensely successful and enjoyable new 500 of 2007. Adapted by designer Roberto Giolito from Dante Giacosa's classic original of fifty years before, the 500 effortlessly reinterpreted Giacosa's immortal concept for a more technological age – and for larger occupants. (Only when you see the 1957 and 2007 models parked together do you realize just how much bigger the new 500 is than its 1950s inspiration.) Built in Poland and Mexico, the 500 brought the Fiat brand back to North America for the first time in twenty-six years. Crucially, Fiat made a virtue of the *Cinquecento*'s flexibility. There were, the car maker proudly announced, over half a million different personalizing permutations for the product, including an American sports version, made in Michigan at a Fiat-owned Chrysler plant; a coupé, devised by Milanese design consultancy Zagato; an upgraded, high-performance global range, marketed under the disinterred Abarth brand;[1] a Start&Stop stop-go version; and, inevitably, an electric adaptation, with a sturdy 75 mile range. There are plans for an estate version. (In the late fifties Giacosa converted the diminutive 500 into the improbable Giardiniera station wagon,[2] which involved lying the engine on its side, lengthening

---

[1] Abarth had been founded in 1949 as a niche racing and sports car manufacturer and was bought by Fiat in 1971. Its most famous model was a sporty version of Giacosa's 500, the Abarth 595.

[2] Literally, 'the small gardener', although the word has also come to denote the Italian

the wheelbase to create a usable rear seat, and fitting better brakes.) A limited edition of two hundred Ferrari 500s were supplied to Ferrari owners as courtesy runabouts while their sports cars were being serviced. There were also custom-built black or white Gucci-styled versions, and a bright pink Barbie edition, made in 2009 to mark the fiftieth anniversary of Mattel's iconic doll. Within three weeks of the 500's launch, the entire year's production of fifty-eight thousand had been sold out. Subsequently, the 500 was showered with awards, including *CAR* magazine's Car of the Year for 2007, European Car of the Year for 2008 and World Car Design of the Year for 2009. Giolito's attempt to emulate his illustrious predecessor seems to have worked brilliantly.

While BMW and Fiat revived two of the most important cars of the 1950s, Ford reworked its most celebrated phenomenon of the sixties. As we have seen, from the 1970s onwards Dearborn allowed its sleek, stylish Mustang to become first a sagging, bloated subcompact-derivative and then a blandly styled, Japanese-looking sedan. In 2005, however, stylist Sid Ramarance – working under the direction of Ford's chief stylist, J. Mays,[1] who had been part of the team behind the New Beetle – introduced a fifth-generation Mustang which finally recaptured the lean muscularity of Bordinat's 1964 car, using an idiom that Mays christened 'retrofuturism'.

Oklahoma-born Mays had been bitten by the automotive bug while working at his father's auto parts store as a boy. Graduating from the prestigious Art Center College in Pasadena, California, in 1980 with a BSc in transportation design, he began his career at Audi in Ingolstadt, where he helped to revamp the Audi 100 and the VW Golf. In 1989 he returned to the US, though still on VAG's payroll, and working at VW's Simi Valley Design Center in California was one of the authors of the New Beetle concept. After spells back in Germany and running his own design consultancy, in 1997 he was made Ford's vice president of design. There

dish of pickled vegetables.
1 His first name is just 'J', and stands for nothing.

he profited from the profligacy of the Nasser years, working on models as diverse as the Aston Martin DB9, the Land Rover Discovery and the short-lived Ford GT of 2005–6. There, too, his exposure to Jaguar and Aston Martin's rich brand heritage helped him to develop his 'retrofuturist' vision, which he subsequently applied not only to the Mustang but also to the Ford Thunderbird. The original fun, sporty T-bird had by the 1990s become a characterless two-door sedan, which was finally (and justifiably) axed in 1997. In 2002 Mays revived the concept in the form of a Jaguar-powered coupé/convertible whose retro lines instantly recalled Earl's original.¹ And where Ford led, GM followed. In 2011 General Motors vowed that the new generation, Kentucky-made C7 Chevrolet Corvette would be a truly global sports car, more like a Ferrari and less like a Chevrolet,² with body styling that returned to Bill Mitchell's classic Sting Ray Corvette of 1963.

Mays's new '02 Thunderbird exploited two of the motoring public's current enthusiasms: retro styling and diminutive size. Indeed, in the early years of the twenty-first century small was, once again, beautiful. Ford led the way in this market sector, too: Jack Telnack and Claude Lobo's cute and modishly styled Ford Ka,³ of 1996, was distinctive, androgynous, and very successful, even though it performed less impressively than its racy lines would suggest. In 2008, however, Ford effectively gave up on the idea; the second incarnation of the model was far more conventional in appearance and was in truth little more than an inferior Fiat 500, using the 500's chassis and engine and being manufactured at Fiat's Polish plant.

Ford's breakthrough in the microcar market was exploited by Mercedes' revolutionary Smart car of 1998. The Smart went a stage further than the Ka; it was so tiny that it could be parked nose-to-kerb like a

---

1 That same year, Mays was canonized by having his 'retrofuturist' car designs made the subject of a major exhibition at the Los Angeles Museum of Contemporary Art.

2 Its C6 predecessor was designed in a very American idiom and gained few sales outside the US.

3 Initially designated the Streetka, the model's name was later abbreviated to just Ka.

motorbike, yet its turbocharged 599cc engine was capable of over 80 mph. This extraordinary miniature car had started life as the Swatchmobile, a concept developed in the late 1980s by the Swiss CEO of Swatch watch-makers, Nicolas Hayek. In 1991 Hayek persuaded Volkswagen to share the substantial costs of the project, but the agreement was hastily terminated two years later by Ferdinand Piëch, newly installed as Volkswagen's CEO, who preferred to develop VW's own microcar. Hayek turned instead to Daimler-Benz, a deal was hammered out, and a new manufacturing plant opened at Hambach, on the Franco-German border in Lorraine, in 1994. However, the Germans soon found themselves at odds with the mercurial watch tycoon, who insisted that his Swatch brand name form some part of the car's identity. Daimler-Benz's management adamantly refused and forced Hayek into a clumsy compromise: Smart, an awkward acronym of Swatch Mercedes Art. The two companies also quarrelled over the car's fuel system. Hayek wanted a hybrid drive train, but the German car maker installed a relatively conventional gasoline engine. At this defeat, Hayek's patience finally snapped; in 1998 Daimler-Benz bought out Swatch's remaining stake in the company and badged the car as a Mercedes.

Daimler-Benz originally envisaged a whole line of Smart models. However, the strange-looking auto struggled in its early years and spin-off variants such as the Roadster, an SUV(!) and a four-seat supermini were soon discontinued. At time of writing, the Fortwo remains the only petrol-powered Smart product – although a rechargeable, electric version was released in 2010, and a roadster version is planned.

The dominant issue in early twenty-first century motoring, however, is not vehicle size or cross-sector adaptability, but fuel flexibility. Gasoline prices in the US rose by over 300 per cent between 1998 and 2008, despite an enormous government subsidy which keeps the cost of the fuel far lower than in the rest of the developed world. US oil production peaked around 1970 (as Shell geologist M. King Hubbert correctly predicted as far back as 1956). Now everyone is speculating when will *world* oil production begin to decline? The debate over Peak Oil is one that haunts not only the oil industry but also governments and car makers across the globe.

Despite long-standing concerns over the future of oil, however, the electric car has not prospered until very recently. Experiments were made with electric cars during the Second World War, when petrol was rationed in most combatant countries, but few of these bizarre contraptions survived into 1946. In France in the 1950s, Casimir Loubières hand-made the electric Symetric car (he then followed it with a bizarre proposal for an atomic-powered variant complete with fluorescent, radioactive rear bumpers); and in 1967 Ford made an experimental two-seater electric car, the Comuta, though only a handful were built. A Ford of Britain executive was perhaps being a little premature when he predicted, 'We expect electrical cars to be commercially feasible within the next 10 years', but he was certainly more prophetic when he added, 'we believe their uses will be primarily as city centre delivery and suburban shopping cars'.

In 1985 the cause of the electric car seemed consigned to the grave following the dismal failure of the over-hyped, battery-powered British three-wheeler, the Sinclair C5. Open to the elements – which was rarely ideal in rain-soaked Britain – and with a top speed of only 15 mph, the C5 rapidly became a national joke. (Sales were not helped when, in a ridiculous PR gambit, the C5 was promoted by former racing driver Stirling Moss.) Sinclair Vehicles went into receivership only nine months after the C5's launch.

In December 1996, however, GM bravely launched the world's first mass-produced electric car, the EV1. Much was promised for, and expected from, this new venture. But after only a few hundred models had been made, and sold only in California, production of the EV1 was halted and the car was mysteriously withdrawn. The debate still rages as to who terminated the EV1 and why – an argument stoked by Chris Paine's incendiary documentary *Who Killed the Electric Car?*, which Japanese-owned Sony Pictures gleefully released in 2006. GM's handling of the debacle showed how little it had learned since Alfred Sloan's retirement. After vowing publicly to save all the EVIs it had built so far, GM's officially sanctioned crushing of unsold EVIs was then caught on camera – precisely at the time the firm was promoting its absurd Hummer, one of the least sustainable private vehicles money could buy. The car maker was thus forced into promising a new electric car to take the EVI's place – a car that was eight years in gestation. And when the Chevrolet Volt did finally appear in 2010 (soon to be joined by its European cousin, the Opel/Vauxhall Ampera), it was not a purely electric vehicle. Technically a hybrid, or at least a hybrid hybrid (or range extender, as GM preferred), it carried a small petrol engine to generate electricity when the battery ran down or when driving at motorway speeds.

Once again, when America faltered, the Japanese stepped in. The electric sensation of 2010–11 was not GM's Volt/Ampera but the Nissan Leaf, the first mass-produced electric car. The Leaf's body styling was dull, but its acceleration and suspension were good and it was cheap to charge – if not to buy; even with government grants it cost almost double its petrol equivalent. Yet since the Leaf, like all electric autos, released no harmful exhaust emissions, its high unit cost could be counterbalanced by more altruistic environmental gains.

The development of the Volt and the Leaf prompted rival car makers into a frenzy of activity. From 2010 every major manufacturer issued an electric car (often adapted from an existing petrol-powered model) or a near-electric model equipped with a small, range-extending petrol engine. Nissan's partner-owner, Renault, unveiled the prototype of its electric Fluence compact executive saloon, boasting an alleged top speed of 84 mph and an impressive 115 mile range; while Renault's French rival, PSA, unveiled two small, four-seat electric city cars, the Citroën C-Zero and its Peugeot sister, the iOn. In 2010 Daimler AG and German energy giant RWE announced a joint project to develop and manufacture environmentally friendly electric cars for Europe, derived from Mercedes' Smart and A- and B-Class cars. The same year VW's chief executive, Martin Winterkorn, told an audience at VW's California Research Center that by 2013 the company would be producing an electric version of the Up and the Golf, together with plug-in hybrid variants of the Golf and the Jetta. In 2011 even Porsche unveiled a prototype for an all-electric Boxster E, using technology VW had developed for the Golf e-motion, demonstrating that electric power and performance were not mutually exclusive. Meanwhile, Ford's electric Focus was unveiled in America in 2011 and in Europe the following year. The Volt's European cousin, the Ampera – equipped with a feisty, 1.4 litre extension engine, which provided impressive acceleration – appeared in 2012. BMW launched its pricey i3 electric city car in 2013. Some of these new electric products actually boasted battery ranges of over 200 miles – although most could not manage more than 120 miles.

The obstacles to the widespread use of electric cars, however, still remain formidable. In Britain, for example, the new coalition government of 2010 announced grants of up to £5,000 to encourage the purchase of electric cars, a subsidy that went some way towards defraying the high sticker price. Ministers also promised £20 million to improve charging infrastructure 'across the UK', rather than just in London, with transport secretary Philip Hammond noting that 95 per cent of UK car journeys involved distances of twenty-five miles or less. However, electric cars remain largely limited to London and a handful of other cities – much as, in the US, electric vehicles flourish in Southern California and New York City but are rarely found elsewhere. Then in 2011 the British government announced it would not, after all, fund a national network of charging points, hoping that most electric car owners would be able to charge their vehicles at home – which many cannot. Increasingly, those consumers who do buy electric cars see their purchase a luxury rather than a necessity, and supplement it with more conventional means of transport. Until governments address the need for a dense grid of charging stations, the electric car will remain shackled to the home.

With all-electric options still hampered by their limited range, more imaginative car makers sought to create a halfway house for those who want to espouse electric power but do not want to sacrifice the advantages of long-distance travel. Thus was born the hybrid car, powered by a combination of an electric motor and a petrol engine.

Hybrids are actually nothing new. The first genuine dual-fuel vehicle appeared as early as 1901, made by the American George Fisher (although, as with the early electric cars, the heavy, leak-prone, lead-acid battery in Fisher's automobile soon proved a fatal handicap). To some extent, too, all cars were technically 'hybrids' following the installation of Charles Kettering's electric starter motor to all automobiles after 1912. Modern hybrids tend to combine a small-capacity petrol engine with an electric motor, usually run from a lithium-ion polymer battery. They can cover up to thirty miles using the electric motor, but then the petrol engine – with all its attendant benefits and faults – cuts in.

The first mass-produced hybrid was, inevitably, Japanese. The Toyota Prius was introduced in Japan in 1997 and in the rest of the world four years later. As the world's first viable hybrid, the Prius captured the imagination in a manner that no dual-fuel vehicles since have been able to match.[1] Film stars traded in their vast SUVs and Hummers and turned up for movie premieres in Priuses. Even Brian Griffin drove one in the animated TV series *Family Guy*. Nevertheless, while it earned worldwide plaudits – among them the European Car of the Year accolade in 2004 – early Priuses sacrificed aesthetics for sustainability, being dowdy, anonymous and utilitarian. It was only with the third generation of 2009, which was far sharper and more aerodynamically styled, that the model was able to challenge its conventional rivals head-on. In 2011 a resurgent Toyota applied the Prius name and shape to an all-electric plug-in model, and introduced a small Lexus hybrid, the CT200, to take on BMW's and Audi's compact family cars, at a time when the reputation of the Prius (from which the CT200 took its powertrain) had been dented by the quality scandal. When Kia announced that it would henceforward concentrate

---

1 In 2000 Honda (for once not the innovator) launched a rival in the shape of the Insight, which looked a bit like a 1970s Citroën. In 2011 Honda's Infiniti marque brought out a hybrid executive saloon, the M35, and a hybrid version of the Jazz supermini.

on producing small hybrids, Toyota raised the stakes by declaring that *all* of their cars would feature a dual-fuel power system by 2020.

Across the Pacific, GM and Ford were predictably slow to enter the hybrid market. Early in 2011, Ford's UK boss candidly admitted that 'we're waiting to see how the market reacts to other electric cars' – an attitude that could see the big American producers fall even further behind their Japanese competitors. The Germans, though, were quick to take up the challenge, applying hybrid technology to luxury and sports models as well as to their more economic products. Audi's hybrid A6 was unveiled in 2012, two years after Porsche had launched a hybrid sports car, the 918, and a hybrid Cayenne SUV based on its VW cousin, the Touareg. In February 2011 Mercedes promised that every future C-Class car would be able to offer a hybrid version.

While hybrids have proved popular in Britain and America, in the rest of Europe diesel engines still remain very much in vogue; 50 per cent of cars sold in Europe carry diesel engines. Accordingly, while the oil companies have been trying to produce cleaner diesel fuels, car makers have also been working on ways to operate with fewer emissions and greater fuel efficiency. Mercedes' Bluetec diesel system of 2006 was the first major step in this direction. Daimler-Benz now share this technology with VAG, owners of Audi, Porsche and Volkswagen, and both firms are installing the system in cars destined for the US market. This latter move may be somewhat optimistic, since in 2011 only 3 per cent of American cars ran on diesel fuel. However, some analysts predict that by 2015 this proportion may be as high as 10 per cent.

Other liquid-fuel alternatives to gasoline have also been cultivated. Shell has developed a gas-to-liquid (GTL) diesel, obtained from natural gas. The gas-to-liquid concept has been known for some time, but has been prohibitively expensive to put into production. Now the imminence of Peak Oil has returned the notion to the top of the 'to-do' list.

Ethanol – motor fuel made from plant-derived alcohol – has also been tried, generally in combination with petrol. Some US states now make such blended gasoline compulsory; it is, for example, particularly popular in Texas. In 2010 Ferrari even unveiled a hybrid version of its 599 flagship Gran Turismo which runs on blended fuel. BP, DuPont and British Sugar have evolved their own biofuel, biobutanol, which, its makers claim, has a higher density and is less volatile than ethanol, and can be made from biological (i.e. organic, but non-food) waste.

Biofuels, however, will never prove a long-term solution to the likely exhaustion of the world's oil reserves. They merely represent a short-term palliative, one that helps – like the hybrid car – to eke out petrol's future. In many ways, the only real alternative to petrol as a means of fuelling vehicles capable of travelling long distances, and imbued with a high degree of sustainability, is hydrogen. Hydrogen fuel cells (linked not to a heavy battery but to a capacitor) allow for quick acceleration, akin to that of a petrol-powered car, and offer a long range – currently up to 400 miles. Equally importantly, emissions from hydrogen cells comprise nothing more than harmful to the planet than oxidized hydrogen – pure, simple water. And the gas can be extracted from a wide variety of sources, ranging from water itself to natural gas (and even urine). On the minus side, hydrogen extraction is expensive and has environmental impacts, and hydrogen is costly and potentially dangerous to store. But this risk is not significantly greater than that faced by producers and retailers of petrol and diesel. Hydrogen cells represent the best option if we want to continue driving cars. However, governments would need to create a service station infrastructure for the fuelling of hydrogen-powered vehicles for such a system to become viable. The world's oil companies are not going to do this for them.

In 2002, encouragingly, the Bush administration in America vowed to invest $1.2 billion in hydrogen car research. Six years later it was, unsurprisingly, Honda that unveiled the world's first hydrogen-cell car, the FCX Clarity. Based on the platform of the Honda Accord, the Clarity featured dashboard monitors for hydrogen consumption, and seat upholstery made from Honda's patent plant-derived Bio-Fabric. Available for lease in the US, Japan and Europe, the Clarity was sold only in Southern California, where the state government had invested in the necessary fast-fill hydrogen service stations. Honda declared it could start mass-producing vehicles based on the FCX Clarity by 2018 – provided more administrations follow California's lead. In response, Hyundai Kia announced that it aimed to build one to two thousand hydrogen-fuelled cars per year on the platform of the Kia Exclusive. Even GM tested a hundred Chevrolet Equinox SUV-cum-saloon hydrogen-powered crossovers in 2011–12. After 130 years of the motor car, it looks as if its salvation may lie in the tiny hydrogen atom.

Further Reading

Below is a selection of useful secondary sources that are widely available in libraries, archives and (in the case of the more recent titles) from book retailers.

Finding the sources for a general history of the motor industry is not as easy as finding information about individual cars. The large car makers have, perhaps understandably, always been very nervous about sharing information, even if it pertains to events that happened decades ago. Many of those company histories that have been allowed to proceed have been somewhat selective in their narrative, clearly guided by commercial concerns. There are, of course splendid exceptions – most notably Robert Lacey's commanding and beautifully written history of Ford. Others are more evidently products of motor manufacturers' public relations departments and have enjoyed a correspondingly short shelf-life.

Primary sources for the car industry are notoriously inconsistent, too. In the 1960s the Ford Motor Company famously destroyed private papers belonging to Henry Ford and his son Edsel, some at the personal behest of Henry Ford II. Towards the end of his life, the titan of General Motors, Alfred Sloan, suddenly got cold feet about publishing his ghosted memoirs and tried to prevent the writer GM had hired for that very purpose from going into print. Sloan, like Ford, also left no private papers; those that did survive his death were destroyed by GM executives. William Morris's papers survive at Nuffield College, Oxford, but they are the exception rather than the rule. In death, as in life, the world's car makers often remain tantalizingly elusive. Hopefully this book has gone some way towards bringing them back into focus.

General

Martin Adeney, *The Motor Makers* (London: Collins, 1988).

Michael L. Beyer, *The Automobile in American History and Culture* (Westport, CN: Greenwood Press, 2001).

David Blanke, *Hell on Wheels* (Lawrence, KA: University Press of Kansas, 2007).

Malcolm Bobbitt, *Austerity Motoring* (Dorchester: Veloce, 2003).

Walter J. Boyne, *Power Behind the Wheel* (London: Conran Octopus, 1988).

John Butman, *Car Wars* (London: Grafton, 1991).

Sally Clarke, *Trust and Power* (Cambridge: Cambridge University Press, 2007).

Tony Davis, *Naff Motors* (London: Century, 2006).

Peter Dunnett, *The Decline of the British Motor Industry* (London: Croom Helm, 1980).

James J. Flink, *The Car Culture* (Cambridge, MA: MIT Press, 1975).

. . ., *The Automobile Age* (Cambridge, MA: MIT Press, 1988).

David Gartmann, *Auto Slavery* (Brunswick, NJ: Rutgers University Press, 1986).

. . ., *Auto Opium: A Social History of American Automobile Design* (London: Routledge, 1994).

Nick Georgano (ed.), *Britain's Motor Industry: The First Hundred Years* (Sparkford: G. A. Foulis, 1995).

. . . (ed.), *The Beaulieu Encyclopaedia of the Automobile*, 3 vols (London: HMSO, 2000–1).

Jonathan Glancey, *The Car: A History of the Automobile* (London: Carlton, 2006).

David Hebb, *Wheels on the Road* (New York: Collier, 1966).

Paul J. Ingrassia and Joseph B. White, *Comeback: The Fall and Rise of the American Automobile Industry* (New York: Simon & Schuster, 1994).

John Jerome, *The Death of the Automobile* (New York: Norton, 1972).

Fred Kaplan, *1959: The Year Everything Changed* (Hoboken, NJ: John Wiley, 2009).

Harold Katz, *The Decline of Competition in the Automobile Industry 1920–1940* (New York: Arno Press, 1977).

. . ., *Shifting Gears* (Cambridge, MA: MIT Press, 1985).

David Kynaston, *Family Britain 1951–7* (London: Bloomsbury, 2007).

. . ., *Austerity Britain 1945–51* (London: Bloomsbury, 2009).

Brian Ladd, *Autophobia* (Chicago: University of Chicago Press, 2008).

James J. Laux, *The European Auto Industry* (Boston: Twayne, 1992).

Wayne Lewchuck, *American Technology and the British Vehicle Industry* (Cambridge: Cambridge University Press, 1986).

Peter Ling, *America and the Automobile* (Manchester: Manchester University Press, 1989).

Jonathan Mantle, *Car Wars* (New York: Arcade, 1995).

Micheline Maynard, *The End of Detroit* (New York: Doubleday, 2003).

Mariana Mazzucato, *Advertising and the Evolution of Market Structure in the US Car Industry* (Milton Keynes: Open University Press, 2001).

Daniel Miller (ed.), *Car Cultures* (Oxford: Berg, 2001).

Ralph Nader, *Unsafe at Any Speed* (New York: Grossman, 1965).

Julian Pettifer and Nigel Turner, *Automania* (London: Collins, 1984).

Anthony Pritchard, *British Family Cars of the 1950s and 60s* (Oxford: Shire, 2009).

John B. Rae, *American Automobile* (Chicago: University of Chicago Press, 1965).

. . ., *The American Automobile Industry* (Boston: Twayne, 1984).

James Ruppert, *The British Car Industry: Our Part in its Downfall* (Maidenhead: Foresight Publications, 2008).

Emma Rothschild, *Paradise Lost: The Decline of the Auto-Industrial Age* (New York: Random House, 1973).

Samuel Saul, 'The Motor Industry in Britain to 1914', *Business History*, 5.1 (December 1962).

Michael Sedgwick, *The Motor Car 1946–56* (London: Batsford, 1979).

L. J. K. Setright, *Drive On!* (London: Granta, 2003).

Richard Sutton, *Motor Mania* (London: Collins and Brown, 1996).

Timothy Whisler, *At the End of the Road* (Greenwich, CN: JAI Press, 1995).

. . ., *The British Motor Industry 1945–94* (Oxford: Oxford University Press, 1999).

Winfried Wolf, *Car Mania* (London: Pluto, 1996).

Peter Wollen and Joe Kerr, *Autopia: Cars and Culture* (London: Reaktion, 2007).

Jonathan Wood, *Wheels of Misfortune* (London: Sidgwick & Jackson, 1988).

. . ., *Coachbuilding* (Oxford: Shire, 2008).

. . ., *The British Motor Industry* (Oxford: Shire, 2010).

Design

C. Edson Armi, *The Art of American Car Design* (Philadelphia: Penn State University Press, 1988).

Ronald Barker and Anthony Harding (eds), *Automobile Design* (Newton Abbot: David & Charles, 1970).

Stephen Bayley, *Sex, Drink and Fast Cars* (London: Faber, 1986).

. . ., *Cars: Freedom, Style, Sex, Power, Motion, Colour, Everything* (London: Conran Octopus, 2008).

. . . and Giles Chapman (eds), *Moving Objects* (London: Eye-Q, 1999).

Ian Beatty, *Automotive Body Design* (Sparkford: Haynes, 1977).

Helen Evenden, *New Directions in Transport Design* (London: V&A, 2007).

Peter Grist, *Virgil Exner: Visioneer* (Dorchester: Veloce, 2007) .

Raymond Loewy, *Industrial Design* (Woodstock, NY: Overlook Press, 1979).

Beryl McAlhone (ed.), *Directors on Design* (London: Design Council, 1985).

L. J. K. Setright, *The Designers* (London: Weidenfeld & Nicolson, 1976).

Penny Sparke, *A Century of Car Design* (London: Mitchell Beazley, 2002).

Paul C. Wilson, *Chrome Dream: Automobile Styling since 1893* (Radnor, PA: Chilton, 1976).

Motoring

Georgine Clarsen, *Eat My Dust: Early Women Motorists* (Baltimore: John Hopkins University Press, 2008).

Frank Coffey and Joseph Layden, *America on Wheels* (Los Angeles: General Publishing, 1996).

Julian Holder and Steven Parissien (eds), *The Architecture of British Transport in the 20th Century* (London and New Haven: Yale University Press, 2004).

John A. Jakle, *Motoring: The Highway Experience in America* (Athens, GA: University of Georgia Press, 2008).

David Jeremiah, *Representations of British Motoring* (Manchester: Manchester University Press, 2007).

D. L. Lewis and Laurence Goldstein (eds), *The Automobile and American Culture* (Ann Arbor: Michigan Press, 1983).

Peter Merriman, *Driving Spaces: A Cultural-Historical Geography of Britain's M1 Motorway* (Oxford: Blackwell, 2007).

Joe Moran, *On Roads* (London: Profile, 2009)

P. D. North, *Fighting Traffic: The Dawn of the Motor Age in the American City* (Cambridge, MA: MIT Press, 2008).

Sean O'Connell, *The Car in British Society* (Manchester: Manchester University Press, 1998).

Dianne Perrier, *Onramps and Overpasses: A Cultural History of Interstate Travel* (Gainesville: University Press of Florida, 2009).

John B. Rae, *The Road and Car in American Life* (Cambridge, MA: MIT Press, 1971).

Graham Robson, *Motoring in the 30s* (Cambridge: Stephens, 1979).

David St Clair, *The Motorization of American Cities* (New York: Praeger, 1986).

Motor Cities

Coventry's Motor Car Heritage (Stroud: History Press, 2011).

John Gallagher, *Re-Imagining Detroit* (Detroit: Wayne State University Press, 2010).

Donald McDonald, *Detroit 1985* (Garden City, NY: Doubleday, 1980).

Kathryn A. Morrison and John Minnis, *Carcapes* (London and New Haven: Yale University Press, 2012)

Johannes F. Spreen and Diane Holloway, *Who Killed Detroit?* (Detroit: iUniverse, 2006).

David Thoms, *The Coventry Motor Industry* (Aldershot: Ashgate, 2000).

Fuels

Iain Carson and Vijay Vaitheeswaran, *Zoom: The Global Race to Fuel the Car of the Future* (London: Penguin, 2008).

David Kirsch, *The Electric Vehicle and the Burden of History* (New Brunswick, NJ: Rutgers University Press, 2000).

Ernest H. Wakefield, *History of the Electric Automobile* (Warrendale, PA: Society of Automotive Engineers, 1994).

Daniel Yergin, *The Prize* (New York: Free Press, 1992).

People

David Abodaher, *Iacocca* (New York: Zebra, 1985).

Martin Adeney, *Nuffield: A Biography* (London: Robert Hale, 1993).

Lee Albert, *Call Me Roger* (Chicago: McGraw-Hill Contemporary, 1988).

Richard Bak, *Henry and Edsel* (Hoboken, NJ: Wiley, 2003).

Neil Baldwin, *Henry Ford and the Jews* (New York: Oxford Publicity Partnership, 2001).

Gillian Bardsley, *Issigonis* (Thriplow: Icon, 2006).

David Bastow, *Henry Royce, Mechanic* (Derby: Rolls-Royce Heritage Trust, 1989).

Malcolm Bobbitt, *W. O. Bentley* (Derby: Breedon, 2003).

John Bullock, *The Rootes Brothers* (Cambridge: Patrick Stephens, 1993).

Walter Chrysler, *Life of an American Workman* (New York: Dodd Mead, 1937).

R. A. Church, *Herbert Austin* (London: Europa, 1979).

Peter Collier and David Horowitz, *The Fords: An American Epic* (New York: Summit, 1989).

Vincent Curcio, *Chrysler* (New York: Oxford University Press, 2000).

Michael Edwardes, *Back from the Brink* (London: Collins, 1983).

Ivan Fallon and James Srodes, *Dream Maker: The Rise and Fall of John Z. DeLorean* (New York: Putnam, 1983).

David Farber, *Sloan Rules* (Chicago: University of Chicago Press, 2002).

Henry Ford, *The International Jew* (Whitefish, MT: Kessinger Publishing, 2003).

. . . [and Samuel Crowther], *Moving Forward* (London: William Heinemann, 1931).

Carol Gelderman, *Henry Ford* (New York: Dial Press, 1981).

Lawrence R. Gustin, *Billy Durant* (Grand Rapids, MI: Eerdmans Publishing, 1973).

Lee Iacocca, *Iacocca* (New York: Bantam, 1984).

Robert Jackson, *The Nuffield Story* (London: Frederick Muller, 1964).

Guy Jellinek-Mercédès, *My Father Mr Mercédès* (London: G. T. Foulis, 1966).

Peter King, *The Motor Men* (London: Quiller, 1989).

David L. Lewis, *The Public Image of Henry Ford* (Detroit: Wayne State University Press, 1976).

Axel Madsen, *The Deal Maker: How William C. Durant Made General Motors* (New York: John Wiley, 1999).

John F. Morris (ed.), *Wealth Well-Given* (Stroud: Alan Sutton, 1994) .

R. J. Overy, *William Morris, Viscount Nuffield* (London: Europa, 1976).

Philip Porter and Paul Skilleter, *Sir William Lyons* (Sparkford: Haynes, 2001).

John Reynolds, *André Citroën,* (Stroud: Alan Sutton, 2006).

Alfred Sloan, *My Years with General Motors* (Garden City, NY: Doubleday, 1964).

Miles Thomas, *Out on a Wing* (London: Michael Joseph, 1964).

Henry Turner, *General Motors and the Nazis* (New Haven: Yale University Press, 2005).

Patrick J. Wright, *On a Clear Day You Can See General Motors* (Grosse Point, MI: Wright Enterprises, 1979).

Peter Wyden, *The Unknown Iacocca* (London: Sidgwick & Jackson, 1988).

Marques and Models

James Ward Arthur, *The Fall of the Packard Motor Car Company* (Stanford: Stanford University Press, 1995).

Martin Bennett, *Rolls-Royce* (Yeovil: Oxford Illustrated, 1983).

. . ., *Rolls-Royce and Bentley* (Sparkford: Haynes, 1998).

Malcolm Bobbitt, *The British Citroën* (Glossop: Transport Publishing, 1991).

. . ., *Rover* (Godmanstone: Veloce, 1994).

. . ., *Rolls-Royce at Derby* (Derby: Breedon, 2002).

. . ., *Citroen DS* (Dorchester: Veloce, 2005).

Chris Brady and Andrew Lorenz, *End of the Road: BMW and Rover, A Brand Too Far* (London: FT Prentice Hall, 2001).

David Burgess-Wise, *Ghia* (London: Osprey, 1985).

. . ., *Ford at Dagenham* (Derby: Breedon, 2001).

Leslie Butterfield, *Enduring Passion: A History of the Mercedes-Benz Brand* (Chichester: Wiley, 2005).

Richard Copping, *VW Beetle* (Dorchester: Veloce, 2006).

Chester Dawson, *Lexus: The Relentless Pursuit* (Chichester: Wiley, 2004).

H. R. Etzold, *VW Beetle: The Chronicle of the People's Car* (Sparkford: Haynes, 1991).

Peter Haguma, *Bentley* (Ferring: Dalton Watson, 2003).

Charles K. Hyde, *Riding the Roller Coaster: A History of the Chrysler Corporation* (Detroit: Wayne State University Press, 2003).

David Kiley, *Driven: Inside BMW, the Most Admired Car in the World* (Hoboken, NJ: Wiley, 2004).

Robert Lacey, *Ford* (London: Pan, 1986).

Karl Ludvigsen, *Battle for the Beetle* (Cambridge, MA: Bentley, 2000).

Horst Mönnich, *The BMW Story* (London: Sidgwick & Jackson, 1991).

George Oliver, *Rolls-Royce* (Sparkford: Haynes, 1988).

..., *The Rover* (London: Cassell, 1971).

Werner Oswald and Jeremy Walton, *BMW: The Complete Story* (Sparkford: Haynes, 1982).

Karen Pender, *Rover SD1* (Marlborough: Crowood, 1998).

Jon Pressnell, *Citroën DS* (Ramsbury: Crowood, 1999).

A. S. Price, *Rolls-Royce* (London: Batsford, 1980) .

Anthony Pritchard, *British Family Cars of the 1950s and 60s* (Oxford: Shire, 2008).

John B. Rae, *Datsun* (New York: McGraw-Hill, 1982).

Dave Randle, *The True Story of Škoda* (Stroud: Sutton, 2002).

Martin Rawbone, *Ford in Britain* (Sparkford: Haynes, 2001).

Edwin M. Reingold, *Toyota* (Harmondsworth: Penguin, 1999).

John Reynolds, *Eighty Years of Citroën in the United Kingdom, 1923–2003* (Ferring: Dalton Watson, 2003).

..., *Citroën 2CV* (Sparkford: Haynes, 2005).

Graham Robson, *Metro* (Sparkford: Haynes, 1982).

..., *Mini* (Sparkford: Haynes, 1986).

..., *The Cars of BMC* (Croydon: Motor Racing Publications, 1987).

..., *BMW* (Sparkford: Haynes, 2005).

... and Richard Langworth, *Triumph Cars: The Complete Story* (Orpington: Motor Racing Publications, 2004).

L. J. K. Setright, *Rolls-Royce* (New York: Ballantine, 1975).

Nigel Tron, *Lancia* (Newton Abbot: David & Charles, 1980).

Martin Wainwright, *Morris Minor* (London: Aurum, 2008).

David Waller, *Wheels on Fire: The True Inside Story of the DaimlerChrysler Merger* (London: Coronet, 2001).

Jeremy Walton, *Capri* (Sparkford: Haynes, 1990).

..., *BMW 3-Series* (London: Osprey, 1993).

..., *Audi Quattro* (Sparkford: Haynes, 2007).

Andrew Whyte, *Jaguar* (Cambridge: Patrick Stephens, 1980).

..., *Cadillac* (London: Octopus, 1986).

..., *Jaguar* (Princes Risborough: Shire, 2007).

Jonathan Wood, *The VW Beetle* (London: Motor Racing Publications, 1983).

..., *MG* (Oxford: Shire, 2000).

..., *The Citroën* (Oxford: Shire, 2003).

..., *Morgan* (Sparkford: Haynes, 2004).

Acknowledgements

I would like to thank all those who have helped me with the ideas, research and illustrations for this book. Particular thanks must go to Richard Milbank, whose idea this was, and whose enthusiasm and wisdom have provided me with invaluable guidance throughout the project.

Index